The Week of Salvation

History and Traditions of Holy Week

James Monti

Our Sunday Visitor Publishing Division
Our Sunday Visitor, Inc.
Huntington, Indiana 46750

Nihil Obstat: Reverend Anthony Sorgie, Ed.C.
                   Censor Deputatus

Imprimatur: † Patrick Sheridan, D.D.
                   Vicar General for the Archdiocese of New York
                   April 19, 1993

The Nihil Obstat and Imprimatur are official declarations that a book or pamphlet is free of doctrinal or moral error. No implication is contained therein that those who have granted the Nihil Obstat and the Imprimatur agree with the content, opinions, or statements expressed.

ISBN: 0-87973-532-5
LCCCN: 93-83256

PRINTED IN THE UNITED STATES OF AMERICA

Cover design by Rebecca J. Heaston
Cover art: "Deposition" by Blessed Fra Angelico
532

To the Immaculata — she whose tears mingled with the cleansing flood flowing from her Son's wounded side that every tear may be wiped away.

Acknowledgments

I WISH TO THANK the entire staff of the Corrigan Memorial Library of Saint Joseph's Seminary in Yonkers, New York for so graciously making available to me their superb collection of books and periodicals. I also wish to express my gratitude to the staff of Saint Vladimir's Orthodox Seminary Library of Tuckahoe, New York, who likewise permitted me to make use of their collection of Eastern Rite literature, as well as to the staff of the Irvington Public Library (New York) who obtained for me several interlibrary loans of books and articles that were quite a challenge to locate. In a special manner, I wish to thank Monsignor James O'Connor of Saint Joseph's Seminary for taking the time to evaluate the first draft of my manuscript and for his continued support and encouragement.

Table of Contents

Introduction

*The Festival of the Passion, Dearly Beloved, so earnestly looked
forward to, so desired of all men, is now here . . . this subject, in that
it is unutterable, gives matter without end for speaking; nor may what
we say fall short, for of what we speak never can there be enough.*

[Saint Leo the Great][1]

HOLY WEEK — THE ANNUAL commemoration of the central
events in the history of mankind's redemption — is a subject so vast in
its scope and significance that one almost hesitates to attempt an overview of it. In a sense, all human history — past, present, and future —
converges upon this one week. The whole life of the Church — the life
of grace and of the Sacraments — flows from the unfolding of the
Paschal Mystery. Is it any wonder, then, that the liturgy of the Church
for Holy Week is so extraordinarily distinctive, or that the faithful have
given expression to their own devotion in so many beautiful ways
during these days? The contemplation of the passion, death, and resurrection of the Son of God can move the heart and mind in ways that no
other subject can; nearly two thousand years of Christian art, literature,
and music amply testify to this fact.

But how should one approach such an all-embracing theme as
the Paschal Mystery? One can begin by going to the holy Scriptures,
where the whole history of salvation is recorded. The four gospels
provide us with a detailed picture of the events of Holy Week; here the
centrality of the cross in our faith becomes immediately apparent, for
the Evangelists all devote a disproportionate amount of space to that
climactic week in Jerusalem. They do not shy away from the grim reality
of our Lord's sufferings, nor do they hesitate to proclaim the astounding
fact of the resurrection. Yet theirs is not the only testimony. On page
after page of the Old Testament we find the passion, death, and resurrection of Christ prefigured and prophesied in innumerable ways. Our
Lord Himself said of the ancient Scriptures:

"If you believed Moses, you would believe me, for he wrote of me."

[Jn 5:46]

Again, following the resurrection, He said to the Apostles:

"These are my words which I spoke to you while I was still with you, that everything written about me in the law of Moses and the prophets and the psalms must be fulfilled."

[Lk 24:44]

Thus it is that the books of the Old Testament in so many passages provide, as it were, a commentary on each event of Holy Week, from our Lord's entry into the City of David on Palm Sunday to His absolute triumph over death on Easter morning. In a number of cases the Evangelists themselves point out specific passages from the prophets or Psalms that predict the events they are describing.

The Scriptures, both from the Old and the New Testaments, are an integral part of the Church's formal public worship, the liturgy. Thus during Holy Week, the Church presents to her children the whole drama of the Paschal Mystery through the Liturgy of the Word. On Palm Sunday one of the three accounts of the passion from the gospels of Saint Matthew, Saint Mark, or Saint Luke is read. On Good Friday the faithful hear the passion narrative from Saint John's gospel. At the Easter Vigil one of the three gospels of Saint Matthew, Saint Mark, or Saint Luke serves to proclaim the resurrection. On each of these days relevant prophetic passages are read from the Book of Isaiah and from Psalms, as well as from other parts of the Old Testament. But it is above all in the liturgy that the Church celebrates the greatest of all the gifts her Divine Spouse has bestowed upon her: the gift of Christ Himself in the holy Eucharist. And is not the holy Eucharist the Paschal Mystery *par excellence*? As Saint Paul reminds us:

For as often as you eat this bread and drink the cup, you proclaim the Lord's death until he comes.

[1 Cor 11:26]

The Mass is the sacrifice instituted in the upper room on the first Holy Thursday and offered on Calvary on Good Friday; in holy Communion we receive the glorified Body of Him Who rose from the Tomb on Easter Sunday. Thus it is during Holy Week that the Liturgy of the Eucharist takes on a heightened significance as we commemorate the events it embodies.

From these considerations it should be obvious that the liturgy

[10]

provides the most perfect means of entering upon the sacred mysteries of Holy Week. The liturgy of Holy Week unites Catholic men and women of every nation on earth in the common worship of our crucified King in word and sacrament. Yet the Church has always recognized that other valid forms of prayer and meditation have their place as well in the lives of her sons and daughters. Legitimate popular devotions provide the faithful with excellent opportunities to further reflect upon the life of Christ and of His Blessed Mother. When prudently conducted, these devotions serve to accentuate the themes of the liturgy. In the observance of Holy Week, such pious exercises as the Stations of the Cross, processions of the passion, and commemorations of the Entombment of Christ and of the Sorrows of the Blessed Virgin Mary help the faithful to retrace the steps of our Lord and to enter upon a deeper understanding of what He suffered for us.

The purpose of the present work is to provide a basic synthesis of the scriptural, liturgical, and devotional dimensions of Holy Week. The author has attempted to interweave these three distinct aspects in order to take the reader on a "pilgrimage" through Holy Week, so as to highlight the link between the original events of that first Holy Week in Jerusalem and the yearly commemorations that have continued down through two millennia to our own day. For when we attend the Mass of the Lord's Supper on Holy Thursday, how much thought do we give to the fact that it was on this very same evening that the Lord sat at table with His disciples and gave them "the bread of life and the cup of eternal salvation"? And when we come forward to kiss the cross on Good Friday afternoon, do we fully reflect that in so doing we join the Blessed Virgin Mary, the Apostle John, and the Magdalene in adoring the Crucified on that first Good Friday? And at each Easter Vigil does not the Church go to the holy sepulchre with the holy women to find the stone rolled aside and her Bridegroom risen from the dead?

This latter point brings us to another consideration. In watching with our Lord in His passion, death, and resurrection, we do not watch alone. There are others with us in Gethsemane, on the way of the cross, and at the tomb. There are the countless other Christians observing Holy Week this very same year as we are, in countries throughout the world. And in virtue of the Communion of Saints, we keep watch with all the many generations before us who have observed Holy Week. For this reason the author has chosen to describe ceremonies from many different places around the world and from past ages, in order to give the reader a more vivid realization of this communal aspect of our observance.

The greater part of this book is taken up with an historical overview of the liturgy and devotions peculiar to Holy Week. Thus the emphasis will be on those features that distinguish the liturgy of this week from that of the rest of the liturgical year. The objective here is to bring to light, at least in a general manner, what is known of the origins and development of the various elements that characterize the liturgy in this special season. The reader may be surprised to learn of the antiquity of so many of these practices; as pointed out by the liturgist Anton Baumstark, Holy Week over the centuries has conserved certain primitive features of the liturgy that would have otherwise disappeared completely.[2] The treatment here of the liturgical history of Holy Week is by no means intended to be exhaustive; such a detailed analysis would require a much larger volume than this. What the author has sought to do is to provide an outline of these liturgical developments, focusing on the aspects that he thinks will be of most interest to the general reader and which can serve to deepen one's appreciation of the richness of the paschal liturgy. The author's intent is very much the same as that expressed so well by the famous Jesuit scholar, Father Herbert Thurston (1856-1939), in his own volume on the subject of Holy Week:

> *One is conscious of a certain feeling of irreverence in turning away from the profound religious emotions awakened in us by the occasion and its surroundings, in order to discuss historical details of ceremonial which in some sense make not for edification. However, as it is not intended that these chapters should take the place of a manual of devotions, or of the Holy Week book [Missal] itself, so I would urge on the other hand that familiarity with the material part of the ritual, and above all, the sense that the ceremonial at which we are assisting has come to us unchanged from the days of the early Fathers and has been sanctified by the participation of unnumbered generations of Christians, believing as we believe and struggling as we struggle, will deepen rather than efface the impressions we wish to cherish.[3]*

Particular attention is given to observances and customs that the author has found to be seldom documented in any significant manner in other standard works on the history of Holy Week. Often the only materials available concerning these practices are eyewitness accounts published in periodicals of the nineteenth and early twentieth centuries. In using such sources it cannot necessarily be determined whether the particular customs described have continued to the present day in the places where they were observed; nonetheless these accounts provide us with detailed information about Holy Week observances that endured for centuries, and which can usually still be found in at least some locales.

It is beyond the scope of this volume to enter upon a thorough, meditative commentary on the gospel narratives of the passion and resurrection; there are a number of other excellent books that approach the subject of the passion from this perspective. Archbishop Alban Goodier's classic works on the life of Christ fill this role superbly. In dealing with Sacred Scripture, the author of the current work simply wishes to present a harmony of the four gospel accounts of the passion and resurrection augmented with Old Testament passages that can serve as a framework for prayer and meditation during Holy Week. The concept of a harmony, that is, the arranging of verses from the four gospels into a unified sequence, is an ancient one. The passion has been read in this form in the Good Friday liturgy of the Eastern rites for many centuries. In determining the proper ordering of passages, the author has for the most part followed the harmony found in the volumes of Archbishop Goodier. However, the selection and arrangement of cor- responding Old Testament verses is the author's own; some of these verses are clearly Messianic prophecies or prefigurations of the Paschal Mystery, while others have been selected because they address the universal themes of sin and suffering. Appropriate passages from the Church Fathers and from Catholic literature, poetry, and hymns have also been used to provide further points for meditation.

In wishing to bring the reader "hour by hour" through Holy Week, the author has generally grouped Scripture passages describing a particular event in the passion with the liturgical and extraliturgical ceremonies conducted on that same day and at that same time. This is done to demonstrate that both the liturgy and the legitimate devotions of Holy Week truly harmonize with the Scriptures in presenting the events of the Paschal Mystery.

Some Final Notes Concerning the Present Volume

In compiling a modest volume on such a vast subject as Holy Week, it is inevitable that there must need be limitations on the range of material covered. Thus the author has chosen not to enter into a discussion of such related topics as the Lenten season in general, or the days of the Easter season following Easter Sunday. In the case of the Divine Office, the official prayer of the Church apart from the Eucharistic liturgy, it has seemed fit to focus upon the most distinctive portion of the Office of Holy Week: the communal recitation of the Office of Readings and Morning Prayer conducted on Holy Thursday, Good Friday, and Holy Saturday (a special triduum of services known as *Tenebrae*). With regard to devotional local customs, the author has generally confined himself to describing only those of an explicitly sacred character. But there are many beautiful practices that fall outside this category, such as the religious symbolism of the various special foods prepared during Holy Week; interesting as these customs are, a discussion of them here would be too much of a digression. The sacred and secular music associated with Holy Week form a whole separate field of study; where appropriate, the texts of certain pieces of music are quoted in the pages that follow, but a comprehensive exposition of this aspect of Holy Week would simply lie beyond the scope of the present work. In a realm all its own is the famous Shroud of Turin, which, regardless of the outcome of the scientific and historical debates concerning its origin, nonetheless gives us a realistic conception of the physical sufferings of our Lord in His passion. Such a complex subject deserves a thorough and in-depth treatment, as is found in the works of Ian Wilson; for this reason the author has not attempted it here.

The descriptions of services according to the current liturgy should be considered as somewhat idealized examples of what can be done under the best of circumstances, such as in an episcopal setting, where numerous clerics are present to give the ceremonies added solemnity. These accounts of the present-day liturgy are based largely upon Holy Week services as conducted in a diocesan seminary where the author has had the opportunity to attend them over the past twelve years. Nevertheless, virtually everything described in this regard can be achieved with a little effort at the parish level as well. Please note that these accounts are intended to highlight the most conspicuous features of each liturgical service and to give the reader a sense of the beauty of the ceremonies. Although the descriptions are written in full accord with the current rubrics, they are not meant to provide the reader with each and every rubric or option available. Such information is given in the *Roman Missal*, the *Caeremoniale Episcoporum* (1985 edition), the 1955 decree *Maxima redemptionis* and the Congregation for Divine Worship's 1988 document, *Circular Letter Concerning the Preparation and Celebration of the Easter Feasts*.

A few comments on sources are in order. Except where otherwise noted, the texts of Sacred Scripture are taken from the Catholic edition of the Revised Standard Version of the *Holy Bible*, published by the Division of Christian Education of the National Council of Churches of Christ in the United States. Biblical texts marked with "JB" are from Doubleday's 1968 "Reader's Edition" of the *Jerusalem Bible*. For Psalms the Hebrew numbering usually found in recent editions of the Bible is followed. In translated quotations from medieval liturgical books, scriptural passages are from the Douay-Rheims version of the Bible. Liturgical texts of the current liturgy are taken from the *Roman Sacramentary*, as reprinted in the *Vatican II Sunday* and *Weekday Missals* of the Daughters of St. Paul; Scripture readings used in the liturgy are from the *Roman Lectionary*, using the New American version of Sacred Scripture and are marked "NAB". The texts of the Liturgy of the Hours (the Divine Office) are taken from *The Office of Readings*, published by the Daughters of St. Paul, and from the Liturgical Press edition of Morning and Evening Prayer entitled *Christian Prayer*. Psalm texts from this work are taken from *The Grail*, published in London. In the four works cited above, all liturgical translations are by the International Committee on English in the Liturgy (ICEL). In citing the early liturgical documents known as the *Roman Ordines*, the author has chosen to follow the numbering system of Jean Mabillon, whose seventeenth-century edition of fifteen such *ordines* is incorporated into J.-P. Migne's standard reference series, *Patrologia Latina* (Vol. 78). Admittedly Michel Andrieu's work, *Les Ordines Romani du Haut Moyen Age*, is widely considered the definitive edition of the *Roman Ordines*, and includes many that Mabillon did not publish; unfortunately, Andrieu's numbering of the *Ordines* differs considerably from that of Mabillon. The wider accessibility of the *Patrologia Latina* series has led the author of the present volume to use Mabillon's classification except where noted otherwise. If Andrieu's is used in a given instance, this will be indicated in parenthesis. All references to the Roman book known as the *Gelasian Sacramentary* are to the edition of this document found in the Vatican manuscript *Vat. Reg. 316* (the "Old Gelasian"). The dating of medieval documents is based largely on that provided by Cyrille Vogel in his work, *The Medieval Liturgy: An Introduction to the Sources*. Finally, references to the current liturgy of the "Byzantine Rite" are to that of the *Catholic* Byzantine Rite.

Endnotes

1. From Sermon 62, "De Passione Domini XI," *The Sunday Sermons of the Great Fathers*, Vols. II and III, edited by M.F. Toal. Copyright © 1958 by H. Regnery Company. Reprinted by special permission of Regnery Gateway, Inc., Washington, D.C.
2. Anton Baumstark, *Comparative Liturgy*, 1957 p. 27.
3. Father Herbert Thurston, S.J., *Lent and Holy Week*, 1904, p. 329.

Ī

An Introductory Overview
of Holy Week

*Just as the week has its beginning and climax in the celebration of
Sunday, which always has a paschal character, so the summit of the
whole liturgical year is in the sacred Easter Triduum of the Passion
and Resurrection of the Lord. . . .*

[Congregation for Divine Worship][1]

Holy Week in the Early Church

*Since our Lord Jesus has made the day glorious by his resurrection
which he had made doleful by his death, let us recall both days in solemn
memorial, keeping vigil in recollection of his death and rejoicing
in celebration of his resurrection. This is our annual feast, and
our pasch. . . .*

[Saint Augustine][2]

FROM THE EARLIEST DAYS of Christianity, the anniversary
of the passion, death, and resurrection of our Lord Jesus Christ has been
observed as the greatest and most solemn feast of the year. Although
surviving records of the life of the Church in the first century are quite
scanty apart from what the Sacred Scriptures themselves tell us, we do
have reason to believe that even in the apostolic era, the commemoration that we call "Easter" was already being observed on an annual
basis. Throughout her long history the Church has always used the
phases of the moon — the lunar calendar — to calculate the anniversary
of Christ's death and resurrection. Our Lord died on the eve of the
Passover, the date of which was determined to coincide with the first
full moon following the vernal equinox (the first day of spring). Such a
method of measuring the passage of the year was a distinctively Jewish
practice in the first century, when most of the Roman Empire was using
the sun for this purpose instead. The first Christians, who were almost
totally of Jewish extraction, would naturally have retained their lunar
method of determining the calendar even after entering the Church. It
is highly probable, then, that the introduction of a feast based upon the
lunar calendar would have had to have been an established fact prior
to the end of the first century, before the Jewish Christians of the Church
were far outnumbered by Gentile Christians, who were accustomed to
calculating with a solar calendar. In confirmation of this theory is the
fact that other Christian feast days not associated with the Easter cycle
and adopted by the Church after the first century, such as Christmas
and the Epiphany, have all been calculated by means of the solar
calendar, and not by the moon.[3]

Be this as it may, the earliest surviving references to the annual
observance of the Pasch (the original term for Easter) do not appear
until the second century. Several of these sources have been preserved
for us by a Church historian of the third and fourth centuries named
Eusebius, who quotes from the relevant documents in his work, the

Ecclesiastical History. These references focus upon a controversy as to whether the Pasch should be celebrated on the "fourteenth day of the moon" — the day on which Christ died and on which the Passover lambs were slain — or on the Sunday after this "fourteenth day" — so that the anniversary of the resurrection might be celebrated on the same day of the week each year, the day on which our Lord rose from the tomb. The Christians of Asia generally favored the former commemoration, and for this reason came to be known as *Quartodecimans* (Latin for "Fourteenth"). The rest of the Church, in conformity with the practice of Rome, always celebrated the Pasch on the first Sunday following the lunar "fourteenth."[4] This dispute was not brought to an end until the fourth century, when the First Ecumenical Council of Nice ruled that from henceforth the "Sunday Pasch" was to be observed universally.[5]

Despite the difference regarding the day of the Pasch, the early Church both in the East and the West observed at least one day of fasting prior to the celebration of the paschal liturgy;[6] the duration of this period of fasting varied, as indicated in a letter of Saint Iranaeus (died A.D. 200) quoted by Eusebius:

> *For some think they ought to fast one day, some two days, some even more; and some reckon as their day (of fasting) forty (consecutive) hours of day and night.*[7]

In these fasting practices we see that already by the second century the Church preceded the joyful celebration of the resurrection with a period of penance, presumably in remembrance of our Lord's death on Calvary; even before this, by the end of the first century, Christians were observing each and every Friday of the year as a day of fasting, according to the *Didache*, a document thought to date from the end of the apostolic era.[8] Undoubtedly we are looking at the germinal stages in the development of the Easter Triduum and of Holy Week.

Perhaps the earliest explicit reference to the commemoration of Good Friday in conjunction with Easter Sunday is provided by the renowned Christian apologist Tertullian (A.D. 160-223). Writing around A.D. 200, he speaks of the distinction the early Christians made between the "Pasch of the Crucifixion," that is, Good Friday, and the "Pasch of the Resurrection," Easter. Of the former he says that it is on "the day of the pasch on which there is a public and almost universal observance of a fast, and on which we very properly lay aside the kiss of peace."[9]

That religious services were held on both of these days is evident from the words of Origen (A.D. 184-254), who while residing at Caesarea in Palestine made the following remark in one of his *Homilies on Isaiah* (ca. A.D. 235-245):

> *There is now a multitude of people on account of the Preparation-day [Good Friday], and especially on the Sunday [Easter Sunday] which commemorates Christ's Passion.*[10]

Later in the third century, we find evidence that the entire week preceding Easter had begun to take on a sacred character; in one of his *Festal Epistles*, Dionysius of Alexandria (ca. A.D. 260) refers to a fast of six days observed by some Christians in preparation for Easter.[11] In another work of the same century, entitled the *Didascalia Apostolorum* (probably of Syrian origin), this week of fasting is referred to as the "days of the Pascha, wherein all the faithful throughout the world fast"; it provides perhaps the earliest detailed outline of Holy Week practices:

> *Therefore you shall fast in the days of the Pascha from the tenth, which is the second day of the week [Monday]; and you shall sustain yourselves with bread and salt and water only, at the ninth hour [three in the afternoon], until the fifth day of the week [Holy Thursday]. But on the Friday [Good Friday] and on the Sabbath [Holy Saturday] fast wholly, and taste nothing. You shall come together and watch and keep vigil all the night with prayers and intercessions, and with reading of the Prophets, and with the Gospel and with Psalms, with fear and trembling and with earnest supplication, until the third hour in the night [nine in the evening] after the Sabbath; and then break your fasts. . .*
> *Especially incumbent on you therefore is the fast of the Friday and of the Sabbath; and likewise the vigil and watching of the Sabbath, and the reading of the Scriptures, and psalms, and prayer and intercession for them that have sinned, and the expectation and hope of the resurrection of our Lord Jesus, until the third hour in the night after the Sabbath. And then offer your oblations; and thereafter eat and make good cheer, and rejoice and be glad, because that the earnest of our resurrection, Christ, is risen.*[12]

Notice in the above passage that within the ambit of Holy Week the Easter Triduum — the period encompassing Good Friday and Holy

Saturday and ending with the celebration of Easter — is already distinguished as a period of particular solemnity, during which an absolute fast is prescribed. The structure of the Easter Vigil is also indicated. Lest there be any doubt as to the reason for the strict fasting, the *Didascalia Apostolorum* further states:

> Fast then on the Friday, because thereon the People killed themselves in crucifying our Saviour; and on the Sabbath also, because it is the sleep of our Lord.[13]

Thus we see that the early Church did indeed observe Good Friday as a day of mourning.

In the fourth century the concept of Holy Week clearly emerges in numerous sources. Among these are two passages from the writings of Saint Athanasius of Alexandria (Egypt), who brings to light the fulfillment of Old Testament "types" in the events of Holy Week. Writing in the year 329, he refers to the severe fasting practiced in the course of "those six holy and great days [preceding Easter Sunday], which are the symbol of the creation of this world."[14] Some parallels between the events of Holy Week and the Genesis account of the "first week" in the history of the world are readily identifiable. Note that on the sixth day God created man (Gen 1:26-31); on Good Friday, the "sixth day" of Holy Week, God redeemed man. On the seventh day "God rested from all his work which he had done in creation" (Gen 2:3); likewise on Holy Saturday, the "seventh day," our Lord "rested" in the tomb. In another of his Festal Letters, written in 331, Saint Athanasius uses Passover imagery in speaking of the week before Easter: ". . . we begin the holy week of the great Easter on the tenth of Pharmuthi (April 5), in which, my beloved brethren, we should use more prolonged prayers, and fastings, and watchings, that we may be enabled to anoint our lintels with precious blood, and to escape the destroyer."[15] Here we see an obvious allusion to the account of the first Passover in the Book of Exodus:

> Then they shall take some of the blood, and put it on the two doorposts and the lintel of the houses in which they eat them. . . . The blood shall be a sign for you, upon the houses where you are; and when I see the blood, I will pass over you, and no plague shall fall upon you to destroy you, when I smite the land of Egypt.
>
> [Ex 12:7, 13]

[21]

The distinction between the two most important days of Holy Week, that is, Good Friday and Easter Sunday, is stressed by another fourth-century writer, Saint Ambrose, Archbishop of Milan (Italy) and a Doctor of the Church (A.D. 340-397), who clarifies the reason for, and significance of, the Good Friday fast practiced since the first century:

> *One shows disbelief in the Resurrection of Christ if he proposes a law of fast on the day of the Resurrection, since the Law says that the Passover should be eaten with bitterness, that is, with sorrow because the Author of our salvation was slain by mankind's great sacrilege. On the Lord's day the Prophet bids us rejoice, saying: "This is the day which the Lord has made, let us be glad and rejoice at it."*
>
> *Consequently, we must observe both the day of the Passion and of the Resurrection, to have a day of bitterness and one of joy, fasting on one day, being refreshed on the other.*[16]

Saint Ambrose's insistence on this distinction is echoed in an Eastern document known as the *Apostolic Constitutions*, composed before A.D. 400, which refers to Good Friday as a "day of mourning, not a day of festive joy."[17]

Undoubtedly the fullest description of Holy Week services from the fourth century is that of a woman pilgrim known to history as Egeria, who is thought to have visited Jerusalem towards the end of the fourth century, probably around 380. In her pilgrimage diary she gives us a detailed liturgical schedule of Holy Week in the city where the events of the Paschal Mystery actually took place. But what makes Egeria's account particularly valuable is that it reveals the ancient roots of so many features of the current liturgy and traditions of Holy Week. These similarities will be made evident as we summarize her descriptions of each of the major services.[18]

On Palm Sunday the people of Jerusalem gathered on the Mount of Olives, where, around five o'clock in the afternoon, one of the gospel accounts of Christ's triumphant entry was read. The faithful then rose and walked in procession down the mountain and into Jerusalem, accompanying the bishop, who represented Christ entering the city. People of all classes participated in this ceremony; all of the children took part, even the smallest, carried on the shoulders of their parents, with palm or olive branches in their hands. The modern Palm Sunday procession is a direct descendant of this practice in fourth-century Jerusalem.

Egeria speaks of many communal services of the Divine Office during Holy Week. For example, on Monday, there were such services at nine o'clock in the morning, at noon, at three o'clock in the afternoon, and in the evening (Vespers). These services are analogous to the solemn celebration of the Divine Office on Holy Thursday, Good Friday, and Holy Saturday that we know as *Tenebrae*.

On Wednesday night of Holy Week, in the *Anastasis* (the ancient church that stood over the holy sepulchre), the gospel account of Judas' arrangement with the chief priests to betray Christ was read to the people. In the current liturgy the Church likewise assigns Saint Matthew's gospel account of the betrayal to the Mass for this day.

On Holy Thursday two Masses were held, the second of which was celebrated in a small chapel immediately behind the cross marking the site of Calvary; only on this one day of the year was Mass held in this chapel. The second liturgy began around four o'clock in the afternoon. Although in later centuries the Mass of the Lord's Supper was shifted to the morning of Holy Thursday, the Church has since returned to the ancient custom of Jerusalem by once more assigning this Mass to the evening hours, around the time of day when the Last Supper would have actually taken place.

Prior to the beginning of the second Mass near Calvary, the archdeacon pronounced a reminder to the faithful: "At the first hour of the night let us assemble at the church which is on the Eleona, for much toil lies ahead of us on this day's night."[19] Thus, following Mass, the people hurried home to eat supper quickly and then gathered in the *Eleona*, a church on the Mount of Olives. There a service of Scripture readings, particularly the gospel accounts of the Last Supper Discourse, together with hymns, antiphons, and prayers, began around seven o'clock and continued to around eleven. At about midnight the people proceeded to another church on the Mount of Olives (the *Imbomon*) to continue their all-night vigil with a second prayer and Scripture service. Around three o'clock in the morning the faithful went in procession from this church to still another marking the site of the Agony in the Garden. Here the gospel account of Christ's agony was read, after which the people slowly moved to another station in Gethsemane, where they heard the gospel account of the arrest of Jesus. The place was illuminated by "over two hundred church candles." In spite of their exhaustion from this long vigil, the faithful had a vivid sense of the events they were commemorating; Egeria tells us that when this last gospel passage was read, there was "such moaning and groaning with weeping from all the people that their moaning can be heard practically as far as the city."[20] She points out that participation in this vigil was universal, encompassing young and old, rich and poor alike. Upon its conclusion (before dawn) the faithful returned to the city, singing hymns along the way.

As can be seen, the Holy Thursday night vigil played an important role in the observance of Holy Week in fourth-century Jerusalem. About eight centuries ago this ancient practice began to reemerge in a new form. The place where the Blessed Sacrament was reserved overnight for holy Communion on Good Friday increasingly became the focal point for devotions following the Mass of the Lord's Supper. The faithful came to realize that this was the ideal place to watch with our Lord, to meditate upon His words and actions at the Last Supper, and to be with Him in His agony in Gethsemane. Even the plants and flowers used to adorn the place of repose are suggestive of the Garden of Gethsemane, and the numerous candles of the repository can be likened to the "two hundred church candles" Egeria mentions in her diary. The use of Scripture for the vigil in Egeria's day is echoed in our own time by the suggestion of the Vatican's Congregation for Divine Worship (*Circular Letter* of Feb 20, 1988) that chapters 13-17 of the gospel of Saint John may be read at the Eucharistic vigil this night.[21]

Shortly after daybreak on Good Friday the people gathered in the courtyard before the site of Calvary to hear the gospel account of the trial before Pilate. Then the bishop addressed them, comforting and encouraging them after an exhausting night of watching and prayer, to be followed by still more exercises of piety this day. Admonishing them to continue their efforts and to place their trust in God, Who would reward them with special graces for their devotion during these holy days, the bishop temporarily dismissed them with these words: "Go, for the time being, each of you, to your homes; sit there awhile, and around the second hour of the day [8:00 a.m.] let everyone be on hand here so that from that hour until the sixth hour [noon] you may see the holy wood of the cross, and thus believe that it was offered for the salvation of each and every one of us. From the sixth hour on we will have to assemble here, before the Cross, so that we may devote ourselves to prayers and scriptural readings until nightfall."[22] The people then went to a place on Mount Sion where was kept the pillar to which our Lord had been bound when He was scourged. There they prayed before returning to their homes to take a short rest. About eight o'clock in the morning the faithful gathered once more in the chapel behind the cross marking Golgotha; with the bishop seated on a throne behind the cross, a linen-veiled table was placed before him. Deacons stationed themselves around the table, after which a "gilded silver casket" containing both the wood of the true cross and the inscription of Pilate ("Jesus of Nazareth, the King of the Jews" — mentioned in Jn 19:19-22) was carried in and opened. These were laid on the table. Then the bishop, remaining seated, gripped the wood with his hands and held it as the faithful came forward to venerate this precious relic of the passion. One by one, the faithful first bowed before the relics, touching the wood and the inscription with both their foreheads and their eyes; they then kissed the wood of the cross and moved on. This service continued until noon.

Jerusalem's ceremonial Veneration of the Cross eventually spread throughout the West, with a cross or crucifix used to represent the true cross; the rite has continued to the present day as part of the Liturgy of the Passion. For many centuries the Veneration of the Cross was held in the morning hours as it had been in fourth-century Jerusalem; in the current liturgy this service is held in the afternoon, in imitation of early Roman practice, usually beginning at three o'clock. As in the Jerusalem ceremony, each of the faithful comes forward to kiss the cross.

At noon on Good Friday, the people of Jerusalem moved out of the chapel to the courtyard in front of the cross marking Golgotha, where a three-hour service of Scripture, prayer, and hymns now began. Readings from both the Old and New Testaments were selected to teach the people that the Old Testament prophecies concerning the Messiah were fulfilled in the passion of Christ. Again, Egeria speaks of the extraordinary devotion with which the people relived the passion: "There is no one, young or old, who on this day does not sob more than can be imagined for the whole three hours, because the Lord suffered all this for us."[23] As three o'clock approached, Saint John's gospel account of the death of our Lord was read; after a concluding prayer the service ended.

The idea of a special service commemorating the three hours Christ spent on the cross first reappeared in the late seventeenth century, when the Jesuit Father Alonso Messia introduced such a ceremony in Lima, Peru.[24] This extraliturgical service was quickly adopted in other Latin countries (and eventually in the United States) and has come to be known as the *Tre Ore* (Three Hours). In its modern form it consists of a series of meditations and sermons on the Seven Last Words of Christ on the cross, and like its fourth-century counterpart, is held from noon until three o'clock on Good Friday afternoon.

As on the other days of Holy Week, a Scripture service was held in the Martyrium (a large church adjoining the courtyard of Calvary) beginning around three o'clock in the afternoon on Good Friday and continuing until about seven. At the end of this the people went to the Anastasis (the church enclosing the holy sepulchre), and there a gospel passage describing the burial of Christ was read. After a concluding prayer the people were dismissed. However, those who still had enough strength after the long services of the last two days now began a vigil near the holy sepulchre that continued through the night. Large numbers of people, and especially the clergy, spent at least some part of the night watching here, as hymns and antiphons were sung.

We know that by the tenth century Christians in places other than Jerusalem were finding ways to symbolically watch at the tomb of Christ. The custom of the "Easter Sepulchre" spread throughout medieval Europe, involving the symbolic burial of a cross or crucifix, and in some cases the Blessed Sacrament. The cross or the holy Eucharist was placed in a structure in the church made to represent a tomb, and there from Good Friday evening through Holy Saturday, clergy and laity kept watch, sometimes in shifts. By the end of the Middle Ages some churches were using a statue of Christ laid out in death for these "burial" ceremonies. The practice has continued in many places to the present day; the Vatican Congregation for Divine Worship's document on Holy Week mentions the placing in church of a statue of Christ in death as a legitimate devotion for Holy Saturday.[25]

Egeria tells us relatively little about the Easter Vigil, for the celebration of it in Jerusalem so closely resembled that of her own native land that she found it unnecessary to describe it at length for her friends at home. However, we do know from other sources that virtually all the distinctive features of the modern Easter Vigil — the blessing of the paschal candle, the numerous readings from the Old Testament relevant to the themes of the Paschal Mystery and Baptism, the administration of the latter sacrament to catechumens, and the culminating Sacrifice of the Mass — were in place by the end of the fourth century, and thus would have been familiar to Egeria. In the centuries that were to follow, each of the ceremonies of Holy Week was to undergo fascinating developments in form and content that expanded upon, rather than altered, the original import of the services. Yet the conservation of ancient practices in the liturgy of Holy Week has been quite remarkable, as we shall see.

The Names for Holy Week

The names that have been given to Holy Week[26] and to the individual days within it have varied somewhat from place to place, but common themes run through all such titles. With regard to the week as a whole, we find in the fourth century such names as "the six days of the Pascha," "Paschal week," "the week of the Passion," "the great week," and "the last week of Lent." During the Middle Ages other titles appear: "Palm-week" in Saxon England, which was superseded in later English times by "Passion-week"; in Germany *Karwoche* (Week of Lamentation); and in France, Italy, and Spain, it is Holy Week. The latter title has become the most common designation for this week in the United States. The name "Great Week" endures in the Byzantine Rite. For centuries the Roman liturgical books have identified this week as *major hebdomas* (greater week).

The more important days of Holy Week have acquired a range of titles over time. Many of these names were derived from the events commemorated on a particular day, or the special liturgical rites peculiar to it. Thus the first day of Holy Week, on which our Lord's entry into Jerusalem is recalled, has been known as "Palm-branch Sunday," "Day of Palms," and the name now most common, "Palm Sunday." Customs related to the reenactment of Christ's entry into Jerusalem on this day have also resulted in such titles as "Sunday of Olives" in the Ambrosian Rite of Milan, Italy, "Sunday of Flowers" in Wales and *Pascua Florida* (Pasch of Flowers) in Spain. In earlier ages Palm Sunday was also the day on which catechumens preparing for Baptism were first taught the words of the Creed, hence the names "Pascha of the Competents," and "the sought (desired) Pascha." The Mass became known as the *Missa in Symboli Traditione* (Mass in Delivery of the Creed). Related either to the ceremonies for the catechumens or to the reading of the gospel concerning Mary of Bethany anointing the feet of our Lord was the term "Day of Unction." The current title in the *Roman Missal* for this day is *Dominica in Palmis de Passione Domini* (literally, "Sunday in Palms of the Passion of the Lord").[27]

In the liturgical books, Monday, Tuesday, and Wednesday of Holy Week have traditionally been identified as *Feria II* ("Day two"), *Feria III* ("Day three"), and *Feria IV* ("Day four") *maioris Hebdomadae* ("of Greater Week"). Wednesday also acquired a more colloquial appellation: "Spy Wednesday" — the day on which Judas went to the Sanhedrin to betray his Master.

The fifth day of Holy Week has been referred to in some instances simply as the "Thursday before Easter" or "Paschal Thursday." But other names touch on the mysteries celebrated. The reconciliation rite for public penitents that used to be conducted on this day resulted in the name, "Day of forgiveness." "Maundy Thursday" was an especially common appellation, taken from the *Mandatum*, the traditional foot-washing ceremony performed by the clergy in imitation of our Lord's action at the Last Supper. The institution of the Eucharist is reflected in the title, *Natalis Calicis* ("birthday of the cup"), and in one of the most frequently used terms for the day, *Feria quinta in Coena Domini* ("Day five upon the Supper of the Lord"), sometimes shortened to *Coena Domini*. In German regions the Thursday before Easter is called *Gründonnerstag* ("Green Thursday"), a name whose origins are obscure. In France, Italy, and Spain the day has been known in more recent times as Holy Thursday, the name with which we are now most familiar in the United States.

The day on which our Lord sacrificed Himself on the cross was identified in the early Church as the *Dies Paschae* ("Day of the Pasch") or *Parasceve* ("Preparation-day"); both terms are a bit ambiguous, for the former was also used to refer to Easter night or Easter Sunday, and the latter could designate any Friday in the Christian calendar. Hence there arose the more specific expressions, "Pascha of the crucifixion" and the term used in the Roman liturgical books, "*Feria Sexta* (Day Six) *in Parasceve*." In the Byzantine East we find the terms *Parasceve* and "Great Friday." Other titles include "Friday of the Lord's Passion," "Long Friday," and in German *Karfreitag* ("Friday of Mourning"). The term "Good Friday" is peculiar to English-speaking countries and Holland.

The two terms most frequently used for the day before Easter — in the West "Holy Saturday," and in the East, "Great Saturday" — can both be traced as far back as the fourth century. But there have been other designations as well, such as "the day of the vigil of Easter"(used by Saint Jerome), "Saturday of the Pasch," "Saturday of the rest of the Lord's Body," "Saturday of Light" (among the Christians of Iraq and Iran) and the English name "Easter Even."

Pascha has been the single most common Latin term for Easter, appearing as part of varied titles used in the liturgical books over the centuries, such as *Dominicum Paschae* ("Sunday of the Pasch" — in the *Gelasian Sacramentary*), *die Paschae* ("Day of the Pasch" — in *Roman Ordo 12*) and *Dominica Paschae in Resurrectione Domini* (literally "Sunday of the Pasch upon the resurrection of the Lord" — in the current *Roman Missal*).[28] It likewise serves as the name for this day in the Romance languages: hence, in French, *Pâques*; in Italian, *Pasqua*; and in Spanish, *Pascua*.[29] The expression "Easter" (in German, *Ostern*), used throughout English-speaking lands and in Germany, is derived from the pagan Teutonic name for the "season of the rising (growing) sun" (that is, spring) — variously appearing as *Eostur*, *Eastur*, *Ostara*, or *Ostar*; this celebration of new life, coinciding as it did with the Paschal Feast of Christianity, was eventually converted into a celebration of the Risen Christ.[30]

A Week Like No Other

Father. . .
The suffering and death of your Son brought life to the whole
world, moving our hearts to praise your glory. The power of the
Cross reveals your judgment on this world and the kingship of
Christ Crucified. . . .

[Preface for Fifth Week of Lent, *Roman Missal*][31]

The fourth century proved to be of landmark proportions in the Church's history. Until the reign of the Roman Emperor Constantine, the Church was constrained to transform men and their society "in hiding," as it were; the state had set itself as her enemy, and at times seemed determined to drive her from the face of the earth. But with Constantine a new age dawned, in which the state was willing to tolerate and even cooperate with the Church. In time Christian rulers appeared, and the opportunity to build a Christian civilization emerged. Thus the natural order could be transformed in ways as never before; all of man's work, his art and literature, and even the laws of the land, were now to be molded by a Christocentric understanding of the world. The Church's liturgical calendar became that of the state as well. In consequence, the state came to recognize, as the Church herself did, that one week above all others should stand at the head of the calendar in terms of its importance — the week in which mankind was redeemed by the King of the Universe: Holy Week.

Both in the East and West Christian emperors set Holy Week apart by forbidding regular work, in order that they and their subjects could devote themselves during these holy days to sacred pursuits; all commerce and labor came to a halt. In A.D. 392 the Roman Emperor Theodosius ordered the suspension of all legal proceedings during Holy Week and Easter Week.[32] During the Middle Ages kings and rulers would lay aside the affairs of the world and withdraw to the seclusion of a monastery, where they could engage in prayer and meditation as they prepared for Easter.

The annual commemoration of the Paschal Mystery also became a special time for forgiveness, clemency, and reconciliation. Christian rulers soon adopted the custom of pardoning and releasing prisoners during Holy Week. One of the earliest references to this practice is to be found in a homily of Saint John Chrysostom (347-407) for Good Friday:

> *Imperial letters are sent forth, enacting that the prisoners' chains be loosed; that, as our Lord, descending into hell, freed all there detained from death, so his servants, imitating as much as may be their Master's clemency, may free men from sensible bands, whom they cannot free from spiritual.*[33]

Saint Gregory of Nyssa (330-395) mentions that the paschal season was often marked by the emancipation of slaves.[34] In later centuries the kings of France would, on Good Friday each year, pardon one prisoner whose crime was otherwise unpardonable.[35] Abbot Guéranger, in his work *The Liturgical Year*, aptly describes this spirit of mercy:

> *The people of the ages of faith had something far more convincing than theory, of the sacredness of their rights. At the approach of those solemn anniversaries which so forcibly remind us of the justice and mercy of God, they beheld princes abdicating, as it were, their sceptre, leaving in God's hands the punishment of the guilty, and assisting at the holy Table of Paschal Communion side by side with those very men, whom, a few days before, they had been keeping chained in prison for the good of society. There was one thought, which, during these days, was strongly brought before all nations: it was the thought of God, in whose eyes all men are sinners; of God, from whom alone proceed justice and pardon. It was in consequence of this deep Christian feeling, that we find so many diplomas and charts of the ages of faith speaking of the days of Holy Week as being the <u>reign of Christ</u>: such an event, they say, happened on such a day, "under the reign of our Lord Jesus Christ": regnante Domino nostro Jesu Christo.*[36]

The desire to respect the special character of Holy Week also inspired an agreement known as the "Truce of God," a practice that originated in the Aquitane region of France during the eleventh century. The agreement stipulated that from Vespers on Wednesday of Holy Week until daybreak on Easter Monday all violence and revenge were to cease. The severest punishments were meted out to any who dared to break this "Truce of God."[37]

Of course, even during the Middle Ages all too many men motivated by ambition and pride became the rulers of the Christian nations of Europe, men who did little more than conform exteriorly to the Church's worship. Yet there were also virtuous men and women who sat on thrones, and some were even saints. Such was the young princess Saint Elizabeth of Hungary (1207-1231), whose love of God and of the poor found expression in her extraordinary zeal for the observances of Holy Week:

> *Nothing can express the fervor, love, and pious veneration, with which she celebrated those holy days, on which the Church, by ceremonies so touching, and so expressive, recalls to the mind of the faithful, the sorrowful and unspeakable mystery of our redemption. On Holy Thursday, imitating the King of kings, who, on this day, rising from table, laid aside his garments, the daughter of the king of Hungary, putting off whatever could remind her of worldly pomps, dressed herself in poor clothes, and, with only sandals on her feet, went to visit different churches. On this day, she washed the feet of twelve poor men, sometimes lepers, and gave to each twelve pieces, a white dress, and a loaf.*
>
> *All the next night she passed in prayer and meditation upon our Lord's passion. In the morning, it being the day on which the divine sacrifice was accomplished, she said to her attendants, "This day is a day of humiliation for all; I desire that none of you do show me any mark of respect." Then she would put on the same dress as before, and go barefoot to the churches, taking with her certain little packets of linen, incense, and small tapers; and, kneeling before one altar, would place thereon of these; and, prostrating herself, would pray awhile most devoutly, and so pass to another altar, till she had visited all. At the door of the church she gave large alms, but was pushed about by the crowd, who did not know her. Some courtiers reproached her for the meanness of her gifts, as unworthy of a sovereign. But though, at other times, her alms-deeds were most*

abundant, so that few ever were more splendidly liberal to the poor, yet a certain divine instinct in her heart taught her, how, in such days, she should not play the queen, but the poor sinner for whom Christ died.[38]

Fasting and Abstinence

As we have discovered already, the most primitive practice associated with the days preceding Easter was the observance of fasting;[39] certainly this was the case by the end of the second century. During the third century a week-long fast emerged, with fasting of a particularly rigorous nature on the Friday and Saturday of the Easter Triduum. But it is not until the fourth century that an extended period of fasting — the season of Lent — appears, serving as a preparation for the more severe fasting of Holy Week.

The concept of just what constituted a fast varied considerably during the earlier centuries of the Church's history. The fifth century historian Socrates speaks of the different kinds of fasting extant in his own age:

> *Some abstain from every sort of creature that has life, while others of all the living creatures eat of fish only. Others eat birds as well as fish, because, according to the Mosaic account of the Creation, they too sprang from the water; others abstain from fruit covered with a hard shell and from eggs. Some eat dry bread only, others not even that; others again when they have fasted to the ninth hour (three o'clock) partake of various kinds of food.*[40]

The most common manner of fasting was to abstain from all nourishment until the evening, when one meal could be taken; at this meal the consumption of meat and (in earlier times) wine was prohibited. A stricter fast, known as the *xerophagia*, was enjoined for Holy Week and especially Good Friday: At the one daily meal only dry food, bread, salt, and vegetables were permitted. Abstinence from *lacticinia* (dairy products) arose at a later date; Pope Saint Gregory I (540-604) speaks of it in a letter to Saint Augustine of Canterbury:

> *We abstain from flesh meat, and from all things that come from flesh, as milk, cheese, and eggs.*[41]

Shortly afterwards, abstinence from *lacticinia* was incorporated into the Church's canon law; nonetheless, during the centuries that followed, many dispensations from this aspect of abstinence were granted.

The time for the one meal permitted on fast days was gradually advanced; already in the fifth century it was considered acceptable to begin the meal as early as three o'clock in the afternoon. By the end of the thirteenth century, theologians such as the Franciscan Richard Middleton had concluded that this meal could be taken as early as noon. Meanwhile another aspect of the fasting law was undergoing relaxation. In the ninth century the Council of Aix la Chapelle (Germany) gave permission for a "collation": those engaged in heavy labor were permitted to have a drink of water or some other beverage in the evening (in addition to the earlier meal). Eventually the definition of the "collation" was widened to include solid food not in excess of eight ounces. In more recent centuries, permission was granted for a third break in the daily fast, an early morning repast consisting of a drink plus a small piece of bread. Abstinence from meat was gradually relaxed to allow its consumption at one meal daily on almost any fast day of Lent except Fridays. This dispensation was extended to include Holy Thursday, which until then had always been a meatless day. However, the consumption of both meat and fish at the same meal during Lent was prohibited. During the last few decades numerous dispensations and modifications to the laws of fasting and abstinence have been granted. Finally, Pope Paul VI, in his Apostolic Constitution *Paenitemini*, issued in February of 1966, revised and considerably simplified the laws in this regard. Many formerly obligatory days of fasting and/or abstinence were abrogated. The provisions of this document stipulate the days of penance retained in the liturgical calendar, as well as the Church's contemporary definition of what constitutes fasting and abstinence; the right of bishops' conferences to substitute other forms of penance in place of fasting and abstinence is also indicated:

> *II.1. The time of Lent preserves its penitential character. The days of penitence to be observed under obligation throughout the Church are all Fridays and Ash Wednesday. . . . Their substantial observance binds gravely.*
>
> *2. Apart from the faculties referred to in VI and VIII regarding the manner of fulfilling the precept of penitence on such days, abstinence is to be observed on every Friday which does not fall on a*

*day of obligation, while abstinence and fast are to be observed on
Ash Wednesday . . . and on Good Friday.*

*III.1. The law of abstinence forbids the use of meat, but not of
eggs, the products of milk or condiments made of animal fat.*

*2. The law of fasting allows only one full meal a day, but does
not prohibit taking some food in the morning and evening, observing — as far as quantity and quality are concerned — approved
local custom.*

*IV. To the law of abstinence those are bound who have com-
pleted their 14th year of age. To the law of fast those of the faithful
are bound who have completed their 21st year and up until the
beginning of their 60th year. . .*

*VI. 1. In accordance with the conciliar decree Christus
Dominus regarding the pastoral office of bishops, number 38,4, it is
the task of episcopal conferences to:*

*A. Transfer for just cause the days of penitence, always taking
into account the Lenten season;*

*B. Substitute abstinence and fast wholly or in part with other
forms of penitence and especially works of charity and the exercises
of piety.*[42]

These laws of fasting and abstinence have since been incorporated into the new *Code of Canon Law,* issued in February of 1983
(Canons 1249 to 1253).[43]

The Liturgical Colors of Holy Week

The liturgical development of Holy Week from the fourth century onward is far too complex a subject to summarize in one chapter,
and thus we will not attempt to do so here; rather, we will explore the
liturgical history of each day separately in the chapters to follow. Yet
there is one feature of the paschal liturgy that can be better addressed
while viewing Holy Week as a whole. This is the selection of "liturgical
colors."[44]

The use of distinctive colors for the different seasons of the liturgical year first arose in the early Middle Ages and became an established
practice in Rome by the time of Pope Innocent III (1198-1216).[45] In fact, one
of our earliest complete accounts of this subject (the treatise, *De sacro altaris
mysterio*) was written by Lothario of Segni (the future Innocent III) before

his election to the See of Peter in 1198.[46] In regard to the liturgy of Holy Week, the selection of particular colors for the vestments of the celebrants was originally determined by the penitential character of the entire Lenten season as contrasted with the jubilant nature of Easter. In *Roman Ordo 13*, a liturgical document of the thirteenth century, we find that in Rome violet was the color used on Palm Sunday, but this same source also mentions that red was worn in many parts of France.[47] Red was used in other places as well, such as in Fleurus, Belgium and at Wells, England. At Paris the color for Palm Sunday was black; in the Spanish cities of Seville and Toledo green was utilized. The mixed motifs of triumph and sorrow that characterize this first day of Holy Week when our Lord entered Jerusalem led to the selection of two colors in some places in order to reflect both moods. Thus at Monte Cassino in Italy and in Palencia, Spain, the celebrants wore white for the "Procession of Palms," but changed into black vestments for Mass, at which the gospel account of the passion was to be read.

On Holy Thursday, the day on which our Lord both instituted the holy Eucharist and entered upon His passion, the question of contrasting themes again arose in the medieval selection of liturgical colors. In many places, as on Palm Sunday, two colors were used, one for the celebration of Mass, and a second for the other observances. At Rome the Mass color has been white for centuries, with violet employed for the recitation of the Divine Office (until recently — a color for the Divine Office is no longer specified). In Paris black was the assigned color for the Divine Office, but red was worn at Mass, at the *Mandatum* (foot-washing) ceremony, and during the rite of reconciliation of penitents. In many instances the use of a more festive color for Mass was contingent upon whether the holy oils (for the administering of the Sacraments) were to be consecrated at the Eucharistic liturgy; such was the case in the Spanish cities of Toledo, Burgo de Osma, and Palencia, where black was worn at all the services, but white was used at those churches holding a Chrism Mass. However, in Milan, Italy, and at the English cathedrals of Salisbury and Wells, as well as throughout most of France, a single color, red, was employed for all the services, even the Chrism Mass, on Holy Thursday.

On Good Friday in the Roman Rite black was used for many centuries, evidently the sole surviving example of an earlier age when this color was worn throughout Lent and Advent. Black was also employed in Spain and in the French cities of Paris, Coutances, Troyes, Chalons, and Senlis, as well as in Eichstadt, Germany. Nonetheless, red was the more common color for this day, especially in Germany and much of France, but also in England at Salisbury and Westminster. In Laon, France we find that saffron (that is, a shade close to yellow) vestments were worn on this one day of the year (during the Mass of the Presanctified), symbolizing the malice of our Lord's enemies. In still another French city, Lyons, violet was employed.

White has always been almost universally associated with the Easter celebrations; however, in the past it was customary to reserve the taking of white vestments during the Easter Vigil until the formal beginning of the "Mass" itself. Thus in the Roman Rite violet was worn during the lighting of the new fire, the Old Testament readings, the blessing of the baptismal font and the recitation of the Litany of Saints up until the chanting of the *Kyrie Eleison*. There was one exception in that the deacon would wear white while singing the *Exultet* at the beginning of the vigil. Elsewhere in medieval Europe we find a similar pairing of a more penitential color (such as violet, blue, red) for the first part of the vigil with the use of white for the Mass. But in at least two Spanish cities — Seville and Burgo de Osma — there existed the now universal practice of wearing only white during the entire Easter Vigil.

In the current liturgy, red vestments are worn both on Palm Sunday and on Good Friday. Purple, the Lenten color, is used on Monday, Tuesday, and Wednesday of Holy Week. White vestments are worn on Holy Thursday and at the Easter Vigil, as well as on Easter Sunday.

The Role of Devotions in the Observance of Holy Week

For centuries extraliturgical devotions have played an important, albeit subordinate, role in the celebration of Holy Week. We will be describing some of these practices in the chapters to follow. It will suffice at this point simply to cite two passages from the Congregation for Divine Worship's *Circular Letter* on the Easter Feasts, which demonstrates the continued value of such exercises in the celebration of the Paschal Mystery. Speaking of observances on Good Friday, the Congregation states:

> *Devotions, such as the Way of the Cross, processions of the Passion, and commemorations of the sorrows of the Blessed Virgin Mary are not, for pastoral reasons, to be neglected. The texts and songs used, however, should be adapted to the spirit of the liturgy of this day. Such devotions should be assigned to a time of day that makes it quite clear*

that the liturgical celebration by its very nature far surpasses them in importance.[48]

In chapter VIII of the same *Circular Letter* the Congregation, in referring to devotions for the Easter Season, further elucidates this subject:

> *According to the differing circumstances of places and peoples, there are found a number of popular practices linked to celebrations of the Easter season, which in some instances attract greater numbers of the people than the sacred liturgy itself; these are not in any way to be undervalued, for they are often well adapted to the religious mentality of the faithful. Let episcopal conferences and local ordinaries therefore see to it that practices of this kind which seem to nourish popular piety, be harmonized in the best way possible with the sacred liturgy, be imbued more distinctly with the spirit of the liturgy, in some way derived from it, and lead the people to it.*[49]

Endnotes

1. Circular Letter Concerning the Preparation and Celebration of the Easter Feasts, 20 Feb 1988, #2, in *L'Osservatore Romano*, Feb 29, 1988, p. 15.
2. Sermo Guelferbytanus 5, #1, in *The Paschal Mystery: Ancient Liturgies and Patristic Texts* (Alba Patristic Library), Andre Hamman, OFM, ed., Vol. 3, pp. 148-149.
3. Reverend John Tyrer, *Historical Survey of Holy Week: Its Services and Ceremonial* (Alcuin Club Collections #29), pp. 17-18.
4. Ibid., pp. 3-10.
5. Ibid., p. 18.
6. Ibid., p. 10.
7. Ibid., p. 7.
8. Monsignor L. Duchesne, *Christian Worship: Its Origin and Evolution*, p. 228.
9. "De Oratione," chapter 18, in Father Herbert Thurston, S.J., "Archdeacon Farrar on the Observance of Good Friday," *The Month*, May 1895, p. 95.
10. Tyrer, p. 23.
11. Father Herbert Thurston, SJ, "Holy Week," *Catholic Encyclopedia*, 1907, Vol. 7, p. 436.

12. Chapter 21, quoted in Tyrer, p. 26.

13. Ibid., p. 26.

14. Festal Letter I, #10, in *A Select Library of Nicene and Post-Nicene Fathers of the Christian Church, Second Series*, Philip Schoff and Henry Wace, eds., 1891, Vol. IV, p. 509.

15. Festal Letter III, in Ibid., #6, Vol. IV, p. 515.

16. Epistle 23 (to the Bishops of Aemelia), in *Saint Ambrose: Letters (Fathers of the Church*, Vol. 26), Sister Mary Melchoir Beyenka, OP, tr., p. 194.

17. Father Francis X. Weiser, SJ, *The Easter Book*, p. 112.

18. The following is based upon the English translation of Egeria's account (chapters 30 to 38) in *Egeria: Diary of a Pilgrimage* (Ancient Christian Writers, #38), George Gingras, ed./tr. pp. 103-114; the text is also provided in *Egeria's Travels*, John Wilkinson, ed./tr., pp. 132-139.

19. Chapter 35, in Gingras, pp. 107-108.

20. Chapter 36, in Gingras, p. 109.

21. Congregation for Divine Worship, Feb 20, 1988, #56, in *L'Osservatore Romano*, Feb 29, 1988, p. 17.

22. Chapter 36, in Gingras, p. 110.

23. Chapter 37, in Gingras, p. 112.

24. Father Herbert Thurston, SJ, "The Devotion of the 'Three Hours,' " *The Month*, March 1899, pp. 249-255.

25. Congregation for Divine Worship, Feb 20, 1988, #74, p. 18.

26. This section based upon Tyrer, pp. 45-46, 69-70, 79-81, 116-117, 143-144, and Weiser, pp. 94, 103-104, 113, 131, except where noted otherwise.

27. *Missale Romanum* (1970 ed.), p. 224.

28. For *Roman Missal* see ibid., p. 266; for *Gelasian Sacramentary* and *Roman Ordo 12* see *Patrologia Latina*, Migne, J.-P., ed., Vol. 74, col. 1113c, and Vol. 78, col. 1077b, respectively.

29. Frederick G. Holweck, "Easter," in *Catholic Encyclopedia*, 1907, Vol. 5, p. 224.

30. Father Francis X. Weiser, SJ, *Handbook of Christian Feasts and Customs: The Year of the Lord in Liturgy and Folklore*, p. 211.

31. *Vatican II Sunday Missal*, Daughters of St. Paul, 1974, p. 635.

32. N. Q. King, *The Emperor Theodosius and the Establishment of Christianity*, p. 110.

33. *De Cruce*, Book 5, quoted in Cardinal Wiseman, *Four Lectures on the Offices and Ceremonies of Holy Week*, ca. 1838, p. 163.

34. *"Hom. iii De Resurrect. Christi,"* cited in Wiseman, p. 164.
35. Wiseman, p. 164.
36. Abbot Guéranger, OSB, *The Liturgical Year*, Vol. 6, pp. 7-8.
37. Wiseman, pp. 174-175.
38. Count Montalembert, in Wiseman, pp. 159-160.
39. Based upon Father Herbert Thurston, SJ, "Lent," *Catholic Encyclopedia*, 1907, Vol. 9, pp. 152-154, except where noted otherwise.
40. *Hist. Eccl.*, V, 22, quoted in Thurston, p. 153.
41. Thurston, p. 153.
42. Chapter 3, *Apostolic Constitution on Penance*, 17 Feb 1966, in *Vatican Council II: More Postconciliar Documents (Vatican Collection, Vol II)*, Austin Flannery, OP, ed., pp. 7-8.
43. Book IV, Part III, Title II, chapter II, in *The Code of Canon Law: In English Translation*, Canon Law Society of Great Britian and Ireland, 1983, p. 218.
44. Based upon J. Wickham Legg, *Notes on the History of the Liturgical Colours*, pp. 21-28, except where noted otherwise.
45. Herbert Norris, *Church Vestments: Their Origin and Development*, p. 70.
46. J. Wickham Legg, *Essays Liturgical and Historical*, pp. 157, 159.
47. *Patrologia Latina*, Vol. 78, col. 1117d.
48. Congregation for Divine Worship, #72, p. 18.
49. Ibid., #106, p. 19.

Dear friends in Christ, for five weeks of Lent we have been preparing, by works of charity and self-sacrifice, for the celebration of our Lord's paschal mystery. Today we come together to begin this solemn celebration in union with the whole Church throughout the world. Christ entered in triumph into his own city, to complete his work as our Messiah: to suffer, to die, and to rise again. Let us remember with devotion this entry which began his saving work and follow him with a lively faith. United with him in his suffering on the cross, may we share his resurrection and new life.

[Introduction, Liturgy of Palm Sunday, *Roman Missal*][1]

II

Palm Sunday

Prelude

Now as the time drew near ... he resolutely took the road for Jerusalem. . . .

[Lk 9:51; JB]

They saw him in the distance, and before he reached them they made a plot among themselves to put him to death. "Here comes the man of dreams," they said to one another. "Come on, let us kill him. . . . Then we shall see what becomes of his dreams."

[Gen 37:18-20; JB]

The chief priests and Pharisees had by now given their orders: anyone who knew where he was must inform them so that they could arrest him.

[Jn 11:57; JB]

Then they said, "Come, let us make plots against Jeremiah, for the law shall not perish from the priest, nor counsel from the wise, nor the word from the prophet. Come, let us smite him with the tongue, and let us not heed any of his words."

[Jer 18:18]

Jesus was going up to Jerusalem, and on the way he took the Twelve to one side and said to them, "Now we are going up to Jerusalem, and the Son of Man is about to be handed over to the chief priests and scribes. They will condemn him to death and will hand him over to the pagans to be mocked and scourged and crucified; and on the third day he will rise again."

[Mt 20:17-19: JB]

*But the Lord is with me as a dread warrior; therefore my persecutors
will stumble, they will not overcome me. They will be greatly shamed,
for they will not succeed.*

[Jer 20:11]

*But they understood none of these things; this saying was hid from
them, and they did not grasp what was said.*

[Lk 18:34]

The Procession of Palms

*When they were near Jerusalem and had come in sight of Bethphage
on the Mount of Olives, Jesus sent two disciples, saying to them, "Go
to the village facing you, and you will immediately find a tethered
donkey and a colt with her. Untie them and bring them to me. If anyone
says anything to you, you are to say, 'The Master needs them. . . .' "*

[Mt 21:1-3; JB]

EVERY YEAR THE CHURCH begins Holy Week by entering
the gates of Jerusalem with her Divine Spouse. For it is on this day that
the celebration of Mass opens with the "Procession of Palms" — a
commemoration of our Lord's triumphant entry into Jerusalem. Indeed,
as we have learned already from Egeria's pilgrimage diary, this
ceremony existed in Jerusalem itself as early as the fourth century. In
the West, it appears for the first time in the *Liber Ordinum*, a liturgical
book of Spain's Mozarabic Rite containing practices of the fifth to
seventh centuries; both the blessing of palms at the altar and a subsequent procession with palms are mentioned.[2] In an eighth-century
document of northern Italy, the so-called *Bobbio Missal*, a prayer for "the
Blessing of Palms and Olives on the altar" is provided, but this missal
says nothing about a procession afterwards; it does, however, indicate
that the people took palms home with them "piously with devotion."[3]
In the next century, the Gallic liturgist Amalarius of Metz (France)
speaks of what is evidently a "Procession of Palms": "In memory of this
[our Lord's entry into Jerusalem] we are accustomed throughout our
churches to carry branches and to cry *Hosanna*."[4] It was during this same
period that the French Bishop Theodolph of Orleans (died A.D. 821)
composed the Palm Sunday hymn, *Gloria laus* ("All glory, laud, and
honor").[5] A Procession of Palms is described in the tenth-century

Regularis Concordia, a document detailing the practices of England's Benedictine monasteries:

> . . .*the gospel* Turba multa *[Jn 12:12-19] shall be read by the deacon as far as the words "Behold, the whole world is gone after him" [Jn 12:19]: the blessing of the palms shall follow. After the blessing the palms shall be sprinkled with holy water and incensed. While the children begin the antiphons* Pueri Hebraeorum *["The children of the Hebrews"] the palms shall be distributed. Then the greater antiphons shall be intoned and the procession shall go forth. As soon as the Mother church is reached the procession shall wait while the children, who shall have gone on before, sing* Gloria laus *with its verses, to which all shall answer* Gloria laus, *as the custom is. When this is finished the cantor shall intone the respond* Ingrediente Domino *["When the Lord entered the Holy City"] and the doors shall be opened.*[6]

Although such ceremonies are not found in the official liturgical books of Rome until the twelfth century, when they appear in *Roman Ordines 11* and *12*,[7] there are indications that the custom may have reached the city long before this time. Three of the earliest Roman liturgical books, the seventh-century *Gelasian Sacramentary* and both the Paduan (seventh century) and the Hadrian (eighth century) editions of the *Gregorian Sacramentary*, refer to the Sunday before Easter as the "*Dominica(o) in(ad) palmas*" ("Sunday for/unto Palms"). Possibly this name arose from the introduction of palm rites in Rome; even so, none of these documents mention such observances.[8] It is more likely that the arrival in Rome of the German liturgical book, the *Romano-Germanic Pontifical of the Tenth Century*, sometime between A.D. 951 and 972,[9] would have led to the introduction of the Procession of Palms into the Roman liturgy, for just such a ceremony is described at great length in this work.[10]

Eventually the Procession of Palms spread throughout medieval Europe, taking on the same general characteristics everywhere,[11] but with certain local variations. Ceremonies began with the blessing of palms at a church or shrine outside of town; from this "station" a procession of clergy and laity wended its way to the city's cathedral or main church. Sometimes the Blessed Sacrament was carried (particularly in England and northern France), a custom that appears to have been introduced by the Norman Abbot Lanfranc in the eleventh century; a Palm Sunday procession featuring the Blessed Sacrament is described in considerable detail in his statutes for

England's Canterbury Cathedral, where he became Archbishop in 1070.[12] A Eucharistic Procession of Palms was held each year in Rouen, France, until the time of the French Revolution (late eighteenth century).[13] In other medieval examples of the Palm Sunday procession the celebrant would carry a crucifix adorned with flowers. The cross was the principle object in the processions at Bayeux and Besancon in France, and in the special Rite of Aquileia, Italy;[14] a medieval book of Egypt's Coptic Rite (fourteenth century) mentions that the cross was borne triumphantly through the villages and countryside on this day.[15] In the tenth century, a wooden sculpture known as the *Palmesel* (Palm Donkey) or *Palmchristus*[16] was introduced into Palm Sunday processions, depicting our Lord mounted on a donkey; the *Palmesel* was particularly common in Germany, where such a figure was in use as early as A.D. 970 in Augsburg (Bavaria).[17] Although this custom generally disappeared following the Middle Ages, a *Palmesel* was evidently still a part of the ceremonies in the Diocese of Constance (France) as late as 1753.[18] In still other medieval Palm Sunday processions the gospel book and even relics of saints were carried. Thus the author of the *Liber de divinis officiis*, a work written sometime before A.D. 950 and formerly attributed to Alcuin, the famous eighth-century Abbot of Tours (France), speaks of the gospel book being borne in a shrine or feretory (portable reliquary).[19]

> *They brought the donkey and the colt, then they laid their cloaks on*
> *their backs and he sat on them.*
>
> [Mt 21:7; JB]

Prior to the arrival of the procession at the city gate, a boys' choir would be stationed either atop the gate or over the porch of the principle church. As the procession neared, the choir would begin the singing of the *Gloria laus* after which all knelt and bowed to the Blessed Sacrament (or the crucifix), before which they spread cloths, carpets, flowers, and branches. As church bells tolled and the *Hosanna* was sung, the procession entered the destination church for Mass.

> *Rejoice heart and soul, daughter of Zion!*
> *Shout with gladness, daughter of Jerusalem!*
> *See now, your king comes to you;*
> *he is victorious, he is triumphant,*
> *humble and riding on a donkey. . . .*
>
> [Zech 9:9; JB]

Certain elements of this ceremony varied from place to place. In England at Winchester (twelfth to thirteenth centuries), the procession upon arriving at the city gate would separate into two groups, one of which served as an entourage for the Blessed Sacrament (which was carried on a bier), the other, only a short distance away, made up of those escorting the bishop. An antiphonal dialogue between the two groups would follow.[20] In Zurich, Switzerland (thirteenth century), where a *Palmchristus* (rather than the Eucharist) was carried, the participants in the procession were likewise divided into two groups, one representing those accompanying Christ into Jerusalem, the other representing the crowds that went out from the City to meet Him. At the climax of the procession, palms would be spread over the *Palmchristus*, after which all the faithful would throw their palms before it.[21] At Essen in Germany (fourteenth century), the procession also featured a *Palmesel*, which was brought into the middle of the church and made to face the east, with carpets strewn before it.[22] In the southwest German town of Biberach (in the years prior to the Protestant Reformation that swept this city in 1531), it was customary for the choir to cast their surplices to the ground before the figure of the *Palmesel*, thus reenacting the action of the crowd that greeted our Lord as He entered Jerusalem, who "spread their garments on the road" (Mt 21:8) before Him.[23] In the *Ordo of Beroldus*, a twelfth-century liturgical text of Milan's Ambrosian Rite (northern Italy), we are told that upon the conclusion of the Blessing of Palms, the archbishop would ride in state on a white horse from the city's Church of San Lorenzo to that of San Ambrogio, carrying a cross of crystal in his left hand while blessing the people with his right.[24] In sixteenth-century Aquileia, Italy, the cross to be carried in procession would be laid upon a carpet at the foot of the altar in the church where the palms were to be blessed; following the blessing, all simultaneously reverenced the cross, after which the celebrant would lift it up and sing, *O Crux, ave, spes unica* ("O Cross, hail, [our] only hope"). A second time all honor the cross — the celebrant, clergy, and cantors prostrating themselves before it; at this point one of the clerics strikes the celebrant on the shoulder with a palm branch and intones the antiphon, *Percutiam pastorem*, from the Book of Zechariah:

> Strike the shepherd,
> that the sheep may be scattered. . . .
>
> [Zech 13:7]

Thereupon the celebrant rises and takes the cross in a triumphant procession to the cathedral, where Mass is then celebrated.[25]

In places where the Blessed Sacrament was borne, the Sacrament would customarily be brought "by stealth" during the night before Palm Sunday to the station where the procession was to begin the next day. This was done so that the faithful would find our Lord waiting for them in the morning when they gathered to accompany Him from this station, symbolizing Bethany, to the destination church, which represented Jerusalem. Confraternities of the Blessed Sacrament participated in the secretive *nocturnal* transfer of the holy Eucharist.[26] For the actual procession on Palm Sunday, the Blessed Sacrament would be carried in a portable reliquary called a "feretory," surrounded by burning lanterns. In the will of an Englishman named William Bruges, dating from 1450, one of these feretories is described in some detail. Bruges had provided a feretory made of gilt wood and silver decorated with jewels and surrounded with images of angels holding emblems of the passion. A small silver cup held the Blessed Sacrament, and this cup in turn was enclosed in a larger second cup of silver. A large silver gilt crown fitted with jewels was used to cover the outer cup.[27]

A number of different customs related specifically to the arrival of the Palm Sunday procession at the door of the church where Mass was to be celebrated. In medieval England the celebrant would sometimes take the cross carried in procession and open the church door with it.[28] In other cases the feretory containing the Blessed Sacrament was lifted in the air to a position above the door, under which the procession then passed into the church; the latter was the practice during the fifteenth century both at the English Cathedral of Hereford and at the French Cathedral of Rouen.[29] In the *Missale Mixtum* of 1500 (Mozarabic Rite of Spain) we find that a dialogue took place upon arrival at the church door. The procession would approach the west face of the Cathedral of Toledo, whereupon the archbishop would knock on the closed door with his staff and say the following words from Psalm 24:

Lift up your gates, O ye princes,
and be ye lifted up, O eternal gates:
and the King of Glory shall enter in.

[verse 7]

From within two canons ask in reply:

[46]

Who is this King of Glory?

[verse 8]

The archbishop then answers them:

The Lord who is strong and mighty. . .

[verse 8]

This dialogue is repeated in a similar manner two more times, after which the door is opened, and the procession enters the cathedral.[30]

> *. . . the crowds who had come up for the festival heard that Jesus was on his way to Jerusalem. They took branches of palm and went out to meet him. . . .*
>
> [Jn 12:12-13; JB]

Gradually the Palm Sunday procession was shortened to a course around the church, with a stop before the church yard crucifix, decorated with flowers. At this point in the procession the congregation would spread out in the church cemetery to kneel in prayer at the graves of their loved ones, while the clergy continued the hymns and antiphons. Afterwards the procession would reassemble and enter the church.[31] A number of English wills from the fifteenth and sixteenth centuries contain requests from the testators to be buried near the Church yard "palm cross."[32] The tradition of visiting graves on Palm Sunday has continued to the present day, especially in England and France,[33] but also in the United States.

Following the issuance in 1570 of the *Roman Missal* for the universal Church by Pope Saint Pius V, the Procession of Palms took on a fixed format throughout the West. The subsequent promulgation of two supplementary liturgical books, the *Caeremoniale Episcoporum* (1600) and the *Memoriale Rituum* (1725), further defined the character of the ceremony in the Roman Rite, which remained virtually unchanged until the middle of the present century.[34] In the morning the church bells are rung in a festive manner, summoning the people. In the sanctuary is a table covered by a white cloth, upon which the palms are laid, veiled under a second, violet cloth. After the celebrant arrives, the violet veil over the palms is removed. Following several opening prayers, a lection from the Book of Exodus (15:27-16:7) and the reading of Saint Matthew's gospel account of Christ's triumphant entry into Jerusalem (Mt 21:1-9), the celebrant sprinkles the palms with holy water three times and censes them. He then sits and delivers a homily suitable to the occasion. Afterwards an assisting cleric takes one of the palms and places it on the *mensa* (top) of the altar, from which the celebrant in turn takes it and kisses it (if another priest is present, the celebrant receives the palm from him instead). Having returned this palm to the other cleric, the celebrant now turns to the congregation and begins to distribute the palms, first to any other priests and clerics present, who kneel on the edge of the topmost altar step (the *predella*) and kiss the palm given them, then the hand of the celebrant. When all the clerics have received their palms, the celebrant descends to the altar rail and likewise distributes the palms to the people, the men first, followed by the women. Each of the faithful kneels at the altar rail and kisses both the palm and the celebrant's hand. Upon the conclusion of the distribution, the assisting cleric ties a palm to the top of the purple-veiled processional cross, using a purple ribbon; he then returns to the celebrant the palm he had given him earlier in the ceremony. The celebrant takes it in his right hand (in his left hand if he is a bishop) and turning toward the people, says, "Let us proceed in peace," to which the other clerics or choir respond, "In the name of Christ. Amen." The procession now begins, moving out of the church through the main door as the bells are rung. The assisting cleric (or a "crossbearer") leads, carrying the processional cross, and followed by the celebrant. Antiphons from the gospels of Saint Matthew (21:1-3, 7, 8, 9) and Saint John (12:12, 13) are chanted along the way. Finally the procession returns to the main door, before which the assisting cleric comes to a stop, while two (or four) chanters or other clerics take a position inside the church behind the closed door. Those inside begin the hymn, *Gloria, laus et honor*, to which the celebrant outside responds antiphonally. Following the last verse, the assisting cleric (or a subdeacon) strikes the lower portion of the church door with the bottom of the staff of the processional cross. Those within open the door and the procession returns to the altar for the beginning of Mass.

In 1955, when the Congregation of Sacred Rites issued the restored Ordo of Holy Week, the ceremony for the Palm Sunday procession was revised and simplified in certain respects, yet not altered thematically, as we shall see shortly.

The plants used as "palms" for the ceremonies this day have varied from one country to another, determined by the availability of suitable foliage. In Italy olive branches have been used, whereas in England, Germany, Poland, and Lithuania willows have commonly served this purpose. In Ireland the yew provided "palms"; other plants that have been utilized in different places include spruce and box.[35] An account of Palm Sunday in Jerusalem dating from 1866 mentions that bundles of fresh green seven-foot palm branches were brought in each year from the Palestinian city of Gaza and placed in the holy sepulchre, where they were blessed, sprinkled with holy water and censed by the patriarch.[36]

> *O God, Who dost gather dispersed things and preserve what Thou hast gathered, Who didst bless the people bearing branches to meet Jesus, bless also these branches of palm and of olive which Thy servants take up in the spirit of faith, that, into whatsoever place they shall be brought, the dwellers in that place may obtain Thy blessing, and that, putting to flight all evil, Thy right hand may protect those who have been redeemed by Jesus Christ, Thy Son, our Lord, Who with Thee liveth and reigneth. Amen.*
>
> [Missale Romanum, 1942][37]

Many of the faithful bring home the palms blessed on this first day of Holy Week and keep them throughout the year, sometimes attaching them to a crucifix or holy image. In Italy blessed palms are exchanged as a token of reconciliation between quarreling parties. Among Poles and Ukrainians there is the custom of *Boze Rany* ("God's Wounds"), in which the faithful tap each other with pussy-willow palms on Palm Sunday in commemoration of the scourging of Christ.[38]

During the afternoon on Palm Sunday, Austrian, Bavarian, and Slavic farmers, together with their families, customarily go through their lands and buildings, praying and singing hymns while they place blessed palms in each plot and structure, so as to obtain God's blessing on their property and harvest.[39]

In Puerto Rico preparations for Palm Sunday begin on the day before when the parish priests give native-grown palm branches to their parishioners. Thus each family spends the whole of Saturday fashioning all sorts of decorations from the palms, ranging from lamps to baby shoes. The decorations are then hung on a palm tree together with ribbons and flowers in a manner analogous to adorning a Christmas tree. On the morning of Palm Sunday the families show their palm creations to the parish priest that he might bless them for the procession that day. But the pastor must also give his judgment as to which family's hand-made art work is the finest. It is considered a great honor to win this distinction. Afterwards, all take their palms in procession to the church.[40]

The manner in which our Lord was welcomed into Jerusalem resembles in several important respects the celebration of the Jewish festival known as the Feast of Tabernacles, which was held in the autumn every year. On each of the seven days of this feast the people would walk in procession with palm branches in their hands around the court surrounding the altar of the temple; making their palms bend towards the altar, they would cry out *Hosanna* ("save now") to the sound of trumpets. Evidently verses 25 and 26 of Psalm 118, containing the expressions *Hosanna* and "Blessed be he who enters in the name of the Lord," served as a kind of responsory for the recitation of the "great Hallel" (consisting of Psalms 113 through 118) used for this event. Interestingly the *Talmud* specified that children old enough to wave palm boughs were also supposed to participate. The palm branches themselves came to be known as *Hosannas*. The similarities to our Palm Sunday commemoration are unmistakable.[41]

The Procession of Palms Today

In the modern Roman liturgy the Mass of Palm Sunday may begin in one of three ways. The First Form is that of a solemn procession that starts outside the church; in the Second Form the whole procession takes place within the church; and with the Third Form the procession is omitted entirely. Naturally the most beautiful and elaborate of these is the first.[42] The priest or priests who are to celebrate the Mass and the faithful gather at a suitable place, such as a church or chapel, away from the church where the procession will end. After an introductory greeting (for text see p. 40), the celebrant, clothed in red vestments, blesses the palms in these words from the *Roman Missal*:

> *Almighty God,*
> *we pray you*
> *bless + these branches*
> *and make them holy.*
> *Today we joyfully acclaim*
> *Jesus our Messiah and King.*
> *May we reach one day the happiness*
> *of the new and everlasting Jerusalem*

by faithfully following him
who lives and reigns for ever and ever.

The celebrant now sprinkles the branches with holy water. One of the gospel accounts of Christ's triumphant entry into Jerusalem is then read; a three-year cycle is used to determine which account (Mt 21:1-11, Mk 11:1-10, Jn 12:12-16, or Lk 19:28-40) will be selected in a given year:

> *The huge crowd spread their cloaks on the road, while some*
> *began to cut branches from the trees and laid them along his path.*
> *The groups preceding him as well as those following kept crying out:*
> *"God save the Son of David!*
> *Blessed be he who comes*
> *in the name of the Lord!*
> *God save him from on high!"*
> *As he entered Jerusalem the whole city was stirred to its depths,*
> *demanding, "Who is this?" And the crowd kept answering, "This is*
> *the prophet Jesus from Nazareth in Galilee."*
>
> [Mt 21:8-11; NAB]

Following the gospel (and an optional brief homily) the celebrant says to the faithful:

> *Let us go forth in peace,*
> *praising Jesus our Messiah,*
> *as did the crowds who*
> *welcomed him to Jerusalem.*

A procession forms, led by an acolyte with a censer, followed by another carrying the cross ("suitably decorated") with two others bearing lighted candles on each side of him. Behind them walks the priest to celebrate Mass, followed by the faithful, all carrying palms. They head for the destination church, singing appropriate hymns and Psalms such as the 24th and 47th:

> *Who is this king of glory?*
> *The Lord of hosts;*
> *he is the king of glory.*
>
> [Ps 24:10]

God mounts his throne amid shouts of joy;
the Lord, amid trumpet blasts.
Sing praise to God, sing praise;
sing praise to our king, sing praise.
For king of all the earth is God;
sing hymns of praise.

[Ps 47:6-8; NAB]

The ninth-century Palm Sunday hymn *Gloria laus* is also sung:

All glory, laud and honor
To thee, Redeemer, King!
To whom the lips of children
Made sweet hosannas ring.
Thou art the King of Israel,
Thou David's royal Son,
Who in the Lord's Name comest,
The King and Blessed One.
The company of angels
Are praising thee on high;
And mortal men, and all things
Created, make reply.

[refrain & vs. 1, 2][43]

As the procession continues, our thoughts return to that first Palm Sunday in Jerusalem, as described in a sermon of Saint Andrew of Crete (A.D. 660-740) used in the Divine Office for this day:

Let us go together to meet Christ on the Mount of Olives.
Today he returns from Bethany and proceeds of his own free will
toward his holy and blessed passion, to consummate the mystery of
our salvation. . .
Let us run to accompany him as he hastens toward his passion,
and imitate those who met him then, not by covering his path with
garments, olive branches or palms, but by doing all we can to
prostrate ourselves before him by being humble and by trying to live
as he would wish. . . . We who have been baptized into Christ must
ourselves be the garments that we spread before him. Now that the
crimson stains of our sins have been washed away in the saving
waters of baptism and we have become white as pure wool, let us

present the conqueror of death, not with mere branches of palms but with the real rewards of his victory. Let our souls take the place of the welcoming branches as we join today in the children's holy song: Blessed is he who comes in the name of the Lord. Blessed is the king of Israel.

["Oratio 9 in ramos palmarum"][44]

Some Pharisees in the crowd said to him, "Master, check your disciples," but he answered, "I tell you, if these keep silence the stones will cry out."

[Lk 19:39-40; JB]

Hero, strap your sword at your side,
in majesty and splendor; on, ride on,
in the cause of truth, religion and virtue!

[Ps 45:3-4; JB]

Then the Pharisees said to one another, "You see, there is nothing you can do; look, the whole world is running after him!"

[Jn 12:19; JB]

Upon entering the church where Mass is to begin, the celebrant goes to the altar, kisses it, and censes it. The procession now ends and after an opening prayer the Liturgy of the Word begins.

The Liturgy of the Word

Throughout Holy Week, we will be hearing passages from the Book of Isaiah describing the "Suffering Servant" — passages that prophesy the redemptive sufferings of the Messiah. Today the Liturgy of the Word begins with a lection from the fiftieth chapter of Isaiah (vs. 4-7); it contains unmistakable references to the scourging, spittle, and buffeting to which our Lord was subjected by His enemies:

I gave my back to those who beat me,
my cheeks to those who plucked my beard;
My face I did not shield
from buffets and spitting.

[Is 50:6; NAB]

[53]

The passion is likewise foreshadowed in the twenty-second Psalm, from which our Lord quoted on the cross (Mt 27:46; Mk 15:34). It is used as the responsorial psalm for the Palm Sunday liturgy (Ps 22:8-9, 17-20, 23-24):

> *All who see me scoff at me;*
> *they mock me with parted lips. . .*
> *Indeed, many dogs surround me,*
> *a pack of evildoers closes in upon me;*
> *They have pierced my hands and my feet;*
> *I can count all my bones.*
>
> [Ps 22:8, 17-18; NAB]

The second reading constitutes one of the most quoted passages from the Epistles of Saint Paul (Phil 2:5-11). This same lection has been used in the liturgy on this day for over twelve hundred years; it is listed in the *Capitulary of Wurzburg,* the oldest surviving Roman lectionary, dating from the seventh or early eighth centuries.[45] In it Saint Paul describes how our Lord humbled Himself for our sake by becoming Man and dying for us:

> *Your attitude must be Christ's:*
> *though he was in the form of God*
> *he did not deem equality with God*
> *something to be grasped at*
> *Rather, he emptied himself*
> *and took the form of a slave,*
> *being born in the likeness of men.*
> *He was known to be of human estate,*
> *and it was thus he humbled himself,*
> *obediently accepting even death,*
> *death on a cross!*
>
> [Phil 2:5-8]

The Reading of the Passion

The second unusual feature of the Mass for Palm Sunday is the solemn reading or chanting of one of the gospel accounts of the passion. This aspect of the Palm Sunday liturgy can be traced back through fifteen hundred years of history. Seven of the sermons of Pope Saint Leo the Great (A.D. 390-461) for the Sunday before Easter focus upon the theme of our Lord's passion,[46] and in one of these he indicates that the gospel account of the passion was heard on this day (as well as on Wednesday of Holy Week):

> But, because it is too much, dearly beloved, for today's sermon to touch on everything, let the rest be deferred till Wednesday, when a Lesson of the Lord's Passion will be read again" [emphasis added].[47]

Our earliest extant Roman lectionary, the *Capitulary of Wurzburg* (seventh to early eighth centuries), specifies the passion according to Saint Matthew (Mt 26:1-27:66) for the first day of Holy Week.[48] Saint Matthew's account remained the only one in the Palm Sunday liturgy of the Roman Rite for centuries to come, up until 1970, when the new *Roman Missal* of Pope Paul VI was issued. A three-year cycle consisting of the gospel accounts of Saint Matthew, Saint Mark, and Saint Luke was adopted, with the passion according to Saint John reserved (as in the past) for the liturgy of Good Friday.

The division of the recitation of the passion among different speakers is a practice with obscure origins. As early as the eighth century we find special markings along the margin of the passion text in the *Bobbio Missal* to distinguish the words of our Lord;[49] similar markings appear in an eighth-century manuscript of Durham, England.[50] However, it does seem that at first such a division was achieved only in a symbolic manner by having a single deacon present the passion in two or three different voices (that is, two or three different pitches and/or volumes) in order to distinguish the words of Christ from those of the evangelist or of others such as Saint Peter or Pilate.[51] The thirteenth-century bishop and liturgist Durandus of Metz speaks of just such a division of voices without mentioning multiple singers,[52] but in another source from this period, the Dominican *Gros Livre*, which dates from 1254, there appears the earliest explicit reference to the distribution of the words of the passion among several cantors.[53] An English *Sarum Gradual* preserved in Parma, Italy, from about the year 1300, specifies five singers for the passion, plus a special cantor to chant the words of Christ on the cross.[54] In Rome, however, the use of more than one reader seems to have been a later development; in the fifteenth century a single deacon was still reading the entire passion at the Papal services, according to *Roman Ordo 15*.[55] In a *Roman Missal* of 1530 the singing of the passion in three different voices — alto, bass, and tenor — is explained at length in the rubrics, but there is no explicit reference to multiple singers.[56] At the beginning of the seventeenth century, we finally find mention of the division of the passion among several cantors in Roman liturgical documents, for both the first edition of the *Caeremoniale Episcoporum* (1600) and an early Decree of the Congregation of Sacred Rites dating from July of 1612 (S.R.C. #299) speak of cantors for the passion in the plural (*Cantoribus*).[57] The practice, as it has existed since, calls for the participation of two or three deacons, each assigned a different part. One deacon assumes the role of narrator, chanting the words of the evangelist in a tenor voice. Another deacon sings the words of Christ in a deep bass voice. A third takes all the other parts, delivering the words in a high contralto voice. This custom continues to the present day, although in many parish churches the division is not among three deacons, but among the lector (as narrator), the priest celebrating Mass (as Christ), a second reader (for other parts), and the congregation (for words spoken by several people at once in the gospel account, such as the shouts of the crowd before Pilate). This format arose following the promulgation of the decree *Plures locorum* of March 25, 1965, which granted permission for the laity to take one or more of the parts.[58] The text of the passion can be delivered in a normal narrative tone, or sung to a special chant that has been used for centuries.

Whether read or sung, there is always a silent and reverent pause in the recitation of the passion when the moment of our Lord's death is reached. The older *Roman Ordines* make no mention of such a practice, but an analogous custom did appear in the early Middle Ages, persisting for several centuries thereafter. The stripping of cloths from the altar, included in the Good Friday rubrics of the eighth-century *Roman Ordines 24* (Andrieu) and *27* (Andrieu),[59] became associated (by the ninth century) with the reading of the words *Partiti sunt vestimenta mea sibi* ("They have parted my garments among them" — Jn 19:24) during the Good Friday recitation of the passion; thus the ninth-century *Roman Ordo 31* (Andrieu) calls for two deacons to strip two cloths from the altar at this point,[60] an action undoubtedly intended to symbolize the stripping of our Lord before His crucifixion. With the introduction of such a dramatic gesture into the reading of the passion, it is not surprising that there would eventually be an attempt to delineate the culminating words of these readings: the moment of Christ's death on the cross. Such was the case in Rome, at least on Good Friday, by the first half of the fourteenth century, as is evident in *Roman Ordo 14*, which prescribes that when the deacon chanting the passion (of John) pronounced the words, *Et inclinato capite tradidit spiritum* ("And bowing his head, he gave up the ghost" — Jn 19:30) the pope and all others present were to genuflect toward the altar, pausing on their knees for the space of one *Pater Noster* (Our Father).[61] Unfortunately this document does not indicate whether there was a similar pause during the reading of the passion on Palm Sunday, but there is evidence concerning the latter day in another fourteenth-century source, the English *Missale Westmonasteriensis*. The text of the passion for Palm Sunday in this Missal is interrupted following the words, *emisit spiritum* ("yielded up the ghost" — Mt 27:50) with a rubric specifying that the priest reading the passion should pronounce the latter words with devotion (*Hic dicit sacerdos deuocionem*); the same rubric appears in the text of Saint John's passion on Good Friday following the phrase *tradidit spiritum*.[62] Finally in *Roman Ordo 15*, from the first part of the fifteenth century, we find both on Good Friday *and* on Palm Sunday (after the words *emisit spiritum*) the same genuflection and pause during the passion mentioned only on Good Friday in *Ordo 14*.[63] The most recent edition of the *Caeremoniale Episcoporum* (1985) continues to call for all to genuflect and pause (*omnes genuflectunt, et pausatur aliquantulum*) at this point in the passion (on both days).[64]

The Liturgy of the Eucharist

As on every Sunday of the liturgical year, so on Palm Sunday the celebration of Mass culminates in the Liturgy of the Eucharist, the climax of the Church's worship. Although this portion of the Palm Sunday liturgy in no way differs from the usual format of other Sundays, the texts of the prayers proper to this day do bear mentioning here. The "Prayer over the Gifts," the "Communion Antiphon" and the "Prayer after Communion" are all dominated by the theme of this day's gospel — our Lord's passion. The preface to the Eucharistic Prayer likewise addresses this motif:

> *Though he was sinless,*
> *he suffered willingly for sinners.*
> *Though innocent,*
> *he accepted death to save the guilty.*
> *By his dying he has destroyed our sins.*
> *By his rising he has raised us up*
> *to holiness of life.*[65]

At the end of Mass the faithful will take palms home with them — a tangible reminder of the mysteries they have commemorated in union with the whole Church on this day. Throughout the upcoming week these palms will serve to direct their hearts and minds to the unfolding of the Paschal Mystery, from the Last Supper to the cross and onward to the empty tomb of Easter morning.

Palm Sunday in the Byzantine Rite

In the Byzantine Rite the solemn reading of the passion has never been part of the observances for Palm Sunday; rather, the theme of our Lord's triumphant entry into Jerusalem dominates the liturgy for this day. The Procession of Palms, which originated in the East, described for the first time in the fourth-century pilgrimage diary of Egeria, was retained in the subsequent books of the Jerusalem liturgy. Thus it appears in the *Armenian Lectionary* (early fifth century),[66] and again, but in greater detail, in the *Georgian Lectionary* (also known as the *Ierusalimskij Kanonar* — fifth to eighth centuries). It is in the latter that for the first time the blessing of the palms prior to their distribution to the people is mentioned. It is also in the *Georgian Lectionary* that we find the earliest evidence of the Jerusalem procession taking on a stational format, with two stops along the route from the place believed to be the site of the Ascension (the *Imbomon*) on Mount Olivet to the Church of the Holy Sepulchre; this trend is likewise evident in the expanded selection of gospel readings, with at least three (and probably all four) gospel accounts of our Lord's entry into Jerusalem utilized.[67] The Procession of Palms in the Jerusalem liturgy reached its fullest stage of development by the tenth century, as found in the *Typicon of the Anastasis*, a document detailing the rites of Holy Week and Easter Week as they existed prior to the takeover of the city and the destruction of its shrines by the caliph Hakim of Egypt in A.D. 1009.[68] The ceremony began in Bethany with the blessing of the palms by the patriarch; all then proceeded to the *Imbomon* on Mount Olivet, where the first gospel passage (Mk 11:1-11) was read, after which the patriarch said a prayer. The procession now moved on to the next station, Gethsemane; the gospel for this stop was that of Saint Luke (19:29-38), once more followed by a prayer. They continued along the route until reaching the vicinity of the *Probatica* (the "Sheep Gate," near the Pool of Bethsaida, mentioned in Jn 5:2), which served as yet another station of Scripture and prayer with a reading from the gospel of Saint John (12:12-18). Finally the procession came to the Church of the Holy Sepulchre, where the fourth and last gospel was read (Mt 21:1-17) at the site of Golgotha.[69]

At Constantinople, the capital of the East's Byzantine Empire, the Procession of Palms was introduced by the ninth or tenth century, for we find it in a liturgical document of the city from this period, the *Typicon of the Great Church*. At daybreak the faithful gathered at the Church of the Forty Martyrs; the patriarch then distributed palms to the clergy and laity. Thereupon all went in procession to the city's huge principle church, the famous Basilica of Santa Sophia, where the patriarch now celebrated Mass.[70] As late as the fourteenth century (the city was conquered by the Turks in 1453) the Palm Sunday procession was still being conducted in Constantinople. According to a book of ceremonies dating from the reign of the Emperor John Cantacuzene (1341-1356) or shortly thereafter, preparations for the procession on the Sunday before Easter began several days ahead and were completed on the night of "Lazarus Saturday." All along the route of the procession, from the Emperor's private apartment to the Basilica of Santa Sophia, flowers were strewn and columns wreathed with palm branches, myrtle, and laurel. The Emperor himself walked in the procession on Sunday morning, preceded by a torch bearer and followed by a retinue of officials; the gospel book, representing Christ Himself in the cortege, was borne by the archdeacon, and followed by the Orthodox Patriarch of Constantinople, as well as by several other patriarchs and by priests carrying icons.[71]

In more recent times Palm Sunday processions were quite common throughout Zsarist Russia prior to the Bolshevik Revolution of 1917; at present the Orthodox Patriarch of Jerusalem leads a Procession of Palms in the Holy City on the first day of the Orthodox Church's Holy Week (their dating of Easter differs somewhat from that of the Catholic Church).[72] In the current Catholic Byzantine Rite there is no Palm Sunday procession, but pussy-willow branches which serve as "palms" are blessed during the Sunday morning service of *Orthros*, the Byzantine Rite's version of Matins (the first "Hour" of prayer in the Divine Office), before the Eucharistic liturgy: the celebrant censes the branches, making the sign of the cross in doing so, after which the "palms" are distributed to the faithful.[73] Children of the Middle-Eastern Maronite Rite carry to Mass their version of the palm branch — the *shahneeny* — a branch of palm, olive, or cedar decorated with flowers and with a variety of candles in different sizes and colors.[74] There is an earlier precedent for the use of candles with palms on this day: in a twelfth-century Typicon of the Byzantine monastery of Evergetes (near Constantinople) we are told that both tapers and palms were distributed to the members of the community during *Orthros*.[75] The Procession of Palms in the current liturgy of Egypt's Coptic Rite likewise includes the carrying of candles, as well as both palm and olive branches.[76]

Other Aspects of the Observance of Palm Sunday

Six nights hence — the great night!
A week hence — the great day!

[Slavic Verse][77]

The "Delivery of the Creed."[78] In the Gallican Rite of early medieval France, in the Mozarabic Rite of Spain, and in the Ambrosian Rite of Milan, Italy, catechumens preparing for Baptism at the Easter Vigil were taught the words of the Creed on the Sunday before Easter. The ceremony, known as the *Traditio Symboli* ("Delivery of the Creed"), was conducted during Mass on this day, according to the Mozarabic Rite's *Liber Ordinum* (fifth to seventh centuries). Following the gospel, the celebrant would recite the Apostles' Creed a clause at a time; the catechumens responded by repeating each clause after him. In honor of the Holy Trinity, the Creed was said in this manner three times, thereby helping the catechumens to retain what they had been taught.

In the Ambrosian Rite the *Traditio Symboli* was eventually transferred from Palm Sunday to the Saturday before it; in the Roman Rite this ceremony was never held on Palm Sunday, but during the fourth week of Lent instead. With time the "Delivery of the Creed" was discontinued almost everywhere; yet in the Mozarabic Rite it was preserved, appearing in the 1500 edition of the Mozarabic Missal — the *Missale Mixtum*[79] — and retained in the official texts of this uniquely Spanish rite into the present century.

Processions of the Passion. In addition to the "Procession of Palms," many Latin countries, and particularly Spain, conduct other special outdoor processions to commemorate the events of Holy Week. Although most of these are held on Good Friday, there are places where such processions are conducted on Palm Sunday and the other days of the week. Covering their heads with hoods and carrying lighted tapers, the members of lay confraternities join in somber parades in which lavishly decorated statues of Christ in His sufferings and the Sorrowful

Virgin Mary are borne through the streets. Many of the participants walk barefoot or in sandals, some with crosses on their shoulders. In some cases these processions are conducted in complete silence, while in others the Rosary is recited or funeral music is played.[80]

The lay brotherhoods that play so prominent a role in the famous Holy Week processions of Seville, Spain first arose during the middle of the sixteenth century, at the outset of the Counter-Reformation that was to spread across the Catholic countries of Europe. During this same age Spain produced some of the greatest saints in the history of the Church, including Saint Ignatius of Loyola, Saint Francis Xavier, Saint Teresa of Ávila, and Saint John of the Cross. One of the manifestations of this Spanish Catholic revival was the emergence of a number of new confraternities specifically founded for the purpose of engaging in penitential exercises, especially processions, during the most solemn week of the Church year, Holy Week. Each such confraternity was named after a particular mystery of the passion. As best as can be determined, Seville's first Holy Week confraternity was founded in 1531, and has continued into the present century under the title, "Confraternity of Our Father Jesus of the Passion and Our Lady *de la Merced*." Shortly thereafter, in 1535, the "Confraternity of the Sacred Decree of the Most Holy Trinity and Christ of the Five Wounds" was established.[81] In the years that followed so many new Holy Week brotherhoods were formed that by the middle of the seventeenth century Seville had forty of them, with a total of fifteen thousand members. Some of these were confraternities originally founded for other pious reasons (and dating as far back as the thirteenth century), but which later decided to merge with or become Holy Week brotherhoods.[82] Even as recently as the late 1950s, there were still forty-seven different Holy Week confraternities in Seville.[83] Over the centuries these brotherhoods have drawn together men of every class, ethnic group, and profession. One example of this is the "Confraternity of the Most Holy Crucifix of the Foundation and Our Lady of the Angels," which originated around the year 1400 as a religious guild for Africans living in Seville (as a result of the iniquitous slave trade) and subsequently became a Holy Week brotherhood in 1554. Eventually Spaniards as well as those of African descent began to join the organization. During the eighteenth century this confraternity excelled all others in devotion, guided by the exceptional zeal of one of its most illustrious members, Salvador de la Cruz, who even succeeded in persuading the cardinal of Seville to become a member in 1766.[84]

Originally the members of the Holy Week confraternities fell

(RNS)

Holy Week in Seville, Spain. Float depicts betrayal of Jesus in the Garden of Gethsemane.

into two broad categories, based upon their manner of doing penance. Some engaged in the mortifying practice of self-flagellation while walking in procession, and hence came to be known as "brothers of blood." Others, the "brothers of light," performed the milder penance of carrying lighted candles in honor of our Lord and the Blessed Virgin Mary. By the end of the nineteenth century the first category had disappeared, and the carrying of lighted tapers in procession had become the usual penitential practice for all of the brothers.[85] The costumes of the Holy Week confraternities, characterized by high-peaked, cone-shaped hoods, worn with special tunics and capes, have varied in color from one brotherhood to another. For example, the confraternity dedicated to Our Lady of Angels have white robes and hoods, with blue belts, while the "Brotherhood of the Convent of San Buenaventura" wear white robes, black hoods, and wide plaited rope belts; the members of the "Tobacco Factory Brotherhood" dress in maroon tunics and hoods, with white capes.[86] Coats of arms are also put on the outfits.[87] The good works of these lay confraternities of Seville are not limited to only one week in the liturgical calendar; members are obligated to engage in particular acts of charity, as well as other religious ceremonies, throughout the year. Thus their activities during Holy Week serve as the culmination of a year of service to God and neighbor.[88]

From their introduction in the sixteenth century, the Holy Week processions of Spain have always featured floats known as *pasos* — sculpted figures mounted on platforms and depicting scenes from the passion. Many of the statues in use at present were made in the late sixteenth, seventeenth, and eighteenth centuries by the famous Spanish sculptors Juan Martinez Montanes (1568-1649), Gregorio Fernandez (1566-1636), Pedro de Mena (1628-1688), and Salzillo (1707-1783). The masterpieces of Baroque art which these men produced reflect not only the piety of the Spanish people in general, but the artists' own devotion as well. Montanes was a daily communicant, de Mena, the father of two priests and three nuns; Salzillo became a Dominican and wished to remain a religious, but was compelled to resume the lay state in order to support his widowed mother.[89] Virtually all of the statues were sculpted in polychrome wood, which was then painted in lifelike colors and dressed in richly embroidered garments; the figures were also adorned with jewels.[90] The custom of lavishly decorating statues with velvets, silks, and laces originated with one of the first Christian kings of Spain many centuries ago.[91] Although the use of these fabrics may seem almost garish to some, it should be remembered that the Spanish people regard this decoration as their way of showing the utmost respect for the holy images. Those tempted to smile at the devotional images of Spanish religious art might do well to consider the power of such images in the life of one of the greatest of mystics, Saint Teresa of Ávila (1515-1582); in her autobiography she tells us:

> It happened to me that one day entering the oratory I saw a statue they had borrowed for a certain feast to be celebrated in the house. It represented the much wounded Christ and was very devotional so that beholding it I was utterly distressed in seeing Him that way, for it well represented what He suffered for us. I felt so keenly aware of how poorly I thanked Him for those wounds that, it seems to me, my heart broke. Beseeching Him to strengthen me once and for all that I might not offend Him, I threw myself down before Him with the greatest out-pouring of tears.[92]

In Seville,[93] five or six parades a day are held on Palm Sunday, "Spy Wednesday," Holy Thursday, and Good Friday. Each of the parish churches of Seville stages a procession with one or more *pasos*; the platforms measure four or five feet square, weigh up to two and a half tons, and hold as many as four or even eight different life-sized figures, surrounded by numerous candles. Each float is borne by up to fifty men, concealed underneath the *paso* by black velvet hangings. The day and time when a church may hold its procession is determined by the order of precedence among the parishes. Each procession begins at the parish church and continues through the streets to the cathedral. The variety of *pasos* seen in Seville on Palm Sunday is evident in an account dating from 1914:

> On the afternoon of Palm Sunday, at two o'clock, the Cofradia of Our Father Christ of Sorrows comes forth from the parish church of San Roque, with a great velvet-robed image of the Saviour bearing His Cross, followed by the gorgeous shrine of Our Lady of Hope. From the church of San Julian, the Brothers of The Most Holy Christ of Happy Death bring a float representing the triumph of the Cross, another representing the Crucifixion and the Magdalen, and a third bearing the finely-sculptured image from the hands of Montanes, the great master of this truly Sevillian art, — Our Lady of the Genesta. At three o'clock, from the gipsy quarter of Triana, issues the paso of Our Lord Beseeching His Eternal Father, escorted by another beautiful image by Montanes, Our Lady of the Star; and at four o'clock, The Most Holy

Christ of the Water, and Our Lady of the Greater Sorrow, set out from
the same parish. From San Juan Bautista, with Our Lady of Sorrows,
appears Our Lord Jesus of Silence — an enormous group of the trial
scene before Herod, with three other floats, The Entry into Jerusalem,
Our Lady of Help, and The Most Holy Christ of Love, a marvelous
illustration of the tragic power of Montanes.[94]

As the Spaniards colonized the New World, they brought their faith and their religious traditions with them; consequently, the custom of Holy Week processions spread throughout Latin America. Among the countries where this practice took root is Guatemala. According to an account from 1942, the Palm Sunday procession in the capital city would pass the cathedral around five o'clock in the afternoon. The men who are to help in carrying the *pasos* work in shifts; on their chests are placards that indicate along what block of the route they are to serve in this capacity. These men, known in Guatemala as *cucuruchos*, are clothed in purple robes and caps, with white gloves on their hands. An Indian leads the procession playing a plaintive melody on a *chirimilla*, thereby adding a distinctively Latin American element to the observances. Among the most colorful of the Guatemalan *pasos* is that of Our Lady of Sorrows, which, unlike the other floats, is carried by women:

The Virgin was pale, with tears streaming down her sad, sweet face.
Her robes were of red velvet and satin and a blue mantle bordered in
gold fell from her shoulders. Long curls, crowned with a golden halo,
reached to her waist. The paso on which she was carried was decorated
with artificial flowers and doves which dipped and swayed as the
women who bore this image stepped, stepped, and paused in time to
the mournful music.[95]

A Final Thought on Palm Sunday

By nightfall the Hosannas
had long since faded
into the silence.
The Holy City had not recognized
what manner of King it had welcomed.
Somewhere near there was a tree,
perhaps already felled,

that was destined
to serve as His throne.
Somewhere there was a thorny vine,
destined to crown His brow.
Somewhere three nails and a Roman spear
awaited their glorious fate.

Endnotes

1. *The Vatican II Sunday Missal*, Daughters of St. Paul, p. 337.
2. John Miller, CSC, "The History and Spirit of Holy Week," *American Ecclesiastical Review*, April 1957, p. 220; Adrian Nocent, OSB, *The Liturgical Year*, Vol. II, p. 189.
3. Reverend John Tyrer, *Historical Survey of Holy Week: Its Services and Ceremonial* (Alcuin Club Collections #29), p. 50 (*Patrologia Latina*, Vol. 72, col. 572a-b).
4. Ibid.
5. Miller, p. 220.
6. *Regularis Concordia: The Monastic Agreement of the Monks and Nuns of the English Nation* (Medieval Classics), Dom Thomas Symons, tr., p. 35 (translations of Jn 12:19, *Pueri Hebraeorum*, and *Ingrediente Domino* added).
7. *Patrologia Latina*, Vol. 78, col. 1039c-1040a (*Ordo 11*), 1071b-1072a (*Ordo 12*) (both summarized in Tyrer, p. 53).
8. Miller, pp. 219-220; for Gelasian text see *Patrologia Latina*, Vol. 74, col. 1093b-1094a; for *Gregorian* texts see *Le Sacramentaire Gregorien: Ses principales formes d'apres les plus anciens manuscrits: I* (Spicilegium Friburgense, Vol. 16), Jean Deshusses, ed., 2nd ed., 1979, pp. 167 (Hadrian), 628 (Paduan).
9. Cyrille Vogel, *The Medieval Liturgy: An Introduction to the Sources*, William G. Storey and Niols Krogh Rasmussen, OP, tr./rev., 1986, pp. 230, 238.
10. *Le Pontifical Romano-Germanique du Dixieme Siecle: Le Texte II* (Studi e Testi, #227), Cyrille Vogel, Reinhard Elze, eds., pp. 40-54.
11. Generalized aspects of the description that follows are taken from Father Francis X. Weiser, SJ, *Handbook of Christian Feasts and Customs: The Year of the Lord in Liturgy and Folklore*, 1958, pp. 189-190.
12. Dom H. Philibert Feasey, OSB, "Palm Sundays," *American Ecclesias-*

tical Review, April 1908, p. 372; *The Monastic Constitutions of Lanfranc*, tr./ed. David Knowles, pp. 22-26.

13. Edmund Bishop, *Liturgica Historica*, 1918, pp. 276-277, 285.

14. Archdale King, *Liturgies of the Past*, 1959, p. 45.

15. Anton Baumstark, *Comparative Liturgy*, 1957, p. 149; for relevant document ("*codex Scaligeri 243*") see A. Baumstark, "Das Leydener griechisch-arabische Perikopenbuch fur die Kar- und Osterwoche," *Oriens Christianus*, Vol. 4, new series, 1914-1915, pp. 40, 48-52, 56. For correct dating of this *Greek-Arabic Pericope Book* see Dom Emmanuel Lanne, OSB, "Textes et rites de la liturgie Pascale dans l'ancienne Eglise Copte," *L'Orient Syrien*, Vol. 6, 1961, pp. 281-282.

16. Elizabeth Lipsmeyer, "The *Liber Ordinarius* by Konrad Von Mure and Palm Sunday Observance in Thirteenth-Century Zurich," *Manuscripta*, 1988, p. 141.

17. R. W. Scribner, "Ritual and Popular Religion in Catholic Germany at the Time of the Reformation," *Journal of Ecclesiastical History*, Jan 1984, p. 56.

18. Ibid.

19. Feasey, p. 372 (footnote); text in *Patrologia Latina*, Vol. 101, col. 1201b-d.

20. Karl Young, *The Drama of the Medieval Church*, 1933, Vol. I, p. 92.

21. Lipsmeyer, pp. 141-143.

22. Young, Vol. I, pp. 94-98.

23. Scribner, p. 55.

24. Tyrer, p. 64.

25. King, p. 45.

26. Father Herbert Thurston, SJ, "Palms," *The Month*, March 1896, p. 385.

27. M. Nesbitt, "Old-Time Holy Week and Easter Customs," *American Ecclesiastical Review*, 1911, p. 398.

28. Tyrer, pp. 59-60.

29. Bishop, p. 286.

30. *Patrologia Latina*, Vol. 85, col. 391a, b, summarized in Tyrer, p. 64.

31. Father Francis X. Weiser, SJ, *The Easter Book*, 1954, p. 92.

32. Feasey, p. 370.

33. Weiser, pp. 92-93.

34. The following is based primarily upon the rubrics of the *Memoriale Rituum*, Title III, chapters 1 and 2, #1-#3, in *The Ritual for Small Churches*, Father Bartholomew Eustace, ed., pp. 27-39; a few details are added from the *Caeremoniale Episcoporum* (Liber II, Cap. XXI, #1-#9) as presented in *Manual of Episcopal Ceremonies*, Reverend Aurelius Stehle, OSB, ed., pp. 166-171.

35. Weiser, p. 93.

36. "Holy Week in Jerusalem," *The Catholic World*, VII, April-Sep 1868, p. 77.

37. *The New Roman Missal: In Latin and English*, Father F. X. Lasance and Father Francis Augustine Walsh, OCD, eds., 1946, p. 393.

38. Weiser, pp. 95-96.

39. Ibid., p. 96.

40. Cynthia Hettinger, "Faith of the Puerto Rican," *America*, April 16, 1960, pp. 66-67.

41. Father Herbert Thurston, SJ, "Palms," *The Month*, March 1896, pp. 375-376.

42. Liturgical texts from *Vatican II Sunday Missal*, pp. 336-344.

43. Ibid., pp. 343-344.

44. *"Oratio 9 in ramos palmarum"* (Second Reading, Office of Readings for Palm Sunday), in *The Office of Readings*, Daughters of St. Paul, eds., 1983, pp. 462-463.

45. Dom Germain Morin, "Le plus ancien *Comes* de l'Eglise Romaine," *Revue Benedictine*, Vol. 27 (1910), pp. 53-54. For description of this lectionary, see Cyrille Vogel, *The Medieval Liturgy: An Introduction to the Sources*, William G. Storey and Niols Krogh Rasmussen, OP, tr./rev., pp. 339-340.

46. Nocent, p. 189.

47. Sermon 54, chapter 5, in Tyrer, p. 74.

48. Dom Germain Morin, "Liturgie et basiliques de Rome au milieu du VII siecle: D'apres les Listes d'Evangiles de Wurzburg," *Revue Benedictine*, Vol. 28 (1911), p. 304.

49. Notes, *The Rosslyn Missal* (Henry Bradshaw Society, Vol. 15), Hugh Jackson Lawlor, ed., p. 128.

50. Father Herbert Thurston, SJ, "Holy Week," *Catholic Encyclopedia*, 1907, Vol. 7, p. 436.

51. Young, Vol. I, pp. 100-101.

52. *Rationale*, VI, lxviii, 6, cited in Lawlor, p. 128.

53. Kurt Von Fischer, "Passion," *The New Grove Dictionary of Music and Musicians*, 1980, Vol. 14, pp. 277-278.

54. Ibid., p. 278.

55. *Patrologia Latina*, Vol. 78, col. 1303c-1304d.

56. Text from *Missale Romanum* of 1530 in *Missale Romanum: Mediolani, 1474: Vol. II: A Collation with Other Editions Printed Before 1570* (Henry Bradshaw Society, Vol. 33), Robert Lippe, ed., 1907, p. 66.

57. *Decreta Authentica Congregationis Sacrorum Rituum*, pub. Typo-

graphia Polyglotta, 1898-1901, Vol. I, pp. 85-86. The text of the decree, which cites the then current edition of the *Caeremoniale Episcoporum*, indicates that a plural term was also used in the latter.

58. *Documents on the Liturgy, 1963-1979: Conciliar, Papal and Curial Texts*, International Commission on English in the Liturgy, 1982, p. 905. *"The passion is proclaimed by deacons or priests, or by lay readers; in the latter case, the part of Christ should be reserved to the priest"* (Congregation for Divine Worship, *Circular Letter Concerning the Preparation and Celebration of the Easter Feasts*, 20 Feb 1988, #33, in *L'Osservatore Romano*, Feb 29, 1988, p. 16).

59. *Les Ordines Romani du Haut Moyen Age: III: Les Textes (Ordines XIV-XXXIV)* (Etudes et Documents, Vol. 24), ed. Michel Andrieu, 1961, pp. 293 (*Ordo 24*), 356 (*Ordo 27*).

60. Ibid., p. 497.

61. *Patrologia Latina*, Vol. 78, col. 1214d-1215a.

62. *Missale ad Usum Ecclesie Westmonasteriensis* (Henry Bradshaw Society, Vol. I), John Wickham Legg, ed., 1891, Vol. I, cols. 239, 282.

63. *Patrologia Latina*, Vol. 78, col. 1304a, 1316c-d.

64. *Caeremoniale Episcoporum*, Typis Polyglottis Vaticanis, 1985, Caput VI, #273, and Caput X, #319, pp. 82, 92.

65. *The Vatican II Sunday Missal*, p. 635.

66. John Wilkinson, ed., *Egeria's Travels*, 1971, p. 266.

67. German translation of original Georgian text of *Georgian Lectionary* for Lent and Holy Week in Theodor Kluge and Anton Baumstark, "Quadragesima und Karwoche Jerusalems im siebten Jahrhundert," *Oriens Christianus*, Vol. 5, new series (1915), pp. 218-220.

68. For dating of this document see Gabriel Bertoniere, *The Historical Development of the Easter Vigil and Related Services in the Greek Church* (Orientalia Christiana Analecta #193), 1972, pp. 12-14.

69. Greek Text of *Typicon of the Anastasis* in *Analekta Hierosolymitikes Stachyologias*, A. Papadopoulos-Kerameus, ed., 1894 (rpt. 1963), Vol. II, pp. 16-22.

70. Greek text with French translation in *Le Typicon de la Grande Eglise: Tome II:Le Cycle des Fetes mobiles* (Orientalia Christiana Analecta #166), ed. Juan Mateos, 1963, pp. 64-67.

71. Anton Baumstark, "La Solennite des Palmes dans l'ancienne et la nouvelle Rome," *Irenikon*, Vol. 13, Jan-Feb 1936, pp. 21-22.

72. Michael J. L. La Civita, "Easter: An Orthodox Perspective," *Catholic Near East*, Vol. 17, April 1991, pp. 26-28.

73. Rubrics in *La Priere des Eglises de Rite Byzantin: II: Les Fetes: II:*

L'Acathiste, la Quinzaine de Paques, l'Ascension et la Pentecote, R. P. E. Mercenier, 1948, pp. 80-81; see also D. Pochin Mould, "Byzantine Holy Week," *Doctrine and Life*, March 1964, p. 178.

74. Father Peter F. Sfeir, "Holy Week Customs in Syria," *The Catholic Mind*, April 22, 1928, pp. 143-144.

75. Baumstark, "La solemnite des palmes," p. 21; for original Greek text see Aleksei Dmitrievskij, *Opisanie liturgitseskich rukopisej*, Vol. I, 1895 (rpt. 1965), p. 542.

76. O. Hadji-Burmester, "Rites and Ceremonies of the Coptic Church: Part XI: Holy Week Services and Ceremonies," *Eastern Churches Quarterly*, Autumn 1956, pp. 321-322.

77. Traditional Polish and Ukrainian verse for Palm Sunday in Weiser, p. 96.

78. Based on Tyrer, pp. 47-49.

79. *Patrologia Latina*, Vol. 85, col. 394b-397a.

80. Weiser, pp. 121-122.

81. "The Lay Brotherhoods of Seville," *The Month*, April 1893, pp. 491-492.

82. Ibid., pp. 492-493.

83. Claudia Andujar, "Holy Week in Seville," *Jubilee*, April 1960, p. 10.

84. "The Lay Brotherhoods of Seville," pp. 493-494.

85. Ibid., pp. 491-492.

86. Andujar, p. 10.

87. Thomas Walsh, "Sevilla of the Images," *The Month*, April 1914, p. 356.

88. "From Our Notebook: Spain," *The Tablet*, April 11, 1953, p. 304; "The Lay Brotherhoods of Seville," p. 499.

89. Victor-Henry Debidour, *Christian Sculpture* (Twentieth Century Encyclopedia of Catholicism, Vol. 122), 1968, p. 164.

90. Ibid., pp. 165-166.

91. Alquien, "Holy Week in Spain," *The Catholic World*, March 1894, pp. 842-843.

92. Autobiography, chapter 9, #1, in *The Collected Works of Saint Teresa of Avila*, Vol. I, Kieran Kavanaugh, OCD and Otilio Rodriguez, OCD, tr., 1976, pp. 70-71.

93. The following is based upon Alquien, pp. 840-843; Andujar, pp. 8, 14; Walsh, pp. 356-357.

94. Walsh, pp. 356-357.

95. L. Hickman and K. Willis, "Holy Week in Guatemala," *Commonweal*, April 3, 1942, pp. 587-588.

III

Monday, Tuesday, and Wednesday of Holy Week

The days of his life-giving death and glorious resurrection are approaching. This is the hour when he triumphed over Satan's pride, the time when we celebrate the great event of our redemption.
[Preface for Monday, Tuesday, and Wednesday of Holy Week, *Roman Missal*][1]

THE EARLIEST RECORDS OF liturgical services on Monday and Tuesday of Holy Week do not appear in Rome until the seventh century, when both the *Gelasian Sacramentary* and the Paduan edition of the *Gregorian Sacramentary* provide Masses for these two days.[2] We can deduce that these Masses must have been introduced no earlier than the second half of the fifth century. According to an Eastern source known as the *Exposition of the Faith*, written by Epiphanius around A.D. 375, there were as yet no Masses between Palm Sunday and the Easter Vigil, except on Holy Thursday, when the Eucharistic sacrifice was celebrated in some churches.[3] Even in the time of Pope Saint Leo I, during the middle of the fifth century, there were evidently still no liturgical services on Monday and Tuesday of Holy Week, at least not in Rome.[4] But this was not necessarily the case elsewhere. In chapters 14 and 25 of his "Epistle 20" to Marcellina, Saint Ambrose implies that at Milan (northern Italy, fourth century) the entire Book of Job was read on Monday of Holy Week, and on Tuesday the entire Book of Jonah. He speaks of giving a sermon on both these days, which suggests that the readings may have been presented in a liturgical setting.[5]

The oldest surviving Roman lectionary, the *Capitulary of Wurzburg* (seventh to early eighth centuries) specifies the Old Testament readings for Monday as Isaiah 50:5-10 and Zechariah 11:12-13:9;[6] in the current liturgy Isaiah 42:1-7 is read on this day, with the former lection from Isaiah 50 used both on Palm Sunday (vs. 4-7) and on Wednesday of Holy Week (vs. 4-9). For Tuesday the *Capitulary* stipulates readings from Jeremiah (11:18-20) and the Book of Wisdom (2:12-22);[7] in the *Roman Missal* of Pope Paul VI (1970), these two lections are assigned to the Fourth Week of Lent (Wisdom on Friday, Jeremiah on Saturday), with Isaiah 49:1-6 now used on Tuesday of Holy Week.

From the time of the *Capitulary of Wurzburg* the gospel for Monday has always been from the beginning of the twelfth chapter of Saint John, although less verses are read now (vs. 1-11) than originally (vs. 1-36).[8] The passage describes an incident that occurred just before our Lord's triumphant entrance into Jerusalem, which we commemorated yesterday. Notice the attitude of Judas and our Lord's reference to his burial — precursors of what will ensue:

> *Six days before Passover Jesus came to Bethany, the village of Lazarus whom Jesus had raised from the dead. There they gave him a banquet, at which Martha served. Lazarus was one of those at table with him. Mary brought a pound of costly perfume made from genuine aromatic nard, with which she anointed Jesus' feet. Then she dried his feet with her hair, and the house was filled with the ointment's fragrance. Judas Iscariot . . . protested: "Why was this perfume not sold? It could have brought three hundred silver pieces, and the money have been given to the poor." . . . To this Jesus replied, "Leave her alone. Let her keep it against the day they prepare me for burial. The poor you always have with you, but me you will not always have."*
>
> [Jn 12:1-5, 7-8; NAB][9]

For Tuesday of Holy Week the *Capitulary of Wurzburg* lists John 13:1-32, while some other early sources mention John 12:24-43 (or 44);[10] however, in the tenth century the passion narrative from the gospel of Saint Mark began to supplant the Johannine selection on this day.[11] Saint Mark's passion was retained in the *Roman Missal* until 1970; in the current liturgy the gospel of St. John is once again used (Jn 13:21-33, 36-38), a reading that describes Christ's predictions during the Last Supper of both the betrayal of Judas and Peter's denials.

Wednesday of Holy Week became a liturgical day in Rome long before the two days preceding it. Ancient sources indicate that originally a *synaxis*, a non-Eucharistic liturgy consisting of Scripture readings, a homily, and intercessions, was held on this day. By the seventh century the Wednesday *synaxis* had been supplanted by a Mass, as found in the *Gelasian* and *Gregorian* (Paduan) *Sacramentaries*.[12] The reading of the passion account from the gospel of Saint Luke was already an established practice prior to the seventh century, and is specified in the *Capitulary of Wurzburg* (Lk 22:1-23:53), along with two readings from Isaiah (62:11-63:7 and 53:1-12).[13] Following the revision of the *Lectionary* of the *Roman Missal* in 1970, the passion of Saint Luke became part of the three-year cycle for Palm Sunday, and in its place a passage describing the betrayal of Judas from the twenty-sixth chapter of Saint Matthew (vs. 14-25) is now read. A similar passage (Mt 26:3-16) was heard on Wednesday of Holy Week in fifth century Jerusalem, according to the *Armenian Lectionary*; such appears to have been the case even in Egeria's day (late fourth century).[14] The two passages from Isaiah have been replaced with another lection from this same prophet (Is 50:4-9).

A Philippine Tradition

In the Philippines there is a special custom unique to the country and associated with the last two weeks preceding Easter. In 1705 a Philippine priest composed a long poem known as the *Ang Pabasa ng Pasyon* ("Reading of the Passion"); this piece relates the entire history of the redemption from Adam and Eve through the Old Testament to the passion, death, and resurrection of Christ. Chanted in a local dialect, it takes twenty-four hours to complete. During Passion Week (the week before Palm Sunday) and Holy Week, it is customary for one or more families in a village to have this poem chanted in their home before an image of Christ resting in death. The home where the *Pasyon* is held opens its doors to all visitors who might wish to come there to pray and pay their respects before the *Christos* lying in state. In poor families a crucifix together with images of the Blessed Mother and Saint Mary Magdalene is used for the *Pasyon*; the poor make tremendous sacrifices in order to afford the upkeep of these beautifully decorated statues passed down from generation to generation.[15]

We have entered into Holy Week. Over the next few days, led by the Church's liturgy, we will relive the mysteries of our salvation. The Easter Triduum is the summit of the liturgical year. In it we recall, with deep and grateful hearts, that by dying Christ destroyed our death and by rising he restored our life.

Let us prepare ourselves to live these upcoming celebrations with intensity, in the clear realization that, if we share now in the sufferings of Christ, we will one day rejoice and exult in the revelation of his glory (cf. 1 Pt 4:13).

[Pope John Paul II][16]

The Lenten Veil

In medieval Europe, especially in England, France, and Germany, there existed a custom known as the "Lenten Veil," also called the "Hunger Cloth"; the practice is thought to have arisen by the tenth or eleventh century. During Lent a large curtain of purple or white fabric, decorated with crosses or scenes of the passion, was hung before the sanctuary to symbolize the separation of the penitent faithful from sight of the altar; in the middle of the veil was an aperture that allowed it to be partially opened for the most important portions of the Mass. The cloth was kept up until Wednesday of Holy Week, when, until recent times, the passion of Saint Luke was read at Mass.[17] What was done with it on this day will be shown shortly.

The Lenten veil did not completely disappear after the Middle Ages. The English scholar John Wickham Legg (1843-1921) observed it still in use in parts of Spain and Sicily; during a trip to Palermo (Sicily) in 1908, he saw several examples of the cloth. Usually these Sicilian veils were situated between the choir and the altar, suspended from the ceiling and long enough to conceal the altar candles from the view of the worshipers; however, the cloths were made of thin, bluish, gauzy material through which the light of the burning candles could be seen. Decorations on the veils ranged from the Old Testament scenes of the bronze serpent (Num 21:9) and of Jonah being thrown overboard (Jonah 1:15), to such New Testament images as a simple cross, the pieta, a crucifixion group with Mary and John, and the descent from the cross. In Palermo the Lenten veils were kept up from Ash Wednesday until Holy Saturday.[18]

It appears that in Seville, Spain, a Lenten veil or something analogous to it was still in use at the cathedral in the late nineteenth century, according to an account dating from 1894. As with medieval examples of the Lenten veil, Seville's veil was "removed" on Wednesday of Holy Week. The city's cathedral is a huge, sprawling edifice, consisting of seven naves, thirty-seven chapels, and eighty altars;[19] on any day the centuries-old edifice is a solemn, imposing place, but much more so on this day, when it was wrapped in darkness, unlit by the many lights usually seen there on feast days. Instead, three black candles were placed on the main altar, which was also veiled in black. The service took a particularly dramatic turn when these words of the passion of Saint Luke were read: ". . . and the curtain of the temple was torn in two" (Lk 23:45). Suddenly a cannon was fired from a cornice overlooking the altar, and immediately the white veil which was draped from the ceiling down to the floor behind the altar was torn down its middle. In the darkness the cannon was repeatedly fired, momentarily shattering the deep silence and lighting up the many pillared arches and aisles of the vast cathedral. Alquien, who witnessed this spectacle, vividly describes it in these terms: "The sudden explosion in the midst of profoundest silence; the momentary flood of light; then darkness denser than before, silence more profound from the contrast, to be followed by another flash and crash again and again, was almost terrifying."[20]

Analogous and perhaps related to the custom of the Lenten veil is the practice of individually veiling statues and crosses during all or part of the Lenten season, including Holy Week; such a custom existed as early as the tenth century.[21] The thirteenth century *Sarum Consuetudinary* provides detailed directions in this regard, stipulating that the veils were to remain on all images and relics from the first Monday of Lent until Easter Monday.[22] Eventually the veiling became associated with the Fifth Sunday of Lent (previously known as "Passion Sunday"), and in particular with the words of the gospel formerly read on this Sunday: ". . . Jesus hid himself, and went out of the temple" (Jn 8:59). Thus virtually all images remained veiled during the two-week period from "Passion Sunday" until the Easter Vigil on Holy Saturday; the crosses were likewise veiled through most of this same period, but the latter were unveiled on Good Friday, during the ceremony of the "Veneration of the Cross."[23] A decree of the Congregation of Sacred Rites dating from 1885 (#3638 ad 2) declared that images of the Stations of the Cross were exempt from this Lenten rubric.[24] Up until 1970 the practice was prescribed for the universal Church in the rubrics of the *Roman Missal*;[25] the current *Roman Missal* of Pope Paul VI leaves the decision of veiling images and crosses to the discretion of the national conferences of bishops, as indicated in the following rubric, which appears after the Mass of Saturday in the Fourth Week of Lent (that is, just before the Fifth Sunday of Lent):

> *The practice of covering crosses and images in the church may be observed, if the episcopal conference decides. The crosses are to be*

covered until the end of the celebration of the Lord's passion on Good Friday. Images are to remain covered until the beginning of the Easter vigil.[26]

Another rubric recommends the veiling of any crosses remaining in the church following the "Mass of the Lord's Supper" on Holy Thursday, a directive which is stated in more detail in the Congregation for Divine Worship's 1988 *Circular Letter* on Holy Week:

> It is fitting that any crosses in the church be covered with a red or purple veil, unless they have already been veiled on the Saturday before the fifth Sunday of Lent. Lamps should not be lit before the images of saints.[27]

Endnotes

1. *The Vatican II Weekday Missal*, Daughters of St. Paul, eds., 1975, p. 883.
2. Reverend John Tyrer, *Historical Survey of Holy Week: Its Services and Ceremonial* (Alcuin Club Collections #29), pp. 74-75; for the Monday and Tuesday Masses of the *Gelasian Sacramentary* see *Patrologia Latina*, Vol. 74, col. 1094a-d; for those of the Paduan see Jean Deshusses (ed.), *Le Sacramentaire Gregorien: Ses principales formes d'apres les plus anciens manuscrits: I* (Spicilegium Friburgense, Vol. 16), p. 629.
3. Tyrer, pp. 33-35, 74.
4. Ibid., p. 74.
5. Ibid., pp. 72-73.
6. Dom Germain Morin, "Le plus ancien *Comes* de l'Eglise Romaine," *Revue Benedictine*, Vol. 27, 1910, p. 54.
7. Ibid.
8. Dom Germain Morin, "Liturgie et basiliques de Rome au milieu du VII siecle: D'apres les Listes d'Evangiles de Wurzburg," *Revue Benedictine*, Vol. 28, 1911, p. 304; Father Herman Schmidt, SJ, *Hebdomada Sancta: Fontes Historici, Commentarius Historicus*, Vol. II, p. 674.
9. *Lectionary For Mass*, Catholic Book Publishing Co., 1970, #258, pp. 368-369.
10. Morin, "Liturgie et basiliques," p. 304; Schmidt, Vol. II, p. 674.
11. Schmidt, Vol. II, pp. 673, 674.
12. Tyrer, pp. 74, 76; Gelasian text in *Patrologia Latina*, Vol. 74, col.

1094d-1095a; Paduan in Deshusses, p. 629.

13. Schmidt, Vol. II, p. 673; Morin, "Liturgie et basiliques," p. 304; Morin, "Le plus ancien *Comes*," p. 54.

14. Egeria refers to the gospel heard on Wednesday as a "passage about Judas Iscariot going to the Jews and fixing what they must pay him to betray the Lord" (*Diary*, chapter 34). There are passages in Matthew, Mark, and Luke that fit this description, yet it seems most likely that Saint Matthew's account was used. See John Wilkinson, *Egeria's Travels*, 1971, pp. 134, 266.

15. Sister Maria del Rey, "Pageant of the Cross," *Sign*, March 1972, pp. 12-14.

16. Talk at General Audience, April 15, 1992, in *L'Osservatore Romano*, April 22, 1992, p. 7.

17. Father Francis X. Weiser, SJ, *Handbook of Christian Feasts and Customs: The Year of the Lord in Liturgy and Folklore*, pp. 176-177.

18. J. Wickham Legg, *Essays Liturgical and Historical*, pp. 166-168.

19. *The Horizon Book of Great Cathedrals*, J. Jacobs, ed., pp. 244-249.

20. Alquien, "Holy Week in Spain," *Catholic World*, March 1894, pp. 843-844.

21. Father Herbert Thurston, SJ, *Lent and Holy Week*, p. 101.

22. Ibid., p. 100 (footnote).

23. P. J. B. De Herdt, *Sacrae Liturgiae Praxis Juxta Ritum Romanum*, Book III, p. 23.

24. *Decreta Authentica Congregationis Sacrorum Rituum*, pub. Typographia Polyglotta, 1898-1901, Vol. III, pp. 173-174.

25. *Roman Missal* (1960 edition), Benziger Bros., 1964, p. 129.

26. *Vatican II Weekday Missal*, Daughters of St. Paul, 1975, p. 615.

27. Congregation for Divine Worship, *Circular Letter Concerning the Preparation and Celebration of the Easter Feasts*, 20 Feb 1988, #57, in *L'Osservatore Romano*, Feb 29, 1988, p. 17.

IV

Holy Thursday

Now is the Son of man glorified,
and in him God is glorified. . .

[Jn 13:31]

Prelude

Then came the day of Unleavened Bread, on which the passover lamb
had to be sacrificed.

[Lk 22:7]

Let us look with the eyes of faith at the paschal events which
begin today, during the Last Supper.
    We lack words to express the depth of the mystery which opens
up before us.

[Pope John Paul II][1]

So Jesus sent Peter and John, saying, "Go and prepare the passover
for us, that we may eat it." They said to him, "Where will you have us
prepare it?" He said to them, "Behold, when you have entered the city,
a man carrying a jar of water will meet you; follow him into the house
which he enters, and tell the householder, 'The Teacher says to you,
Where is the guest room, where I am to eat the passover with my
disciples?' And he will show you a large upper room furnished; there
make ready." And they went, and found it as he had told them; and
they prepared the passover.

[Lk 22:8-13]

Tenebrae

ON THE MORNINGS OF Holy Thursday, Good Friday, and Holy Saturday, the Church engages in a solemn communal version of the Divine Office (the Breviary), an ancient service that has been known since the ninth century (or even earlier) as *Tenebrae* (Darkness).[2] We have reason to believe that this special celebration of the Liturgy of the Hours already existed in the sixth century;[3] we know for certain that it was in use in Rome by the eighth century, appearing in *Roman Ordo I*,[4] *Roman Ordo 30B*[5] (Andrieu — from the "Collection of Saint Amand"), and *Roman Ordo 23*[6] (Andrieu — also called the *Ordo of Einsiedeln*); it is described in considerable detail in the first two documents. These sources indicate that the service began at midnight and consisted of three *nocturns* made up of selections of psalms, antiphons, and readings, followed by Lauds, the Morning Prayer of the Church; the first *nocturn* featured passages from the Lamentations of Jeremiah, the second, from the writings of Saint Augustine, and the third, from the Epistles of Saint Paul. On Holy Thursday the service was conducted with normal lighting. But on Good Friday the lights were successively extinguished, so that by the end only one candle was left burning, which was afterwards hidden behind the altar and there reserved for the following day. At midnight on Holy Saturday the third of these services commenced in almost total darkness, with only a single lamp burning for the sake of the lector.[7]

By the twelfth-century, Rome had adopted the Gallican custom of using the dramatic successive extinguishing of lights during the Divine Office not only on Good Friday, but on all three days of the Easter Triduum.[8] This use of light was rich in symbolic implications, as attested by Amalarius of Metz, a ninth-century Gallican liturgist:

> *That the lights of the church are extinguished on these nights seems to me to be in commemoration of the Sun of Justice Himself, who is buried for three days and three nights. . . . Our church is illuminated with twenty-four candles and at each song — where we might otherwise rejoice — we choose sadness because our true Sun has set; and thus during the individual hours the lack of the sun is increased until complete extinction. This happens three times because it recalls the three-day burial of the Lord.*[9]

It is due to this putting out of lights that the Office of the Easter Triduum acquired the name of *Tenebrae*. Until recently, *Tenebrae* was performed during the afternoon or evening preceding the day to which it was assigned liturgically. Thus *Tenebrae* for Holy Thursday would be held on Wednesday evening; similarly, for Good Friday and Holy Saturday *Tenebrae* was held in the evening on Holy Thursday and Good Friday respectively.

The lights extinguished during the Office of *Tenebrae* are mounted on the triangular top of a large candelabrum known as a "hearse." The two rows of candles lining both sides of the triangular frame resemble the spikes of a harrow, resulting in the name "hearse," which is ultimately derived from the Latin word for a harrow, *herpex*. At medieval funerals a similar structure was used both to support the pall over the coffin and to hold numerous candles; this eventually led to the association of the word "hearse" with vehicles that bear the deceased to the grave.[10] During the Middle Ages the number of candles mounted on the *Tenebrae* hearse varied considerably from place to place, as witnessed by the thirteenth-century writer William Durandus, Bishop of Metz (France), who speaks of as little as seven in some churches and as many as seventy-two in others.[11] At Salisbury Cathedral in pre-Reformation England there were twenty-four candles, at York and Hereford (also in England), twenty-five;[12] in France, nine tapers were used at Nevers, thirteen at Paris and Reims, twenty-six at Amiens, and forty-four at Coutances.[13] But the most common number has been fifteen. Usually the *Tenebrae* hearse was positioned on the "epistle side" (typically the south side) of the sanctuary. Significantly this was the same location specified in Mosaic law for the seven-branched candle stand used in the Temple of Jerusalem.[14] The hearse itself (at least in more recent times) would usually be made of wood or iron;[15] at the Cathedral of Seville, Spain (1876), a bronze hearse twelve feet in height was used, its triangular frame arrayed with sixteen images of saints.[16]

Although there is no longer any mention of the *Tenebrae* hearse in the current edition of the *Roman Breviary* (issued in 1972), and the hitherto detailed rubrics regarding this and other aspects of *Tenebrae* have been eliminated from the most recent edition of the *Caeremoniale Episcoporum* (1985), there has not been any directive calling for the termination of this venerable custom. Indeed, in 1956, shortly after the restored Order of Holy Week was promulgated, the Congregation of Sacred Rites was asked whether the use of the *Tenebrae* hearse was to be continued; the Congregation replied in the affirmative.[17] Of course, in view of the changes in the liturgical books this practice is no longer required, yet neither has it been prohibited. Thus the tradition has been retained in some places.

The Tenebrae hearse.

Tenebrae Today

As we enter the church for *Tenebrae*,[18] we immediately notice a massive wooden candelabrum at the front of the sanctuary; the top is of a triangular shape and is mounted with fifteen candles. This is the hearse; prior to the beginning of *Tenebrae*, all fifteen candles are alight. The doors of the chapel are then closed; the silence is broken by a priest intoning the opening words of the Divine Office:

O Lord, open my lips.

The congregation responds:

And my mouth will proclaim your praise.

A hymn is now sung to the accompaniment of the organ, during which we begin to feel the distinctive atmosphere of the upcoming days gently enveloping us. At its conclusion Psalm 69 is intoned as it is assigned to the Office of Readings for Holy Thursday:

Save me, O God,
for the waters have risen to my neck.
I have sunk into the mud of the deep
and there is no foothold.
I have entered the waters of the deep
and the waves overwhelm me.

[Ps 69:2-3]

In today's office, Psalm 69 is presented in three parts (vs. 2-13, 14-22, 30-37). At the end of the first portion, as the "Glory be" is chanted, two acolytes rise from their places at opposite sides of the altar and proceed to the front of the sanctuary; standing before the hearse, they extinguish the two lowest candles on it and then return to their seats. Throughout the service, as each Psalm is completed, succeeding pairs of candles will be put out. The second part of Psalm 69 is now sung:

Save me from the waters of the deep
lest the waves overwhelm me.
Do not let the deep engulf me
nor death close its mouth on me. . .
You know how they taunt and deride me;
my oppressors are all before you.
Taunts have broken my heart;
I have reached the end of my strength.
I looked in vain for compassion,
for consolers; not one could I find.
For food they gave me poison;
in my thirst they gave me vinegar to drink.

[vs. 16, 20-21, 22]

Two more candles are put out. One tradition associates the extinguishing of the hearse candles with the desertion of the Apostles, who fled when our Lord was arrested in the garden.[19]

Upon completion of the third and final portion of the 69th Psalm, there is a brief period of silence. A cantor then comes forward to a lectern flanked by two candles, situated in the central aisle. Here begins what has been for centuries a most moving and dramatic part of

Tenebrae, the chanting of the Lamentations of Jeremiah:

ALEPH.   *How lonely sits the city*
                that was full of people!
                How like a widow has she become,
                she that was great among the nations!

[Lam 1:1]

The Lamentations once constituted an essential element of the Office of Matins (the first "Hour" of *Tenebrae*) for Holy Thursday, Good Friday, and Holy Saturday; however, when the revised *Roman Breviary* was issued in 1972, they were no longer included in the Office for Holy Week. Nonetheless, they continue to be used in some places as an extraliturgical addendum to the official Liturgy of the Hours, indeed a most appropriate and valid addition considering that the Lamentations have been heard on these days since the eighth century (or earlier). The first four of the five Lamentations of Jeremiah are in the form of alphabetic acrostic poems; in the original Hebrew text, each verse of these acrostics (in the case of Lam 3, every third verse) begins with a different letter of the Hebrew alphabet (Aleph, Beth, Ghimel, and so on).[20] Before intoning a verse the cantor chants the letter assigned to it.

DALETH.   *The roads to Zion mourn,*
                for none come to the appointed feasts;
                all her gates are desolate,
                her priests groan. . . .

[Lam 1:4]

The part of the Lamentations to be chanted on this morning is divided into three portions (Lam 1:1-5, 6-9, 10-14),[21] the first and third of which are set to one melody, while the second portion is set to a different one.

ZAIN.   *Jerusalem remembers*
                in the days of her affliction and bitterness
                all the precious things
                that were hers from days of old.
                When her people fell into the hand of the foe,
                and there was none to help her,

the foe gloated over her,
mocking at her downfall.

[Lam 1:7]

One of the melodies most often used for the Lamentations is so ancient that it may date back to Jewish antiquity; its origins have been lost to history.[22] Another less used but extraordinarily beautiful tone is that assigned to the Lamentations for Good Friday in the *Gregorian Antiphonary of Silos,* a Spanish liturgical book dating from the late twelfth or early thirteenth centuries.[23] In some places both tones are utilized.

HETH.   *Jerusalem sinned grievously,*
            therefore she became filthy;
            all who honored her despise her. . . .

[Lam 1:8]

The verses evoke many images. They bring to mind Jerusalem's rejection of Christ and the subsequent fall of Jerusalem in A.D. 70.

TETH.   *Her uncleanness was in her skirts;*
            she took no thought of her doom;
            therefore her fall is terrible,
            she has no comforter. . . .

[Lam 1:9]

There is also much in these verses that can be applied to the sufferings of the Church down through the ages, especially in difficult times such as the present.

CAPH.   *All her people groan*
            as they search for bread;
            they trade their treasures for food
            to revive their strength. . . .

[Lam 1:11]

At the end of each of the three portions of the Lamentations, the cantor ends with a plea:

Jerusalem, Jerusalem, return to the Lord your God.

In nineteenth-century Jerusalem, *Tenebrae* for Holy Thursday began at three o'clock in the afternoon on Wednesday in the Church of the Holy Sepulchre; the hearse candle stand was set up at the right side of the door to the tomb. The patriarch, as well as many priests, seminarians, friars, choirboys, and a large number of the laity would attend. The service took on a particular poignancy in the Holy City:

> *The chanting of the Lamentations was most impressive; and when the words, "Jerusalem, Jerusalem, convertere ad Dominum Deum tuum!" were uttered, it seemed that this plaintive entreaty even now could be addressed with fitness to the city that once was full of people, but is solitary, and made tributary to her enemies. There was a wild pathos and deep earnestness in the chant when the summons to turn to the Lord God was made, as if the singer knew that today there is need for the city to listen and obey.*[24]

Do not these words written over one hundred and twenty years ago still ring true for Jerusalem, torn by strife in our own day?

Upon completion of the Lamentations, the Office continues with a reading from the Letter to the Hebrews (4:14-5:10). On this day on which the Church commemorates our Lord's institution of the priesthood at the Last Supper, we hear Christ described as the "great high priest who has passed through the heavens":

> *Even Christ did not glorify himself with the office of high priest;*
> *he received it from the One who said to him,*
> *"You are my Son;*
> *today I have begotten you";*
> *just as he says in another place,*
> *"You are a priest forever,*
> *according to the order of Melchizedek."*
>
> [Heb 5:5-6; NAB]

The second reading is from an Easter homily of Saint Melito of Sardis (died A.D. 190), who speaks of how the passion of Christ is prefigured in the events of the Old Testament:

> *He is the One who covered death with shame and cast the devil into mourning, as Moses cast Pharaoh into mourning. . . .*
> *It is He who endured every kind of suffering in all those who*

*foreshadowed Him. In Abel He was slain, in Isaac bound, in Jacob
exiled, in Joseph sold, in Moses exposed to die. He was sacrificed in
the Passover lamb, persecuted in David, dishonored in the prophets.*

The psalms, canticles, and reading assigned to Morning Prayer (Ps
80, Is 12:1-6, Ps 81, Heb 2:9-10, Lk 1:68-79 [the Canticle of Zechariah]) now
follow. By the end of *Tenebrae*, only one candle remains burning on the top
of the hearse. This lone candle has traditionally been seen as representing
Christ; in past ages it was removed from the stand at this point and hidden
behind the altar to symbolize His death and burial. The church was left in
such total darkness that afterwards the candle had to be brought out once
more so that those present could find their way out.

The Mass of Chrism

On this same morning there is celebrated a special Mass in each
diocese for the consecration of the holy oils used in the administration
of the Sacraments; the local ordinary (that is, the bishop of the diocese)
concelebrates this Mass together with priests from throughout his
diocese. Three separate oils are blessed, the most important of which is
called "chrism," a mixture of oil and balsam (or other "sweet smelling
matter") used for Baptism and Confirmation; only a bishop is allowed
to consecrate chrism.[25] The two other oils are for anointing catechumens
(that is, those to be baptized) and for Extreme Unction (what is now
known as the Sacrament of the Anointing of the Sick). Traditionally,
olive oil has been used for all three of the "holy oils."

The Apostle Saint James the Less speaks of anointing the sick with
oil in the fifth chapter of his epistle (James 5:14), and thus we know that
oils were used from apostolic times. One of the very earliest references to
the actual blessing of the holy oils dates from the first part of the third
century, and is found in the *Apostolic Tradition* of Saint Hippolytus:

*At the hour which is determined for baptizing let the Bishop give
thanks over the oil and put it into a vessel and call it the "oil of the
thanksgiving"; and take also other oil and exorcize it and call it "the
oil of exorcism."*[26]

It is evident from this passage that in Hippolytus' time the
blessing of the oils took place not on Holy Thursday, but at the Easter

(Courtesy of St. Joseph's Seminary, Yonkers; Chris Sheridan, Catholic New York)

Chrism Mass, St. Patrick's Cathedral, Archdiocese of New York. *"Grant to those who are to come to the cleansing of spiritual rebirth purification of mind and body through anointing with this your creature."*

Vigil, where they would be put to immediate use. Notice that Saint Hippolytus refers to the chrism as the "oil of the thanksgiving," and that the bishop consecrates it by "giving thanks" over it. The prayers that have been used through the centuries for this consecration of the chrism have thus come to be known as "eucharistic prayers," for the word "eucharist" means "thanksgiving." Of course, these prayers must be clearly distinguished from the regular Eucharistic Prayers of the Mass, which contain the words of institution of *the holy Eucharist*, the Sacrament of the Body and Blood of our Lord. Nevertheless, these two different kinds of eucharistic prayers do resemble each other in overall format; in fact, from at least the time of Saint Cyprian (died A.D. 258) the consecration of chrism has taken place during Mass.[27] Another point of interest in the above account of Saint Hippolytus is the reference to the "oil of exorcism"; this is what we know as the "oil of catechumens." Hippolytus' name for it stems from the fact that it is used in the exorcism of any evil spirits from the catechumens anointed with it. This role of the "oil of catechumens" is evident in the prayer for blessing it as found in the *Roman Pontifical* of Pope Clement VIII (1596):

> Grant to those who are to come
> to the cleansing of spiritual rebirth
> purification of mind and body
> through anointing with this your creature.
> If any defilement of hostile spirits remains in them,
> may it depart at the touch of this holy oil,
> and leave no place for wicked spirits,
> no opportunity for the powers
> that have been put to flight,
> no freedom for lurking evils.[28]

The blessing of the third of the holy oils, the "oil of the sick," is also described by Hippolytus in his *Apostolic Tradition*.[29]

By the end of the fifth century the blessing of the holy oils had been transferred to Holy Thursday; a document from this period purporting to be a biography of Pope Saint Silvester states that on this day chrism was consecrated "throughout the world."[30] The *Gelasian Sacramentary* of Rome (seventh century) contains three Masses for Thursday of Holy Week, during the second of which the oils were blessed.[31]

From a number of sources of varying antiquity — the *Gelasian* and *Gregorian* (Hadrian) Sacramentaries, *Roman Ordo I*, the writings of

Amalarius and an *Ordo* from the "Collection of Saint Amand" (*Roman Ordo 30B* in Andrieu) — we are able to form a picture of the special blessing ceremonies at the Mass of Chrism as they existed in ninth-century Rome.[32] Prior to Mass the pope himself would prepare a vessel of chrism by mixing balsam with oil in the sacristy; a second vessel was filled with oil for anointing catechumens. The laity brought to the church and placed on the altar rail the vessels of oil that were to be blessed for use in anointing the sick. During Mass, as the pope neared the end of the Canon (the Eucharistic Prayer), deacons brought several of these latter vessels of oil to him. He would bless them and then resume saying the Canon. The rest of the vessels on the altar rail were blessed by priests and any other bishops present. After the pope received holy Communion, the two *ampullae*, that is, the two vessels of oil and chrism in the sacristy, were now brought out, wrapped in white silk. An archdeacon would then hold the *ampulla* of chrism before the pope who, standing in front of the altar, faced east. The pontiff breathed three times on the vessel and made the sign of the cross over it, after which he said a "eucharistic prayer" to consecrate the chrism. Afterwards an acolyte took the *ampulla* of chrism into his hands and held it as the pope and the deacon kissed it. The vessel was now covered, and the rest of the clergy likewise venerated it. Another deacon then brought the oil of catechumens to the pope who breathed on it three times and recited the Prayer of Exorcism. After both *ampullae* were returned to the sacristy, Mass continued with holy Communion for the clergy and laity.

The modern liturgy of the Chrism Mass as found in the *Roman Missal* of Pope Paul VI follows virtually the same format described above for ninth-century Rome.[33] The three oils are brought to the sanctuary in the offertory procession, along with the bread and wine for Mass, and then set on a table. The oil for anointing the sick is blessed shortly before the conclusion of the Eucharistic Prayer; when Eucharistic Prayer I is said, this blessing comes just prior to the words, "Through Christ our Lord you give us all these gifts." As the vessel is held before him the bishop blesses it, saying the appropriate prayer. Following holy Communion, the bishop goes to the table holding the oil of catechumens and the chrism, where the other priests concelebrating form a semicircle around him. First he blesses the oil of catechumens:

> *Lord God,*
> *protector of all who believe in you,*
> *bless + this oil*

and give wisdom and strength
to all who are anointed with it
in preparation for their baptism.
Bring them to a deeper understanding of the gospel,
help them to accept the challenge of Christian living,
and lead them to the joy of new birth
in the family of your Church.
We ask this through Christ our Lord. Amen.

It is now time to consecrate the chrism. If the balsam or perfume has not already been mixed with the oil for the chrism, it is put in at this point by the bishop. Then he breathes upon the chrism and extending his hands, consecrates it, saying:

God our maker,
source of all growth in holiness,
accept the joyful thanks and praise
we offer in the name of your Church.
In the beginning, at your command,
the earth produced fruit-bearing trees.
From the fruit of the olive tree
you have provided us with oil for holy chrism.
The prophet David sang of the life and joy
that the oil would bring us
in the sacraments of your love.
After the avenging flood,
the dove returning to Noah with an olive branch
announced your gift of peace.
This was a sign of a greater gift to come. . .
After your Son, Jesus Christ our Lord,
asked John for baptism in the waters of Jordan,
you sent the Spirit upon him
in the form of a dove
and by the witness of your own voice
you declared him to be your only, well-beloved Son.
In this you clearly fulfilled the prophecy of David,
that Christ would be anointed
with the oil of gladness beyond his fellow men.

Now the other priests concelebrating extend their right hands toward the chrism. The bishop continues:

> *And so, Father, we ask you to bless + this oil you have created.*
> *Fill it with the power of your Holy Spirit*
> *through Christ your Son.*
> *It is from him that chrism takes its name*
> *and with chrism you have anointed*
> *for yourself priests and kings,*
> *prophets and martyrs.*
> *Make this chrism a sign of life and salvation*
> *for those who are to be born again*
> *in the waters of baptism.*
> *Wash away the evil they have inherited*
> *from sinful Adam,*
> *and when they are anointed with this holy oil*
> *make them temples of your glory,*
> *radiant with the goodness of life*
> *that has its source in you. . . .*

At the end of Mass, the holy oils are carried in procession, immediately behind the cross, back to the sacristy, where the bishop may instruct his priests about the reverent use and safekeeping of these blessed unctions. The oils are afterwards distributed to each parish, where they are placed in the *ambry*, a special coffer constructed for this purpose, mounted in or on the wall of the sanctuary.

Several other features of the Mass of Chrism should be noted. The first reading and the gospel are taken from the Book of the Prophet Isaiah (chapter 61:1-3, 6, 8-9) and the gospel of Saint Luke (chapter 4:16-21) respectively, both of which touch on the motif of our Lord as "the Anointed," as does the responsorial psalm (Ps 89: 21-22, 25, 27). The second reading, from the Book of Revelation (Rev 1:5-8), speaks of Christ as the One who "has made us a royal nation of priests," but it also returns us to a pervading theme of Holy Week:

> *Every eye shall see him,*
> *even of those who pierced him.*
> *All the peoples of the earth*
> *shall lament him bitterly.*
> *So it is to be! Amen!*

[Rev 1:7; NAB]

The gospel describes our Lord in the synagogue of Nazareth, standing before the congregation to read a passage from the Book of Isaiah (61:1-2) that prophesies the work of the Messiah:

> *The spirit of the Lord is upon me;*
> *therefore he has anointed me.*
> *He has sent me to bring glad tidings to the poor. . . .*
>
> [Lk 4:18; NAB]

Following the reading, He applies Isaiah's words to Himself, saying:

> *"Today this Scripture passage is fulfilled in your hearing."*
>
> [Lk 4:21; NAB]

Pope Paul VI introduced a totally new element into the Mass of Chrism: the "Renewal of Commitment to Priestly Service." This beautiful practice highlights one of the most important themes of Holy Thursday: the institution of the Priesthood at the Last Supper. The renewal is made following the homily, before the offertory; the bishop begins by addressing the priests:

> *My brothers,*
> *today we celebrate*
> *the memory of the first eucharist,*
> *at which our Lord Jesus Christ*
> *shared with his apostles and with us*
> *his call to the priestly service of his Church.*
> *Now, in the presence of your bishop*
> *and God's holy people,*
> *are you ready to renew your own dedication*
> *to Christ as priests of his new covenant?*

The priests answer in unison, "I am." The bishop continues:

> *At your ordination*
> *you accepted the responsibilities of the priesthood out of love for*
> *the Lord Jesus and his Church.*
> *Are you resolved to unite yourselves*
> *more closely to Christ*

and to try to become more like him
by joyfully sacrificing
your own pleasure and ambition
to bring his peace and love
to your brothers and sisters?

The priests respond, "I am." The bishop asks:

Are you resolved
to be faithful ministers
of the mysteries of God,
to celebrate the eucharist
and the other liturgical services
with sincere devotion?
Are you resolved to imitate Jesus Christ,
the head and shepherd of the Church,
by teaching the Christian faith
without thinking of your own profit,
solely for the well-being of the people
you were sent to serve?

Once more the priests answer, "I am." The bishop concludes by asking the people to pray for their priests, and then for himself, their bishop.

The Reconciliation of Penitents

The conversion of sinners is a matter that goes to the very heart of the Paschal Mystery. When our Lord gave us the holy Eucharist at the Last Supper, He spoke of His Blood as "poured out for many for the forgiveness of sins" (Mt 26:28). On Calvary He asked forgiveness for His enemies and promised paradise to the repentant thief dying at His side (Lk 23:34,43). And on Easter Sunday, shortly after showing Himself to the Apostles in His risen glory, our Lord instituted the Sacrament of Penance: ". . . he breathed on them, and said to them, 'Receive the Holy Spirit. If you forgive the sins of any, they are forgiven; if you retain the sins of any, they are retained' " (Jn 20:22-23). It is easy, therefore, to understand why the Church in earlier times selected Holy Thursday, the first day of the Easter Triduum, for the reconciliation of public penitents. One of the oldest references to a special reconciliation service for penitents on this day appears in an epistle of Pope Innocent I, dating from A.D. 416: "With regard to penitents . . . if no illness intervenes, the custom of the Roman Church proves that they are to be absolved on the Thursday before Easter."[34] The first of the three Masses listed for Holy Thursday in the seventh-century *Gelasian Sacramentary* was intended for the reconciliation of penitents; at this liturgy the reconciliation ceremony took the place of the first part of Mass, and was followed immediately by the offertory.[35] The reconciliation rite is described in considerable detail in the *Pontifical of Durand*, a liturgical document from the late thirteenth century.[36] The bishop enters the church and prostrates himself before the altar; outside the penitents, holding unlit tapers, kneel down before the church door. The Litany of the Saints is sung, during which there are three pauses; at each of the first two pauses the bishop dispatches two sub-deacons with lit candles, who go to the penitents and chant a versicle that serves as a message of encouragement. On the first occasion the versicle is, "As I live, says the Lord, I want the sinner not to die but to be converted and live," after which the subdeacons extinguish their tapers and return to the bishop. On the second occasion they chant, "The Lord says: Do penance, for the kingdom of God is at hand"; again they put out their candles and return. But when the third pause in the litany comes, the bishop sends a deacon with a tall lit candle, who upon reaching the penitents chants the versicle, "Lift up your heads, for your redemption is at hand." The candles of the penitents are now lit from the large candle brought by the deacon, who then returns with it to the bishop. Following the conclusion of the litany, the archdeacon delivers an address at the threshold of the church; a beautiful English translation of the text of this same address is found in Frederick Warren's edition of the 1526 *Sarum Missal* of England:

> *The accepted time is come, O venerable prelate, the day of divine propitiation and salvation of men; when death was abolished, and eternal life begun; when a planting of new vines is so to be made in the vineyard of the Lord of Sabaoth, that the blindness of the old man may be purged away. For, albeit no time is devoid of the riches of the goodness of God, yet now forgiveness of sins is more ample by reason of his indulgence, and the admission of those who are beginning a new life is more numerous by reason of his grace. By those to be regenerated we are increased in numbers, by those who return [to the unity of the Church] we are increased in strength. Waters wash; tears wash; hence*

there is joy over the receiving of those that are called, and there is joy over the absolution of penitents. . . .[37]

Following this address, according to the *Pontifical of Durand*, the bishop approaches the door himself and speaks to the penitents about God's mercy and His forgiveness; he concludes by chanting the antiphon, "Come, come, come, children, listen to me and I will teach you the fear of the Lord." He reenters the church, and takes his place at a distance from the door; the penitents now enter the church for the first time since Ash Wednesday and kneel down before him. At the proper moment the penitents rise and the bishop takes the hand of one of them; all the other penitents join hands in a chain to the first penitent. The bishop then leads them to the middle of the church where once more they kneel. Following the antiphon, "My son, you should rejoice because your brother was dead and is alive again, was lost and has been found," the prelate says several prayers, concluding with a prayer of absolution for the penitents. He then sprinkles them with holy water, censes them, and says, "Rise up, sleeper! Rise from the dead, and Christ will enlighten you!" The bishop ends the penitential rite by giving them appropriate indulgences and then blesses them.

Upon the conclusion of these services, the penitents, until now barefoot and dressed in sackcloth, would quickly return to their homes to bathe and to clothe themselves once again in their normal attire after forty days of penance.[38]

Although public reconciliation services gradually disappeared after the Middle Ages, the rite was retained in the *Roman Pontifical* up until the Second Vatican Council.[39] Nevertheless, the theme of repentance has by no means been thrust aside, for penance is the key motif of Lent, the season that leads us into Holy Week. In restoring the liturgy of Holy Week in 1955, the Congregation of Sacred Rites emphasized the importance of Sacramental Confession as a preparation for the celebration of Easter:

> *Moreover, the faithful should be admonished to approach the Sacrament of Penance in time during Holy Week. . . . Let those who have the responsibility for souls zealously see to it that the faithful have ready access to the sacrament of Penance during the whole of Holy Week and especially on the last three days of that week.*[40]

The Church's recent *Circular Letter* concerning Holy Week observances likewise stresses the role of the Sacrament of Reconciliation in the fruitful observance of Lent and Holy Week:

> *The faithful are to be encouraged to participate in an ever more intense and fruitful way in the Lenten liturgy and in penitential celebrations. They are to be clearly reminded that both according to the law and tradition, they should approach the Sacrament of Penance during this season, so that with purified heart they may participate in the paschal mysteries.*[41]

And in another place:

> *It is fitting that the Lenten season should be concluded, both for the individual Christian as well as for the whole Christian community, with a penitential celebration, so that they may be helped to prepare to celebrate more fully the paschal mystery.*
>
> *These celebrations, however, should take place before the Easter Triduum, and should not immediately precede the evening Mass of the Lord's Supper.*[42]

Several Holy Thursday Traditions

Thus far in our discussion of Holy Thursday, we have focused upon a number of different liturgical celebrations associated with this day; in the next chapter we will explore the evening Mass of the Lord's Supper at great length. But there are also cherished extraliturgical customs associated with Holy Thursday; naturally, the subject of the Last Supper has inspired several of these traditional practices. On the Mediterranean island of Malta there is a Holy Thursday custom known as the "Last Supper Table," a table laden with food provided by the faithful for subsequent distribution among the poor. In parts of Latin America, especially in Mexico, the dialogue of the Last Supper is reenacted in church on this day, with a priest assuming the role of Christ and twelve men or boys dressed as the Apostles.[43]

On Holy Thursday, as on other days of Holy Week, there are processions in the Spanish city of Seville.[44] Families fill the streets, the women dressed in long velvet skirts and black mantillas worn especially on this day. Many of the men will participate in the processions as members of any one of over forty different brotherhoods; they will spend up to twelve hours on their feet, totally abstaining from all food or drink. Men of every class and profession have walked in these religious parades, including famous bullfighters. It is the longshoremen who have the distinction of carrying the *pasos*, which can weigh up to two and a half tons. From time to time, as a *paso* depicting the Sorrowful Virgin passes by, one of the onlookers serenades her with a haunting chant known as the *saeta*, a style of singing in couplets peculiar to the Andalusian people of southern Spain, the sound of which has been described as "a cross between Gregorian plain chant and Arabic lament."[45] As the *paso* of the Mother of Dolors moves on, the people scatter roses, carnations, and violets before her.

The Spanish city of Valencia is blessed with a most tangible reminder of the first Holy Thursday, for it is in one of the chapels of Valencia's cathedral that there is kept an ancient chalice that for centuries has been venerated by many as the actual vessel used by our Lord Himself at the Last Supper. The Chalice of Valencia is believed to be one of the more important sources of inspiration for the famous medieval legends of the "Holy Grail," which tell of this sacred object being kept in a mysterious mountaintop sanctuary guarded by a military religious order of knights dedicated to its service. Indeed, the Chalice of Valencia is thought to have been kept at a series of locations in the mountains of northeastern Spain from the year 712 up until 1399, when it was transferred to Saragossa and to Valencia twenty-five years later.[46] A number of Catholic scholars have seen the Grail legends as an allegorical expression of the increasing Eucharistic devotion of the Middle Ages, which underwent considerable development during the very same period that produced the earliest surviving Grail narratives.[47] Both the Chalice of Valencia and the legends associated with it have been directly linked to the annual observances of Holy Week. Thus in Richard Wagner's nineteenth-century music drama *Parsifal*, which is based on one of the most important of the medieval Grail stories, that of Wolfram von Eschenbach (composed around 1215),[48] the entire third act takes place on Good Friday. The presence of certain allusions to the liturgy and penitential exercises of Good Friday in Chretien de Troyes' twelfth-century version of the Parsifal legend was emphasized in a recent study.[49] For its part, the Chalice of Valencia has played a prominent role in the Holy Week ceremonies of the city where it is kept; up until the year 1744 (when the relic was damaged in an accident) the chalice was used for carrying one of the Hosts consecrated at the Mass of the Lord's Supper on Holy Thursday to the *Monumento* (the repository) where the Host, resting within the chalice, was reserved until the next day. On Good Friday the vessel with the Eucharist was carried back to the altar for the Communion of the celebrant at the Mass of the Presanctified. This practice echoes an element of the Grail legends, which speak of a dove bringing a Host down from Heaven each year on Good Friday and placing it upon the Holy Grail.[50]

Endnotes

1. Homily, Chrism Mass, Holy Thursday, March 31, 1988, *L'Osservatore Romano*, April 11, 1988, p. 11, #3.
2. Father Herbert Thurston, SJ, "Holy Week," *The Catholic Encyclopedia*, Vol. 7, 1907, p. 437.
3. Pierre Batiffol, *History of the Roman Breviary*, p. 92 (footnote).
4. *Patrologia Latina*, Vol. 78, col. 951a-b, 953a-b, 954c.
5. *Les Ordines Romani du Haut Moyen Age: III: Les Textes (Ordines XIV-XXXIV)* (Etudes et Documents, Vol. 24), pp. 467, 470, 471.
6. Ibid., p. 269.
7. Summarized in Batiffol, pp. 92-93. Edmund Bishop asserts that there was no successive extinguishing of lights on Good Friday in Rome; rather, the service was conducted in almost total darkness as on Holy Saturday (*Liturgica Historica*, 1918, pp. 158-159). All three documents (*Roman Ordines I, 23* [Andrieu] and *30B* [Andrieu]) stipulate the omission during the Easter Triduum of the "Glory be" (*Gloria patri*) which was ordinarily said at the conclusion of every Psalm in the Divine Office. This "suppression" of the "Glory be" was retained in the Roman Rite until the issuance of the *Roman Breviary* of 1972, when it was discontinued.
8. We find this Gallican custom at Rome's Lateran Basilica in the *Ordo Bernardi* (ca. 1120). See Mario Righetti, *Manuale di Storia Liturgica*, Vol. II, p. 156.
9. O. B. Hardison, *Christian Rite and Christian Drama in the Middle Ages*, pp. 117-118.
10. Leo A. Kelly, "Hearse," *Catholic Encyclopedia*, 1907, Vol. 7, p. 162.
11. Father Herbert Thurston, SJ, "Tenebrae," *Catholic Encyclopedia*, Vol. 14, 1907, p. 506.
12. Reverend John Tyrer, *Historical Survey of Holy Week: Its Services and Ceremonial* (Alcuin Club Collections #29), p. 82.
13. H. J. Heuser, "Tenebrae and the New Light of the Holy Fire," *American Ecclesiastical Review*, March 1907, p. 228.

14. Ibid., pp. 228-229.
15. Peter F. Anson, *Churches: Their Plan and Furnishing*, p. 213.
16. "Seville," *The Catholic World*, Oct 1876, p. 15.
17. Decision of 18 June 1956, in "Questions and Answers: Tenebrae," *Clergy Review*, March 1958, p. 170.
18. Liturgical texts reproduced here are from the *The Office of Readings*, Daughters of St. Paul, 1983, pp. 472-475, 732-734, and *Christian Prayer: The Liturgy of the Hours*, Liturgical Press, 1976, pp. 354-355, 866-869, unless otherwise noted. Texts of the Lamentations of Jeremiah are from the Revised Standard Version — see copyright page.
19. Pius Parsch, *The Church's Year of Grace*, 2nd ed., 1953, Vol. 2, p. 306.
20. Father John Steinmueller and Kathryn Sullivan, RSCJ, *Catholic Biblical Encyclopedia: Old Testament*, 1959, p. 547.
21. John Marquess, tr., *The Roman Breviary*, Vol. II, 1908 (Spring), pp. 365-366.
22. Parsch, Vol. 2, p. 304.
23. Casiano Rojo, OSB, "The Gregorian Antiphonary of Silos and the Melody of the Spanish Lamentations," *Speculum*, 1930, pp. 309, 312, 318; the tone itself appears on p. 318 of Rojo's article.
24. "Holy Week in Jerusalem," *The Catholic World*, VII, April-Sep 1868, pp. 77-78.
25. Congregation for Divine Worship, *Rite of the Blessing of Oils; Rite of Consecrating the Chrism*, Decree of Dec 3, 1970; #1, #4, #6, #23, in *The Rites of the Catholic Church*, 1976, pp. 518, 519, 524.
26. Tyrer, pp. 96-97.
27. Ibid., p. 97.
28. "De Officio in Feria V. Coenae Domini: Benedictio olei catechumenorum," *Pontificale Romanum Summorum Pontificum* (edition of Pope Benedict XIV) 1873, Part III, p. 74; English translation from "Mass of the Chrism," #13, in Appendix to *The English-Latin Sacramentary for the United States of America*, 1966, p. 39A.
29. J. D. Crichton, *The Liturgy of Holy Week*, p. 37.
30. Ibid., pp. 34, 36.
31. *Patrologia Latina*, Vol. 74, col. 1099b-1102a.
32. Based upon Tyrer, pp. 99-101.
33. Texts and rubrics of Chrism Mass from Congregation for Divine Worship, #13-#28, pp. 521-527; readings from *Lectionary for Mass*, Catholic Book Publishing Co., 1970, pp. 86-87. Text of "Renewal of Commitment to Priestly Service" in *The Vatican II Weekday Missal*, Daughters of St. Paul, 1975, pp. 664-666.

34. Epistle 25, c. 7., in Tyrer, p. 87 (Latin text in *Patrologia Latina*, Vol. 20, col. 559a).

35. *Patrologia Latina*, Vol. 74, col. 1095b-1099b (summarized in John H. Miller, CSC, "The History and Spirit of Holy Week," *American Ecclesiastical Review*, April 1957, p. 223).

36. The following description of the "Reconciliation of Penitents" in the *Pontifical of Durand* is based upon Adrian Nocent, OSB, *The Liturgical Year*, Vol. II, pp. 206-213, except where noted otherwise.

37. *The Sarum Missal in English* (1526 edition), Frederick Warren, tr., Part I, pp. 236-237.

38. Father Francis X. Weiser, SJ, *The Easter Book*, pp. 107-108.

39. Nocent, Vol. II, p. 206.

40. *Instruction on the Correct Use of the Restored Ordo of Holy Week*, Nov 16, 1955, #2, *American Ecclesiastical Review*, Jan 1956, p. 56.

41. Congregation for Divine Worship, *Circular Letter Concerning the Preparation and Celebration of the Easter Feasts*, 20 Feb 1988, #15, in *L'Osservatore Romano*, Feb 29, 1988, p. 15.

42. Ibid., #37, p. 16. Please note, however, that the Sacrament of Penance is by no means prohibited during the Easter Triduum; see "The Celebration of the Sacraments During the Easter Triduum," *Bishops' Committee on the Liturgy Newsletter*, Vol. 14, Jan 1978, p. 97, as well as p. 209 of the present volume.

43. Weiser, p. 109.

44. The following description is based upon several accounts: Claudia Andujar, "Holy Week in Seville," *Jubilee*, April 1960, pp. 10-14; Maura Laverty, "Holy Week in Seville," *Ave Maria*, March 14, 1931, pp. 333-334; Alquien, "Holy Week in Spain," *The Catholic World*, March 1894, p. 844.

45. Philip Robinson, "From Our Notebook: 'Jesus Del Gran Poder,' " *The Tablet*, April 1, 1961, p. 303.

46. Juan Angel Onate Ojeda, *El Santo Grial: Su Historia, Su Culto y Sus Destinos*, pp. 34-41.

47. See, for example, Father Herbert Thurston, SJ, "The Blessed Sacrament and the Holy Grail," *The Month*, Dec 1907, pp. 622-632. See also A. D. Horgan, "The Grail in Wolfram's *Parzival*," *Medieval Studies*, Vol. 36, 1974, pp. 354-360.

48. Dating for Eschenbach's text in Thurston, p. 623.

49. Bonnie Buettner, "The Good Friday Scene in Chretien de Troyes' Perceval," *Traditio*, Vol. 36, 1980, pp. 415-426.

50. Ojeda, pp. 49-50.

$\overline{V}$

Evening on Holy Thursday: The Easter Triduum Begins

The greatest mysteries of the Redemption are celebrated yearly by the Church beginning with the evening Mass of the Lord's Supper on Holy Thursday until Vespers of Easter Sunday. This time is called "the triduum of the crucified, buried and risen"; it is also called the "Easter Triduum" because during it is celebrated the Paschal mystery, that is, the passing of the Lord from this world to his Father. The Church by the celebration of this mystery, through liturgical signs and sacramentals, is united to Christ, her Spouse, in intimate communion.

[Congregation for Divine Worship][1]

Prelude

Go, my brother, go forward, and with all the love of your soul follow Christ wheresoever He may go. . . .

And follow Him to the Last Supper, in which He bequeathed, and to His Disciples, the Holy Mysteries, and ponder earnestly why it was that He there washed the feet of His Disciples, and moved within you by the profound reflection of untroubled faith, with fear and wonder exclaim: God the Creator of all things, who of His grace made man from the dust has washed the feet of His own image, of His own creation! Ponder earnestly within you, O Brethren, and praise and adore His infinite goodness.

And lovingly behold Him as taking bread into His Hands, He blesses it, and breaks it, as the outward form of His own Immaculate Body; and the chalice which He blessed as the outward form of His Precious Blood, and gave to His Disciples; and be you also a partaker of His Sacraments.

And going from there, and descending to the court of the im-

pious and unjust Caiphas, enter in with your Lord, and stand there firmly, so that you may witness the insults He suffers for you, that you may then become a more perfect lover of your Lord. Follow Him still further, and stand at the place of His Cross, as a faithful servant by his Lord. Behold how blood flowed from His side, and water, for the redemption of your soul, O my Brother! And also look carefully where they laid Him, when taken down from the Cross. And go in the morning early; go with the women to His tomb, and see the stone rolled back from above Him, and see the Angels standing there. Listen to what the Angels say to the women: The Lord is truly risen: as he told you.

[Saint Ephraem][2]

The Still Days

IT WAS WITHIN THE ambit of three days — only seventy-two hours — that the greatest events of our redemption were accomplished — the triduum of the crucified, buried, and risen. From at least as far back as the eighth century,[3] the Sacred Easter Triduum has been seen as a time of silence, during which the Church mourns the sufferings and death of her Divine Spouse. In Anglo-Saxon times this period from Holy Thursday through Good Friday and Holy Saturday was known as "the still days," a term explained in a twelfth-century English homily:

Between His passion and His resurrection He [Christ] lay in the sepulchre and was still, and for that cause the three days before Easter are called "still-days."[4]

Perhaps the most notable custom in this regard has been the silencing of bells from the conclusion of the *Gloria* at Mass on Holy Thursday until the "return" of the *Gloria* at the Mass of the Easter Vigil. This practice already existed in the eighth century: *Roman Ordo I* specifies that the bells were to fall silent following the beginning of Matins (said at midnight) on Holy Thursday.[5] In his work *De Ecclesiasticis Officiis* the French liturgist Amalarius of Metz (died A.D. 850) speaks of the three-day suspension of bell-ringing and the use of wooden soundmakers in their place beginning on Holy Thursday (although he does not explicitly mention the immediate association of the bells with the *Gloria*).[6] It likewise appears in the eleventh-century monastic *Constitutions* of the Norman Abbot and Archbishop Lanfranc for England's Canterbury Cathedral. Thus on Holy Thursday, as the monks walked in procession from the cloister to the church, singing the *Miserere* (Psalm 51), the striking of boards took the place of bells:

> *Meanwhile the sacristan and other brethren standing with him shall beat the boards slowly, in the same manner as the bells are rung on feast days.*[7]

Throughout the Triduum these "boards" were used to summon the monks to the liturgical functions, to prayers, and to meals. It seems likely that the term "boards" in this case refers to a wooden clapper, a device that dates back to the early Church. According to the twentieth-century liturgist Anton Baumstark, the use of these clappers during the Easter Triduum represents, as with so many other elements of the Holy Week liturgy, the sole surviving example of an ancient usage.[8]

According to England's *Sarum Consuetudinary* (ca. 1210) bells could be rung on Holy Thursday only until morning Mass, remaining silent thereafter until the *Gloria* on Holy Saturday.[9] In a later English document, the *York Missal* (fifteenth or sixteenth centuries), we finally find it specifically stated that the bells are to be rung during the *Gloria* on Holy Thursday.[10] With the issuance of the *Roman Missal* of Pope Saint Pius V in 1570, the Church throughout the West adopted this custom, which has continued to the present day.[11]

> *And I will make to cease from the cities of Judah and from the streets of Jerusalem the voice of mirth and the voice of gladness, the voice of the bride-groom and the voice of the bride. . . .*
>
> [Jer 7:34]

In the Christian culture of medieval Europe, secular institutions often sought to echo the practices of the Church; this was certainly the case with the Easter Triduum, during which, as we have already seen, all commerce was brought to a halt. Thus the unique character of these holy days was not confined within the walls of cathedrals and monasteries; rather, emanating from these places, it transformed all aspects of life. With the onslaught of the Reformation and the upheavals that followed in its wake, this harmony in society was in large part shattered; yet, in a few regions it has managed to survive into the present century.

In the city of Palma, on the western Mediterranean island of Mallorca (1942), everything would come to a halt on Holy Thursday. All shops and businesses are closed, and all streetcars and vehicles are pulled from the streets. Everyone, rich and poor alike, walks to the services this day, dressed in black. The stillness continues in this city of over eighty thousand people through Good Friday and into Holy Saturday. On government buildings, in the parks, in the harbor, and on many homes, flags are lowered to half mast. The only sound to be heard above the quiet shuffling of the devout crowds is that of the cooing of doves, and occasionally a bird song.[12]

In rural regions of Germany and Austria the stillness of the triduum pervades the countryside. In accordance with the suppression of church bells after the singing of the *Gloria* at the Mass of the Lord's Supper, all bells used on the farms fall silent during the triduum; calls for dinner are made with wooden clappers.[13]

The Mass of the Lord's Supper

And when the hour came, he sat at table, and the apostles with him. And he said to them, "I have earnestly desired to eat this passover with you before I suffer. . . ."

[Lk 22:14-15]

On the night on which our Lord instituted the holy Eucharist, it is only natural that the Church would wish to commemorate this event in the most appropriate way of all: by celebrating the Mass. The earliest references to such an evening Mass on Holy Thursday appear in the fourth century in the writings of Saint Augustine, reflecting the practice of northern Africa,[14] and in the account of services in Jerusalem provided by the pilgrim Egeria (mentioned earlier). The celebration of an evening Mass of the Lord's Supper must have reached Europe, and even Rome itself, by the seventh century, for the *Gelasian Sacramentary* mentions this Mass as the last of three held on Holy Thursday; there is likewise reference to an evening Mass for this day in the seventh-century Paduan edition of the *Gregorian Sacramentary*.[15] However, by the tenth century such an *evening* Mass had apparently disappeared;[16] the celebration of the institution of the holy Eucharist was transferred to an earlier hour, and eventually came to be celebrated in the morning. Originally the Mass of the Lord's Supper on Holy Thursday was well-attended, and on this day large numbers received holy Communion. Even when the Mass was moved to the morning hours, attendance did not significantly diminish at first, because during the Middle Ages, Holy Thursday was then a holy day of obligation on which all work was laid aside. However, changing social conditions during the seventeenth century compelled Pope Urban VIII to cancel the universal "Holy Day" status of Holy Thursday, Good Friday, and Holy Saturday in his Apostolic Constitution *Universa per Orbem*, issued in 1642.[17] With services held during the morning hours when most now had to go to work, attendance dropped drastically. But in 1955 the Congregation of Sacred Rites, as part of their restoration of the liturgy of Holy Week, returned the Holy Thursday Mass to the evening hours[18] where it truly belongs; many more of the faithful around the world would now be able to attend it at this time of day.

From the *Armenian Lectionary*, which is thought to be representative of the liturgy of fifth-century Jerusalem, we learn that the two readings used at the evening Mass of Holy Thursday were from the first Letter to the Corinthians (11:23-32) and from the gospel of Saint Matthew (26:17-30). Both of these passages describe the institution of the holy Eucharist, and thus their selection confirms that the evening Mass at Jerusalem was specifically intended to commemorate the anniversary of the Last Supper.[19] In the West the oldest Roman Lectionary, the *Capitulary of Wurzburg* (seventh to early eighth centuries), assigns virtually the same epistle from 1 Corinthians 11 (vs. 20-32) to the Mass for Holy Thursday.[20] But the gospel for this day in the Western liturgy differs from that of fifth-century Jerusalem: Saint John's account of Christ washing the feet of His disciples (Jn 13:1-15) is specified in several sources from the eighth century and it has been assigned to the Holy Thursday Mass in the West ever since,[21] together with the aforementioned epistle. In recent times an Old Testament reading has been added — the account of the Passover meal from chapter 12 of the Book of Exodus — a passage that clearly prefigures the Paschal Mystery and the holy sacrifice of the Mass. This selection has been used for centuries in the liturgy of Good Friday and at the Easter Vigil, so in a sense it has simply been transferred to the first night of the Easter Triduum, where it seems particularly appropriate.

This Mass includes two unusual features that endow it with an especially distinctive character. These are: 1) the *Mandatum*, or the washing of feet in imitation of our Lord's action at the Last Supper; and 2) the solemn Eucharistic procession to the repository. The first of these two practices follows the homily, and the second follows Communion. Both will be treated separately in the course of our description of the current liturgy below.

The Mass Begins

When evening came. . . .

[Mt 26:20; JB]

It is near twilight when we enter the church for the Mass of the Lord's Supper. The high altar is splendidly arrayed in white and gold for the celebration of tonight's liturgy; yet, as at the Last Supper, joy is tinged with sadness. One immediately notices the open, emptied tabernacle and the extinguished sanctuary lamp, for the hour is fast approaching "when the bridegroom is taken away" (Lk 5:35). All about us the stained-glass windows seem especially poignant on this sacred evening. The setting sun brightly illuminates a multihued depiction of our Lord at table with His Apostles; there comes a deepening realization that this night and that portrayed in the glass are indeed one and the same.

> *Before the Heavenly Friend forth to His Passion goes*
> *He, urged by His sacred love, gives up Himself*
> *Unto His own to feed their souls*
> *On their pilgrimage here on earth.*
> *Ready to offer Himself, here He doth consecrate*
> *A sacrificial feast that for all time shall last*
> *And proclaim His love for aye*
> *Unto the ransomed race of men.*
>
> [*Oberammergau Passion Play*, 1930][22]

The silence is broken by the forceful sound of the organ as Mass begins with a triumphant entrance hymn. Through the open doors of the chapel the celebrants enter in procession headed by an acolyte walking at a measured pace down the center aisle, carrying a swaying *thurible*. Directly behind him is the processional cross, borne by a second acolyte flanked by two others with lighted candles. They are followed by a deacon who carries the gospel book, the Word of God, holding it aloft as he slowly passes through the church. Finally come the priests in double file, robed in festive white vestments; at the very end of the procession is the principal celebrant of tonight's Mass. As the priests reach the main altar, they kiss the stone two at a time and then take their places in the sanctuary.

"Now is the judgment of this world, now shall the ruler of this world be cast out. . ."

[Jn 12:31]

The Easter Triduum has begun.

The splendor with which Mass begins reaches its climax in the *Gloria*, sung to the accompaniment of bells; but when it is ended the bells fall silent, not to be heard again until the Easter Vigil.

The first reading is from the Book of Exodus (12:1-8, 11-14); in it we see the Old Testament prefiguration of the Sacrifice of Calvary, the same Sacrifice that is the Mass:

The Lord said to Moses and Aaron in the land of Egypt, "This month shall stand at the head of your calendar; you shall reckon it the first month of the year. Tell the whole community of Israel: On the tenth of this month every one of your families must procure for itself a lamb, one apiece for each household. . . . The lamb must be a year-old male and without blemish. . . . You shall keep it until the fourteenth day of this month, and then, with the whole assembly of Israel present, it shall be slaughtered during the evening twilight. They shall take some of its blood and apply it to the two doorposts and the lintel of every house in which they partake of the lamb. That same night they shall eat its roasted flesh with unleavened bread and bitter herbs. . . . It is the Passover of the Lord. For on this same night I will go through Egypt, striking down every first-born of the land, both man and beast, and executing judgment on all the gods of Egypt — I, the Lord! But the blood will mark the houses where you are. Seeing the blood, I will pass over you; thus, when I strike the land of Egypt, no destructive blow will come upon you."

[Ex 12:1-3, 5-8, 11-13; NAB]

The reading ends with a reminder never to forget the events of this night when Christ delivered Himself into the hands of men as the Passover Lamb:

This day shall be a memorial feast for you, which all your generations
shall celebrate with pilgrimage to the Lord, as a perpetual institution.

[Ex 12:14; NAB]

During the Passover supper, through Christ's choice, through his
perfect freedom and his perfect love, the figure of the paschal lamb had
reached the height of its meaning.

[Pope John Paul II][23]

This night's second reading is from Saint Paul's first Letter to
the Corinthians (11:23-26). The reason for its selection over so many
centuries is obvious: In it Saint Paul describes the institution of the holy
Eucharist at the Last Supper and then impresses upon us the unity
between Holy Thursday and Good Friday:

Every time, then, you eat this bread and drink this cup, you proclaim
the death of the Lord until he comes!

[1 Cor 11:26; NAB]

The Liturgy of the Word culminates with the reading of John
13:1-15; so intimately linked is this gospel with the action that follows
it in tonight's liturgy that we will present the text from it as part of our
description of the "Washing of the Feet," the *Mandatum*.

The *Mandatum*

Before the feast of Passover, Jesus realized that the hour had come
for him to pass from this world to the Father. He had loved his own in
this world, and would show his love for them to the end.

[Jn 13:1; NAB]

These are the words with which this night's gospel begins. They
touch upon the one explanation for everything our Lord was to do and
say on this night — and all that He would willingly endure on the
morrow. Thus these words set the stage for all that was to follow, as the
renowned English martyr Saint Thomas More (1478-1535) points out:

In these words the holy evangelist Saint John . . . the disciple that
Jesus loved, declareth here what a manner of faithful lover our holy

Saviour was. . . . For unto those words he putteth and forthwith joineth, the rehearsing of his bitter passion, beginning with his maundy, and therein his humble washing of his disciples' feet, the sending forth of the traitor, and after that his doctrine, his prayer, his taking, his judging, his scourging, his crucifying, and all the whole piteous tragedy of his most bitter passion. Before all which things he setteth these afore rehearsed words, to declare that all these things that Christ did, in all this he did it for very love.

[*A Treatise upon the Passion*][24]

Our Lord chose to reveal what was in His heart with a visible manifestation of love that the Apostles would never forget. How extraordinary it is that God should stoop to earth to wash the feet of sinful men:

The devil had already induced Judas, son of Simon Iscariot, to hand Jesus over; and so, during the supper, Jesus — fully aware that he had come from God and was going to God, the Father who had handed everything over to him — rose from the meal and took off his cloak. He picked up a towel and tied it around himself. Then he poured water into a basin and began to wash his disciples' feet and dry them with the towel he had around him.

[Jn 13:2-5; NAB]

What could be stranger than this? What more awesome? He Who is clothed with light as with a garment [Ps 104:2] is girded with a towel. He Who binds up the waters in his clouds [Job 26:8], Who sealed the abyss by His fearful Name, is bound with a girdle. He Who gathers together the waters of the sea as in a vessel [Ps 33:7] now pours water into a basin. He Who covers the tops of the heavens with water [Ps 104:3] washes in water the feet of His Disciples; and He Who hath weighed the heavens with his palm, and the earth with three fingers [Is 40:12] now wipes with undefiled palms the soles of His servants. He before Whom every knee should bow, of those that are in heaven, on earth, and under the earth [Phil 2:10] now kneels before His servants.

[Saint Cyril of Alexandria][25]

Within one hundred to three hundred years of the time of the pilgrim Egeria, whose diary provides us with our first detailed records of the Procession of Palms and the Good Friday Veneration of the Cross, there appeared yet another rite in the celebration of Holy Week that has likewise endured — the *Mandatum.* Although the washing of feet was a common gesture of charity in the early centuries of the Church, going back even to the time of Saint Paul (1 Tm 5:10),[26] it is not until the seventh century that we find in the West unambiguous evidence of a *Mandatum* ceremony peculiar to Holy Thursday and specifically intended to imitate our Lord's action at the Last Supper. A liturgical document from this period, the "Roman Ordo *in Coena Domini*," states that on Holy Thursday the pope himself washed the feet of his chamberlains (attendants).[27] Likewise in A.D. 694 the Seventeenth Council of Toledo (Spain) spoke in criticism of those priests that had begun to omit the foot-washing rite:

> *Since Our Lord has not disdained to wash the feet of His disciples, why should we refuse to emulate the example He gives us? It now happens that, partly from slackness, partly from custom, in sundry churches the priests no longer wash the feet of the brethren on Maundy Thursday. . . .*[28]

The above passage implies that the *Mandatum* was an established tradition, at least in Spain, for many years prior to the time of the council; the presence of a Holy Thursday *Mandatum* rite in the Spanish *Liber Ordinum,* which contains practices of the fifth to seventh centuries, lends credence to this supposition.[29] In fact it seems plausible that the Holy Thursday Washing of the Feet had arisen by the fifth century, for it is similarly found in an ancient monastic work, the *Regula Magistri* (fifth to seventh centuries), as well as in at least one of four surviving manuscripts of the *Georgian Lectionary,* a book of the liturgy of Jerusalem (fifth to eighth centuries).[30] Indicative of the importance given to the ceremony is the fact that the Seventeenth Council of Toledo threatened to excommunicate any priests or bishops who continued to neglect it.[31]

During the Middle Ages the *Mandatum* spread throughout the West, and became quite common in the monasteries of Europe; thus the *Regularis Concordia* testifies to its existence in the Benedictine communities of tenth-century England.[32] A particularly detailed description of the *Mandatum* is found in the eleventh-century monastic *Constitutions* of Lanfranc, Archbishop of Canterbury. At the appointed time a selected group of poor men would be led into the cloister of the monastery and seated in a row. The monks then enter, each one taking his place, standing before the poor man assigned to his care. The abbot is given two poor men. In an expression of love prompted by our Lord's words, ". . . as you did it to one of the least of these my brethren, you did it to me" (Mt 25:40), the monks now offer the poor a sign of respect accorded only to the Lord Himself and to royalty:

> Then the prior shall strike the board thrice at the abbot's command, and genuflecting and bowing down they shall adore Christ in the poor.

Each of the monks now washes the feet of the man before him, wipes the feet with a towel, kisses them and touches them to his own forehead. Afterwards the monks serve beverages to the poor men, kissing their hands, and then giving them each two pence. Upon the conclusion of this first *Mandatum* ceremony, the abbot says a final prayer:

> Assist, we beseech thee, O Lord, this work of our service, and since thou didst vouchsafe to wash the feet of thy disciples, despise not the work of thy hands, which thou hast commanded us to imitate; that as the outward stains are washed away by them, so all our inward sins may be washed away by thee.

Later the monks reconvene in the chapter-house for a second *Mandatum* among themselves; girt with linen cloths, the abbot and prior go down on their knees to wash, dry, and kiss the feet of their subjects. When finished, the abbot and prior take turns washing each other's feet.[33]

> "The kings of the Gentiles exercise lordship over them; and those in authority over them are called benefactors. But not so with you; rather let the greatest among you become as the youngest, and the leader as one who serves. For which is the greater, one who sits at table, or one who serves? Is it not the one who sits at table? But I am among you as one who serves."
>
> [Lk 22:25-27]

Although as we have already seen the *Mandatum* appears to have been introduced in Rome as early as the seventh century, it is not mentioned again in the surviving records of the Roman liturgy until the twelfth century. *Roman Ordo 11* (dating from between 1140 and 1143) describes the pope washing the feet of twelve subdeacons following Mass,[34] while another document of this period, *Roman Ordo 12*, composed only about fifty years later (ca. 1188-1197), mentions not only the Papal *Mandatum* of subdeacons, but also a second *Mandatum* ceremony conducted in the private apartments of the pontiff, at which the pope washed the feet of thirteen poor men.[35] However this arrangement did not last; the second ceremony was eventually discontinued(perhaps as early as the thirteenth century),[36] and by the fifteenth century the one that remained, that of the subdeacons, was being conducted in the afternoon, having become separated from the Eucharistic liturgy, which was celebrated in the morning.[37] Nonetheless the concept of a *Mandatum* for the poor was not forgotten: the *Caeremoniale Episcoporum*, first issued in 1600, permitted either thirteen paupers or thirteen canons to be selected for the liturgical foot-washing rite.[38] The *Mandatum* gradually fell into disuse in many places, although it was never officially discontinued; the popes themselves continued to perform it. The famous English Prelate, Cardinal Nicholas Wiseman (1802-1865), speaks of the pope in his time washing the feet of "thirteen priests, generally poor, of different nations, who are afterwards by him served at table, in a hall upstairs."[39] Bishops, abbots, and religious superiors also maintained the practice, faithfully observing the ceremony as specified by the *Roman Missal* of 1604:

> . . . *the prelate puts off his cope and, fastening a towel around him, he kneels before each one of those who are chosen for the ceremony, washes, wipes and kisses the right foot.*[40]

We read in a nineteenth-century account that on Holy Thursday of each year, at one o'clock in the afternoon, the Catholic Patriarch of Jerusalem would wash the feet of a number of pilgrims in front of the holy sepulchre and give each of them a roughly hewn wooden cross, about seven inches in length, with little cavities for inserting relics from the Via Dolorosa. Many considered this cross among the most precious of keepsakes they could bring back from the Holy Land because of the unforgettable circumstances of time and place in which they received it.[41]

> *"Then the King will say to those at his right hand, 'Come, O blessed of my Father, inherit the kingdom prepared for you from the foundation of the world; for I was hungry and you gave me food, I was thirsty and*

you gave me drink, I was a stranger and you welcomed me, I was naked and you clothed me, I was sick and you visited me, I was in prison and you came to me.' "

[Mt 25:34-36]

At the parish level, the *Mandatum* became an increasingly rare phenomenon, but at least some parish priests continued the tradition. In Tasco, Mexico (nineteenth century) the ceremony was performed around three o'clock in the afternoon. Twelve poor men, dressed to represent the Apostles, would be seated on two benches in the middle of the church; each is clothed in a brightly colored tunic, with a leafy wreath on his head and a stave in his hand. Barefoot and wearing an alb and purple stole, the parish priest kneels before each of the men and washes, dries, and kisses their feet; the vicar and another priest follow him and likewise kneel to kiss the feet of the beggars. They in turn are followed by twelve to fifteen of the most prominent men of Tasco, who perform this same act of humility. Afterwards, the parish priest delivers a homily on the humility of our Lord in what He did at the Last Supper.[42]

" 'Lord, when did we see thee hungry and feed thee, or thirsty and give thee drink? And when did we see thee a stranger and welcome thee, or naked and clothe thee? And when did we see thee sick or in prison and visit thee?' And the King will answer them, 'Truly I say to you, as you did it to one of the least of these my brethren, you did it to me.' "

[Mt 25:37-40]

In our own day, the *Mandatum* has once more become a universally observed practice, thanks to the restoration of the Holy Week liturgy in 1955, when the *Mandatum* was rejoined to the Mass of the Lord's Supper and inserted between the homily and the offertory, thus giving it a more prominent place than ever before.

The clergy's performance of this service of love over a period of more than thirteen centuries has inspired many Christian monarchs down through the ages to imitate their example. To cite one extraordinary case, King Robert II of France (996-1031) on at least one occasion washed the feet of 160 members of the clergy on this day.[43] Throughout the Middle Ages, and in some instances up to the present century, reigning monarchs and lords would wash the feet of a group of poor people and then wait upon them at table. As mentioned earlier the

Pope John Paul II, *Mandatum* ceremony. *"Come, O blessed of my Father, inherit the kingdom prepared for you from the foundation of the world. . ." (Mt 25:34).*

young Hungarian princess Saint Elizabeth of Hungary (thirteenth century) sometimes chose twelve lepers to receive this service from her.

An especially interesting example of these royal *Mandatum* ceremonies comes to us from an account of Holy Week ceremonies as they were observed in April of 1885 in the city of Madrid, where the Spanish monarchy faithfully performed the washing each year. Following Mass at the Chapel Royal, the king and queen would proceed to the Hall of Columns. Arriving there at two o'clock in the afternoon, the king (Alfonso XII)[44] entered in full ceremonial uniform, decked with all his medals of state, together with his queen (Maria Christina), who was dressed in a fine gown and flowing train, with a white mantilla and a diamond diadem on her head. In the center of the hall stood two platforms; on one twelve poor elderly men were seated, clothed in new suits provided by the king; on the other platform were twelve elderly women, likewise dressed in new clothing provided by the queen. Nearby stood an altar on which was placed a crucifix and two lighted candles. The bishop who was Patriarch of the Indies then went before this altar and read Saint John's gospel account of Christ washing the feet of His disciples at the Last Supper. Following the reading, a small gold-fringed, embroidered band was tied around the king's waist, symbolizing the towel that Christ tied around His waist on this occasion. The king now mounted the first platform, accompanied by his steward, who brought a golden basin and ewer. He then knelt down before each of the men seated there and poured water over their feet, wiped them, and kissed them. Likewise the queen performed this service on her knees for the poor women. Some years earlier, as Queen Isabella II (reigned 1833-1868) was washing the feet of one woman, a beautiful diamond bracelet she was wearing fell from her arm into the basin. The other woman reached down and took it out of the water to return it to the queen, but the monarch handed it back to her, saying: "Keep it, *hija mia*; it is your luck."

Upon completing the *Mandatum*, the king would lead the twelve elderly men down from the platform to a long table prepared for them where, after they had taken their places, the king set before each of them a sumptuous fifteen-course fish dinner, plus fifteen *entremets* and a large flagon of wine. Similarly, the queen led the poor women to a second table, where she served them in the same manner. The food, together with all the flatware, glasses, and utensils with which it was served, was then packed into twenty-four large baskets, so that these poor people could take their rich banquet home with them. In addition, each was given a purse containing twelve gold pieces.[45]

> *Beloved, let us love one another;*
> *for love is of God, and he who*
> *loves is born of God and knows God.*

[1 Jn 4:7]

Let us return now to the liturgical *Mandatum* as it is conducted in the current liturgy. After the gospel and a homily on the mysteries of this evening (the institution of the holy Eucharist and of the priesthood, and Christ's command to love one another), twelve men[46] assemble before the sanctuary and are seated. Then the chief celebrant, assisted by a priest concelebrating with him, removes his chasuble; the acolytes bring out a basin and towels. He kneels to wash the feet of each of the twelve men, while the choir sings the eighth-century hymn *Ubi Caritas*:

> *Where are charity and love,*
> *God is there.*
> *The love of Christ hath gathered us together.*
> *Let us exult and be joyful in Him.*
> *Let us fear and love the living God.*
> *And let us love one another with sincere hearts.*
> *Being, therefore, assembled together.*
> *Let us beware of being divided in mind.*
> *Let malicious upbraidings cease,*
> *let wranglings cease.*
> *And may Christ, our God,*
> *be in the midst of us.*

[antiphon and vs. 1-8][47]

> *Thus he came to Simon Peter, who said to him, "Lord, are you going to wash my feet?" Jesus answered, "You may not realize now what I am doing, but later you will understand." Peter replied, "You shall never wash my feet!" "If I do not wash you," Jesus answered, "you will have no share in my heritage." "Lord," Simon Peter said to him, "then not only my feet, but my hands and head as well." Jesus told him, "The man who has bathed has no need to wash [except for his feet]; he is entirely cleansed, just as you are; though not all." (The reason he said, "Not all are washed clean," was that he knew his betrayer.)*

[Jn 13:6-11; NAB]

After washing the feet of the twelve, the celebrant is revested with his chasuble and returns to his seat in the sanctuary, while the acolytes prepare the altar for the offertory of the Mass.

> *After he had washed their feet, he put his cloak back on and*
> *reclined at table once more. He said to them:*
>   *"Do you understand what I just did for you?*
>   *You address me as 'Teacher' and 'Lord,'*
>   *and fittingly enough,*
>   *for that is what I am.*
>   *But if I washed your feet —*
>   *I who am Teacher and Lord —*
>   *then you must wash each other's feet.*
>   *What I just did was to give you an example:*
>   *as I have done, so you must do."*
>
>   [Jn 13:12-15; NAB]

> *The love of Christ hath gathered us together.*
> *Let us fear and love Christ the Lord.*
> *Where are charity and love, God is there.*
> *Behold how good and how pleasant it is*
> *for brethren to dwell together in unity.*
>
>   [*Congregavit Nos in Unum*, plus Ps 133:1][48]

The Liturgy of the Eucharist

> *Do not labour for the food which perishes, but for the food which*
> *endures to eternal life, which the Son of man will give to you. . . .*
>
>   [Jn 6:27]

On this, the anniversary of the Institution of the Holy Eucharist,[49] it seems particularly appropriate to pause to consider the origins of the various elements of the Eucharistic liturgy. Of course the most important aspects of this liturgy were established at the Last Supper itself. Yet in addition, almost every other feature of the Eucharistic liturgy as we know it today has ancient roots in the life of the early Church, even if not demonstrably traceable to the first Mass in the Cenacle. For the sake of brevity we will confine our discussion to only a few of these elements.

The earliest explicit reference to the presentation of the gifts of bread and wine with which the offertory of the modern Mass begins is found in the *First Apology* of Saint Justin Martyr, written around A.D. 155.[50] The Offertory Prayers in the current *Roman Missal* are based largely on a passage in the first-century document known as the *Didache*.[51] The bread used by our Lord for the first Mass was almost certainly unleavened, but, probably for practical reasons, the early Church utilized leavened loaves instead; since the eleventh century, the Church in the West has resumed using unleavened bread.[52] The mingling of a little water with the wine during the offertory goes back to the Last Supper; in our Lord's day wine was never consumed without first mixing water with it.[53] The so-called *Sursum corda* ("Lift up your hearts. . .") which follows the offertory and serves as an introduction to the Eucharistic Prayer first appears in the *Apostolic Tradition*, a work of Saint Hippolytus dating from around A.D. 218; the wording is almost identical to what it is today.[54] Now we come to the heart of the Mass, the Eucharistic Prayer itself, containing the words of consecration with which our Lord instituted the Sacrament. Except for the actual words of consecration, the early Church used a variety of different formulas for the rest of the Eucharistic Prayer. One of these emerged to become what we now refer to as the "First Eucharistic Prayer," also known as the "Roman Canon." Evidence suggests that at least the core of the Roman Canon was already in existence by the second half of the fourth century; a significant portion of it is found in the *De Sacramentis* of Saint Ambrose (A.D. 340-397).[55] By around A.D. 600 the entire text of the Roman Canon as we know it today had been formulated;[56] it has changed little over almost fourteen centuries, during most of which it was the only Eucharistic Prayer used by the Church in the Roman Rite. The Roman Canon is now one of four different Eucharistic Prayers provided by the current *Roman Missal* of Pope Paul VI. Another of these, the second, is an abbreviated and somewhat modified version of a canon found in the *Apostolic Tradition* of Saint Hippolytus (ca. A.D. 218); thus it constitutes the oldest surviving version of a Eucharistic Prayer.[57] We know that the Our Father had been incorporated into the Eucharistic liturgy, at least in some places, by the end of the fourth century; both Saint Cyril of Jerusalem (315-386) and Saint Augustine (354-430) mention this use of the prayer.[58] But it may be that the insertion of the Our Father into the Mass is almost as ancient as the Eucharistic Sacrifice itself, for Pope Saint Gregory I (reigned 590-604), in an epistle to the Bishop of Syracuse, asserts that this tradition originated with the Apostles.[59] The words that follow shortly after the Our Father, "For the kingdom, the power, and the glory are yours. . . ," date from the apostolic age, appearing as part of what are evidently Mass prayers in the first-century *Didache*.[60] The sign of peace is first mentioned around A.D. 155 by Saint Justin Martyr.[61] The *Agnus Dei* ("Lamb of God, you take away the sins of the world. . . .") was introduced into the Roman liturgy under Pope Saint Sergius (reigned 687-701).[62] The prayer, "Lord, I am not worthy to receive you. . . ", was not inserted into the Mass until the Middle Ages, but the text is taken almost word for word from Sacred Scripture (Mt 8:8).[63] The words of the priest in distributing holy Communion ("The body of Christ"), and the response of "Amen" given by the faithful have been part of the Communion rite since the third century, if not earlier; the *Apostolic Tradition* of Hippolytus gives only a slightly more elaborate version of the formula used today.[64]

This night's Liturgy of the Eucharist follows the same format as does the holy Sacrifice on any other day; but the fact that this Mass is taking place on the very same night as that first Mass at the Last Supper gives everything an added significance:

> *Blessed are you, Lord, God of all creation. Through your goodness we have this bread to offer, which earth has given and human hands have made. It will become for us the bread of life.*
>
> [Offertory]

Following the offertory, all the priests concelebrating gather around the altar as they make ready for the most sacred moment of this and every Mass: the consecration.

> *He is the true and eternal priest who established this unending sacrifice. He offered himself as a victim for our deliverance and taught us to make this offering in his memory. . . .*
>
> [Preface for Holy Thursday, *Roman Missal*]

The Eucharistic Prayer

> *For the bread of God is that which comes down from heaven, and gives life to the world.*
>
> [Jn 6:33]

Although on this night the Church allows any of the four

Eucharistic Prayers to be used, she deems the selection of the first, the Roman Canon, to be "particularly apt" in virtue of the three special formularies composed for insertion into this prayer on Holy Thursday;[65] these insertions entered the Holy Thursday liturgy at least thirteen hundred years ago, with all three appearing in the seventh century *Gelasian Sacramentary* as well as in both the Paduan (seventh century) and the Hadrian (eighth century) editions of the *Gregorian Sacramentary*.[66] The texts remind us just what night this is:

In union with the whole Church
we celebrate that day
when Jesus Christ, our Lord,
was betrayed for us. . .

Father, accept this offering
from your whole family
in memory of the day
when Jesus Christ, our Lord,
gave the mysteries of his body and blood
for his disciples to celebrate. . .

The day before he suffered
to save us and all men, that is today,
he took bread into his sacred hands
and looking up to heaven,
to you, his almighty Father,
he gave you thanks and praise.
He broke the bread,
gave it to his disciples, and said:

TAKE THIS, ALL OF YOU, AND EAT IT:
THIS IS MY BODY WHICH WILL BE GIVEN UP FOR YOU.

When supper was ended, he took the cup.
Again he gave you thanks and praise,
gave the cup to his disciples, and said:

TAKE THIS, ALL OF YOU, AND DRINK FROM IT:
THIS IS THE CUP OF MY BLOOD,
THE BLOOD OF THE NEW AND EVERLASTING
COVENANT.
IT WILL BE SHED FOR YOU AND FOR ALL
SO THAT SINS MAY BE FORGIVEN.

DO THIS IN MEMORY OF ME.

[Eucharistic Prayer I]

At every Mass we return in spirit to the upper room in Jerusalem where this great Sacrament was instituted by our Savior, but it is especially on this night, at the Mass of the Lord's Supper, that our thoughts converge upon that mysterious room of which Saint Ephraem (died 373) speaks so eloquently:

O blessed spot, thy narrow room may be set against all the world. That which is contained in thee, though bounded in narrow compass, filleth the universe. Blessed is the dwelling-place in which with holy hand the bread was broken. In thee the grape which grew on Mary's vine was crushed in the chalice of salvation.[67]

Holy Communion

"I am the living bread which came down from heaven; if any one eats of this bread, he will live for ever; and the bread which I shall give for the life of the world is my flesh."

[Jn 6:51]

From the earliest times Holy Thursday has been a day on which the faithful have received holy Communion in very large numbers. The sons and daughters of the Church have instinctively sensed the importance of commemorating the anniversary of the Last Supper by uniting themselves with Christ in this most perfect manner.

"He who eats my flesh and drinks my blood abides in me, and I in him."
[Jn 6:56]

As the faithful silently make their thanksgiving following holy Communion, the remembrance of our Lord's words in the Cenacle cannot be far from their minds:

"If anyone loves me he will keep my word,
and my Father will love him,
and we shall come to him
and make our home with him."

[Jn 14:23; JB]

[121]

The Stripping of the Altar

The Mass of the Lord's Supper ends abruptly with a short concluding prayer, and with it the joyful mood that pervades this evening liturgy seems to end just as suddenly. There is no final blessing as on other days; instead there is silence as the chief celebrant leaves his place to stand before the main altar, on which is the ciborium containing the Hosts consecrated for Good Friday. After putting incense into a *thurible*, he kneels and censes the Blessed Sacrament three times. The procession to the repository, to the place prepared for the reservation of the holy Eucharist, is about to begin. But before continuing further with this subject, with which we will be dealing at some length, it is necessary to pause here to consider one other action that follows this night's Mass and expresses in a particularly striking manner the transition from the Last Supper to Gethsemane.

It is in seventh-century Spain that we encounter two of the earliest references to the stripping and washing of the altars following Mass on Holy Thursday: Saint Isidore of Seville (560-636) tells us that on this day "the altars and walls and floors of the church are washed," and the Seventeenth Council of Toledo (694) mentions that on Holy Thursday "after the usual manner the altars are wont to be stripped."[68] Although this custom may have originated for practical reasons (to have everything cleaned in time for Easter), the practice was found to be consonant with the atmosphere of desolation associated with the first two days of the Easter Triduum. In Spain at least, the practice took on dolorous connotations almost from the beginning, for the *Liber Ordinum*, a Spanish liturgical book of the fifth to seventh centuries, prescribed that during the stripping of the altar Psalm 109 ("... I am gone, like a shadow at evening; I am shaken off like a locust. ..." [verse 23]) was to be chanted with the antiphons *Ecce venit hora* ("Behold the hour is at hand, and the Son of man shall be betrayed into the hands of sinners. ...") and *Tristis est anima* ("My soul is sorrowful even unto death. ..."), as twelve candles held by twelve deacons standing around the altar were extinguished.[69] In later centuries the stripping and washing took on even more ceremonial elements in other parts of Europe. Thus the *Sarum Processional* of pre-Reformation England specifies that the water to be used for the washing should first be blessed. Two priests and their attendants would walk in procession from one altar to another, at each of which the priests poured wine and water onto the five crosses in the altar slab; their attendants followed, pouring water on the slabs. At each of these altars responsory and versicle prayers were chanted.[70]

Altar-washing ceremonies such as the one described above were, after the Middle Ages, discontinued almost everywhere. In the *Roman Missal* of Pope Saint Pius V (1570), there is no mention of the washing of altars, but a simple ceremony for the stripping of the altars is prescribed for the universal Church. Following Vespers, the presiding priest and his assistants strip the altar cloths while reciting Psalm 22 together with the antiphon, "They parted my garments amongst them; and upon my vesture they cast lots."[71]

In the current *Roman Missal* of Pope Paul VI there is no longer a formal ceremony for the stripping of the altar, but the actual stripping itself is still required:

> *Then the altar is stripped and, if possible, the crosses are removed from the church. It is desirable to cover any crosses which remain in the church.*[72]

At Saint Peter's Basilica in Rome the medieval altar-washing ceremony was retained into the present century. In an account written in 1909, Dom Bede Camm, OSB, describes the washing of the papal altar following *Tenebrae* on the evening of Holy Thursday. Prior to the beginning of the washing rite, all the clergy and seminarians that had sat in choir for *Tenebrae* are given "curious mops made of shavings." In a procession led by officials carrying maces, followed by a veiled cross, the numerous clerics make their way through the basilica from the "Altar of the Chair" where *Tenebrae* was held to the high altar, the papal altar, which has already been stripped of its cloths. A row of silver cruets containing water and wine are set on this latter altar. As the procession arrives and begins to mount the altar steps, the participants start Psalm 22 ("O God, my God . . . why hast thou forsaken me? . . ."), together with the antiphon, "They parted my garments amongst them; and upon my vesture they cast lots." The recital of this Psalm and antiphon continues through the rest of the service. The clerics line up on one side of the altar; eleven priests in black and gold stoles, plus a twelfth in a black and gold cope, now approach it, and taking the silver cruets, pour water and wine onto the *mensa* (the flat top of the altar), spreading the mixture over the whole stone surface with their mops. They then retire to the bottom altar step, after which a cardinal approaches the altar, wipes it with his mop, and moves on. This action is repeated by each of the other clerics present, from the Latin Patriarch of Constantinople (Istanbul) to the seminarians. Finally, when all have taken their turn wiping the *mensa*, the twelve priests that poured the water and wine return to the altar and dry the stone top with sponges that are subsequently wrapped in cloths and borne away. Each carrying their own mops, the cardinal, the patriarch, and all the other participants leave the altar in procession, bringing the ceremony to an end.[73]

The Eucharistic Procession to the Repository

"Rise, let us go hence."

[Jn 14:31]

> *April 20th. — Holy Thursday . . . we went down to the Church of the Holy Sepulchre. . . . There the impressive service of Holy Thursday was carried out with great precision. . . . At the procession we marched thrice around the rotunda of the Holy Sepulchre, the third time going out around the so-called stone of unction by the entrance of the church. About seventy-five priests were in the procession. . . .*
>
> *After the procession the Host consecrated for the Ceremony of the Presanctified was placed in the Holy Sepulchre on the slab covering the . . . grave of Christ.*
>
> [A. E. Breen, *A Diary of My Life in the Holy Land*][74]

Already in the seventh century, the Blessed Sacrament was being reserved overnight on Holy Thursday for holy Communion on Good Friday; this practice is mentioned both in the *Gelasian Sacramentary* and later in the eighth-century *Roman Ordo I*. However, these sources refer to the practice in only the briefest of terms; the *Gelasian Sacramentary* merely says:

> *They communicate and reserve of this sacrifice until the morrow; and thence let them communicate.*

And on Good Friday:

> *. . . the deacons go into the sacristy. They proceed with the body and blood of the Lord which remained the day before, and place it upon the altar.*[75]

"I am the living bread which came down from heaven. . ." (Jn 6:51).

The rubrics in *Roman Ordo I* provide no additional information in this regard;[76] but an eighth-century appendix to this *Ordo*, of Gallican provenance (that is, from France), speaks of an established custom being followed:

> *Mass being finished they communicate in the appointed order, and reserve of the Sancta until the morrow according to custom.*[77]

Does this passage simply mean that the practice of reserving the holy Eucharist was itself "customary" on this day, or does it suggest that the *manner* of reserving the sacrament followed an established form — that there was a *customary ceremony* for bringing the Blessed Sacrament to the place of repose? The latter may be the case. The French Benedictine liturgist Jean Mabillon (1632-1707), in the *Commentarius* accompanying his landmark edition of the *Roman Ordines* known as the *Museum Italicum*, quotes the following passage regarding the Holy Thursday reservation rite from what he terms an "old missal of the most famous Bishop of Rieux" (*Rivensis* — what is now Toulouse, France), which he dates around A.D. 600:

> *Let it [the Eucharist] be carried with veneration by a priest and deacon with the other ministers holding a white cloth over it. And let*

this be done without the [Precious] Blood, and with thurible and light preceding, until it is in the place of repose; and never let it be without a light.[78]

In the above passage we find three features that were to characterize many later versions of the Holy Thursday Eucharistic procession: the use of light, incense, and a canopy. There is reason to be highly skeptical of Mabillon's dating in this case; but even if the document were actually written as late as the tenth century, it would still constitute the earliest record of such a formal Holy Thursday procession. We do not find other examples of the reservation rite with this degree of ceremony until the eleventh century. According to the *Constitutions* of Abbot Sigibert of the Monastery of Cluny (France), dating from this latter period, the Eucharistic procession consisted of a deacon, a "secretary," and a number of lay brethren, carrying candles and a *thurible*. The Blessed Sacrament was placed in a chalice and paten, covered by a second paten and wrapped in linen. It was then borne away to another altar or "a most clean coffer," where a light was set before it through the night until Matins (that is, until midnight, when Matins, the first "Hour" of the Divine Office, was said).[79]

In Rome a formal procession is first mentioned during the thirteenth century: *Roman Ordo 10* specifies that before the end of the Holy Thursday Mass the holy Eucharist, enclosed in a pyx, is carried from the altar by the junior cardinal priest to "the place prepared," with a cross and lights borne before him and a canopy over him.[80]

During the Middle Ages this procession became increasingly elaborate. In *Roman Ordo 15* (early fifteenth century) the cleric who carries the Eucharist in the procession is no longer a lesser assistant priest or deacon as in earlier Roman documents; instead, the celebrant, in this case the pope himself, performs the office.[81] Another liturgical document, the *Ceremoniale sanctae romanae Ecclesiae* (1516), lists an extensive retinue of participants in the papal Eucharistic procession; it also specifies the singing of the *Pange, lingua* on the way to the place of reposition, a tradition that has remained in the liturgical books to the present day.[82] By the early seventeenth century the procession reached its fullest stage of development; in the *Roman Missal* of 1604 the Eucharistic procession is described in considerable detail. At the end of Mass torches are lit; the celebrant, dressed in a white cope, genuflects before the Eucharist and censes it. He then takes the chalice, containing a single Host, into his hands and covering it with the ends of a veil around his shoulders, proceeds to the place of repose, under a canopy, and flanked by a deacon and subdeacon; two acolytes continually cense the Sacrament along the way. Upon arriving at the repository the deacon takes the chalice from the celebrant and places it on the altar. The celebrant kneels and censes the Blessed Sacrament again before putting it into the special coffer used for this occasion.[83]

In the Mozarabic Rite (Spain) there were some additional customs, as found in the *Missale Mixtum* of 1500. Along the path of the procession green branches were strewn and a small bell rung. At the place of repose a cross, a missal or Bible, a bell, a censer, and an incense-boat with incense were also placed into the repository tabernacle (called the *monumentum* in the Mozarabic Rite), which was then double-locked and double-sealed.[84]

The recent liturgical reforms of the 1950s and 1960s have hardly altered the Holy Thursday procession in the Roman Rite from what it was in the *Roman Missal* of 1604. The only notable differences regard the canopy and the vessel in which the Sacrament is carried. A canopy is no longer specified for the procession in the rubrics of the current *Roman Missal* of Pope Paul VI (1970). And with the reinstitution of a general Communion on Good Friday in 1955, it has become necessary to use a ciborium (which can hold numerous Hosts) rather than a chalice for conveying the holy Eucharist to the repository.[85]

In the older liturgical documents, the destination of these Holy Thursday processions was usually referred to in veiled terms, such as "the place prepared." Often this meant the sacristy, which during the Middle Ages was elaborate and chapel-like, unlike the purely functional sacristies we see in modern churches. In what is perhaps our earliest detailed description of the reservation ceremony, that of the "old missal" of Rieux (as cited by Mabillon and quoted above), we read that a candle or oil lamp was to be kept burning at the place of repose (*nunquam sine lum ine remaneat*).[86] However, it is difficult to determine just when or where the adornment of the repository began to take on more developed forms. In the eleventh century statutes of England's Canterbury Cathedral, composed by its archbishop, Lanfranc (1005-1089), and also thought to reflect practices at the Benedictine Monastery of Bec (northern France) where Lanfranc had previously been the abbot, the repository of Holy Thursday is referred to as the "appointed place *most fittingly prepared*" (*locum constitutum decentissime praeparatum —* emphasis added);[87] this phrase does seem to suggest a specially furnished setting for the reservation of the holy Eucharist. Lanfranc likewise stipulates that a "lamp shall burn without ceasing before the spot." Another eleventh-century monastic document, the *Liber de Officiis Ecclesiasticis* of John of Avranches, Archbishop of Rouen (France), speaks of "the brightest linen cloths" being used for the reposition of the Blessed Sacrament on this day.[88] A further interesting clue is provided by a document prescribing the austere rule of the Carthusian monks, dating from around 1130; in reference to the Mass on Holy Thursday, it states:

> *One host of the larger size ought to be consecrated in this mass for Good Friday, and this we wish put back in the usual place at the high altar, and forbid sepulchres to be made for the reserving of it after the manner of the seculars, or other preparations not fitting for our solitude"* [emphasis added].[89]

This passage implies that already by the twelfth century the repository for Holy Thursday, here referred to as the "sepulchre,"[90] was becoming a focal point of popular devotion in some places. In another twelfth-century source, the *Ordo of Beroldus*, a document of the Ambrosian Rite of Milan, Italy, we are told that following Mass on Holy Thursday the Archbishop of Milan would enter the sacristy "where he bids the sub-deacons diligently guard the Sacrament of the body and blood of the Lord."[91] This clearly means that some sort of watch was mounted at the repository; and it was the concept of watching at the place of repose that served as the nucleus for the increasing attention given to this Holy Thursday reservation of the Sacrament in the centuries that followed. In the thirteenth-century (and perhaps as early as the mid-twelfth century) we begin to find references to an extended "watch" of forty hours observed in the city of Zara (what is now Zadar) on the Adriatic coast of western Yugoslavia. According to a will dating from 1270, a vineyard was given "to defray the expenses of the prayer of forty hours in Holy Week (*hebdomada dolorosa*) in the Chapel of St. Silvester"; another even earlier bequest from 1214 likewise provides for the support of the "forty hours" devotion as conducted by the fraternity of the *Verberati* at this same chapel.[92] In an entry in a diary dated March 22, 1380, we learn that this watch indeed began on Holy Thursday, evidently around eight o'clock in the evening, and involved relays of watchers:

> *. . . upon the evening of Maundy Thursday, a popular disturbance broke out in the little square in front of the Chapel of St. Silvester,*

*belonging to the confraternity of the Verberati, just before the public
prayer of the Forty Hours. I, with the other two magistrates of the city
of Zara, put an end to the disturbance and restored tranquility at the
first summons, so that even this year also the prayer took place in due
form, being distributed according to ancient custom among different
persons from hour to hour and lasting until Gloria Saturday at noon.*[93]

Although the passage above does not explicitly mention that the
Blessed Sacrament was the object of this "watch," such seems to have
been the case in view of the fact that the devotion began on Holy
Thursday, the day on which the institution of this sacrament is commemorated, and thus would have coincided with the ceremonial reservation of the Eucharist on this day; the existence in other places of a
similar Eucharistic watch of approximately forty hours from Good
Friday until Easter morning (see chapter IX) in commemoration of our
Lord's entombment likewise lends credence to this supposition. In the
Ambrosian Rite, where as we have seen the Holy Thursday reservation
had been introduced by the twelfth century, and where the custom of
"interring" the Eucharist in a "sepulchre" (along with a cross) on Good
Friday appeared as early as the eleventh century,[94] we find evidence in
later centuries that these two reservation rites may have melded into
one in some places. Significantly, there has never been a formal Mass
of the Presanctified (Communion service) on Good Friday in the
Ambrosian Rite;[95] the Holy Thursday reservation mentioned by the
twelfth century *Ordo of Beroldus* was for the Communion of the clergy
alone, which took place in the sacristy after the Good Friday liturgy had
concluded.[96] Eventually this private Communion rite was discontinued,
so that by the sixteenth century the Eucharist was being kept at the
repository without interruption from Mass on Holy Thursday until the
Easter Vigil on Holy Saturday, a period of roughly forty hours.[97] Might
not the "Forty Hours" devotion in Zara have been in some way derived
from or related to the customs in Milan? We do know that the modern
Eucharistic devotion of the *Quarant 'Ore* (Forty Hours), which is held
at different times in various places throughout the year, can be traced
back to sixteenth-century Milan.

Although the thirteenth-century *Roman Ordo 10* does refer to the
repository tabernacle as an "adorned" coffer (*adornata capsis*),[98] by and
large the Roman liturgical books up until the beginning of the seventeenth century provide no information on the adornment of the
repository and do not even mention whether a watch was held. How-

ever, the increasingly elaborate rubrics in these books with regard to the Eucharistic procession of Holy Thursday strongly suggest that the repository was playing an ever-increasing role in the devotions of the clergy and faithful. Indeed, there is evidence that such developments were actually taking place. Thus in the *Consuetudines* of Giovanni Orsini, Archbishop of Naples (Italy), dating from 1337, we are told that on Holy Thursday in the Basilica of Santa Restituta the Blessed Sacrament was brought in procession to this saint's altar for reposition there;[99] it is significant that such a prominent altar (that of the church's patron saint) should be selected for this purpose. From a text in the capitular Archives of Vich, Spain, we learn that in 1463 the practice was introduced of assigning twelve priests, dressed as the Apostles, to keep continuous watch at the repository while chanting Psalms.[100] This custom brings to mind our Lord's admonition to the Apostles to watch with Him while He prayed in Gethsemane. The rubrics of the *Missale Mixtum* of Toledo, Spain, published in 1500, do not describe the place of repose, but significantly the Missal states:

> And when the tomb [Repository] is reached, let the bishop or priest ascend vested in superhumerals. . . .[101]

Evidently the celebrant had to ascend steps, suggesting that the Eucharist was to be reserved not in an inconspicuous place but on an altar or special structure erected for the purpose. We know that later in the sixteenth century a massive repository was constructed for the Cathedral of Seville, Spain (see below).

By the early seventeenth century we find the place of repose described in the way we now know it:

> Today let a suitable place be prepared in some chapel of the church, or on an altar, and let it be adorned as fairly as possible with veils and lights that the chalice with the reserved host . . . may be reposed there.
> [*Roman Missal*, 1604][102]

In addition to this description in the *Roman Missal*, the 1853 edition of the *Memoriale Rituum* (a supplemental guide to ceremonies for parish priests first issued in 1725) states that the repository — a place apart (*distinctus*) from the main altar — may be adorned with flowers as well as lights (*luminibus ac floribus ornatus*) and with veils made of precious materials (*velis pretiosis*);[103] the 1886 edition of the *Caeremoniale*

Episcoporum (a volume governing ceremonies in cathedrals and collegiate churches) stipulates the use of "many lights" (*multis luminibus*).[104] Since the seventeenth century the Congregation of Sacred Rites has provided further specifications, many of which were aimed, not at forbidding the faithful from meditating upon the passion during the Eucharistic vigil, but rather at keeping the *burial* connotations of the Holy Thursday reservation (to be explained in due course) on a purely symbolic level. Thus in 1662 it prohibited the use of darkly colored or black decorations inside or immediately outside the repository (#1223).[105] In 1705 it prohibited exposition in a monstrance of the Host reserved in the repository (#2148 ad 6).[106] In 1835 it forbade the hanging from a cross of draperies representing winding cloths down over the *capsa* (that is, the repository tabernacle) (#2734 ad 1).[107] As early as 1631, the Congregation had ruled that the *capsa* was to be securely locked and the key kept by the priest who was to celebrate the Good Friday liturgy (#579),[108] but in 1844 it prohibited the affixing of a seal to the door of the vessel as if it were a tomb (#2873 ad 1).[109] In 1868 it prohibited the placing of the *capsa* on the floor of the repository in a cave-like representation of Gethsemane, as well as the use of statues as decorations in the repository (#3178),[110] but in 1896 the congregation ruled that in places where there exists an ancient custom of placing images of the passion around the repository, such as statues of Our Lady of Sorrows, Saint Mary Magdalene, Saint John, and the Roman Guards (this was particularly the case in Spain[111]), the local bishop may permit the continuance of this practice, so long as it is not introduced anywhere else (#3939 ad 2).[112] Chalices, pyxes, and *ostensoria* are not to be used as ornaments for the altar of repose (#4077 ad 10),[113] nor is the *capsa* to have a transparent door (#3660 ad 1).[114] We must stress that these regulations were by no means intended to dampen the tremendous devotion that for centuries the laity have manifested on Holy Thursday, "the day when God wants to repose among the flowers and the scents of spring," as Eugenie de Guerin described it.[115] They should be seen rather as an expression of the zealous care with which the Church protects her Divine Bridegroom's gift of Himself in this sacrament. Within the limits circumscribed above, there has still been considerable latitude for variety in the adornment of the repository, as we shall see.

Writing in 1909, Dom Bede Camm, OSB, provides us with a description of the chapel of repose at Rome's Basilica of the Holy Apostles, where the relics of Saint James the Less and Saint Philip are entombed:

> On the altar itself there are no flowers, for it is entirely covered with gilded candlesticks; but all around, filling the whole chapel except the approach to the altar, are magnificent palms, great tree-ferns, azaleas, and other flowering shrubs in pots. Among the foliage and the flowers gleam countless colored lamps. The effect of the whole is positively indescribable. . . .[116]

In Belgium (nineteenth century) it was customary to suspend a precious diadem of gold or silver over the place where the Sacrament was reserved on Holy Thursday.[117] In the Latin countries of Europe and South America the place of repose has been referred to for centuries as the *monumento* (tomb). A scaffold would be erected supporting a series of steps to form a multitiered "sacred hill," nearly reaching the ceiling. The Blessed Sacrament is placed atop this large structure and surrounded with innumerable candles, palms, orchids, and lilies, as well as other decorations.[118]

In nineteenth-century Havana (Cuba) the repository was set up in the south transept of the cathedral; from Palm Sunday until Holy Thursday, this part of the church was concealed behind a huge white curtain, which was removed for the Mass of the Lord's Supper:

> . . . the great white curtain had been removed from before the southern transept, and there was now to be seen a magnificent golden sepulchre, under a white and gilded dome supported by columns. The statue of a kneeling angel adorned each side of this monument, to which the officiating priest ascended by six carpeted steps. Innumerable wax tapers in silver candlesticks were arranged on each side, their soft light reflected by the silver and gold drapery that lined the vault.[119]

Two of the *Roman Ordines* of the later Middle Ages, *Ordo 14* (fourteenth century) and *Ordo 15* (early fifteenth century), refer to the special tabernacle used for the place of repose as the *armariolum* (little chest), a term believed to be of Gallican origin.[120] Subsequently this name was superseded by the terms *capsula* (small box) in the *Roman Missal* of 1570[121] and *sepulchrum* (sepulchre) or *urnula* (small urn) in other documents, including a turn-of-the-century decree of the Congregation of Sacred Rites (#4049, Dec 9, 1899).[122] The *Memoriale Rituum* (1853 edition) specifies that the *capsula* be of an elegant design (*capsula elegans*).[123] In the current *Roman Missal* of Pope Paul VI (1970), the vessel for reservation is identified simply as a *tabernaculum* (tabernacle) or *capsa repositionis* (literally, box of reposition).[124]

> *The Majesty of our God has withdrawn to that mysterious sanctuary, into which we enter not but with silence and compunction.*
> [Abbot Guéranger][125]

In the Cathedral of Palma on Mallorca (1942), the Eucharistic procession following the Mass of the Lord's Supper would head to a side altar which had been prepared as the place of repose. Sixteen canons, thirty priests, several hundred seminarians, and a number of acolytes, as well as the governor general and his officials would participate. The chief celebrant carrying the Eucharist goes up the steps in front of the repository and places the sacrament inside a beautiful casket that serves as the *capsa repositionis*, ornamented with intricate carvings and jewels. He then locks the first of three different hasps on the casket. A deacon and a subdeacon lock the second and third hasps respectively. The gold key used to lock these hasps is then put into a little case hanging from the neck of the celebrant.[126]

Undoubtedly the most extraordinary repository of all is that of the Cathedral of Seville, Spain, a monument of epic proportions first built in the sixteenth century. Several accounts from the late nineteenth and early twentieth centuries provide us with the details. Following the Mass of the Lord's Supper, the Blessed Sacrament would be borne in procession from the high altar, accompanied by cardinals, bishops, and priests, as well as by members of the Spanish royal family, all carrying lighted candles. The holy Eucharist is brought to the *monumento*, an immense white and gold three-story wooden structure temporarily erected in time for Holy Week in the center of the cathedral (over the tomb of Ferdinand Columbus, son of the renowned explorer of the New World), where it remains hidden behind a white veil until the reading of the gospel at the Mass of the Lord's Supper. Designed by Antonio Florentin and first constructed in the years 1543-1554, this four-sided edifice is truly a work of architecture, with the Doric style used for the first story, Ionic on the second, and Corinthian on the third. Each story is supported by sixteen columns, four per side; the sides are decorated with images of the patriarchs. The figures on the top story are huge, with a great cross so tall that it reaches the ceiling of the cathedral, giving the structure a total height of over one hundred feet. Located on the first story is a *custodia*, a large solid silver vessel ten feet high and shaped just like the *monumento* structure it is mounted on, with three stories and four sides. In a joint venture the silversmith Juan de Ribera and the famed humanist Francisco Pacheco spent seven years designing this sacrament house, so copiously adorned with images and theological symbols. The Blessed Sacrament is placed in a diamond-studded solid gold *capsa* weighing twenty-five pounds, located in the middle section of the larger silver *custodia*; round about it 336 oil lamps are hung. All three stories of the *monumento* are filled with thousands of burning wax candles, thus transforming the structure into "one blaze of light, gold, and silver." From the very moment the Blessed Sacrament is enthroned here, all vehicles are forbidden to travel through the streets of Seville. Soldiers are instructed to carry their arms reversed, as they do at a funeral, nor are they to salute anyone with their arms, even the king. Flags are lowered to half-mast, and clappers used in place of the bells now silenced.[127]

> . . . *he went forth with his disciples across the Kidron valley, where there was a garden, which he and his disciples entered.*
>
> [Jn 18:1]

Over the years the Holy Thursday repository has been known by such names as the "Throne," the "Paradise" (in France) and the "Garden" (in Flanders).[128] As we have already seen, this place has also been referred to as the "sepulchre," reflecting the fact that following the Last Supper our Lord entered upon His passion in Gethsemane. Remember that by Jewish reckoning a new day began at sunset on what we would term the previous day, and thus it was already Good Friday as our Savior prayed in the Garden; that same "day," then, He was to die and be laid in the tomb. The symbolic association of the reservation of the Blessed Sacrament with the burial of Christ appears to have ancient roots. In the earlier centuries of the Church's history, vessels intended for the reservation of the Eucharist were often fashioned in the shape of a tower (*turris*),[129] a design resembling the original structure built by the Emperor Constantine over the holy sepulchre itself in Jerusalem.[130] This same emperor donated just such a vessel for the Eucharist — "a tower of the purest gold" — to the Church during the reign of Pope Saint Sylvester (A.D. 314-335), as attested by the *Liber Pontificalis*.[131] But it is not until the seventh century that the sepulchral symbolism of this design is stated explicitly in a document from France, the *Explanation of the Gallican Mass*: "The body of the Lord is carried in towers because the tomb of the Lord was cut out of the rock in the shape of a tower."[132] The association of Eucharistic vessels with the tomb of our Lord is expressed in other sources as well. Both the eighth-century *Missale Francorum* and the eleventh-century *Leofric Missal* refer to the Eucharistic vessel as "a new sepulchre of the body of Christ."[133] And it is during the eleventh century that we see this symbolism applied specifically to the practices on Holy Thursday: a sacramentary from the Albi region of France states that the "Body of the Savior" is reserved on Holy Thursday "in memory of His burial."[134] During the centuries that followed, this concept manifested itself in a number of ways. Thus in Rome in the fifteenth century the rubrics of *Roman Ordo 15* for Holy Thursday stipulated that the Host was to be carried to the place of repose not in a pyx but in a chalice, a vessel that during the Middle Ages was particularly seen to represent the tomb of Christ;[135] this manner of carrying the Sacrament on Holy Thursday was retained in the Roman Rite until the revision of the Holy Week liturgy in 1955. In the *Missale Mixtum* of Spain's Mozarabic Rite (1500) the repository is referred to as the *monumentum*, that is, the tomb;[136] likewise in Milan's *Ambrosian Missal* of 1594, it is identified as the *scurolo* (sepulchre).[137] In 1896 the Congregation of Sacred Rites reiterated this symbolic tradition, affirming that the Holy Thursday reservation commemorated both the institution of the holy Eucharist and the entombment of Christ.[138] As recently as 1981 the burial connotations of the place of repose were mentioned in *L'Attivita Della Santa Sede*, a Vatican publication that chronicles the actions of the Holy Father for each given year. In the 1981 edition there is a description of the Holy Thursday Mass of the Lord's Supper at the Roman Basilica of Saint John Lateran, celebrated by Pope John Paul II, that includes the following passage:

> . . . the Pope carries the remaining consecrated Hosts into one of the side chapels of the Basilica, named the "Reposition," adorned with plants and with flowers, in which the most holy Sacrament remains exhibited to the adoration of the faithful for the rest of the evening and there it will remain until the celebration on Good Friday of the Passion of the Lord. The Pope lingers in prayer, having knelt before a special tabernacle that is popularly called "the Sepulchre," in memory of the deposition of Christ in the tomb after His death. . . . [author's translation].[139]

However, the association with burial has since been discontinued, at least in any explicit sense, and the Church now discourages

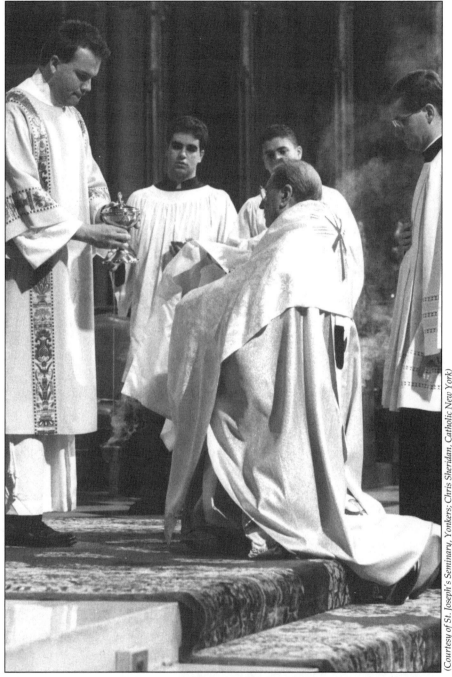

***John Cardinal O'Connor, St. Patrick's Cathedral, Archdiocese of New York:
Eucharistic procession, Mass of the Lord's Supper.*** *"At the same time, it should be
obvious that the motif of the passion cannot be dissociated from this solemn adoration
of the Blessed Sacrament. . . ."*

the use of the term "sepulchre" for the place of repose, as stated in the Congregation for Divine Worship's 1988 *Circular Letter* on the liturgy of Holy Week: "The place where the tabernacle or pyx is situated must not be made to resemble a tomb, and the expression 'tomb' is to be avoided. . . ."[140] The burial concept was somewhat anachronistic, in that our Lord this night is not yet in the tomb; indeed, there are devotions for Good Friday and Holy Saturday that more appropriately commemorate the entombment, as we shall see. At the same time, it should be obvious that the motif of the passion cannot be disassociated from this solemn adoration of the Blessed Sacrament, for it takes place within the ambit of the Easter Triduum; as the famous Jesuit liturgist Father Josef Jungmann (1889-1975) has pointed out, "meditation on Christ's Passion is not, indeed, alien to the Holy Thursday liturgy."[141] Significantly, the 1988 *Circular Letter* stipulates that a "sobriety appropriate to the liturgy of these days" should govern the decoration of the repository; in addition, exposition of the Blessed Sacrament in a monstrance is strictly forbidden on this night.[142] Clearly, these directives point to an atmosphere quite distinct from the jubilant celebration of the Feast of Corpus Christi. On this night, we celebrate the institution of the holy Eucharist, but we cannot forget the circumstances under which it was instituted; the cross looms so near. The Hosts we adore this night will be given to us in holy Communion on the morrow, at the very hour that our Lord was laid in the tomb. Thus in the chapel of repose we find ourselves, as it were, upon the threshold of Good Friday; the themes of love, suffering, and the "kingship of Christ crucified," present throughout Holy Week, are so strikingly intertwined in this chapel of mysterious beauty, where for centuries so many have come to be with our Lord in His passion.

Then Jesus went with them to a place called Gethsemane, and he said to his disciples, "Sit here, while I go yonder and pray."

[Mt 26:36]

The Eucharistic Procession Today

Let us now follow the reservation ceremony in its current form. The celebrant of the Mass just ended goes to the main altar, on the middle of which is a large ciborium containing the consecrated Hosts for tomorrow's Communion. After putting incense into a *thurible*, he kneels before the altar and censes the sacrament three times. Upon rising he takes the ciborium into his hands, wrapping it with the ends of a humeral veil draped across his shoulders. A procession forms, led by an acolyte carrying the processional crucifix; the clergy who have concelebrated the Mass follow. At the end of this cortege is the principal celebrant carrying the holy Eucharist; immediately before him is an acolyte gently swaying a burning *thurible*, flanked by two other servers bearing lit candles.

> *And walk in love, as Christ loved us and gave himself up for us, a fragrant offering and sacrifice to God.*
>
> [Eph 5:2]

As the procession wends its way from the main altar of the church, the thirteenth-century Eucharistic hymn *Pange, lingua* is sung. Does not this procession remind us of the departure of our Lord from the Cenacle with His Apostles, and their journey to the Garden of Gethsemane?

> *And when they had sung a hymn, they went out to the Mount of Olives.*
>
> [Mt 26:30]

> *I shall praise the Savior's glory,*
> *Of his flesh the mystery sing,*
> *And the blood, all price excelling,*
> *Shed by our immortal King:*
> *God made man for our salvation,*
> *Who from Virgin pure did spring.*
>
> *On the night before he suffered,*
> *Seated with his chosen band,*
> *Jesus, when they all had feasted,*
> *Faithful to the law's command,*
> *Far more precious food provided:*
> *Gave himself with his own hand.*
>
> [*Pange, lingua,* vs. 1, 3][143]

> *Then the Lord will go forth and fight. . . . On that day his feet shall stand on the Mount of Olives which lies before Jerusalem on the east. . . .*
>
> [Zech 14:3-4]

As verse after verse of Saint Thomas Aquinas' famous hymn is

The capsa. "*Jesus, when they all had feasted, faithful to the law's command, far more precious food provided: Gave himself with his own hand*" *(Pange, lingua).*

sung, the procession continues at a somber pace to the place set apart, the chapel of repose. Upon entering the darkened chapel, we immediately notice a small altar covered with a white frontal and surrounded by lilies as well as other white and red flowers. It is flanked by four large candelabra, each mounted with seven unlit candles. Such multi-branched candle stands are a common sight on Holy Thursday night, serving to remind us of the furnishings surrounding the Ark of the Covenant:

> *And you shall make a lampstand . . . and there shall be six branches going out of its sides, three branches of the lampstand out of one side of it and three branches of the lampstand out of the other side of it. . . . And you shall make the seven lamps for it. . . .*
>
> [Ex 25:31-32, 37]

On the altar itself, between two more small candelabra, is a majestic, urn-shaped gold vessel; this is the *capsa*. On the molded door of this tabernacle is depicted the cross with a winding sheet across its arms; affixed to each side of the *capsa* are two molded angels keeping watch. Those in the procession move aside as the celebrant arrives with the Blessed Sacrament in his hands. While the acolytes light the thirty-four candles around the altar, the celebrant comes forward and enthrones our Savior: Pushing aside a little curtain inside the door of the *capsa,* the celebrant places the large ciborium inside. Before closing the vessel, he kneels and censes it, as the last two verses of *Pange, lingua* — the portion known as the *Tantum ergo* — are sung; afterwards he spends a few moments in quiet prayer. Then he and the other clergy return to the sacristy. The chapel is now silent, cast in the soft light of numerous candles. The vigil of Gethsemane has begun.

Holy Thursday in the Byzantine Rite

As we have already seen from the pilgrimage diary of Egeria, the institution of the holy Eucharist on this day was commemorated with a special evening Mass (the second Mass of the day) in Jerusalem as early as the fourth century. By the first half of the fifth century a third Holy Thursday service had been added to the day's liturgical horarium in the Holy City — a rite conducted at the actual site of the Last Supper itself on Mount Sion. This service, mentioned for the first time in the *Armenian Lectionary*, included readings from the First Letter to the Corinthians (11:23-32) and the gospel of Saint Mark (14:1-26); both readings concern the institution of the Eucharist, and thus it seems at least possible that the liturgy at Sion was actually a third Mass.[144] In a later Jerusalem book, the *Georgian Lectionary* (fifth to eighth centuries), we find only one Mass for Holy Thursday,[145] but in the tenth century *Typicon of the Anastasis,* two Masses are specified — one near Golgotha in the Church of the Holy Sepulchre, the other, celebrated in the evening by the Patriarch of Jerusalem, in the church on Mount Sion; the readings for the latter (1 Cor 11:23-32 and Mk 14:12-26) are nearly identical to those assigned to the service at Sion in the *Armenian Lectionary.*[146] In medieval Constantinople, the capital of the Byzantine Empire, an evening Mass was likewise celebrated on this day in the Basilica of Santa Sophia, as indicated in the *Typicon of the Great Church* (ninth to tenth centuries); the epistle was the same as that in the Mass at Sion (1 Cor 11:23-32), but the gospel consisted of a "harmony" of passages describing the Last Supper from three of the four Evangelists — Mt 26:2-20, Jn 13:3-17, Mt 26:21-39, Lk 22:43-44, and Mt 26:40-27:2.[147] The evening Mass for Holy Thursday in the current liturgy of the Byzantine Rite has retained this very same gospel harmony.[148]

In the East, the consecration of chrism has been conducted on

Holy Thursday for over twelve hundred years. The *Codex Barberini* (*Barberini gr. 336*, Vatican Library), an eighth-century *Euchologion* (an Eastern liturgical book containing directions and prayer texts for various ceremonies) largely reflecting the usages of the patriarchate of Constantinople (although some believe it to be of Palestinian origin),[149] provides rubrics for this ceremony, as conducted during the Mass on Holy Thursday. The chrism was brought to the altar during the offertory procession and placed on the *mensa* together with the unconsecrated bread and wine for the Eucharistic liturgy. The chrism would subsequently be consecrated at the end of the Eucharistic Prayer.[150] The *Typicon of the Great Church* (ninth to tenth centuries) likewise testifies to the consecration of the chrism on Holy Thursday at Constantinople's Basilica of Santa Sophia.[151] In Jerusalem the rite appears for the first time in the tenth century *Typicon of the Anastasis*; it was performed within the context of a special non-Eucharistic liturgy separate from the two Masses celebrated on the same day. This service had its own series of readings: Ex 30:22-38, 1 Sm 16:1-13, Is 61:1-6, Sg 1:1-4, Rom 11:13-36, and Mt 26:6-16.[152] In the current liturgy of the Byzantine Rite the consecration of the chrism is still performed by patriarchs during Mass on Holy Thursday, following the same overall format as that given in the *Codex Barberini*.[153]

The washing of the altars on this day can be found in the East as early as the ninth to tenth centuries in Constantinople's *Typicon of the Great Church*.[154] The present-day ceremony of the Byzantine Rite takes place before Mass, as did that of tenth-century Constantinople; the altar is first stripped by the patriarch with other clerics assisting, as three Psalms (51, 26, and 84) are recited. They wash the *mensa* with warm water, wiping the surface with linen napkins. The patriarch now sprinkles rose water on the surface of the holy table, after which it is dried with sponges and then covered anew in altar cloths. Finally he censes the altar; the sponges are afterwards distributed to the people as a memento of the ceremony.[155]

The *Mandatum*, the washing of the feet, has existed in the Holy Thursday liturgy of the East for at least twelve hundred years; although such a ceremony is mentioned neither by the pilgrim Egeria nor by the *Armenian Lectionary*,[156] it does evidently appear in at least one manuscript of a subsequent Jerusalem book, the *Georgian Lectionary* (fifth to eighth centuries).[157] It is also found at an early date in another Eastern source, the eighth-century *Codex Barberini*; the latter provides very brief rubrics and three prayers for the rite, including one for blessing the water for the footwashing.[158] The *Mandatum* as practiced in Constantinople is described in more detail in the *Typicon of the Great Church* (ninth to tenth centuries). On Holy Thursday, following the first part of Vespers (Evening Prayer of the Divine Office), but before the evening Eucharistic liturgy, the city's patriarch would wash the feet of twelve clerics: three subdeacons, three deacons, three priests, an archbishop, and two metropolitans. During the washing there was a lection — the gospel account of our Lord performing this action at the Last Supper (Jn 13:3-11). When the patriarch was finished, the concluding portion of the relevant gospel was read (Jn 13:12-17: ". . . Do you know what I have done to you? . . .").[159] A similar format was followed in tenth-century Jerusalem, according to another document of this period, the *Typicon of the Anastasis*. The ceremony was performed on Holy Thursday evening, following Mass, in the upper room, the very place on Mount Sion traditionally believed to have been the actual site of the Last Supper. With a linen cloth tied about his waist the patriarch would wash the feet of three deacons, three subdeacons, three priests, two bishops, and one metropolitan, the latter assuming the role of the Apostle Saint Peter.[160]

The *Mandatum* was similarly introduced into other Eastern Rites, including that of Egypt, appearing in two fourteenth-century documents of the Coptic Church, Abu'l Barakat's *The Lamp of the Darkness*[161] and the *Greek-Arabic Pericope Book* (*codex Scaligeri 243*, University of Leiden); in the latter, two readings are provided for the ceremony — 1 Tm 4:9-5:10 and Jn 13:1-30.[162]

The Byzantine Rite has retained the *Mandatum* up to the present day (it is also observed in the Maronite, Coptic, and Ethiopian Rites). The elements of religious drama evident in the tenth-century ceremony of Jerusalem appear in a more developed form in the service as it now exists, performed by bishops and in Byzantine monasteries; in the evening at the end of Mass the celebrant reenacts the actions of our Lord literally step by step as each verse of Saint John's gospel account of the *Mandatum* is read. Thus at the words, "laid aside his garments," the celebrant removes his *mandhyas* (a black cloak); likewise at the words "poured water into a basin," he pours the water for the footwashing. Among the twelve brethren chosen for the *Mandatum* are two in the roles of Judas and Saint Peter respectively. When the celebrant approaches the latter the dialogue between our Lord and Saint Peter is reenacted ("Lord, do you wash my feet? . . .").[163] This dialogue is also recreated in the *Mandatum* ceremony of the Maronite Rite.[164]

The Eucharistic Watch

But David went up the ascent of the Mount of Olives, weeping as he went, barefoot and with his head covered; and all the people who were with him covered their heads, and they went up, weeping as they went.

[2 Sm 15:30]

And taking with him Peter and the two sons of Zebedee, he began to be sorrowful and troubled. Then he said to them, "My soul is very sorrowful, even to death; remain here, and watch with me."

[Mt 26:37-38]

As we have seen already, the reservation of the holy Eucharist on the night of Holy Thursday was originally instituted exclusively for the purpose of providing for Communion on Good Friday. But with time there came the realization on the part of the faithful that in the chapel of reposition they could keep watch with our Lord in a most intimate manner on this first night of the Easter Triduum. This venerable tradition has continued to the present day. In its latest document on Holy Week, the Congregation for Divine Worship has reiterated the Church's desire that her children participate in tonight's Eucharistic vigil:

The faithful should be encouraged after the Mass of the Lord's Supper to spend a suitable period of time during the night in the church in adoration before the Blessed Sacrament that has been solemnly reserved. Where appropriate, this prolonged eucharistic adoration may be accompanied by the reading of some part of the gospel of Saint John (ch. 13-17).

[Congregation for Divine Worship][165]

It was a night of watching by the Lord, to bring them out of the land of Egypt; so this same night is a night of watching kept to the Lord by all the people of Israel throughout their generations.

[Ex 12:42]

How very much the saints loved this night! Saint Margaret Mary Alacoque (1647-1690) spent the whole night "from seven in the evening until the next morning" kneeling motionless before the altar of repose;

when asked what she thought about during these hours she answered, "I am then so occupied with the Lord's Passion that I do not know that I have a body."[166] We know that Saint Thérèse of Lisieux (1873-1897) likewise desired to remain this entire night before the Blessed Sacrament; only her poor health at the time prevented her from doing so.[167] Of Saint Paul of the Cross (1694-1775), the founder of the Passionists, whose devotion to the solemn rites of Holy Week knew no bounds, it is recorded that on one occasion, after he had celebrated the Mass of the Lord's Supper and the Eucharist had been placed in the "urn of the Holy Sepulchre" (that is, the *capsa*), he tenderly kissed the key to the urn and said: "This is the key that contains my Treasure, my Love, my God!"[168] The devotion of Saint John Vianney, the "Curé of Ars" (1786-1859), to this holy vigil is particularly noteworthy:

> *On Maundy Thursday, in order to commemorate the institution of the holy Eucharist, M. Vianney insisted on providing a splendid altar of repose, and his heart rejoiced at [the] sight of the decorations which enhanced the majesty of the tabernacle. The whole of the chancel, which had been considerably enlarged in 1845, was draped with banners. Numerous and tastefully arranged lights transfigured the scene. However, he took every precaution lest these decorations should be a hindrance instead of a help to the interior recollection of the people. The day was spent in adoration by the whole parish. In the evening he held the exercise of "the Holy Hour." The whole night from Maundy Thursday to Good Friday was spent by him on his knees, for he refused to sit down for a single moment.[169]*

Prior to the issuance of the revised order of Holy Week in 1955, which moved the Mass of the Lord's Supper to the evening hours, Mass was held in the morning, and therefore the period for adoration at the altar of repose following this Mass lasted all day long and continued through the night. It was common for the faithful to arrange to keep constant watch at the repository in relays, so that our Lord was never left alone. Thus in an account of Holy Week in the year 1933 at the Benedictine Abbey of Steenbrugge, Belgium, we read that the laity came in successive one-hour shifts to maintain a Eucharistic watch from about a quarter past seven in the morning on Holy Thursday (when Mass ended) until two o'clock on the afternoon of Good Friday, when the Good Friday Liturgy of the Passion took place. Four hundred young men volunteered to participate in shifts through the night, from eight o'clock in the evening until morning on Good Friday, while over eight hundred women offered to keep watch during the daylight hours.[170] The idea of a constant watch at the repository is specifically recommended in the 1853 edition of the *Memoriale Rituum*, and repeated in the 1920 edition:

> *Care will be taken that, in so far as possible, there will be always some persons adoring the Blessed Sacrament in the chapel of the Sepulchre, and that a proper number of candles are lighted there.*[171]

Bishop Francis Xavier Ford, MM, the famous American missionary who died a martyr's death in a Chinese Communist prison in 1952, has left us a record of the great devotion of the Catholics of China for the services of Holy Week. In one of his essays, entitled "Holy Week in the Orient," published in 1933, he tells how, even in the interior of this vast country where priests are scarce and the chapels are by necessity of simple design, the liturgy of the universal Church is nevertheless observed as faithfully as possible under the circumstances. To attend in these places many of the people must make an arduous journey of four to five days on foot. Despite the difficulties, "Holy Week is the best observed of the Church's feasts in China." Regarding the reposition of the holy Eucharist he says:

> *The Christians are especially fervent on Holy Thursday. In all the churches where the Blessed Sacrament is reserved there is nocturnal adoration, and as sometimes the Christians are very few it means three and four hours of adoration for each. They pass the entire night in vocal prayer, chanting the litanies and special prayers to our Lord, or reciting the Rosary aloud, or singing hymns in Chinese.*[172]

The above description was written years before the Communist takeover of the country gradually forced the Church in China underground. Yet we have good reason to believe that the fervor of the people has not been diminished, for in an account from 1950 we learn that despite the first waves of persecution and mass murder under Mao Tse-tung, the Catholics of the city of Suchow attended Holy Week services that year in "standing room only" numbers, thus defying a government order that forbade them to do so.[173]

In Latin countries there has been a long-standing custom of visiting not just one, but several repositories on Holy Thursday; most accounts speak of the faithful making a series of seven visits. Such was the case in nineteenth-century Madrid, Spain, where the king and queen would engage in a formal procession from church to church, visiting seven repositories. Embarking at four o'clock in the afternoon, the royal couple traveled on foot through the streets, accompanied by their entire court. Once the procession was under way it could not be terminated, even if it began to rain.[174]

On the Mediterranean island of Malta, where the churches use their finest silver ornaments to decorate the place of repose, entire families and pious associations say the Rosary as they travel from one church to another, making the round of seven repositories.[175]

In Naples, Italy, on Holy Thursday (early twentieth century) a large thoroughfare in the heart of the city called the *Via Roma* would be closed to all vehicles. During the day and well into the night vast numbers of pedestrians thronged the avenue, making the round of the seven churches to be visited with their beautiful chapels of repose, somberly adorned with small floor lamps as well as with white-stemmed flowers and plants grown without sunlight. This annual event came to be known as *Lo Struscio*, a name resulting from the sound of the rustling silk garments of the crowds.[176]

In the Cenacle: Points for Meditation

I have loved you with an everlasting love. . . .

[Jer 31:3]

The Eucharistic vigil affords us an opportunity not only to be with Christ in Gethsemane, but also to reflect upon His intimate words at the Last Supper. No doubt the Apostles must still have been pondering this extraordinary discourse as they lay in the garden, awaiting our Lord as He prayed. He intended these words for us as well; thus the reader will want to take the time to meditate upon all or at least part of Saint John's narrative of the Last Supper discourse, as contained in chapters 13-17 of his gospel. So beautiful are these pages of our Savior's words that just a verse or two can more than suffice for an hour of reflection. It is here that He assures us that He is going to prepare a place for us in His Father's House (Jn 14:2), and that just as a mother forgets the pain of childbirth when her child is born, so shall our sorrow be turned into joy (Jn 16:20-22). Here He reveals Himself as our Way, our

Truth, and our Life (Jn 14:6), and as the Vine, with His Father as the vine-dresser and with us as the branches, reminding us that apart from Him we can do nothing (Jn 15:1-5). And here He tells us that as the Father has loved Him, so has He, the Christ, loved us (Jn 15:9), inviting us to abide in Him (Jn 15:4). Here He sets the ultimate criterion for our love of others: that we should love one another as He has loved us (Jn 13:34). Warning us of persecutions to come, He points out that if the world hates us, we should remember that the world has hated Him before us (Jn 15:18), yet we should not fear, for He has overcome the world (Jn 16:33).

> *On that Passover night Jesus leads his disciples into the mystery of the new covenant. His words already announce Good Friday. Tomorrow his words about blood shed for the world's sinners will become a redeeming reality. . . .*
>
> *Listen to him! Let us listen to what he says.*
>
> *Echoing the words pronounced by Jesus in the upper room, St. Paul states: "For as often as you eat this bread and drink the cup, you proclaim the death of the Lord until he comes" (1 Cor 11:26).*
>
> *Christ's words, through the events of Good Friday, affect the future of humanity until the end of the world.*
>
> *What will take place tomorrow and will soon begin at the foot of the Mount of Olives, all that the Passover of the new covenant means, accompanies humanity, journeys with it until the end of its earthly destiny, when Christ will come again to bring the history of salvation to completion.*
>
> *What will happen tomorrow, Good Friday?*
>
> *What does the cup of the new covenant in the blood of Christ mean?*
>
> *It means death on the cross. It means his heart pierced by the lance.*
>
> *It means the hour of Christ's passing from this world to the Father; it means the love with which he loved his own in the world: "He loved them to the end" (Jn 13:1).*
>
> *The cup of the new covenant then means life, "for stern as death is love" (Song 8:6). . . .*
>
> *In the Upper Room on Passover evening the Apostles were with Christ. Like them, we too gather around the Eucharistic table and commemorate everything the Lord said and did.*
>
> *He who loves us, who "has freed us from our sins by his blood"*

(Rev 1:5), is with us. Let us relive the Passover of the new and eternal covenant in his blood.

"For stern as death is love."
He, the One, he who dies no more.
God is love!

[Pope John Paul II][177]

The Agony in the Garden

Sunk in a sea of overwhelming sadness,
With heavy load His head bowed down to the earth,
Drenched with the bloody sweat of anguish —
He fights His fiercest fight on Olivet.

[Oberammergau Passion Play, 1930][178]

As we continue our vigil before the altar of repose, evening deepens into night and our thoughts return to Gethsemane. The stillness of the chapel merges with the quiet of the garden on that paschal night nearly two thousand years ago. In a very real sense we are there with Him. Through the centuries many a pilgrim has journeyed to Jerusalem to get some sense of what that first Holy Thursday was like:

In the evening at 8:30 we went down to the Garden of Gethsemane. . . .
We remained until towards midnight in silent prayer and meditation in the garden.
It was a beautiful night. The full moon rose over the summit of the Mount of Olives and flooded the garden with light. Nothing in Jerusalem has impressed me as did these hours in the stillness of this garden. There kneeling on the ground under these gigantic old olive trees, the realization grew wondrous strong of that mysterious event when Jesus fell prostrate on that ground, and prayed the wondrous prayer so intensely human, and so intensely divine.[179]

There are eight ancient olive trees still standing in the Garden of Gethsemane in our own day. No one has yet been able to determine just how long they have been there, but they are at least a thousand years old. They may well have witnessed the Holy Thursday vigil of the fourth-century Christians of Jerusalem described by the pilgrim

Egeria; they could be the descendants of the trees that threw their shadows across the face of the Savior on that first Holy Thursday night.[180]

In rural areas of Austria (1954), where the church clocks are stopped on Holy Thursday, the passage of time on this quiet evening is marked by the sound of boys with wooden clappers announcing the hours. Every hour they sing a different stanza in memory of an episode from the passion. The traditional stanza for nine o'clock on Holy Thursday night is:

> We beg you, people, hear and hark!
> It's nine o'clock, and fully dark.
> O, think of the pain which Christ has felt,
> When, praying for us, in the garden He knelt.
> In agony fretting,
> Blood and water sweating,
> He suffers in darkness who is our Light:
> Remember it, folks, at nine o'clock night![181]

The Royal Hours

On this night the Eastern rites used to observe a special vigil known as the *Pannuchida* (all-night service); it acquired another name, the "Royal Hours," in Constantinople, where the Byzantine emperors attended the service many centuries ago.[182] As early as the fourth century a vigil was being observed during the night of Holy Thursday to Good Friday in the East. The pilgrim Egeria speaks of it as the practice in Jerusalem, and Epiphanius in his *Exposition of the Faith* (ca. A.D. 375) attests to its existence elsewhere at this time.[183] We know from Egeria that the Jerusalem vigil was clearly stational in nature, with numerous Psalms and gospel readings along a route from the Church of the Eleona on Mount Olivet to the site of Calvary.[184] The *Armenian Lectionary* (early fifth century) gives the specific readings for this vigil in the Holy City: the service featured a series of fifteen Psalms, followed by seven gospel lections during the course of the night, taken from all four Evangelists, beginning with the Last Supper Discourse (Jn 13:16-18:1) and ending with the trial before Pilate (Jn 18:28-19:16).[185] By the time of the *Georgian Lectionary* (fifth to eighth centuries) some changes had been made in the selection of lections for this service,[186] but it is in the tenth-century *Typicon of the Anastasis* that the Jerusalem vigil appears in its most highly developed form, with a route closely matching that taken by our Lord Himself during the last hours before His crucifixion. Beginning on Mount Sion (site of the Last Supper), the participants headed out "across the Kidron valley" (Jn 18:1) to Mount Olivet and the Garden of Gethsemane, thereafter returning to the city, where they stopped at a location associated with the "Repentence of Peter" not far from the House of Caiaphas the High Priest, then proceeded to Pilate's Praetorium, and thence to Golgotha. There was a total of eleven gospel lections, the first of which was the Last Supper Discourse (Jn 13:31-18:1), read quite appropriately in its original historical setting on Mount Sion; the gospel passages concluded with the Burial of Christ (Jn 19: 38-42), which was followed by a unique ceremony not even alluded to in the other liturgical books of Jerusalem. The patriarch would enter the Relic Chapel immediately behind Calvary and reemerge with a relic of the true cross tied to his shoulders; an archdeacon "pulled" the patriarch forward as they proceeded to the "Holy Prison," presumably the site where it was believed our Lord had been held during the night before His crucifixion. There was a special reading from the Old Testament assigned to this unusual rite (Zech 11:10-13), a passage that presages Judas casting the thirty silver pieces into the temple upon realizing what He had done in betraying His Master (Mt 27:3-5).[187]

The Pannuchida of Holy Thursday to Good Friday likewise appears in the *Typicon of the Great Church*, one of the earliest liturgical books of Constantinople (ninth to tenth centuries). There is nothing in this document to suggest that the service in Byzantium's capital took on anything approaching the stational format of Jerusalem, but it did feature twelve gospel readings, almost all of which correspond to the lections given in the *Typicon of the Anastasis*.[188]

The ceremony as it exists today in the Byzantine Rite is no longer held during the night; instead, it is conducted on the morning of Good Friday.[189] A cross is placed in the middle of the choir section of the church and encircled with candles; a lectern is set before it. Around the cross the clergy take their places; after the gospel book is solemnly borne to the lectern, readers take turns chanting or reciting a series of Scripture passages concerning the passion, arranged in twelve "chapters":

1: Jn 13:31-18:1	7: Mt 27:33-54
2: Jn 18:1-28	8: Lk 23:32-49
3: Mt 26:57-75	9: Jn 19:25-37
4: Jn 18:28-19:16	10: Mk 15:43-47
5: Mt 27:3-32	11: Jn 19:38-42
6: Mk 15:16-32	12: Mt 27:62-66

These readings serve as a gospel "harmony," for they are selected and arranged to provide a complete account of the passion drawn from all four Evangelists; they are identical to the lections specified for the "Royal Hours" in the medieval *Typicon of the Great Church*. The faithful are provided with candles that are lit for each "chapter" reading, then extinguished, as chants follow. In Zsarist Russia (pre-1917) the people took home their candles from this night service and employed them to kindle the lamps that were kept continuously burning before family religious icons.[190]

Gethsemane: Points for Meditation

Be gracious to me, O Lord, for I am in distress;
my eye is wasted from grief,
my soul and my body also.

[Ps 31:9]

And going a little farther he fell on his face and prayed, "My Father,
if it be possible, let this cup pass from me; nevertheless, not as I will,
but as thou wilt."

[Mt 26:39]

As though to a festival you have
summoned terrors from every side. . . .

[Lam 2:22; JB]

There, then, in that most awful hour, knelt the Saviour of the world,
putting off the defenses of His divinity, dismissing His reluctant
Angels, who in myriads were ready at His call, and opening His arms,
baring His breast, sinless as He was, to the assault of His foe, — of a
foe whose breath was a pestilence, and whose embrace was an agony.
There He knelt, motionless and still, while the vile and horrible fiend

*clad His spirit in a robe steeped in all that is hateful and heinous in
human crime, which clung close round His heart, and filled His
conscience, and found its way into every sense and pore of His mind,
and spread over Him a moral leprosy, till He almost felt Himself to be
that which He never could be, and which His foe would fain have made
Him. . . . And adversaries such as these gather around Thee, Blessed
Lord, in millions now; they come in troops more numerous than the
locust or the palmer-worm, or the plagues of hail, and flies, and frogs,
which were sent against Pharaoh. Of the living and of the dead and of
the as yet unborn, of the lost and of the saved, of Thy people and of
strangers, of sinners and of saints, all sins are there. Thy dearest are
there, Thy saints and Thy chosen are upon Thee; Thy three Apostles,
Peter, James, and John; but not as comforters, but as accusers, like the
friends of Job, "sprinkling dust towards heaven," and heaping curses
on Thy head. All are there but one. . . . She will be near Thee on the
Cross, she is separated from Thee in the garden. She has been Thy
companion and Thy confidant through Thy life . . . but her virgin ear
may not take in, nor may her immaculate heart conceive, what now is
in vision before Thee. . . . It is the long history of a world, and God
alone can bear the load of it. Hopes blighted, vows broken, lights
quenched, warnings scorned, opportunities lost; the innocent betrayed,
the young hardened, the penitent relapsing, the just overcome, the aged
failing; the sophistry of misbelief, the wilfulness of passion, the ob-
duracy of pride, the tyranny of habit, the canker of remorse, the wasting
fever of care, the anguish of shame . . . nay, the haggard faces, the
convulsed lips, the flushed cheek, the dark brow of the willing slaves of
evil, they are all before Him now; they are upon Him and in Him. . . .
He cries to His Father as if He were the criminal, not the victim. . . .*

[John Cardinal Newman][191]

*My soul is shut out from peace;
I have forgotten happiness.*

[Lam 3:17; JB]

*And he came and found them sleeping, and he said to Peter, "Simon,
are you asleep? Could you not watch one hour?"*

[Mk 14:37]

. . . I found no one to console me.

[Ps 69:20c; JB]

"Watch and pray that you may not enter into temptation; the spirit indeed is willing, but the flesh is weak."

[Mt 26:41]

Again, for the second time, he went away and prayed, "My Father, if this cannot pass unless I drink it, thy will be done."

[Mt 26:42]

And there appeared to him an angel from heaven, strengthening him.

[Lk 22:43]

Prone in Gethsemane upon His face, —
His eyelids closed, — lay Christ of all our world, —
The winds with endless sorrows seemed enswirled;
A little fountain murmured of its pain
Reflecting the pale sickle of the moon; —
Then was the hour when the Angel brought
From God's high throne the Cup of bitter boon,
While on His hands tears trembling fell like rain.

Before the Christ a cross arose on high;
He saw His own young body hanging there
Mangled, distorted; knotted ropes half-tear
The sinews from their sockets; saw He nigh
The jagged nails' hot rage, the direful Crown
Upon His head, and every dripping thorn
Red-laden, as in fury of its scorn
The thunder battered all kind voices down.
He heard the pattering drops, as from the cross
A piteous sobbing whispered and grew still.
Then Jesus sighed, and every pore did spill
A bloody sweat —

Blackness of night came on, and in a sea
Of ashes swam a lifeless sun and dim;
The agony He read upon the face turned grim
Unto the tossing struggle death must win.
There near the cross the three knelt silently;
He saw them gray as clouds of darkling mist;
He heard the stirring of their heavy breath.

The tremor cloaked within their doleful tryst.
Oh, where is love that knows the flame of His?
His mother, oh! — His piercing glance knew well;
The blood of man, checked in His veins a spell,
Was then in copious sweat poured faster forth.
["Gethsemane," Annette von Droste-Hulshoff (Excerpts)][192]

And being in an agony he prayed more earnestly; and his sweat
became like great drops of blood falling down upon the ground.
[Lk 22:44]

My face is red with tears,
and a veil of shadow hangs on my eyelids.
[Job 16:16; JB]

And again he came and found them sleeping, for their eyes were
heavy. So, leaving them again, he went away and prayed for the third
time, saying the same words.
[Mt 26:43-44]

A flash across the night and radiant stood
The cross resplendent with its signs of woe;
He saw a million hands outstretch and go
Clinging in anguish to the bloody wood,
Yes, hands and tiny fingers from afar,
And myriad souls unborn that thronging came. . . .
["Gethsemane," Annette von Droste-Hulshoff (Excerpt)][193]

The Arrest in Gethsemane

It is near midnight. Our time in the Eucharistic presence of our Lord grows short. There is a sense of sadness in our hearts as we watch the candles extinguished one by one, signaling the end of this sacred vigil. Only one candle will be left burning here through the night. But we must go:

From midnight onwards, however, the adoration should be made
without external solemnity, for the day of the Lord's passion has begun.
[Congregation for Divine Worship][194]

Our Lord is now hidden in darkness, just as the darkness enveloped Him on that first Holy Thursday so long ago. As we leave the chapel and go out into the night yet another reminder of His agony confronts us. High above, the Passover moon sheds its soft illumination on the world below. Was it not this same light that revealed the bloody sweat of our Savior to the Apostles on the Mount of Olives?

But there were other lights on that first night. They came not to dispel the darkness but to deepen it all the more. They were torches and lanterns in the hands of His enemies, led by one whom He had once called His own:

Then he came to the disciples and said to them, "Are you still sleeping and taking your rest? Behold, the hour is at hand, and the Son of man is betrayed into the hands of sinners. Rise, let us be going; see, my betrayer is at hand."

[Mt 26:45-46]

Even my bosom friend in whom I trusted,
who ate of my bread,
has lifted his heel against me.

[Ps 41:9]

While he was still speaking, Judas came, one of the twelve, and with him a great crowd with swords and clubs, from the chief priests and the elders of the people.

[Mt 26:47]

I am not afraid of ten thousands of people who have set themselves against me round about.

[Ps 3:6]

Then Jesus, knowing all that was to befall him, came forward and said to them, "Whom do you seek?" They answered him, "Jesus of Nazareth." Jesus said to them, "I am he." Judas, who betrayed him, was standing with them. When he said to them, "I am he," they drew back and fell to the ground.

[Jn 18:4-6]

The mountains saw thee, and writhed;
the raging waters swept on;

[155]

the deep gave forth its voice,
it lifted its hands on high.
The sun and moon stood still in their habitation
at the light of thine arrows as they sped,
at the flash of thy glittering spear.

[Hab 3:10-11]

Again he asked them, "Whom do you seek?" And they said, "Jesus
of Nazareth." Jesus answered, "I told you that I am he; so, if you seek
me, let these men go." This was to fulfil the word which he had spoken,
"Of those whom thou gavest me I lost not one."

[Jn 18:7-9]

The good shepherd lays down
his life for the sheep.

[Jn 10:11]

Now the betrayer had given them a sign, saying, "The one I shall
kiss is the man; seize him." And he came up to Jesus at once and said,
"Hail, Master!" And he kissed him.

[Mt 26:48-49]

Where hatred is there are dissembling lips,
but deep within lies treachery. . . .

[Prov 26:24; JB]

"Judas, would you betray the Son of man with a kiss?"

[Lk 22:48]

It is not an enemy who taunts me —
then I could bear it;
it is not an adversary who deals insolently with me —
then I could hide from him.
But it is you . . .
my companion, my familiar friend.
We used to hold sweet converse together;
within God's house we walked in fellowship.

[Ps 55:12-14]

And when those who were about him saw what would follow, they *said, "Lord, shall we strike with the sword?"*

[Lk 22:49]

Then Simon Peter, having a sword, drew it and struck the high priest's slave and cut off his right ear.

[Jn 18:10]

Then Jesus said to him, "Put your sword back into its place; for all who take the sword will perish by the sword. Do you think that I cannot appeal to my Father,and he will at once send me more than twelve legions of angels?"

[Mt 26:52-53]

Oh, that you would tear the heavens open and come down — at your presence the mountains would melt . . . to make known your name to your enemies, and make the nations tremble at your Presence. . . .

[Is 64:1-2; JB]

"But how then should the scriptures be fulfilled, that it must be so?"

[Mt 26:54]

". . . shall I not drink the cup which the Father has given me?"

[Jn 18:11]

And he touched his [the servant's] ear and healed him.

[Lk 22:51]

*Return, O faithless sons,
I will heal your faithlessness.*

[Jer 3:22]

Then Jesus said to the chief priests and captains of the temple and elders, who had come out against him, "Have you come out as against a robber, with swords and clubs? When I was with you day after day in the temple, you did not lay hands on me. But this is your hour, and the power of darkness."

[Lk 22:52-53]

This is your short hour. This is that mad and ungovernable power which brings you armed to take an unarmed man, which brings the fierce against the gentle, criminals against an innocent man, a traitor against his lord, puny mortals against God.

[Saint Thomas More, *De Tristitia Christi*]¹⁹⁵

Then all the disciples forsook him and fled.

[Mt 26:56]

He has put my brethren far from me,
and my acquaintances
are wholly estranged from me.

[Job 19:13]

So the band of soldiers and their captain and the officers of the Jews seized Jesus and bound him.

[Jn 18:12]

He was oppressed, and he was afflicted,
yet he opened not his mouth;
like a lamb that is led to the slaughter,
and like a sheep that before its shearers is dumb,
so he opened not his mouth.

[Is 53:7]

And a young man followed him, with nothing but a linen cloth about his body; and they seized him, but he left the linen cloth and ran away naked.

[Mk 14:51-52]

Peter followed at a distance. . . .

[Lk 22:54]

My friends and my companions shrink from my wounds, even the dearest of them keep their distance. . . .

[Ps 38:11; JB]

Gethsemane Commemorated in Mexico

The Spanish missionaries who evangelized Latin America brought many of the devotional customs of their native land to the New

World; such customs, intended for the instruction and edification of the souls entrusted to their care, often took highly representational forms in order to help the faithful visualize the great events of salvation recorded in the Sacred Scriptures. A particularly colorful example relevant to our current subject is found in a nineteenth-century account of Holy Week in the Mexican city of Tasco, where on this night the arrest of Christ would be vividly reenacted. In the square in front of the parish church a "garden" was set up on one side of the door, containing a life-size statue of Christ in His agony. Shortly after six o'clock in the evening, the parish priest would mount a pulpit in front of the church door and deliver a sermon on the agony in Gethsemane and the arrest of our Lord. Following this talk a company of "Roman soldiers," directed by a man playing Judas, entered the garden and seized the statue of Christ there. The silence was now broken by the sound of drums and the discordant tones of the *chirimia*, a musical instrument with a sound similar to a fife or whistle and capable of only two notes. As the people looked on in silence, the statue was tied with ropes and loaded down with chains, after which it was hoisted onto a framework shouldered by six men. A procession now began and continued until midnight, with over two thousand of the faithful walking in double file and carrying candles. Those in the role of "Roman soldiers" carried torches, lanterns, clubs, spears, and staves, in accordance with the Scriptures (Mt 26:47 and Jn 18:3). The statue of Christ, clothed in soiled and torn garments, was borne slowly through the streets of Tasco, as the drums and *chirimias* continued their sad accompaniment:

> *Let it not be imagined that all this is merely a curious and idle show for the thousands of spectators: it is for them a real religious ceremony, which speaks very forcibly to their feelings. This fact is well proved by the behavior of a good Mexican priest who was witnessing this strange scene. When the image of our Lord passed before him, surrounded by the wild and savage soldiery, two large tears rolled down his cheeks, and he exclaimed: Asi en verdad llevaron al mansisimo Cordero de Dios! "Thus, indeed, did they lead the most gentle Lamb of God!" He was a man of learning, who had filled important Government positions before embracing the priesthood. He had witnessed many a desperate struggle, and himself had gone through many a hair-breadth escape of his life in the troubled times of revolution which have so long afflicted his native land.[196]*

The Trial Before Caiaphas and the Sanhedrin:
Points for Meditation

. . . I suffer insult for your sake.

[Jer 15:15b; JB]

First they led him to Annas; for he was the father-in-law of Caiaphas, who was high priest that year. . . .
Simon Peter followed Jesus, and so did another disciple. As this disciple was known to the high priest, he entered the court of the high priest along with Jesus, while Peter stood outside at the door. So the other disciple . . . went out and spoke to the maid who kept the door, and brought Peter in.

[Jn 18:13, 15-16]

Be wary . . .
because you are walking with your own downfall.

[Sir 13:13; JB]

The high priest then questioned Jesus about his disciples and his teaching. Jesus answered him, "I have spoken openly to the world; I have always taught in synagogues and in the temple, where all Jews come together; I have said nothing secretly. Why do you ask me? Ask those who have heard me, what I said to them; they know what I said."

[Jn 18:19-21]

. . . the Lord God helps me;
therefore I have not been confounded;
therefore I have set my face like a flint,
and I know that I shall not be put to shame;
he who vindicates me is near.

[Is 50:7-8]

When he had said this, one of the officers standing by struck Jesus with his hand, saying, "Is that how you answer the high priest?" Jesus answered him, "If I have spoken wrongly, bear witness to the wrong; but if I have spoken rightly, why do you strike me?"

[Jn 18:22-23]

Who will contend with me?

Let us stand up together.
Who is my adversary?
Let him come near to me.
Behold, the Lord God helps me;
who will declare me guilty?

[Is 50:8-9]

Now the chief priests and the whole council sought testimony against Jesus to put him to death; but they found none. For many bore false witness against him, and their witness did not agree.

[Mk 14:55-56]

Behold, the wicked man conceives evil,
and is pregnant with mischief,
and brings forth lies.

[Ps 7:14]

And some stood up and bore false witness against him, saying, "We heard him say, 'I will destroy this temple that is made with hands, and in three days I will build another, not made with hands.'" Yet not even so did their testimony agree.

[Mk 14:57-59]

. . . false witnesses have risen against me, and breathe out violence.

[Ps 27:12; JB]

And the high priest stood up and said, "Have you no answer to make? What is it that these men testify against you?" But Jesus was silent.

[Mt 26:62-63]

Behold what I suffer from those who hate me. . . .

[Ps 9:13]

. . . when they had kindled a fire in the middle of the courtyard and sat down together, Peter sat among them.

[Lk 22:55]

Beware lest you err with your tongue, lest you fall before him who lies in wait.

[Sir 28:26]

Then a maid, seeing him as he sat in the light and gazing at him, said, "This man also was with him." But he denied it, saying, "Woman, I do not know him."

[Lk 22:56-57]

Who was it you dreaded . . .
that you should disown me
and not remember me . . . ?

[Is 57:11; JB]

And when he went out to the porch, another maid saw him, and she said to the bystanders, "This man was with Jesus of Nazareth." And again he denied it with an oath, "I do not know the man."

[Mt 26:71-72]

. . . are you not ashamed to wrong me?

[Job 19:3]

After a little while the bystanders came up and said to Peter, "Certainly you are also one of them, for your accent betrays you."

[Mt 26:73]

Lying is an ugly blot on a man. . . .

[Sir 20:24; JB]

One of the servants of the high priest, a kinsman of the man whose ear Peter had cut off, asked, "Did I not see you in the garden with him?"

[Jn 18:26]

Thou hast caused my companions to shun me; thou hast made me a thing of horror to them.

[Ps 88:8]

Then he began to invoke a curse on himself and to swear, "I do not know the man."

[Mt 26:74]

My kinsfolk and my close friends have failed me; the guests in my house have forgotten me. . . .

[Job 19:14-15]

And immediately, while he was still speaking, the cock crowed. And the Lord turned and looked at Peter. And Peter remembered the word of the Lord. . . . And he went out and wept bitterly.

[Lk 22:60-62]

Have mercy on me, O God, in your goodness,
in your great tenderness wipe away my faults;
wash me clean of my guilt,
purify me from my sin.

[Ps 51:1-2; JB]

And the high priest said to him, "I adjure you by the living God, tell us if you are the Christ, the Son of God."

[Mt 26:63]

Then Moses said to God, "I am to go, then, to the sons of Israel and say to them, 'The God of your fathers has sent me to you.' But if they ask me what his name is, what am I to tell them?" And God said to Moses, "I Am who I Am. . . ."

[Ex 3:13-14; JB]

And Jesus said, "I am; and you will see the Son of man sitting at the right hand of Power, and coming with the clouds of heaven."

[Mk 14:62]

And when Jeremiah had finished speaking all that the Lord had commanded him to speak to all the people, then the priests and the prophets and all the people laid hold of him, saying, "You shall die!"

[Jer 26:8]

Then the high priest tore his robes, and said, "He has uttered blasphemy. Why do we still need witnesses? You have now heard his blasphemy. What is your judgment?" They answered, "He deserves death."

[Mt 26:65-66]

. . . there is no one to befriend me.
All help is denied me,
no one cares about me.

[Ps 142:4; JB]

The Mocking Following the Trial Before Caiaphas

Now arrogant men, God, are attacking me,
a brutal gang hounding me to death:
people to whom you mean nothing.

[Ps 86:14; JB]

Then they spat in his face, and struck him; and some slapped him. . . .

[Mt 26:67]

. . . let him give his cheek to the smiter, and be filled with insults.

[Lam 3:30]

. . . they also blindfolded him and asked him, "Prophesy! Who is it that struck you?"

[Lk 22:64]

. . . I did not cover my face
against insult and spittle.

[Is 50:6; JB]

And they spoke many other words against him, reviling him.

[Lk 22:65]

Yahweh, you have heard their insults,
all their plots against me,
my opponents slandering me
under their breath all day long.

[Lam 3:61-62; JB]

And the guards received him with blows.

[Mk 14:65]

Final Thoughts for Holy Thursday

Behold, of dreams
the best will I tell,
That met me at midnight,

the while men rest.
I saw, methought,
a marvelous tree
Lifted aloft, light illumined;
Of all beams brightest
that beacon was.
Gilded with gold, agleam with gems
Fairest on the face of earth.
Five there shone On the shoulder-span. . .
Souls of the saved, men upon earth,
and all earth's creatures upon it gazed.

Fair was that victory-tree;
I, foul with vice,
Wounded with wickedness,
witnessed the glory-tree,
Sheathed in splendor,
wondrously shining
With gems and gold, garmented nobly,
this tree of the forest.

[*The Dream of the Rood*][197]

Endnotes

1. *Circular Letter Concerning the Preparation and Celebration of the Easter Feasts*, 20 Feb 1988, #38, in *L'Osservatore Romano*, Feb 29, 1988, p. 16.
2. *Vossio S. Ephraim, Tome 3, Oratio 17*, in *The Sunday Sermons of the Great Fathers*, M. F. Toal, ed., Vol. III, pp. 121-122.
3. Father Herbert Thurston, SJ, "Holy Week," *Catholic Encyclopedia*, 1907, Vol. 7, p. 437.
4. Father Herbert Thurston, SJ, *Lent and Holy Week*, 1904, p. 282 (footnote).
5. *Patrologia Latina*, Vol. 78, col. 951a (Thurston, p. 279).
6. Liber IV, Caput XXI, in *Patrologia Latina*, Vol. 105, col. 1201b.
7. *The Monastic Constitutions of Lanfranc* , David Knowles, tr./ed., p. 33.
8. Anton Baumstark, *Comparative Liturgy*, p. 29.
9. Thurston, p. 280 (footnote).
10. Ibid., p. 280. There are several different manuscripts of the *York*

Missal, only one of which is from the fifteenth century (the "Sidney Sussex Manuscript"); the others date from the first half of the sixteenth century. Unfortunately, Father Thurston does not indicate which of these he is quoting.

11. *Missale Romanum: Mediolani, 1474* (Henry Bradshaw Society, Vol. II), Robert Lippe, ed., 1907, p. 72.
12. G. E. Karmany, "Holy Week Memories of Palma de Mallorca," *Ave Maria*, March 28, 1942, pp. 399-400.
13. Father Francis X. Weiser, SJ, *The Easter Book*, p. 111.
14. Epistle 54 to Januarius, cited in Reverend John Tyrer, *Historical Survey of Holy Week: Its Services and Ceremonial* (Alcuin Club Collections #29), pp. 113-114.
15. *Gelasian* text in *Patrologia Latina*, Vol. 74, col. 1102b-1103a; Paduan text in *Le Sacramentaire Gregorien: Ses principales formes d'apres les plus anciens manuscrits: I* (Spicilegium Friburgense, Vol. 16), Jean Deshusses, ed., p. 630.
16. Tyrer, p. 114.
17. *Maxima redemptionis*, Nov 16, 1955, Introduction, in *American Ecclesiastical Review*, Jan 1956, p. 52.
18. Ibid., Section II, #7, p. 54.
19. J. D. Crichton, *The Liturgy of Holy Week*, pp. 37-38.
20. Dom Germain Morin, "Le plus ancien *Comes* de l'Eglise Romaine," *Revue Benedictine*, Vol. 27 (1910), p. 54.
21. Father Herman Schmidt, SJ, *Hebdomada Sancta: Fontes Historici, Commentarius Historicus*, Vol. II, 1957, pp. 674-675.
22. *The Passion Play at Oberammergau, 1930: The Complete English Texts of the Play* (1930), p. 150.
23. Homily at Mass of the Lord's Supper, April 8, 1982, #2, in *Pope John Paul II: Daily Meditations*, Valeria Caprioglio et al., eds., 1985 p. 105.
24. *The Complete Works of Thomas More: Vol. 13: Treatise on the Passion, Treatise on the Blessed Body, Instructions and Prayers*, G. Haupt, ed. 1976, pp. 82-83 (spellings modified).
25. Homily 10, *Homiliae Diversae*, in Toal, Vol. III, p. 158.
26. Father John H. Miller, CSC, "The History and Spirit of Holy Week," *American Ecclesiastical Review*, April 1957, p. 225.
27. Antoine Chavasse, "A Rome, le Jeudi-Saint, au VII Siecle, d'apres un Vieil Ordo," *Revue D'Histoire Ecclesiastique*, Vol. 50, 1955, pp. 28, 35; also cited in P. M. Gy, OP, "Les Origines Liturgiques du Lavement des Pieds," *La Maison-Dieu*, Vol. 49, 1957, p. 51.
28. Canon III, 17th Council of Toledo, quoted in Ernest Graf, OSB, "The

Washing of Feet on Maundy Thursday," *Homiletic and Pastoral Review*, Feb 1945, p. 350.

29. For Latin text of *Mandatum* in *Liber Ordinum*, see Dom Henri Leclercq, "Lavement de la Tete, des Mains, des Pieds," *Dictionnaire d'archeologie chretienne et de liturgie*, 1929, Vol. 8, Part 2, col. 2005-2007 (summarized in Tyrer, p. 111).

30. *Regula Magistri*, Caput 53, in *Patrologia Latina*, Vol. 88, col. 1015c (for dating and provenence see P. B. Corbett, "Regula Magistri," *New Catholic Encyclopedia*, 1967 ed., Vol. 12, p. 208). Although the Holy Week texts of two manuscripts of the *Georgian Lectionary* translated by T. Kluge and A. Baumstark (1915) contain no *Mandatum* (probably because of a *lacuna*), it is evident from a comment of Dom Emmanuel Lanne, OSB, that the *Mandatum* is found in at least one of two additional manuscripts utilized in Father Michael Tarchnischvili's more recent Latin translation of this ancient Lectionary (*Le Grand Lectionnaire de l'Eglise de Jerusalem*, Corpus Scriptorum Christianorum Orientalium #189, Scriptores Iberici 10, 1959); see E. Lanne, OSB, "Textes et rites de la liturgie Pascale dans l'ancienne Eglise Copte," *L'Orient Syrien*, Vol. 6, 1961, pp. 285, 291.

31. Graf, p. 350.

32. *Regularis Concordia: The Monastic Agreement of the Monks and Nuns of the English Nation* (Medieval Classics), Dom Thomas Symons, tr., pp. 39, 40-41.

33. Knowles, pp. 30-35.

34. *Patrologia Latina*, Vol. 78, col. 1040d-1041a.

35. Ibid., col. 1074a-1075a.

36. Chavasse, p. 35. The second *Mandatum* is mentioned neither in the thirteenth-century *Roman Ordo 10* nor in the fourteenth-century *Roman Ordo 14* (*Patrologia Latina*, Vol. 78, col. 1013a (Ordo 10), 1207b-d, 1210c-1211a (Ordo 14)).

37. Miller, pp. 225-226. See *Roman Ordo 15* in *Patrologia Latina*, Vol. 78, col. 1307b, 1310c-1312b, 1363d-1364a.

38. Liber II, Caput XXIV, #1, #2 (1886 Edition), p. 244.

39. "Lecture the First," *Four Lectures on the Offices and Ceremonies of Holy Week*, ca. 1838, p. 19.

40. Weiser, p. 108.

41. "Holy Week in Jerusalem," *The Catholic World*, VII, April-Sep 1868, p. 78.

42. J. V. Amor,"Holy Week at Tasco, Mexico," *The Month*, April 1885, p. 513.

43. Tyrer, p. 112. This practice of King Robert ("the Pious") is recorded

by the Benedictine monk Helgaud (died ca. 1048) in his *Epitoma Vitae Regis Rotberti Pii* (*Patrologia Latina*, Vol. 141, col. 924b-c).

44. King Alfonso died just seven months later on Nov 25, 1885.

45. Alquien, "Holy Week in Spain," *The Catholic World*, March 1894, pp. 850-852.

46. The use of the noun *viri* ("men," "masculine persons") in the original Latin of the current editions of the *Roman Missal* ("Missa vespertina in Cena Domini," #6), the *Ceremoniale Episcoporum* (#301) and in the 1988 *Circular Letter Concerning the Preparation and Celebration of the Easter Feasts* (#51) indicates that only men or boys are to be selected for the liturgical *Mandatum* rite.

47. *The New Roman Missal: In Latin and English*, Father F. X. Lasance and Father Francis Augustine Walsh, OCD, eds., p. 468.

48. Jacket notes, *Paschale Mysterium: Holy Week* (*Gregorian Chant I*), Konrad Ruhland, cond., Capella Antiqua Munich and Choralschola, 1981.

49. Liturgical texts from *The Vatican II Sunday Missal*, Daughters of St. Paul, 1974, pp. 598, 602-605, 644-645.

50. Pius Parsch, *The Liturgy of the Mass*, pp. 27-28, 31.

51. Father John A. Hardon, SJ, *Christianity in the Twentieth Century*, pp. 149-150.

52. Parsch, p. 173.

53. Ibid., p. 174.

54. Ibid., pp. 32-33, 215.

55. Father Josef A. Jungmann, SJ, *The Mass of the Roman Rite: Its Origins and Development*, Vol. I, pp. 51-53.

56. Parsch, p. 192.

57. Enrico Mazza, *The Eucharistic Prayers of the Roman Rite*, 1986, pp. 90, 96.

58. Parsch, p. 281.

59. Epistle 9, cited in ibid., pp. 282-283.

60. Ibid., pp. 25-26.

61. Ibid., pp. 28, 297.

62. Ibid., p. 295.

63. Ibid., p. 304.

64. Ibid., p. 36.

65. *General Instruction on the Roman Missal*, #322a, in *Documents on the Liturgy, 1963-1979*, International Commission on English in the Liturgy, tr., 1982, p. 529.

66. *Gelasian Sacramentary* in *Patrologia Latina*, Vol. 74, col. 1099a, b;

Gregorian texts in Deshusses, pp. 172 (Hadrian), 630 (Paduan).

67. Saint Ephraem, quoted in Father Herbert Thurston, SJ, "Archdeacon Farrar on the Observance of Good Friday," *The Month*, May 1895, p. 102.

68. Saint Isidore, *De Ecclesiasticis Officiis*, Liber I, #29, and 17th Council of Toledo, Canon II, both cited in Tyrer, p. 107.

69. Latin text in Leclercq, col. 2006 (summarized in Tyrer, p. 108).

70. Tyrer, pp. 108-109.

71. Rubrics of 1570 *Roman Missal* in Lippe, Vol. I, p. 158, Vol. II, p. 73. The stripping of the altars in Rome on Holy Thursday is mentioned as early as the eighth century in *Roman Ordo I* (*Patrologia Latina*, Vol. 78, col. 953a).

72. *Roman Missal*, "Evening Mass of the Lord's Supper," #19, in *Revised Rites of Holy Week*, Catholic Book Publishing Co., 1971, p. 67.

73. "A Good Friday in Rome," *Ave Maria*, April 3, 1909, pp. 418-419.

74. P. 501.

75. *Patrologia Latina*, Vol. 74, col. 1102a, 1105c, d; English translation of these passages is from W. Lockton, *The Treatment of the Remains at the Eucharist After Holy Communion and the Time of the Ablutions*, p. 75.

76. *Patrologia Latina*, Vol. 78, col. 952c, 954a, b (Lockton, p. 75).

77. Ibid., Vol. 78, col. 961a, b (Lockton, pp. 75-76).

78. Ibid., Vol. 78, col. 889d-890a; English translation (slightly modified) is from O. B. Hardison, *Christian Rite and Christian Drama in the Middle Ages*, 1965, p. 125.

79. Lockton, pp. 76-77.

80. *Patrologia Latina*, Vol. 78, col. 1012c, d (English trans. in Lockton, pp. 82-83).

81. Ibid., Vol. 78, col. 1309a, b (Lockton, pp. 84-85).

82. Lockton, pp. 88-90.

83. Ibid., pp. 95-96.

84. *Patrologia Latina*, Vol. 85, col. 418b-419a; English translation in Hardison, pp. 125-126.

85. *The Revised Ordo of Holy Week* (*Ordo Hebdomadae Sanctae Instauratus*, Jan 1956) specifies a ciborium for the transfer of the Eucharist (*The Rites of Holy Week*, Frederick R. McManus, JCD, ed., 1957, pp. 76, 78).

86. *Patrologia Latina*, Vol. 78, col. 890a.

87. Knowles, p. 31 (translation slightly modified).

88. *Patrologia Latina*, Vol. 147, col. 50b.

89. Lockton, p. 77.

90. The term "sepulchre" has also been used to refer to a medieval practice concerning the "deposition" of the Eucharist on Good Friday in a structure symbolizing the Lord's tomb (this custom is discussed at length in chapters IX and X). However, the passage here quoted clearly speaks of the reservation of only one Host — that which will be consumed at the Mass of the Presanctified on Good Friday. If the reference here were to the Good Friday "sepulchre," it would mention the reservation of two Hosts, one for the Good Friday liturgy and the second for "deposition" afterwards in the Good Friday sepulchre.

91. Lockton, p. 96; Latin text reprinted in Mario Righetti, *Manuale Di Storia Liturgica*, Vol. II, p. 439.

92. Father Herbert Thurston, SJ, "Easter Sepulchre, or Altar of Repose?," *The Month*, April 1903, pp. 404-405.

93. Ibid., p. 405.

94. Archdale King, *Eucharistic Reservation in the Western Church*, 1965, p. 145.

95. Righetti, Vol. II, p. 440.

96. King, p. 72; Righetti, Vol. II, pp. 440-441.

97. King, p. 217; Righetti, Vol. II, p. 439.

98. *Patrologia Latina*, Vol. 78, col. 1013b.

99. Domenico Mallardo, "La Pasqua e La Settimana Maggiore a Napoli dal Secolo Val XIV," *Ephemerides Liturgicae*, 1952, pp. 31-32.

100. Richard Donovan, CSB, *The Liturgical Drama in Medieval Spain*, p. 87.

101. *Patrologia Latina*, Vol. 85, col. 418c; English translation is from Hardison, p. 126.

102. Lockton, p. 95.

103. Titulus IV, Caput I, p. 30. The new *Caeremoniale Episcoporum* of 1985 also specifies flowers and lights (#299).

104. Liber II, Caput XXIII, #2, p. 239.

105. *Decreta Authentica Congregationis Sacrorum Rituum*, pub. Typographia Polyglotta, 1898-1901, Vol. I, p. 252. Summarized in English by William Thomas Cavanaugh, CP, *The Reservation of the Blessed Sacrament*, 1927, p. 87.

106. Ibid., Vol. I, pp. 480-481 (Cavanaugh, p. 89).

107. Ibid., Vol. II, p. 260 (Cavanaugh, p. 88).

108. Ibid., Vol. I, p. 138 (Cavanaugh, p. 88).

109. Ibid., Vol. II, p. 320 (Cavanaugh, p. 88).

110. Ibid., Vol. II, pp. 464-465 (Cavanaugh, pp. 87-88).

111. Ibid., Commentary, Vol. IV, pp. 424-425.

112. *Decreta*, Vol. III, pp. 323-324 (Cavanaugh, pp. 87-88).

113. Cavanaugh, p. 87.

114. *Decreta*, Vol. III, pp. 181-182 (Cavanaugh, p. 88).

115. From the *Journal* of Eugenie de Guerin, quoted in Francois Mauriac, *The Eucharist: The Mystery of Holy Thursday*, p. 30.

116. Camm, p. 420.

117. Commentary, *Decreta*, Vol. IV, p. 427.

118. Weiser, pp. 106-107.

119. "The Holy Week of 1869 in Havana" (Part One), *The Catholic World*, April 1870, pp. 60, 65.

120. Lockton, p. 81.

121. Lippe, Vol. II, pp. 81-82.

122. "Answers to Questions: The Repository on Holy Thursday," *American Ecclesiastical Review*, June 1949, p. 510; Latin text of Decree #4049 in *Decreta*, Vol. III, p. 374.

123. *Memoriale Rituum*, Titulus IV, Caput I, p. 30.

124. *Missale Romanum*, Typis Polyglottis Vaticanis, 1970, "Missa vespertina in Cena Domini," #17, p. 248.

125. *The Liturgical Year*, 1952, Vol. 6, p. 395.

126. Karmany, pp. 400-401.

127. Alquien, p. 845; Thomas Walsh, "Sevilla of the Images," *The Month*, April 1914, pp. 354-355; E. Boyle O'Reilly, *Heroic Spain*, pp. 311-312; "Semana Santa," *Encyclopedia Universal Ilustrada*, 1927 ed., Vol. 55, p. 88.

128. Eugene Viale,"Le Reposoir du Jeudi Saint," *La Maison-Dieu*, Vol. 41, 1955, pp. 51, 54.

129. Karl Young, *The Drama of the Medieval Church*, 1933, Vol. I, p. 116.

130. See pp. 308-309 for description.

131. Joan Hazelden Walker, "Further Notes on Reservation Practice and Eucharistic Devotion: The Contribution of the Early Church at Rome," *Ephemerides Liturgicae*, May-Aug 1984, p. 403.

132. Ibid., pp. 403-404.

133. King, pp. 41, 145.

134. Viale, p. 48. A somewhat similar comment appears in the eleventh-century *Ordinarium Canonicorum Regularium* of John of Avranches (*Patrologia Latina*, Vol. 147, col. 175a,b).

135. Commentary, *Decreta*, Vol. IV, pp. 419-421; for rubrics of *Roman Ordo 15* see *Patrologia Latina*, Vol. 78, col. 1308d-1309b.

136. *Patrologia Latina*, Vol. 85, col. 418c-419a.

137. King, p. 217.

138. "Answers to Questions: Holy Thursday Repository or Sepulchre," *American Ecclesiastical Review*, April 1946, p. 299.

139. "16 Aprile — Giovedi Santo," p. 275.

140. Congregation for Divine Worship, 1988, #55, p. 17.

141. Father Josef A. Jungmann, SJ, *Pastoral Liturgy*, 1962, p. 237.

142. Congregation for Divine Worship, #49, #55, p. 17.

143. Translation of Edward Caswall, adapted by Anthony G. Petti, in *Christian Prayer: The Liturgy of the Hours*, Liturgical Press, 1976, Hymn #108.

144. John Wilkinson, *Egeria's Travels*, p. 267.

145. Theodor Kluge and Anton Baumstark, "Quadragesima und Karwoche Jerusalems im siebten Jahrhundert," *Oriens Christianus*, Vol. 5, new series (1915), p. 222.

146. *Analekta Hierosolymitikes Stachyologias*, A. Papadopoulos-Kerameus, ed., 1894 (rpt. 1963), Vol. II, pp. 105-108.

147. *Le Typicon de la Grande Eglise: Tome II: Le Cycle des Fetes Mobiles* (Orientalia Christiana Analecta #166), Juan Mateos, ed., pp. 74-77.

148. I.-H. Dalmais, "*Le Triduum Sacrum* dans la liturgie Byzantine," *La Maison-Dieu*, Vol. 41, 1955, p. 120.

149. M. Arranz, SJ, "Les Sacrements de l'ancien Euchologe Constantinopolitain (1): Etude preliminaire des sources," *Orientalia Christiana Periodica*, Vol. 48, 1982, pp. 295-296 (outline of contents of *Codex Barberini*, pp. 296-298). In some older sources this same manuscript is identified as "*Vat. grec. 366.*" Recent studies generally agree in dating the *Codex* to the eighth century.

150. Stefano Parenti, "Nota sull'impiego del Termine 'Proskomide' nell'Eucologio Barberini gr. 336 (VIII sec.)," *Ephemerides Liturgicae*, Vol. 103 (1989), p. 410.

151. Mateos, pp. 76-77.

152. Papadopoulos-Kerameus, Vol. II, pp. 99-105.

153. Maximilian, Prince of Saxony, *Praelectiones de Liturgiis Orientalibus*, 1908, Vol. II, p. 108.

154. Mateos, pp. 72-73.

155. Maximilian, Vol. II, pp. 107-108.

156. Wilkinson, p. 267.

157. See p. 110 and note 30 of this chapter.

158. Greek text with Latin translation in Jacobus Goar, *Euchologion sive Rituale Graecorum*, 1730, (rpt. 1960), p. 595 (cited, with English translation, in Dennis R. Rhodes, "The Service of the Washing of

Feet on Holy Thursday: An Historical and Theological Investigation," Diss. Saint Vladimir's Orthodox Theological Seminary 1977, pp. 7, 47-49).

159. Mateos, pp. 72-75.

160. Papadopoulos-Kerameus, Vol. II, pp. 108-116.

161. Lanne, pp. 291-292.

162. Anton Baumstark, "Das Leydener griechisch-arabische Perikopenbuch fur die Kar- und Osterwoche," *Oriens Christianus*, Vol. 4, new series, 1914-1915, pp. 40, 44, 53; for correct dating of this document see Lanne, pp. 281-282.

163. Maximilian, Vol. II,pp. 109-111.

164. Father Peter F. Sfeir, "Holy Week Customs in Syria," *The Catholic Mind*, April 22, 1928, pp. 146-148.

165. Congregation for Divine Worship, 1988, #56, p. 17.

166. Right Reverend E. Bougaud, *Life of Saint Margaret Mary Alacoque*, 1920, pp. 121-124.

167. *The Autobiography of Saint Thérèse of Lisieux: The Story of a Soul*, John Beevers, tr., 1957, p. 116.

168. P. Enrico Zoffoli, *S. Paolo Della Croce: Storia Critica*, 1963-1968, Vol. II, p. 1175.

169. Abbe Francis Trochu, *The Curé d'Ars: Saint Jean-Marie-Baptiste Vianney*, 1927 (rpt. 1977), pp. 226-227.

170. Dom Donatien, OSB, "Holy Week in a Flemish Abbey," *Orate Fratres*, March 24, 1934, pp. 212-214.

171. *Memoriale Rituum*, Title IV, chapter II, Part 4, #9, in *Ritual for Small Churches*, Father Bartholomew Eustace, ed., 1935, p. 58 (1920 edition); in 1853 edition, Titulus IV, Caput II, Section IV, #11, p. 42.

172. *Stone in the King's Highway*, Most Reverend Edmund Lane, MM, ed., pp. 110-111; essay originally printed in *The Field Afar*, April 1933, pp. 98-101.

173. Gretta Palmer, *God's Underground in Asia*, p. 90.

174. Alquien, pp. 852-853.

175. Father James Monks, SJ, *Great Catholic Festivals*, p. 49.

176. Karl Baedeker, *Baedeker's Southern Italy and Sicily*, 1930, p. 38; Monks, p. 48.

177. Homily at Mass of the Lord's Supper, April 8, 1993, #2-#4, in *L'Osservatore Romano*, April 14, 1993, p. 2.

178. Prologue, Act VII, *The Passion Play at Oberammergau, 1930*, p. 165.

179. Breen, p. 501.

180. Wolfgang Pax, *In the Footsteps of Jesus*, 1970, p. 172; Father John

Steinmueller and Kathryn Sullivan, RSCJ, *Catholic Biblical Encyclopedia: New Testament*, 1959, p. 255.

181. Weiser, p. 111.

182. Ibid., pp. 109-110. See also Nicolaus Nilles, SJ, *Kalendarium Manuale Utriusque Ecclesiae Orientalis et Occidentalis*, 1896-1897 (rpt. 1971), Vol. II, pp. 241-242.

183. Chapter 22, cited in Tyrer, pp. 33-35.

184. See chapter I, pp. 23-24.

185. Wilkinson, pp. 267-269.

186. Kluge and Baumstark, pp. 223-225.

187. Papadopoulos-Kerameus, Vol. II, pp. 116-147.

188. Mateos, pp. 76-79.

189. The following is based upon D. Pochin Mould, "Byzantine Holy Week," *Doctrine and Life*, Vol. 14, March 1964, pp. 179-180, and Weiser, p. 109.

190. Weiser, p. 110.

191. "Discourse XVI: Mental Sufferings of Our Lord in His Passion," in John Henry Cardinal Newman, *Discourses Addressed to Mixed Congregations*, 1909 (originally published 1849), pp. 336-339.

192. Translated by George N. Shuster from the original German of Annette von Droste-Hulshoff (1797-1848), in *The Catholic Anthology: The World's Great Catholic Poetry*, Thomas Walsh, ed., 1943, p. 243.

193. Ibid., p. 244.

194. *Circular Letter Concerning the Preparation and Celebration of the Easter Feasts*, Feb 20, 1988, #56, *L'Osservatore Romano*, Feb 29, 1988, p. 17. It should be noted that this passage does not prohibit adoration after midnight; it only requires that the formal public adoration following the Mass of the Lord's Supper be ended by this hour, when Good Friday begins. In view of this it may be appropriate to remove some of the festive decorations from the chapel of repose after twelve o'clock. In the United States the churches are commonly closed at or before midnight.

195. Excerpt, in *The Complete Works of Thomas More: Vol. 14: De Tristitia Christi, Part I: The Valencia Manuscript: Facsimiles, Transcription and Translation*, Clarence H. Miller, ed./tr., pp. 541-543.

196. Amor, pp. 513-515.

197. Excerpt, eighth-century English poem, in Walsh, p. 31.

VI

Good Friday

Do you not know what holy day this is?
No? Then whence come you?
Among what heathen have you dwelt,
not to know that today
is the supremely holy Good Friday?
Lay down your weapons!
Do not offend the Lord, who today,
bereft of all arms, offered His holy blood
to redeem the sinful world!

It is the tears of repentant sinners
that today with holy dew
besprinkle field and meadow:
thus they make them flourish.
Now all creation rejoices
at the Saviour's sign of love
and dedicates to Him its prayer.

[Richard Wagner, *Parsifal*][1]

Good Friday is a day of extreme suffering and the mysterious confrontation of God's infinite love with mankind's sin; it recalls the dramatic passion of Christ, which already began the evening before with his agony in the Garden of Gethsemane, and it concludes with his death on the cross.

For the Christian this day cannot be other than an intense participation: after having followed Jesus from Gethsemane to the religious and civil tribunals, after having accompanied him on his climb to Calvary with the wood of the cross on his shoulder, the believer stands with the apostle John, with Mary Most Holy, and the women at his feet at Golgotha in order to reflect on these dramatic yet exalting events. In contemplating the crucifix, it is pos-

sible to measure the depth of the truth of Jesus' words: "God so loved the world that he gave his only Son . . . that the world might be saved through him" (Jn 3:16-17).

[Pope John Paul II][2]

(John Zierten)

Prelude: Dawn on Good Friday

The standards of the King appear,
the mystery of the Cross shines out in glory,
the Cross on which Life suffered death
and by that death gave back life to us.

The words of David's true prophetic song
were fulfilled, in which he announced
to the nations: "God has reigned from a tree."

Tree of dazzling beauty,
adorned with the purple of the King's blood,
and chosen from a stock
worthy to bear limbs so sacred!

[*Vexilla Regis*, vs. 1, 3, 4][3]

Woe to those who devise wickedness
and work evil upon their beds!
When the morning dawns, they perform it. . . .

[Mic 2:1]

When day came, the assembly of the elders of the people gathered together, both chief priests and scribes; and they led him away to their council, and they said, "If you are the Christ, tell us." But he said to them, "If I tell you, you will not believe; and if I ask you, you will not answer. But from now on the Son of man shall be seated at the right hand of the power of God." And they all said, "Are you the Son of God, then?" And he said to them, "You say that I am." And they said, "What further testimony do we need? We have heard it ourselves from his own lips."

[Lk 22:66-71]

O my people,
what have I done to you?
In what have I wearied you?
Answer me!

[Mic 6:3]

Tenebrae

AS ON HOLY THURSDAY, the Church begins her observance of Good Friday with the Office of *Tenebrae*.[4] Once again, upon entering the chapel, our attention is drawn to the stark form of the hearse with its fifteen candles burning. But in one very important way the chapel is different from the previous morning. The tabernacle is empty:

"The days will come, when the bridegroom is taken away from them, and then they will fast in that day."

[Mk 2:20]

The stripped altar reminds us that today the Church is in mourning. *Tenebrae* begins with a hymn appropriate to the mysteries of this day:

O Cross of Christ, immortal tree
On which our Savior died,
The world is sheltered by your arms
That bore the Crucified.

From bitter death and barren wood
The tree of life is made;
Its branches bear unfailing fruit
And leaves that never fade.

O faithful Cross, you stand unmoved
While ages run their course;
Foundation of the universe,
Creation's binding force.

[*O Cross of Christ*, vs. 1-3][5]

As on Holy Thursday, a series of Psalms are now chanted, the first of which speaks of the folly of Christ's enemies:

Why this tumult among nations,
among peoples this useless murmuring?
They arise, the kings of the earth,
princes plot against the Lord and his Anointed. . . .

He who sits in the heavens laughs;
the Lord is laughing them to scorn.
Then he will speak in his anger,
his rage will strike them with terror.
"It is I who have set up my king
on Zion, my holy mountain."

[Ps 2:1-2, 4-6]

The next Psalm is the twenty-second (vs. 2-23), the Psalm that our Lord Himself quoted while on the cross:

My God, my God, why have you forsaken me?
You are far from my plea and the cry of my distress.

O my God, I call by day and you give no reply;
I call by night and I find no peace.

Do not leave me alone in my distress;
come close, there is none else to help.

Many dogs have surrounded me,
a band of the wicked beset me.

Save my life from the jaws of these lions,
my poor soul from the horns of these oxen.

[Ps 22:2-3, 12, 17, 22]

Psalm 38 is now chanted, and like Psalm 22, it also gives us a vivid picture of our Savior's sufferings:

O Lord, do not rebuke me in your anger; —
do not punish me, Lord, in your rage. —

I am bowed and brought to my knees.
I go mourning all the day long.

All my frame burns with fever;
all my body is sick.

But I am like the deaf who cannot hear,
like the dumb unable to speak.
I am like a man who hears nothing,
in whose mouth is no defense.

My wanton enemies are numberless
and my lying foes are many.
They repay me evil for good
and attack me for seeking what is right.

[Ps 38:2, 7-8, 14-15, 20-21]

This morning the Lamentations (Lam 2:8-15) once more speak of the ruin of Jerusalem; as on Holy Thursday the cantor prefaces each strophe of the Lamentations with a letter of the Hebrew alphabet:

[179]

TETH.	Her gates have sunk into the ground;
	he has ruined and broken her bars;
	her king and princes are among the nations;
	the law is no more,
	and her prophets obtain
	no vision from the Lord.

IOD.	. . . the maidens of Jerusalem
	have bowed their heads to the ground.

CAPH.	. . . infants and babes faint
	in the streets of the city.

LAMED.	They cry to their mothers,
	"Where is bread and wine?"
	as they faint like wounded men
	in the streets of the city,
	as their life is poured out
	on their mothers' bosom.

[Lam 2:9, 10, 11-12]

Today we also hear verses from the third of these Lamentations (Lam 3:1-9), in which the "man who has seen affliction" speaks:

BETH.	. . . he has besieged and enveloped me with bitter-ness and tribulation;

BETH.	he has made me dwell in darkness like the dead of long ago.

[Lam 3:5-6]

We have provided only limited excerpts from the Lamentations for the present in order that other verses may serve as points for meditation in subsequent sections of this work.

As on Holy Thursday, the first reading today is from the Letter to the Hebrews, continuing the theme of Christ as the Eternal High Priest:

When Christ came as high priest of the good things which have come to be, he entered once for all into the sanctuary, passing through the greater and more perfect tabernacle not made by hands, that is, not belonging to this creation. He entered, not with the blood of goats and calves, but with his own blood, and achieved eternal redemption.

[Heb 9:11-12; NAB]

In the second reading Saint John Chrysostom (in his "Catechesis 3") speaks of "the power of Christ's blood," describing how the blood of the paschal lamb that protected the children of Israel from death on the first Passover was but a prefiguration of the Blood of Christ:

In those days, when the destroying angel saw the blood on the doors he did not dare to enter, so how much less will the devil approach now when he sees, not that figurative blood on the doors, but the true blood on the lips of believers, the doors of the temple of Christ.

Morning Prayer from the Divine Office now follows, beginning with Psalm 51, known as the *Miserere*:

Have mercy on me, God, in your kindness.
In your compassion blot out my offense. . .

Against you, you alone, have I sinned;
what is evil in your sight I have done.

O purify me, then I shall be clean;
O wash me, I shall be whiter than snow.

A pure heart create for me, O God,
put a steadfast spirit within me.
Do not cast me away from your presence,
nor deprive me of your holy spirit.

[Ps 51:1, 4, 7, 10-11]

In the past (before 1955), the *Miserere* was used not only as the first Psalm of Morning Prayer (Lauds) on Good Friday, but was also sung near the end of the *Tenebrae* services on all three days (thus it was heard twice on Good Friday). Although the rubrics of the *Caeremoniale Episcoporum* merely specified that this Psalm was to be chanted in a "mournful tone" (*flebili voce*) prior to the concluding prayer of *Tenebrae*,[6] it was nevertheless often given a highly dramatic musical setting. Thus the Spanish writer Emilio Castelar (1832-1899), a skeptic prone to anti-Catholic Voltairian attitudes, was so moved by the chanting of the *Miserere* during *Tenebrae* in Saint Peter's Basilica in Rome that he wrote of it in these terms:

> *No pen can describe the solemnity of the "Miserere." The night advances. The basilica is in darkness. Its altars are uncovered. Through the open arches there penetrates the uncertain light of dawn, which seems to deepen the shadows. The last taper of the "Tenebrario" is hidden behind the altar. The cathedral resembles an immense mausoleum, with the faint gleaming of funereal torches in the distance. The music of the "Miserere" is not instrumental. It is a sublime choir, admirably combined. Now it comes like the far-off roar of a tempest, as the vibration of wind upon ruins or among the cypresses of tombs; again like a lamentation from the depths of the earth or the moaning of heaven's angels, breaking into sobs and sorrowfully weeping. . . . This profound and sublime lament, this mourning of bitterness, dying away into airy circles, penetrates the heart by the intensity of its sadness.[7]*

In this morning's service, Psalm 51 is followed by a canticle from the Book of Habakkuk (3:2-4, 13a, 15-19); the eighth-century *Roman Ordo I* indicates that this same Old Testament canticle was sung between readings at the Good Friday Liturgy of the Passion.[8] The words bring to mind the awesome power of Christ crucified:

> *O Lord, I have heard your renown,*
> *and feared, O Lord, your work. . .*
> *in your wrath remember compassion! . . .*
>
> *His splendor spreads like the light;*
> *rays shine forth from beside him,*
> *where his power is concealed.*
> *You came forth to save your people,*
> *to save your anointed one.*
>
> *You tread the sea with your steeds*
> *amid the churning of the deep waters.*
> *I hear, and my body trembles;*
> *at the sound, my lips quiver.*

[Hab 3:2, 4, 13, 15-16; NAB]

Morning Prayer continues with the chanting of Psalm 147 (vs. 12-20), followed by a reading from the Book of Isaiah (Is 52:13-15). Upon its conclusion a schola of singers chants in Latin an antiphon known as the *Christus factus est*:

> *For our sake Christ was obedient,*
> *accepting even death,*
> *death on a cross.*

These words are taken from the Letter of Saint Paul to the Philippians (2:8-9). The antiphon was already a part of the liturgy of the Easter Triduum in Rome by the eighth century, for it appears in *Roman Ordo 23* (Andrieu — ca. 700-750).[9] The *Regularis Concordia* testifies to its use in monasteries during the tenth century; by A.D. 1000 the *Christus factus est* had spread throughout western Europe.[10] Traditionally this antiphon has been sung in three different "stages" on the three days of the Easter Triduum; on Holy Thursday, the shortest form is used:

> *For our sake Christ was obedient,*
> *accepting even death.*

In the past this version was heard at *Tenebrae* for Holy Thursday, but as of 1972, when the revised Liturgy of the Hours was issued, the *Christus factus est* was limited to Evening Prayer and Night Prayer on the first day of the triduum; even so, the "shortened form" has been retained for these two Offices. On Good Friday the antiphon appears with the added phrase, "death on a cross," thereby emphasizing the mystery commemorated on this day:

> *For our sake Christ was obedient,*
> *accepting even death,*
> *death on a cross.*

The *Christus factus est* has been retained in the Morning Prayer of Good Friday, and thus remains part of the current *Tenebrae* service for the day. But it will not be until *Tenebrae* on Holy Saturday that we will hear the antiphon in its most complete form, ending with an expression of the triumph of Easter:

> *For our sake Christ was obedient,*

accepting even death,
death on a cross.
Therefore God raised him on high
and gave him the name
above all other names.

At this morning's service, the *Christus factus est* is followed by the Canticle of Zechariah. After intercessions and the Our Father, *Tenebrae* ends with a brief prayer and blessing.

The Stations of the Cross

The Way of the Cross is one of the most well known of all devotional exercises;[11] throughout the year many of the faithful engage in this practice, in which a series of fourteen episodes associated with our Lord's carrying of the cross to Golgotha are commemorated with prayer and meditation:

1. Christ is sentenced by Pilate.
2. Christ is given His cross.
3. Christ falls under the cross for the first time.
4. Christ meets His Mother.
5. Simon the Cyrenean is compelled to carry the cross for Christ.
6. Veronica wipes the bloodied face of Christ.
7. Christ falls a second time.
8. Christ meets the women of Jerusalem.
9. Christ falls a third time.
10. Christ is stripped of His clothes.
11. Christ is nailed to the cross.
12. Christ dies on the cross.
13. Christ is taken down from the cross.
14. Christ is laid in the Tomb.

In its current form the Way of the Cross is no more than four hundred years old; twelve of the fourteen stations are mentioned in *Jerusalem sicut Christi tempore floruit*, a book published in 1584, the work of an author named Adrichomius. However, the concept of following the steps of our Lord to Calvary is far more ancient. There is even a tradition claiming that the Blessed Virgin Mary herself daily visited the various sites in Jerusalem connected with her Son's passion. In fourth-century Jerusalem several of the most important sites were regularly visited by pilgrims, as attested by Egeria in her diary from this period; even so, she makes no mention of a commemoration of the Way of the Cross. As early as the fifth century the desire to bring the shrines of Jerusalem "closer to home" led Saint Petronius, the Bishop of Bologna (Italy), to erect a complex of connected chapels representing these shrines at Bologna's Monastery of San Stefano. In accounts of pilgrimages to Jerusalem from the twelfth, thirteenth, and fourteenth centuries there are references to a *Via Sacra*, a course along which the pilgrims were led from one shrine to another, but there is no evidence

"My eyes weep ceaselessly, without relief until Yahweh looks down and sees. . ." (Lam 3:49-50; JB).

that this was meant to be a Way of the Cross. Jerusalem's *Via Dolorosa* as we understand it does not begin to emerge until the fifteenth century; such a route (albeit with some important differences) is described by an English pilgrim named William Wey, who visited Palestine both in 1458 and in 1462. The devotion of the Way of the Cross spread across Catholic Europe during the sixteenth, seventeenth, and eighteenth centuries, largely through the efforts of the Franciscans, the custodians of the original holy sites in Jerusalem.

In 1750 Pope Benedict XIV became the first pontiff to lead the Stations of the Cross held on Good Friday at the Colosseum.[12] With very few exceptions, each of his successors faithfully continued to lead the Stations every year until 1870, when the invasion of Rome by the anticlerical forces of Victor Emmanuel compelled Pope Pius IX to suspend this custom.[13] But on Good Friday of 1964 Pope Paul VI restored the practice, and Pope John Paul II has continued the tradition.[14] On the evening of Good Friday he goes to the Colosseum and there leads the Stations, carrying a large wooden cross. He is accompanied by two torchbearers. Thousands of Romans and pilgrims attend this service.

Passion Plays

Among the many works of religious drama produced during the course of the Middle Ages, we find a surprisingly small number that treat of the events of our Lord's sacred passion. The drama scholar Karl Young surmises that the men of the Middle Ages must have felt more often than not that any merely human effort to present the great immolation on Calvary would be utterly eclipsed by the holy sacrifice of the Mass, thus rendering such attempts fruitless.[15] Nevertheless, the subject was sometimes presented, no doubt inspired in part, by the chanting of the gospel accounts of the passion during Holy Week.[16] The earliest of the surviving medieval religious dramas of the West to venture a portrayal of our Lord's sufferings on Calvary is the twelfth-century Monte Cassino Passion Play from the Italian Benedictine Monastery of this name.[17] A brief excerpt from the text of this play demonstrates how the drama follows but also elaborates on the gospel narratives ("stage directions" are in italics); here we encounter a moving addendum to our Lord's conversation with the Good Thief (Lk 23:39-43):

. . . and continuing on let the robber say to Jesus:
"Lord, remember me when you shall come to the kingdom of
God where you rule forever."
and let Jesus answer him and say:
"Amen, I say to you, thief, you will come
with me today into holy paradise.
    . . . the mother . . . standing with John and the other women
before the cross . . . toward him . . . as if showing him the womb in
which she carried Christ . . . calls out to her crucified son with a
powerful cry, and says before the armed men:
"*. . . .* Why did I carry you in my womb, when I see you dying
now. Remember <u>me</u> in your kingdom" [emphasis added].[18]

The Passion Play achieved its greatest development during the
fifteenth and early sixteenth centuries.[19] Often these dramas encompassed not only the passion, but also the resurrection and other events
of our Lord's public ministry as well; in some cases even Old Testament
scenes were included as "prefigurations."[20] The Lucerne Passion Plays
of Switzerland covered the entire sweep of Salvation history from the
creation of mankind to the Descent of the Holy Spirit on Pentecost; the
Passion Play at Bozen (Bavaria) took seven days to perform.[21] The
earliest Passion Plays seem to have been performed by the clergy, but
by the later Middle Ages pius confraternities had become responsible
for the production of these dramas, which were actually viewed as a
form of worship. Usually the stage was set up in a public square; some
productions required the participation of over two hundred actors.[22]
    Passion Plays went into a sharp decline during the sixteenth
century, largely through the introduction of vulgar nonreligious elements into the dramas that vitiated the formerly sacred character of
these productions; the Reformation likewise contributed to their suppression.[23] Yet the Passion Play did manage to survive in some remote
hamlets and in the monasteries, especially in Bavaria and Austria. Thus
it is that in 1633 we discover the earliest mention of the most renowned
Passion Play of all, that of the southern Bavarian village of Oberammergau, where the townspeople had made a vow to perform the play every
ten years if they were relieved from the ravages of the Black Death. The
oldest extant text of this play is thought to date from about 1600, but it
has undergone numerous revisions over the last four centuries;[24] the
latest production was mounted in 1990.
    Closely related to the medieval Passion Play was an extralitur-

gical composition known as the *Planctus,* a lament delivered by one of those present on Calvary as an expression of their sentiments on this occasion. Usually the speaker is the Blessed Virgin herself, expressing her grief as she watches her Son suffer and die on the cross; such is the case with the earliest extant examples, which like the Monte Cassino Passion Play date from the twelfth century.[25] Among the most important of these Marian laments is the *Planctus ante nescia* (twelfth century), which is thought to have exerted a major influence on the development of the Passion Play. In this piece the Blessed Virgin expresses her grief in the very first verse and then addresses her Son, speaking of their mutual suffering. After mentioning Simeon's prophecy of the sword that would pierce her heart, she appeals to death to take her in place of her Son. She ends by seeking compassion from the women of Jerusalem.[26] In other examples of the *Planctus* we find something of a dialogue with more than one speaker, as in a text from a book published in Venice in 1523 (the *Planctus* it contains is undoubtedly older than the sixteenth century). The lament opens with Mary appealing to those passing by for sympathy, evocative of a passage from the Lamentations of Jeremiah (Lam 1:12); she then begs mercy from the judges and implores the Apostle John to intervene on her Son's behalf, but the Apostle responds by gently reproving her for increasing her Son's sufferings by giving way to her grief. She cannot help but continue her lament. Finally our Lord speaks to her, declaring John her new son and entrusting her to his care, as described in the gospel (Jn 19:25-27).[27] The *Planctus* was often associated with the various rites of Good Friday. Thus we find that it was sung following the ninth responsory of Matins during *Tenebrae* on Good Friday at the Cathedral of Palma on Mallorca (fourteenth century); evidence suggests that there was a similar practice during the thirteenth century in Toulouse, France.[28] The Mallorcan *Planctus* was performed by three singers vested in black or violet dalmatics and with their faces veiled. They would proceed through the church in three stages: during each stage one of them would chant a stanza, after which all three genuflected and sang a refrain. Upon reaching the sanctuary they entered the pulpit and there each sang two additional stanzas for a total of nine verses; when the *Planctus* was completed, the Office of Lauds was begun.[29] The *Planctus* could also appear within the context of the Good Friday Veneration of the Cross, as at Regensburg (Germany) in the fifteenth century, where it was sung by two clerics (representing the Blessed Virgin and Saint John) following the unveiling of the cross.[30] In Italy the *Planctus* was incorporated into extraliturgical commemorations of the Burial of Christ, and exerted an influence on the development of these rites in southern Europe, where the image of Our Lady of Sorrows was to become an integral element of Good Friday processions in the centuries that followed (see chapter IX).

A Good Friday Tradition of Corsica

On the Mediterranean island of Corsica, in the town of Sartene (1962), a sort of Passion Play has been held each year on this day since the Middle Ages. In an outdoor procession known as the *Catenacciu*, an actor in the role of Christ carries a heavy cross and drags a long, burdensome chain (*catena*) as he walks barefoot along the cobblestone pavement. In past centuries the men chosen to assume the parts of Christ and of Simon the Cyrenean were criminals seeking to expiate their crimes with this penitential exercise. Their identities were concealed and recorded in a padlocked book to which only the parish priests had access.[31]

Now with him they were also leading out two other criminals to be executed.

[Lk 23:32; JB]

Midmorning on Good Friday: Points for Meditation

The Trial Before Pilate

I shall proclaim your decrees to kings without fear of disgrace.
[Ps 119:46; JB]

Then they led Jesus from the house of Caiaphas to the praetorium. It was early. They themselves did not enter the praetorium, so that they might not be defiled, but might eat the passover. So Pilate went out to them and said, "What accusation do you bring against this man?" They answered him, "If this man were not an evildoer, we would not have handed him over."

[Jn 18:28-30]

In return for my friendship, they denounce me,
though all I had done was pray for them;
they pay me back evil for kindness
and hatred for friendship.

[Ps 109:4-5; JB]

Pilate said to them, "Take him yourselves and judge him by your own law." The Jews said to him, "It is not lawful for us to put any man to death."

[Jn 18:31]

Now arrogant men, God, are attacking me,
a brutal gang hounding me to death:
people to whom you mean nothing.

[Ps 86:14; JB]

And they began to accuse him, saying, "We found this man perverting our nation, and forbidding us to give tribute to Caesar, and saying that he himself is Christ a king."

[Lk 23:2]

Lying witnesses take the stand . . .
they repay my kindness with evil,
there is desolation in my soul.

[Ps 35:11-12; JB]

Now Jesus stood before the governor; and the governor asked him, "Are you the King of the Jews?" Jesus said to him, "You have said so." But when he was accused by the chief priests and elders, he made no answer. Then Pilate said to him, "Do you not hear how many things they testify against you?" But he gave him no answer, not even to a single charge; so that the governor wondered greatly.

[Mt 27:11-14]

Pilate entered the praetorium again and called Jesus, and said to him, "Are you the King of the Jews?" Jesus answered, "Do you say this of your own accord, or did others say it to you about me?" Pilate answered, "Am I a Jew? Your own nation and the chief priests have handed you over to me; what have you done?"

[Jn 18:33-35]

Though princes put me on trial,
your servant will meditate
on your statutes. . . .

[Ps 119:23; JB]

Jesus answered, "My kingship is not of this world; if my kingship
were of this world, my servants would fight, that I might not be handed
over to the Jews; but my kingship is not from the world." Pilate said
to him, "So you are a king?" Jesus answered, "You say that I am a
king. For this I was born, and for this I have come into the world, to
bear witness to the truth. Every one who is of the truth hears my voice."
Pilate said to him, "What is truth?"

[Jn 18:36-38]

The fool says in his heart,
"There is no God!"

[Ps 14:1; JB]

And Pilate said to the chief priests and the multitudes, "I find no
crime in this man." But they were urgent, saying, "He stirs up the
people, teaching throughout all Judea, from Galilee even to this place."

[Lk 23:4-5]

They have turned to me their back
and not their face; and though
I have taught them persistently
they have not listened
to receive instruction.

[Jer 32:33]

When Pilate heard this, he asked whether the man was a Galilean. And
when he learned that he belonged to Herod's jurisdiction, he sent him over
to Herod, who was himself in Jerusalem at that time. When Herod saw
Jesus, he was very glad, for he had long desired to see him, because he had
heard about him, and he was hoping to see some sign done by him. So he
questioned him at some length; but he made no answer. The chief priests
and the scribes stood by, vehemently accusing him. And Herod with his
soldiers treated him with contempt and mocked him; then, arraying him
in gorgeous apparel, he sent him back to Pilate.

[Lk 23:6-11]

Now therefore, O kings, be wise;
be warned, O rulers of the earth.
Serve the Lord with fear,
with trembling kiss his feet,
lest he be angry, and you perish in the way;
for his wrath is quickly kindled.

[Ps 2:10-11]

Now at the feast the governor was accustomed to release for the crowd any one prisoner whom they wanted. And they had then a notorious prisoner, called Barabbas. So when they had gathered, Pilate said to them, "Whom do you want me to release for you, Barabbas or Jesus who is called Christ?" For he knew that it was out of envy that they had delivered him up.

[Mt 27:15-18]

Israel loved Joseph more than all his other sons. . . . But his brothers, seeing how his father loved him more than all his other sons, came to hate him. . . .

[Gen 37:3-4; JB]

. . . while he was sitting on the judgment seat, his wife sent word to him, "Have nothing to do with that righteous man, for I have suffered much over him today in a dream."

[Mt 27:19]

Immediately the fingers of a man's hand appeared and wrote on the plaster of the wall of the king's palace, opposite the lampstand; and the king saw the hand as it wrote. Then the king's colour changed, and his thoughts alarmed him. . . .

[Dan 5:5-6]

Now the chief priests and the elders persuaded the people to ask for Barabbas and destroy Jesus. The governor again said to them, "Which of the two do you want me to release for you?" And they said, "Barabbas." Pilate said to them, "Then what shall I do with Jesus who is called Christ?" They all said, "Let him be crucified." And he said, "Why, what evil has he done?" But they shouted all the more, "Let him be crucified."

[Mt 27:20-23]

All are lurking for blood. . . .

[Mic 7:2; JB]

So when Pilate saw that he was gaining nothing, but rather that a riot was beginning, he took water and washed his hands before the crowd, saying, "I am innocent of this righteous man's blood; see to it yourselves."

[Mt 27:24]

Though you wash yourself with lye
and use much soap,
the stain of your guilt is still before me. . . .

[Jer 2:22]

And all the people answered, "His blood be on us and on our children!"

[Mt 27:25]

They have set their faces harder than rock,
they have refused to repent.

[Jer 5:3b; JB]

Then he released for them Barabbas. . . .

[Mt 27:26]

. . . you denied the Holy and Righteous One,
and asked for a murderer to be granted to you,
and killed the Author of life. . . .

[Acts 3:14-15]

The Scourging at the Pillar

But he was wounded for our transgressions,
he was bruised for our iniquities. . .
and with his stripes we are healed.

[Is 53:5]

Then Pilate took Jesus and scourged him.

[Jn 19:1]

A herd of bulls surrounds me,
strong bulls of Bashan close in on me;
their jaws are agape for me,
like lions tearing and roaring.

[Ps 22:12-13; JB]

I offered my back to those who struck me. . . .

[Is 50:6; JB]

. . . strangers I never even knew
with loud cries tear me to pieces. . . .

[Ps 35:15; JB]

How many times will you come rushing at a man, all of you, to bring him down like a wall already leaning over, like a rampart undermined?

[Ps 62:3; JB]

He has wasted my flesh and skin away. . . .

[Lam 3:4; JB]

In my back he has planted his darts. . . .

[Lam 3:13; JB]

He has torn me in his wrath. . .
. . . he set me up as his target,
his archers surround me. . . .
He breaks me with breach upon breach. . . .

[Job 16:9,12-14]

. . . I am worn out with the blows you deal me.

[Ps 39:10; JB]

. . . there is no soundness in my flesh. . . .

[Ps 38:7; JB]

Why is thy apparel red,
and thy garments like his that
treads in the wine press?
"I have trodden the wine press alone,

and from the peoples no one was with me . . .
their lifeblood is sprinkled upon my garments,
and I have stained all my raiment.
For . . . my year of redemption has come.
I looked, but there was no one to help;
I was appalled, but there was no one to uphold;
so my own arm brought me victory. . . ."

[Is 63:2-5]

The Crowning With Thorns

They surround me like a flood all day long;
they close in upon me together.

[Ps 88:17]

Then the soldiers of the governor took Jesus into the praetorium, and
they gathered the whole battalion before him. And they stripped him
and put a scarlet robe upon him, and plaiting a crown of thorns they
put it on his head, and put a reed in his right hand.

[Mt 27:27-29]

He has made a yoke for me,
has encircled my head with weariness.

[Lam 3:5; JB]

He has filled my paths
with briars and torn me,
he has made me a thing of horror.

[Lam 3:11; JB]

And kneeling before him they mocked him. . . .

[Mt 27:29]

They surrounded me,
surrounded me on every side. . . .
They surrounded me like bees,
they blazed like a fire of thorns. . . .

[Ps 118:12]

. . . they came up to him, saying, "Hail, King of the Jews!" and struck him with their hands.

[Jn 19:3]

Men have gaped at me with their mouth,
they have struck me insolently upon the cheek,
they mass themselves together against me.
God gives me up to the ungodly,
and casts me into the hands of the wicked.

[Job 16:10-11]

And they spat upon him, and took the reed and struck him on the head.

[Mt 27:30]

I have become a byword among the people,
and a creature on whose face to spit.

[Job 17:6; JB]

Pilate went out again, and said to them, "Behold, I am bringing him out to you, that you may know that I find no crime in him."

[Jn 19:4]

. . . I am a worm, and no man. . . .

[Ps 22:6]

The Verdict

Who is this coming from Edom,
from Bozrah in garments
stained with crimson. . . ?

[Is 63:1; JB]

So Jesus came out, wearing the crown of thorns and the purple robe. Pilate said to them, "Here is the man!"

[Jn 19:5]

. . . he had no form or comeliness
that we should look at him,
and no beauty that we should desire him.

[196]

He was despised and rejected by men;
a man of sorrows, and acquainted with grief;
and as one from whom men hide their faces
he was despised, and we esteemed him not.

[Is 53:2-3]

When the chief priests and the officers saw him, they cried out,
"Crucify him, crucify him!"

[Jn 19:6]

To every one of my oppressors I am contemptible,
loathsome to my neighbors,
to my friends a thing of fear.

[Ps 31:11; JB]

Pilate said to them, "Take him yourselves and crucify him, for I find
no crime in him." The Jews answered him, "We have a law, and by
that law he ought to die, because he has made himself the Son of God."

[Jn 19:6-7]

When the waters saw thee, O God,
when the waters saw thee, they were afraid,
yea, the deep trembled.

[Ps 77:16]

When Pilate heard these words, he was the more afraid; he entered
the praetorium again and said to Jesus, "Where are you from?"

[Jn 19:8-9]

God came from Teman,
and the Holy One from Mount Paran.
His glory covered the heavens,
and the earth was full of his praise.

[Hab 3:3]

But Jesus gave no answer. Pilate therefore said to him, "You will
not speak to me? Do you not know that I have power to release you,
and power to crucify you?" Jesus answered him, "You would have no
power over me unless it had been given you from above. . . ."

[Jn 19:9-11]

[197]

As the crowds were appalled on seeing him —
so disfigured did he look
that he seemed no longer human —
so will the crowds be astonished at him,
and kings stand speechless before him. . . .

[Is 52:14-15; JB]

Upon this Pilate sought to release him, but the Jews cried out, "If
you release this man, you are not Caesar's friend; every one who makes
himself a king sets himself against Caesar."

[Jn 19:12]

For now they will say:
"We have no king,
for we fear not the Lord,
and a king, what could he do for us?"

[Hos 10:3]

When Pilate heard these words, he brought Jesus out and sat down
on the judgment seat at a place called The Pavement, and in Hebrew,
Gabbatha. Now it was the day of Preparation of the Passover; it was
about the sixth hour. He said to the Jews, "Here is your King!" They
cried out, "Away with him, away with him, crucify him!" Pilate said
to them, "Shall I crucify your King?" The chief priests answered, "We
have no king but Caesar."

[Jn 19:13-15]

They hunted me . . .
they who hate me for no reason.
They tumbled my life into a pit,
they threw stones down on me.
The waters went over my head;
I said, "I am lost."

[Lam 3:52-54; JB]

Then he handed him over to them to be crucified.

[Jn 19:16]

Thou goest, our Propitiation, to be slain for all! And doth not Peter
come to Thee, he who said he would die with Thee? Hath Thomas left

Thee, who said, Let us die with Him? What, not one of them? But Thou art led away to death alone, Thou who hast preserved me in chastity, My Son and My God! Though they promised that they would go with Thee into prison and to death, they have forsaken Thee and fled!

[Responsory, Medieval Office of Holy Saturday][32]

The Carrying of the Cross

And Abraham took the wood of the burnt offering, and laid it on Isaac his son; and he took in his hand the fire and the knife. . . . And Isaac said to his father Abraham, "My father!" And he said, "Here am I, my son." He said, "Behold, the fire and the wood; but where is the lamb for a burnt offering?" Abraham said, "God will provide himself the lamb for a burnt offering, my son."

[Gen 22:6-8]

So they took Jesus, and he went out, bearing his own cross. . . .

[Jn 19:17]

I am the man familiar with misery . . .
I am the one he has driven and forced to walk
in darkness, and without any light . . .
. . . he has made my chains heavy . . .
He has blocked my ways with cut stones,
he has obstructed my paths . . .
He has broken my teeth with gravel,
he has given me ashes for food.

[Lam 3:1, 2, 7, 9, 16; JB]

Those who see me in the street hurry past me. . . .

[Ps 31:11; JB]

. . . thy hand has come down on me.
. . .I am ready to fall,
and my pain is ever with me.

[Ps 38:2, 17]

Now I have fallen, they crowd around delighted,
flocking to jeer at me. . . .

[Ps 35:15; JB]

. . . thou dost lay me in the dust of death.

[Ps 22:15]

Surely he has borne our griefs
and carried our sorrows;
yet we esteemed him stricken,
smitten by God, and afflicted . . .
upon him was the chastisement that made us whole. . . .
All we like sheep have gone astray;
we have turned every one to his own way;
and the Lord has laid on him
the iniquity of us all.

[Is 53:4-6]

I was pressed, pressed, about to fall,
but Yahweh came to my help. . . .

[Ps 118:13; JB]

And they compelled a passer-by, Simon of Cyrene, who was coming in
from the country, the father of Alexander and Rufus, to carry his cross.

[Mk 15:21]

"If any man would come after me, let him deny himself and take up
his cross daily and follow me. For whoever would save his life will lose
it; and whoever loses his life for my sake, he will save it."

[Lk 9:23-24]

And there followed him a great multitude of the people, and of
women who bewailed and lamented him.

[Lk 23:27]

My eyes weep ceaselessly,
without relief
until Yahweh looks down
and sees. . . .

[Lam 3:49-50; JB]

But Jesus turning to them said, "Daughters of Jerusalem, do not weep for me, but weep for yourselves and for your children. For behold, the days are coming when they will say, 'Blessed are the barren, and the wombs that never bore, and the breasts that never gave suck!' Then they will begin to say to the mountains, 'Fall on us'; and to the hills, 'Cover us.' For if they do this when the wood is green, what will happen when it is dry?"

[Lk 23:28-31]

Take up weeping and wailing for the mountains,
and a lamentation for the pastures of the wilderness,
because they are laid waste
so that no one passes through,
and the lowing of cattle is not heard;
both the birds of the air and the beasts
have fled and are gone.

[Jer 9:10]

". . . he who does not take his cross
and follow me is not worthy of me."

[Mt 10:38]

Down in the dust I lie prostrate:
revive me as your word has guaranteed.

[Ps 119:25; JB]

"If any one serves me, he must follow me;
and where I am, there shall my servant be also. . . ."

[Jn 12:26]

. . . . The shadow of the cross
He bears falls upon her
through the dim day's glow.
Wrapped in blue, calm,
with stately tread
she follows close,
close — so very close
she feels the terrible heat
of His tortured heart
upon her own.

[201]

Her shoulders shrink
beneath her gown
as He stumbles and falls
and the tree sinks deep
in open wounds.
But no sign of pain
mirrors in her cold
still face;
No gasping cry parts
her carved, white lips.
He is silent.
So is she. . . .

["Our Lady on Calvary," Sister Michael Marie][33]

. . . . Jesus too suffered outside the gate to sanctify the people with his own blood. Let us go to him, then, outside the camp, and share his degradation.

[Heb 13:12-13; JB]

Endnotes

1. Libretto, Act III, excerpts, Lionel Salter, tr., in *Parsifal*, Herbert Von Karajan, cond., Berlin Philharmonic, Deutsche Grammophon, pp. 47, 50.
2. "Participation in the Paschal Mystery" (Talk at General Audience), March 27, 1991, #3, in *L'Osservatore Romano*, April 2, 1991, p. 11.
3. *The Hours of the Divine Office in English and Latin: Vol. Two: Passion Sunday to August*, Liturgical Press, 1964, pp. 154-155.
4. Liturgical texts taken from *The Office of Readings*, Daughters of St. Paul, 1983, pp. 475-480, and *Christian Prayer: The Liturgy of the Hours*, Liturgical Press, 1976, pp. 358-362.
5. Stanbrook Abbey, Callow End, England. Reprinted with permission.
6. *Caeremoniale Episcoporum* (1886 ed.), Liber II, Cap. XXII, #13, p. 238.
7. Castelar, quoted in "Some Non-Believers on Easter in Rome," *The Catholic World*, April 1885, pp. 120-121.
8. *Patrologia Latina*, Vol. 78, col. 953c.
9. *Les Ordines Romani du Haut Moyen Age: III: Les Textes (Ordines XIV-XXXIV)* (Etudes et Documents, Vol. 24), Michel Andrieu, ed., 1961, p. 269.

10. Romanus Rios, OSB, "The Great Antiphon of the *Triduum Domini*," *Clergy Review*, Vol. 23, 1943, pp. 161-162; see also *Regularis Concordia: The Monastic Agreement of the Monks and Nuns of the English Nation* (Medieval Classics), Dom Thomas Symons, tr., 1953, pp. 36-37.
11. Based upon G. Cyprian Alston, "Way of the Cross," *Catholic Encyclopedia*, 1907, Vol. 15, pp. 569-571, except where noted otherwise.
12. *L'Attivita Della Santa Sede, Nel 1988*, Libreria Editrice Vaticana, p. 236.
13. Ibid.
14. Ibid.
15. Karl Young, *The Drama of the Medieval Church*, 1933, Vol. I, p. 492.
16. Robert Edwards, *The Monte Cassino Passion and the Poetics of Medieval Drama*, 1977, p. 23.
17. Ibid., p. 1.
18. Ibid., pp. 20-21.
19. Anselm Salzer, "Passion Plays," *Catholic Encyclopedia*, 1907, Vol. 11, p. 533.
20. Ibid., pp. 532-533.
21. Ibid., p. 533.
22. Ibid.
23. Ibid.
24. Ibid., pp. 533-534.
25. Young, Vol. I, pp. 492-493, 496, 538.
26. Ibid., Vol. I, pp. 496-498.
27. Ibid., Vol. I, pp. 500-503.
28. For Toulouse see ibid., Vol. I, pp. 503, 698.
29. Richard Donovan, CSB, *The Liturgical Drama in Medieval Spain*, 1958 pp. 135-137.
30. Young, Vol. I, pp. 503-506.
31. Geoffrey Wagner, "The Catenacciu: Holy Week in Corsica," *The Tablet*, April 21, 1962, p. 375.
32. Tr. in Pierre Batiffol, *History of the Roman Breviary*, p. 94, footnote #1.
33. Excerpt, in *I Sing of a Maiden: The Mary Book of Verse*, Sister M. Therese, ed., p. 368.

(John Zierten)

VII

Noon on
Good Friday

"And as Moses lifted up the serpent in the wilderness, so must the Son of man be lifted up, that whoever believes in him may have eternal life."

[Jn 3:14-15]

The *Tre Ore*

Oh come and mourn with me awhile!
See, Mary calls us to her side;
Oh come and let us mourn with her;
Jesus, our Love, is crucified!

Seven times He spoke, seven words of love,
And all three hours His silence cried
For mercy on the souls of men;
Jesus, our Love, is crucified!

[Father Frederick William Faber][1]

THE *TRE ORE* ("THREE Hours"), a devotional service of meditation focusing upon our Lord's agony on the cross, and held during the early afternoon on Good Friday, first emerged in its current form in Peru during the seventeenth century, introduced by a native priest, Father Alonso Messia, SJ (1665-1732);[2] yet in spirit it harks back to the three-hour afternoon service held in Jerusalem on Good Friday over sixteen centuries ago (discussed earlier). In Egeria's account of the Jerusalem service, there is little mention of the specific readings used, but we are able to determine what these were from the *Armenian Lectionary*, which reflects the liturgy of the Holy City in the early fifth century (within half a century of Egeria's time). The service featured eight sets of readings; each of the first four sets consisted of a Psalm, an excerpt from an Old Testament book and a passage from the New Testament letters of Saint Paul. The last four sets of readings followed this same format but each ended with a passage from the gospel accounts of the passion. The actual selections for the eight sets were as follows:[3]

Psalm	Old Test. Book	Epistle	Gospel
Ps 35	Zech 11:11-14	Gal 6:14-18	—
Ps 38	Is 3:9b-15	Phil 2:5-11	—
Ps 41	Is 50:4-9	Rom 5:6-11	—
Ps 22	Amos 8:9-12	1 Cor 1:18-31	—
Ps 31	Is 52:13-53:12	Heb 2:11-18	Mt 27:1-56
Ps 69	Is 63:1-6	Heb 9:11-28	Mk 15:1-41
Ps 88	Jer 11:18-20	Heb 10:19-31	Lk 22:66-23:49
Ps 102	Zech 14:5-11	1 Tm 6:13-16	Jn 19:17-37

All of the selections above are particularly well-suited to the theme of the passion; in fact, both the passage from Isaiah and the Psalm included in the fifth set of readings are now used as the first lection and the responsorial psalm respectively at the afternoon Liturgy of the Passion in the Roman Rite (to be described later). The reader may also notice that many verses from the Old Testament passages and Psalms in the above list appear in the scriptural portions of the present volume.

Sacred Scripture likewise provided the basis for the *Tre Ore* as originally practiced in Peru. At noon a crucifix would be put on the altar, together with an appropriate number of lights. The priest presiding then enters the pulpit (or stands in front of the altar), and after making the sign of the cross and invoking the Holy Spirit, exhorts the faithful to participate fervently in this devotional exercise. The service focuses on the seven last words of Christ on the cross (Lk 23:34; Lk 23:43; Jn 19:26-27; Mt 27:46; Jn 19:28; Jn 19:30; Lk 23:46);[4] for each of these Last Words an address is given, after which the people kneel, sing a hymn, and say ten Our Fathers and ten Hail Marys. There is also a period of silence for each of the Seven Words, so that the faithful can engage in quiet meditation on the sufferings of Christ. Just before three o'clock the choir begins to sing the Creed, timed in such a way that the words *Crucifixus et mortuus est* are pronounced at the very moment when the hour strikes. At this point the priest rises from his place and exclaims in a loud but tender voice:

> *Jesus Christ is dead!*
> *Our Redeemer has expired!*
> *Our Father has ceased to live!*

The service ends with a concluding sermon, followed by recital of an Act of Contrition.[5]

> *Ye pious souls, rise up and go,*
> *With grateful penitence aglow,*
> *With me to Golgotha, and see*
> *What shall be done your souls to free*
> *See how the Mediator dies*
> *The atoning death of sacrifice.*
>
> [*Oberammergau Passion Play*, 1930][6]

The *Tre Ore* service soon spread from Peru to other Latin American countries, such as Chile, Ecuador, Colombia, and Mexico; it also appeared in Italy and Spain, and thereafter, in the United States and England.[7] In the various places where the *Tre Ore* was adopted, efforts were made to enhance the dramatic setting provided for the service by the stripped altars and shrouded statues that characterized the church interior on Good Friday. This penchant for the dramatic is evident in the eyewitness accounts of the *Tre Ore* that follow. Our first example comes from the pen of the famous Austrian composer Franz Joseph Haydn, who has left us a description of the *Tre Ore* as observed in the Spanish city of Cadiz:

About fifteen years ago (1786) I was requested by a canon of Cadiz to compose instrumental music on The Seven Last Words of our Saviour on the Cross. It was customary at the Cathedral of Cadiz to produce an oratorio every year during Lent, the effect of the performance being not a little enhanced by the following circumstances. The walls, windows, and pillars of the church were hung with black cloth, and only one large lamp hanging from the center of the roof broke the solemn darkness. At midday, the doors were closed and the ceremony began. After a short service the bishop ascended the pulpit, pronounced the first of the seven words (or sentences) and delivered a discourse thereon. This ended, he left the pulpit, and prostrated himself before the altar. The interval was filled by music. The bishop then in like manner pronounced the second word, then the third, and so on, the orchestra following on the conclusion of each discourse.[8]

Our Lord Jesus Christ placed as our Heavenly Master on the seat of the Cross, and having till then kept a profound silence, opened His Divine lips to teach the world in seven words the most sublime doctrine of His love.

[Father Alonso Messia, SJ][9]

Spain is also the setting for our second example of the *Tre Ore*. In nineteenth-century Madrid, the service was held each year beginning at noon in the Chapel Royal:

The Chapel Royal is so dark that on entering one can see literally nothing. After awhile, however, as the eyes become accustomed to the darkness, one begins to distinguish, far in the distance, the outlines of

three life-sized crucified figures, our Saviour between the two thieves.
The altar has been taken away, and nothing is to be seen but mountains
and rocks behind the three mournful figures. After each "word" is
preached the choir sings, to full orchestral accompaniment, Haydn's
"Seven Words."

During the last, "Into thy hands I commend my spirit," there is a
rolling as of thunder, and flashes as of lightning through the church.[10]

Heywood Broun gives us a picture of the *Tre Ore* in twentieth-
century Venezuela (1939):

Some few years ago I went on a spring cruise. The steamer
touched the northern tip of South America and paused for a day at
the port so that the passengers might travel up the mountain to
Caracas. When we reached Venezuela word came that Gomez, the
old dictator, lay dying in the capital. And, as we went up the wind-
ing road, . . . I noticed that all those who walked along the highway
were clad in black or purple. Young and old all seemed to be hurry-
ing to some central point. And, naturally, it was my notion that
they were hurrying to the palace to learn the fate of Gomez. . . .

But at the door of the cathedral the driver stopped and said
something to my companion. My friend translated and explained,
"The driver says this is the service to mark the three hours of agony
on the cross."

And it came to me that they mourned not for Gomez, but for
the Son of God. Out of bright sunlight I came into cool darkness
flecked, but not wholly broken, by the light of many flickering
candles. And all about the walls and statues and across the
shoulders of the worshipers I saw the Holy Week badge of purple.

I have seen church services in far and near places, and many
were impressive, but here for the first time I saw a people who
seemed to feel that the Passion of the Lord was actually occurring
again.

Pilate was not a famous dead procurator of Judea who washed
his hands in an ancient city long ago. It was but yesterday that
Jesus stood before the Romans on trial for His life and was con-
demned. And at the very moment the living Christ hung on the
cross.

An Indian woman, older than any being I had ever seen before,
lifted her head from the floor as she prayed that death should not

achieve its victory. Children in their purple smocks looked at the
dancing lights and wondered. But they were silent.

It was as if some one of their own lay dying in a room at home.
And all of them lived in a world in which each year Jesus again
walked the earth and Judas brought betrayal in a pleasant garden.
Many stood outside upon the steps under the hot sun and peered
through the doors and down the dark aisles. They waited for some
word from the mourners. Almost they seemed to say, "What is the
news? How fares our Lord on Calvary?"[11]

In a relatively recent account from 1972 we learn that in the Philippines, where the weather is unbearably hot and humid on Good Friday, the faithful nonetheless pack the large Spanish-built churches for the *Tre Ore* service. In the sanctuary a huge crucifix is erected, twenty-five to thirty feet in height, featuring a life-size image of the crucified. Each of the seven Last Words from the gospels is first chanted once, after which the customary sermon expanding upon it is delivered. Following each sermon the choir sings, and then the gospel verse is chanted once more. At three o'clock the head of the corpus on the crucifix is made to tip forward, to the sound of thunder.[12]

O Father . . . remember not, O Lord, that they have crucified Me,
but rather that I die for them: — instead of their sins, remember My
love. . . .

[Father Alonso Messia, SJ][13]

A Good Friday Custom of Pope John Paul II. Each year on Good Friday, during the early afternoon, Pope John Paul II enters a confessional in Saint Peter's Basilica and there applies the merits of our Lord's sufferings on the cross to the souls that come to him to receive the Sacrament of Penance. On Good Friday of 1988, for example, the Holy Father began hearing confessions shortly after noon and continued until half past one, administering the sacrament to eleven men and women from four different countries.[14]

. . . without the shedding of blood there is no forgiveness of sins.

[Heb 9:22]

On the Cross: Points for Meditation

See, my servant shall prosper,
he shall be lifted up, exalted,
rise to great heights.

[Is 52:13; JB]

And when they came to the place which is called The Skull, there
they crucified him. . . .

[Lk 23:33]

Soften your branches, noble tree,
relax your taut fibers
and let your natural hardness
give way to yielding suppleness,
and so offer yourself as a gentle support
for the body of the King of heaven.

[*Pange, lingua, gloriosi*, verse 9][15]

He has bent his bow and taken aim,
making me the target for his arrows.

[Lam 3:12; JB]

. . . they have pierced
my hands and feet. . . .

[Ps 22:16]

Your arrows have pierced deep. . . .

[Ps 38:2; JB]

Then marked I the Maker of mankind
Hastened with courage high,
me He would mount.
There then I durst not
against the decree of God
Bow nor break.
I beheld tremble
The face of the earth. . .
The young Hero stripped Him there,
He that was mighty God,

Strong and stout-hearted,
strode He up to the gallows of shame,
Steadfast in sight of all;
man He would save.
I trembled as tenderly this Man touched me
nor dared I however to bow to earth.
A rood I was raised;
aloft I lifted the King of rank,
Lord of high heaven,
nor dared to bow.

[*The Dream of the Rood*][16]

"When you have lifted up the Son of man,
then you will know that I am he. . . ."

[Jn 8:28]

So when Joseph came to his brothers,
they stripped him of his robe,
the long robe with sleeves that he wore;
and they took him and cast him into a pit.

[Gen 37:23-24]

When the soldiers had crucified Jesus they took his garments and
made four parts, one for each soldier; also his tunic.

[Jn 19:23]

He has stripped from me my glory. . . .

[Job 19:9]

But the tunic was without seam, woven from top to bottom; so they
said to one another, "Let us not tear it, but cast lots for it to see whose
it shall be."

[Jn 19:23-24]

. . . they divide my garments among them
and cast lots for my clothes.

[Ps 22:18; JB]

Pilate also wrote a title and put it on the cross; it read, "Jesus of
Nazareth, the King of the Jews." Many of the Jews read this title, for

the place where Jesus was crucified was near the city; and it was written in Hebrew, in Latin, and in Greek. The chief priests of the Jews then said to Pilate, "Do not write, 'The King of the Jews,' but, 'This man said, I am King of the Jews.'" Pilate answered, "What I have written I have written."

[Jn 19:19-22]

And you, who were dead in trespasses and the uncircumcision of your flesh, God made alive together with him, having forgiven us all our trespasses, having cancelled the bond which stood against us with its legal demands; this he set aside, nailing it to the cross.

[Col 2:13-14]

And they shall say to him: What are these wounds in the midst of thy hands? And he shall say: With these I was wounded in the house of them that loved me.

[Zech 13:6][17]

"Father, forgive them; for they know not what they do."

[Lk 23:34]

He who suspended the earth is himself suspended; he who fixed the heavens is himself transfixed; he who made all things fast is made fast upon the tree. The Master has been outraged. God has been slaughtered. The King of Israel has been slain by Israel's right hand.

O strange murder! O strange injustice! The Master has been insulted, his body stripped naked, and he has not been deemed worthy of a covering to keep him concealed. That is why the lights of heaven have been turned off, and the day darkened, to hide him who was naked on the cross, to drape, not the body of the Lord, but the eyes of mankind.

[Saint Melito of Sardis][18]

"And on that day," says the Lord God,
"I will make the sun go down at noon,
and darken the earth in broad daylight."

[Amos 8:9]

Now from the sixth hour there was darkness over all the land until the ninth hour.

[Mt 27:45]

I dress the heavens in black,
make sackcloth their covering.

[Is 50:3; JB]

We looked for light and all is darkness,
for brightness and we walk in the dark.
Like the blind we feel our way along walls
and hesitate like men without eyes.
We stumble as though noon were twilight. . . .

[Is 59:9-10; JB]

Tell us, sun, why did you darken your rays when the Lord was crucified? Was it that the crucified one was a mere man? Should you not have done the same when Abel the Just was put to death? . . . The sun exclaims: My Lord was crucified in the flesh. Terrified by the splendor of his divinity I withdrew my rays.

[Saint Proclus of Constantinople][19]

I am poured out like water,
and all my bones are out of joint;
my heart is like wax,
it is melted within my breast. . . .

[Ps 22:14]

More misfortunes beset me than I can count. . . .

[Ps 40:12; JB]

. . . evening, morning, noon, I complain, I groan. . . .

[Ps 55:17; JB]

I have no food but tears, day and night;
and all day long men say to me,
"Where is your God?"

[Ps 42:3; JB]

There were also many women there, looking on from afar, who had followed Jesus from Galilee, ministering to him; among whom were Mary Magdalene, and Mary the mother of James and Joseph, and the mother of the sons of Zebedee.

[Mt 27:55-56]

Yahweh, remember what has happened to us;
look on us and see our degradation.
We are orphans, we are fatherless;
our mothers are like widows.

[Lam 5:1, 3; JB]

. . . I have become an object of derision,
people shake their heads at me in scorn.

[Ps 109:25; JB]

. . . my enemies insult me all day long, those who used to praise me
now use me as a curse.

[Ps 102:8; JB]

All that pass by despoil him; he has become the scorn of his neighbours.

[Ps 89:41]

And those who passed by derided him, wagging their heads and
saying, "You who would destroy the temple and build it in three days,
save yourself! If you are the Son of God, come down from the cross."

[Mt 27:39-40]

More people hate me for no reason
than I have hairs on my head. . . .

[Ps 69:4; JB]

My enemies say of me in malice:
"When will he die, and his name perish?". . .
All who hate me whisper together about me;
they imagine the worst for me.
They say, "A deadly thing has fastened upon him;
he will not rise again from where he lies."

[Ps 41:5, 7-8]

So also the chief priests, with the scribes and elders, mocked him,
saying, "He saved others; he cannot save himself. He is the King of
Israel; let him come down now from the cross, and we will believe in
him. He trusts in God; let God deliver him now, if he desires him; for
he said, 'I am the Son of God.' "

[Mt 27:41-43]

... all who see me jeer at me,
they toss their heads and sneer,
"He relied on Yahweh, let Yahweh save him!
If Yahweh is his friend,
let him rescue him!"

[Ps 22:7-8; JB]

They open wide their mouths against me;
they say, "Aha, Aha!
our eyes have seen it!"

[Ps 35:21]

The soldiers also mocked him, coming up and offering him vinegar,
and saying, "If you are the King of the Jews, save yourself!"

[Lk 23:36-37]

They gave me poison for food,
and for my thirst
they gave me vinegar to drink.

[Ps 69:21]

One of the criminals who were hanged railed at him, saying, "Are
you not the Christ? Save yourself and us!" But the other rebuked him,
saying, "Do you not fear God, since you are under the same sentence
of condemnation? And we indeed justly; for we are receiving the due
reward of our deeds; but this man has done nothing wrong." And he
said, "Jesus, remember me when you come in your kingly power." And
he said to him, "Truly, I say to you, today you will be with me in
Paradise."

[Lk 23:39-43]

... I will not forget you.
Behold, I have graven you on the
palms of my hands. ...

[Is 49:15-16]

O new and unheard of happening! He is stretched out upon a Cross
Who by His word stretched out the heavens (Is. 51:13). He is held fast
in bonds Who has set the sand a bound for the sea (Jer. 5:22). He is
given gall to drink Who has given us wells of honey. He is crowned

[215]

with thorns Who has crowned the earth with flowers. With a reed they struck His Head Who of old struck Egypt with ten plagues, and submerged the head of Pharaoh in the waves. That countenance was spat upon at which the Cherubim dare not gaze.

[Saint Amphilochius of Iconium][20]

. . . whenever I heave a sigh,
my bones stick through my skin.

[Ps 102:5; JB]

I can count every one of my bones. . . .

[Ps 22:17; JB]

. . . there is no soundness in my flesh:
numbed and crushed and overcome,
my heart groans, I moan aloud.
. . . my heart is throbbing, my strength deserting me,
the light of my eyes itself has left me.

[Ps 38:7-8, 10; JB]

For my life is spent with sorrow, and my years with sighing; my strength fails because of my misery, and my bones waste away.

[Ps 31:10]

. . . all your waves, your breakers,
have rolled over me.

[Ps 42:7; JB]

But standing by the cross of Jesus were his mother, and his mother's sister, Mary the wife of Clopas, and Mary Magdalene.

[Jn 19:25]

In his winepress the Lord has trampled
the virgin daughter of Judah.

[Lam 1:15; JB]

Is it nothing to you, all you who pass by?
Look and see if there is any sorrow like my sorrow
which was brought upon me,
which the Lord inflicted

on the day of his fierce anger.
From on high he sent fire;
into my bones he made it descend;
he spread a net for my feet;
he turned me back;
he has left me stunned,
faint all the day long.

[Lam 1:12-13]

My eyes are spent with weeping;
my soul is in tumult;
my heart is poured out in grief. . . .

[Lam 2:11]

". . . a sword will pierce your own soul too — so that the secret thoughts of many may be laid bare."

[Lk 2:35; JB]

Woe is me, my mother, that you bore me, a man of strife and contention to the whole land! I have not lent, nor have I borrowed, yet all of them curse me.

[Jer 15:10]

When Jesus saw his mother, and the disciple whom he loved standing near, he said to his mother, "Woman, behold, your son!"

[Jn 19:26]

The man named his wife "Eve" because she was the mother of all those who live.

[Gen 3:20; JB]

Then he said to the disciple, "Behold, your mother!" And from that hour the disciple took her to his own home.

[Jn 19:27]

What can I say for you, to what compare you,
O daughter of Jerusalem?
What can I liken to you, that I may comfort you,
O virgin daughter of Zion?

For vast as the sea is your ruin;
who can restore you?

[Lam 2:13]

If they persecuted me,
they will persecute you too. . . .

[Jn 15:20; JB]

All who pass along the way
clap their hands at you;
they hiss and wag their heads
at the daughter of Jerusalem. . .
All your enemies
rail against you;
they hiss, they gnash their teeth,
they cry: "We have destroyed her!
Ah, this is the day we longed for;
now we have it; we see it!"

[Lam 2:15, 16]

Cry aloud to the Lord!
O daughter of Zion!
Let tears stream down like a torrent
day and night!
Give yourself no rest,
your eyes no respite!

[Lam 2:18]

Slain are mother here and Son,
Stricken by this blow as one,
Clasped in final union
On one cross of dread.

[Fra Jacopone da Todi][21]

"Behold, I am the handmaid of the Lord;
let it be to me according to your word."

[Lk 1:38]

I said, In the noontide of my days I must depart;
I am consigned to the gates of Sheol

for the rest of my years. . . .
My dwelling is plucked up and removed from me
like a shepherd's tent;
like a weaver I have rolled up my life
he cuts me off from the loom;
from day to night thou dost bring me to an end;
I cry for help until morning. . . .
Like a swallow or a crane I clamour,
I moan like a dove.
My eyes are weary with looking upward.
O Lord, I am oppressed;
be thou my security!

[Is 38:10, 12-14]

Save me, O God!
For the waters have come up to my neck.
I sink in deep mire, where there is no foothold;
I have come into deep waters,
and the flood sweeps over me.
I am weary with my crying; my throat is parched.
My eyes grow dim with waiting for my God.

[Ps 69:1-3]

He has given me my fill of bitterness,
he has made me drunk with wormwood.

[Lam 3:15; JB]

I have passed out of mind
like one who is dead;
I have become like a broken vessel.

[Ps 31:12]

. . . now darkness is my one companion left.

[Ps 88:18; JB]

And about the ninth hour Jesus cried with a loud voice, "Eli, Eli, la'ma sabach-tha'ni?" that is, "My God, my God, why hast thou forsaken me?"

[Mt 27:46]

My heart flutters,
dread makes me tremble,
the twilight I longed for
has become my horror.

[Is 21:4; JB]

And some of the bystanders hearing it said, "This man is calling Elijah."

[Mt 27:47]

Oh come and rescue me, God,
Yahweh come quickly and help me!

[Ps 70:1; JB]

Already the splendor of the Resurrection can be foreseen precisely
because the darkness of the Passion is almost at its height.

[Blessed Miguel Pro][22]

. . . my soul is all troubled,
my life is on the brink of Sheol;
I am numbered among those
who go down to the Pit,
a man bereft of strength:
a man alone, down among the dead,
among the slaughtered in their graves. . . .

[Ps 88:3-5; JB]

After this Jesus, knowing that all was now finished, said (to fulfil
the scripture), "I thirst."

[Jn 19:28]

. . . my strength is dried up like a potsherd,
and my tongue cleaves to my jaws. . . .

[Ps 22:15]

A bowl full of vinegar stood there; so they put a sponge full of the
vinegar on hyssop and held it to his mouth.

[Jn 19:29]

Didst thou feel thirst
more keenly than all that bitter pain?

[220]

Or rather, our salvation didst thou so thirst to gain?

[*Sarum Missal*, 1526][23]

But the others said, "Wait, let us see whether Elijah will come to save him."

[Mt 27:49]

My spirit is broken, my days are extinct,
the grave is ready for me.

[Job 17:1]

The Death of Our Lord

O saving hour of the Passion! O hour of None, favored with richest graces! O hour of hours! O beloved Spouse of souls, kiss us at this hour from thy cross, for the cross is the trophy of thy victory.

[*Oratio ad Nonam*, Gallican Liturgy][24]

. . . love is strong as death. . . .

[Sg 8:6]

When Jesus had received the vinegar, he said, "It is finished." . . .

[Jn 19:30]

The cords of death encompassed me. . .
the cords of Sheol entangled me,
the snares of death confronted me.

[Ps 18:4-5]

Then Jesus, crying with a loud voice, said, "Father, into thy hands I commit my spirit!"

[Lk 23:46]

From his temple he heard my voice,
and my cry to him reached his ears.

[Ps 18:6]

And having said this he breathed his last.

[Lk 23:46]

Then the earth reeled and rocked;
the foundations also of the mountains trembled
and quaked, because he was angry. . .
He reached from on high, he took me. . .
He delivered me from my strong enemy,
and from those who hated me. . . .

[Ps 18:7, 16-17]

And behold, the curtain of the temple was torn in two, from top to
bottom; and the earth shook, and the rocks were split. . . .

[Mt 27:51]

I looked to the earth, to see a formless waste;
to the heavens, and their light had gone.
I looked to the mountains, to see them quaking
and all the heights astir.

[Jer 4:23-24; JB]

Death on that mount have I endured
Through grievous fate.
Saw I the God of hosts
Stretched severely.
Darkness deepened,
Covered with clouds
the corpse of the King;
Shadow shrouded its splendor bright.
Wrapped in clouds wept all creation,
Wailed the King's death,
Christ on the cross.

[*The Dream of the Rood*][25]

For this the earth shall mourn,
and the heavens above be black. . . .

[Jer 4:28]

. . . for a short time the stars of heaven were falling when they viewed
stretched on the cross him who was before the morning star. For a time
the sun's fire was extinguished, the great Light of the world suffered
eclipse. Then the earth's rocks were rent, crying to ungrateful Israel:
you have not recognized the spiritual rock which you followed and from

which you drank (cf. 1 Cor 10:4). *The veil of the temple was rent in sympathy, bearing witness to the true High priest of the heavens, and the world would have been dissolved in confusion and fear at the passion if the great Jesus had not expired saying: Father, into your hands I commit my spirit (Luke 23:46). The whole universe trembled and quaked with fear. . . .*

[Saint Hippolytus][26]

. . . when they look on him whom they have pierced,
they shall mourn for him,
as one mourns for an only child,
and weep bitterly over him
as one weeps over a first-born.
On that day the mourning in Jerusalem
will be as great as the mourning
for Ha'dad-rim'mon in the plain of Megid'do.

[Zech 12:10-11]

When the centurion and those who were with him, keeping watch over Jesus, saw the earthquake and what took place, they were filled with awe, and said, "Truly this was the Son of God!"

[Mt 27:54]

Sunset to sunrise changes now,
For God doth make his world anew:
On the Redeemer's thorn-crown'd brow
The wonders of that dawn we view.

E'en though the sun withholds its light,
Lo! a more heav'nly lamp shines here,
And from the cross on Calvary's height
Gleams of eternity appear.

Here in o'erwhelming final strife
The Lord of life hath victory;
And sin is slain, and death brings life,
And sons of earth hold heav'n in fee.

[*Sunset to Sunrise*, Saint Clement of Alexandria][27]

And all the multitudes who assembled to see the sight, when they saw what had taken place, returned home beating their breasts.

[Lk 23:48]

He was the true peacemaker, reconciling the world to God. From His cross comes the peace given by all the absolutions of nineteen centuries. From His cross comes the peace procured through every Mass to the end of time. The peace of the Crucified can make every desolation sweet, every weakness strong.

[Reginold Garrigou-Lagrange, OP][28]

Since it was the day of Preparation, in order to prevent the bodies from remaining on the cross on the sabbath (for that sabbath was a high day), the Jews asked Pilate that their legs might be broken, and that they might be taken away. So the soldiers came and broke the legs of the first, and of the other who had been crucified with him; but when they came to Jesus and saw that he was already dead, they did not break his legs.

[Jn 19:31-33]

He keeps all his bones;
not one of them is broken.

[Ps 34:20]

On that day there shall be a fountain opened for the house of David and the inhabitants of Jerusalem to cleanse them from sin and uncleanness.

[Zech 13:1]

But one of the soldiers pierced his side with a spear, and at once there came out blood and water.

[Jn 19:34]

. . . and behold, water was issuing from below the threshold of the temple toward the east (for the temple faced east) . . . and the water was coming out on the south side.

[Ez 47:1, 2]

He who saw it has borne witness — his testimony is true, and he knows that he tells the truth — that you also may believe.

[Jn 19:35]

. . . so everything will live where the river goes. . . . And on the banks, on both sides of the river, there will grow all kinds of trees for food. Their leaves will not wither nor their fruit fail, but they will bear fresh fruit every month, because the water for them flows from the sanctuary. Their fruit will be for food, and their leaves for healing.

[Ez 47:9, 12]

. . . the thorns, nails and lance pierce
His tender body; water and blood flow out.
In this stream the whole world, earth,
sea and sky are purified.

[*Pange, lingua, gloriosi*, verse 7][29]

So the Lord God caused a deep sleep to fall upon the man, and while he slept took one of his ribs and closed up its place with flesh. . . .

[Gen 2:21]

If you desire further proof of the power of this blood, remember where it came from, how it ran down from the cross, flowing from the Master's side. . . . Now the water was a symbol of baptism and the blood, of the holy eucharist. The soldier pierced the Lord's side, he breached the wall of the sacred temple, and I have found the treasure and made it my own. . .
. . . . Since the symbols of baptism and the eucharist flowed from his side, it was from his side that Christ fashioned the Church, as he had fashioned Eve from the side of Adam. . . . God took the rib when Adam was in a deep sleep, and in the same way Christ gave us the blood and the water after his own death.

[Saint John Chrysostom][30]

Rivers of blood most precious
the Saviour's fountains give;
With speedy steps run hither,
O sinner's soul, and live.

[*Sarum Missal*, 1526][31]

Endnotes

1. *Jesus Crucified*, vs. 1, 5, *Hymns*, American ed., Murphy & Co., 1880, pp. 113,114.
2. Father Herbert Thurston, SJ, "The Devotion of the 'Three Hours,' " *The Month*, Vol. 93, March 1899, pp. 249-254.
3. John Wilkinson, *Egeria's Travels*, 1971, p. 269.
4. Texts of seven Last Words are as follows:
    1) "Father, forgive them; for they know not what they do."
    2) "Truly, I say to you, today you will be with me in Paradise."
    3) "Woman, behold, your son! . . . Behold, your mother!"
    4) "My God, my God, why hast thou forsaken me?"
    5) "I thirst."
    6) "It is finished."
    7) "Father, into thy hands I commit my spirit!"
5. Thurston, pp. 254-255.
6. Prologue, Act XV, excerpt, *The Passion Play at Oberammergau*, 1930, p. 231.
7. Thurston, pp. 253-254, 257-258, 260.
8. Foreword to composition, *The Seven Last Words* (vocal version), 1801, quoted in H. C. Robbins Landon, Jacket Notes, Franz Joseph Haydn, *The Seven Last Words*, Academy of St. Martin-in-the-Fields, Neville Marriner, cond., 1978.
9. "Devotion of the Three Hours," in Thurston, p. 258.
10. Alquien, "Holy Week in Spain," *The Catholic World*, March 1894, p. 854.
11. "Good Friday in Venezuela," *Catholic Digest*, April 1941, pp. 99-100.
12. Sister Maria del Rey, "Pageant of the Cross," *Sign*, March 1972, p. 14.
13. "Devotion of the Three Hours," in Thurston, p. 259.
14. *L'Attivita Della Santa Sede, Nel 1988*, Libreria Editrice Vaticana, p. 234.
15. *The Hours of the Divine Office in English and Latin*, Vol. II, Liturgical Press, 1964, p. 148.
16. Excerpt, *The Catholic Anthology: The World's Great Catholic Poetry*, Thomas Walsh, ed., rev. ed., p. 32.
17. From *The Holy Bible: Douay Rheims Version*, 1899, rpt. 1971, p. 1021 (Old Testament).

18. "Paschal Homily," in *The Paschal Mystery: Ancient Liturgies and Patristic Texts* (Alba Patristic Library, Vol. 3), Andre Hamman, OFM, ed., p. 38.

19. Sermon 13, #4, in Hamman, pp. 115-116.

20. Oratio V, #2, *The Sunday Sermons of the Great Fathers*, M. F. Toal, ed., 1958, Vol. II, p. 192.

21. "Christ and His Mother at the Cross," Verse 9, in Walsh, p. 79.

22. Quoted in Helen Homan, *Letters to the Martyrs*, 1951, p. 179.

23. Excerpt, sequence, "Mass of the Five Wounds," *The Sarum Missal in English*, Frederick Warren, tr., 1911, Part II, p. 68.

24. From the Office for Good Friday, quoted in Abbot Guéranger, OSB, *The Liturgical Year*, 1952, Vol. 6, p. 518.

25. Excerpt, Walsh, p. 32.

26. "The Pasch History," #2, in Hamman, p. 66.

27. Paraphrased by Howard Robbins, in *The Hymnal of the Protestant Episcopal Church in the United States of America*, The Church Pension Fund, 1943, Hymn #81.

28. *The Love of God and the Cross of Jesus*, Vol. I, p. 202.

29. *The Hours of the Divine Office*, Vol. II, p. 148.

30. Catechesis 3 (used in Office of Readings for Good Friday as part of *Tenebrae*), in *The Office of Readings*, Daughters of St. Paul, 1983, pp. 479-480.

31. Excerpt, sequence, "Mass of the Five Wounds," in Warren, Part II, p. 69.

VIII

It Is Consummated

The Liturgy of the Passion

FROM THE EARLIEST AGES, the Church on Good Friday has omitted the celebration of Mass, as a sign of mourning. A special liturgy is held instead — the Liturgy of the Passion — consisting of three basic elements: 1) a Liturgy of the Word, ending with general intercessions; 2) the ceremony of the "Veneration of the Cross"; 3) a service for reception of the holy Eucharist as previously consecrated at the evening Mass on Holy Thursday. The most primitive of these, the first, constitutes a classic example of the *synaxis*, a service of Scripture readings and prayers originating in the Sabbath services of the Jewish Synagogue and adopted by the early Christians.[1] The *synaxis* was held as a complete liturgy of its own on those days when Mass was not celebrated; on days with the Eucharistic liturgy the *synaxis* served as an opening service for the latter. From the *First Apology* of Saint Justin (ca. A.D. 155) we learn that the *synaxis* consisted of readings from the Apostles and prophets, followed by a homily and concluding with the intercessory "Prayer of the Faithful."[2] Our earliest records of the Western liturgy suggest that at Rome the *synaxis* was the one and only liturgical service held on Good Friday up until the seventh century.[3] A particularly striking feature of the Roman *synaxis* was the way it began: The celebrant would enter silently and prostrate himself before the altar. Thus we find it in the eighth-century *Roman Ordo 23* (Andrieu).[4] To this very day the Good Friday liturgy begins with this prostration, an action meant to symbolize both "the abasement of 'earthly man' " and "the grief and sorrow of the Church."[5]

Our earliest records of what Scripture readings were used for the Good Friday *synaxis* of the Roman Rite indicate that there were two readings from the Old Testament — Hosea 6:1-6, which prophesies the resurrection, and Exodus 12:1-11, which describes the Passover meal; the gospel was Saint John's account of the passion (Jn 18:1-19:42). All three lections are specified in the *Capitulary of Wurzburg* (seventh to early eighth centuries).[6] These selections remained in the Good Friday liturgy for a period of over twelve hundred years, up until the recent revisions in the Holy Week liturgy. The reading from Hosea has been replaced with a longer passage from the Book of the Prophet Isaiah (Is 52:13 to 53:12), every line of which prophesies the passion; the latter selection is identical to the second reading assigned to the Good Friday liturgy in the ancient Spanish liturgical book of the fifth to seventh centuries, the *Liber Ordinum* (which interestingly also prescribes the reading of a harmony of all four gospel accounts of the passion on this day).[7] The first two verses of Hosea 6 are now part of the Roman Rite's Divine Office for Holy Saturday.[8] The reading from Exodus has been transferred to the Mass of the Lord's Supper on Holy Thursday, and in its place there is now a reading from the New Testament, from the Letter to the Hebrews (Heb 4:14-16; 5:7-9), which speaks of Christ as the great High Priest. The gospel selection, from Saint John, has not been replaced, thus maintaining a continuity with earlier ages.

In the Roman Rite the moment of our Lord's death on the cross in the reading of the passion is, as on Palm Sunday, marked by a pause and the kneeling of the entire congregation (the history of this practice has already been discussed with regard to Palm Sunday).[9] In the Good Friday liturgy of Milan's Ambrosian Rite, as described in the *Ufficiatura della Settimana Santa* of 1831, the custom in this regard is unusually dramatic. The passion is taken from the gospel of Saint Matthew (27:1-56) rather than that of Saint John and is chanted by a single deacon; at the words *emisit spiritum* ("yielded up the ghost" — Mt 27:50) the archbishop rises from his throne and kneels in the middle of the sanctuary as the rest of the clergy likewise fall on their knees and the bells of the cathedral are solemnly rung. All the lights in the church are now extinguished as two subdeacons strip the altar of its furnishings and a dark curtain marked with three crosses is lowered behind it. Cloth coverings and hangings are removed from the rest of the church as well.[10]

The basic content and form of the Solemn Prayers — the general intercessions of the Good Friday *synaxis* — appear to have remained relatively unchanged for at least fifteen hundred years. A listing of petitions remarkably similar to those currently in use in our Good Friday liturgy has been found in a passage written in the fifth century and appended to a letter of Pope Celestine I dating from around 431. It includes petitions for catechumens, for the Jewish people, for heretics and for pagans.[11] The latter three intentions likewise appear in another fifth-century source, the anonymous treatise *de Vocatione omnium gentium*.[12] From the seventh century (when they appear both in the *Gelatian Sacramentary* and in the Paduan edition of the *Gregorian Sacramentary*)[13] until the time of the Second Vatican Council there were nine intercessions and their actual wording (with the exception of the fourth) underwent virtually no change at all. The wording of the third intercession (prior to 1965) hints at just how ancient these petitions may be:

> Let us pray also for all Bishops, Presbyters, Deacons, Subdeacons, Acolytes, Exorcists, Readers, Door-keepers, Confessors, Virgins, Widows, and for all God's holy People. Let us pray.[14]

An identically ordered listing of the different Ecclesiastical Orders from that of bishop to that of door-keeper is found in a letter of Pope Cornelius to Fabius of Antioch, dating from A.D. 251. Thus at least some of the intercessions may have already been formulated by the third century.[15] In 1965, the Good Friday Solemn Prayers were modified somewhat for ecumenical reasons,[16] but their subject matter and basic thrust have not been significantly altered. The current practice of kneeling at intervals during the Good Friday general intercessions dates back to the sixth century or earlier; in two sermons of Saint Caesarius of Arles (died A.D. 542) there is mention that when the deacon signaled the people to pray, they would respond by genuflecting.[17]

> Faithful Cross, tree that is alone
> in its glory among all other trees;
> no forest ever yielded its equal
> in leaf, flower and fruit.
> Loving nails and loving wood
> bear a loving burden.
>
> [*Crux fidelis*][18]

The second element of the current Good Friday liturgy, the Veneration of the Cross, originated in Jerusalem following the discovery there of the true cross in the fourth century. We have already described this Good Friday veneration in the Holy City as observed by the pilgrim Egeria (see chapter I). Perhaps our earliest witness to this practice in the West is that of Spain's *Liber Ordinum* (fifth to seventh centuries), which speaks of a relic of the cross being placed in a paten

John Cardinal O'Connor, Veneration of the Cross, St. Patrick's Cathedral, Archdiocese of New York. *"Christ became obedient for us even to death, dying on the cross. Therefore God raised him on high and gave him the name above all other names"* *(Christus factus est).*

on the altar of Toledo's principal church and then carried in procession to "Holy Cross Church," where it was kissed by the clergy and laity; as in Jerusalem the ceremony took place in the morning, beginning at nine o'clock.[19] In Rome the Veneration of the Cross was added to the city's Good Friday liturgy by the seventh century, for it is mentioned in the *Gelasian Sacramentary*[20] and later in the eighth-century *Roman Ordo 23*

(Andrieu). In the latter document the Roman veneration is described in some detail. At two o'clock the pope, barefooted, would embark upon a procession from the Basilica of Saint John Lateran to the Church of Santa Croce in Gierusalemme, carrying a censer before a relic of the true cross, which was enclosed in a "capsa of gold adorned with gems" and was borne by a deacon. Upon arrival at Santa Croce, the reliquary would be set on the altar, where the pontiff opened it, prostrated himself before it, and kissed it. The rest of the clergy came forward and likewise venerated the relic of the true cross, after which it was brought near the altar rail so that the faithful could venerate it as the service continued with readings, Psalms, and prayers.[21]

In another eighth-century source, *Roman Ordo I*, the antiphon *Ecce lignum crucis* ("Behold the wood of the cross") is mentioned as an antiphon for the singing of Psalm 119 during Veneration of the Cross.[22] This antiphon was to figure prominently in later versions of the veneration, as it does today.

The dramatic character of the Good Friday Veneration of the Cross was heightened with the introduction into the Roman liturgy of a composition known as the *Improperia* (Reproaches), a work consisting of three distinct features: 1) the *Trisagion* ("Holy God, holy and strong, have mercy on us. . ."); 2) a series of three Reproaches, based upon the words of the prophets Micah, Jeremiah, and Isaiah; and 3) a second series of nine Reproaches, based partially upon Reproaches found in the apocryphal fourth Book of Esdras, but also influenced by Saint Paul (Acts 13 and 1 Cor 10:1-13) and by the ritual narrative of the Jewish Passover known as the *Haggadah*.[23] As the name suggests, the Reproaches are verses in the form of accusations addressed by our Lord to His own people and to all mankind; in the words of Jerome Gassner, OSB, "They are Christ's elegy on the ingratitude of His people, answered by the faithful with an act of adoration, and with a prayer for mercy. . . ."[24] The *Trisagion* is an ancient Greek hymn, perhaps of apostolic origin, for it is found in all of the Eastern liturgies; certainly it already existed in the East by the fifth century.[25] By the seventh century the *Trisagion* had reached the West, appearing first in Gallican sources such as the *Explanation of the Gallican Mass*, a work formerly attributed to Saint Germanus of Paris.[26] At Rome the *Trisagion* was introduced sometime before 1200, for it appears in a twelfth-century Papal Pontifical.[27] The insertion of the *Trisagion* into the Roman liturgy in its original Greek, rather than in Latin, suggests that Rome adopted it prior to the Photian Schism of the ninth century.[28] It came to be utilized as a refrain

[232]

for the chanting of the original series of three Reproaches; the earliest evidence for the use of these *Improperia* in the liturgy of Good Friday appears in the fifth- to seventh-century *Liber Ordinum* of Spain.[29] All three Reproaches are found in conjunction with the *Trisagion* for the first time in an Antiphonary of Senlis (France) dating from around A.D. 880.[30] The second set of nine Reproaches may be at least partially traceable to the liturgy of Jerusalem, for they are similar in certain respects to two of twelve *Troparia* (special Eastern Rite antiphons) in the Good Friday services of the Holy City as found in the *Georgian Lectionary* (fifth to eighth centuries).[31] In the West the nine additional *Improperia* first appear with the other three Reproaches and the *Trisagion* in the eleventh century (in Benevento, Italy), but the complete series of twelve does not emerge in Rome until the fourteenth or fifteenth centuries;[32] all of them are included in the *Roman Missal* of 1474.[33]

Although the earliest examples of the veneration of the cross all focused upon a relic of the true cross, the practice eventually arose of using images of the cross in churches that did not possess such a relic. Thus the ninth-century liturgist Amalarius says of this derived usage:

> *Although every church cannot possess it [the true cross], yet the virtue of the holy cross is not wanting to them in those crosses which are made after the likeness of the Lord's cross.*[34]

The concept of a "likeness of the Lord's cross" was taken a step further with the introduction into the Good Friday liturgy of the "crucifix," that is, a cross with an image of the crucified corpus of Christ fastened upon it. It is difficult to determine just when this change took place, since the term *crux* (cross) has frequently been used in liturgical books to designate a crucifix; such was the case in the *Roman Missal* of Pius V (1570), which speaks only of a *crux* for the Good Friday veneration.[35] Nonetheless, the crucifix had already begun to appear in the Good Friday veneration ceremony in some places by the end of the eleventh century; we find what may be one of the oldest references to such a usage in the *Constitutions* of Lanfranc, Archbishop of Canterbury:

> *Carpets shall be laid before the altar, and on these the abbot and the vested ministers shall prostrate themselves; meanwhile others shall approach to take the place of those holding the cross, and then others still, in due order. They shall not lie in adoration for long, but praying*

briefly and simply, and then each one shall kiss the feet of the crucifix and return to choir [emphasis added].[36]

The phrase *osculetur pedes crucifixi* in the Latin text of the above passage leaves no doubt as to the nature of the object venerated. The repeated use of the word *crux* in other portions of Lanfranc's description of the rite[37] serves to demonstrate that the "cross" was often assumed to mean a crucifix, and indeed the word "crucifix" is seldom encountered in the liturgical documents of the centuries that followed. In another monastic document of the eleventh century, the *Ordinarium Canonicorum Regularium* of John of Avranches, Archbishop of Rouen (France), the use of a crucifix for this ceremony is mentioned three times; it too speaks of the worshipers coming forward to kiss the "feet of the crucified Lord" (*crucifixi Domini pedes*).[38] There is reason to believe that the crucifix supplanted the cross in many more places during the thirteenth and fourteenth centuries, for by this time most processional crosses had become crucifixes.[39] Another explicit reference to the crucifix does appear at the beginning of the fifteenth century; in the *Ordinal* of the Benedictine Nuns of England's Barking Abbey, which dates from 1404 but which reflects practices already existing in the late fourteenth century, we are told that during the veneration the abbess would prostrate herself before the cross and then "kiss, with reverence and devotion, the feet and hands and right side of the Crucified," thus honoring the Five Wounds of our Lord (the devotion of the Five Wounds was quite common in medieval England). In turn the other nuns came forward and did likewise.[40] A century later, the nature of the *crux* is unambiguously specified in the *Missale Mixtum* of Spain's Mozarabic Rite, dating from 1500, which twice uses the term *Crucifixus* in describing the cross for Good Friday.[41] The 1886 edition of the *Caeremoniale Episcoporum*, which was first issued in 1600, speaks of the unveiling of the *caput figurae crucifixi* (head of the figure of the Crucified), thereby requiring that the *crux* be a crucifix.[42] Likewise, in the 1853 edition of the *Memoriale Rituum* (first published in 1725), the term *caput Crucifixi* appears.[43] The fourteenth rubric of the Liturgy of the Passion in the 1960 edition of the *Roman Missal* specifies that a "sufficiently large cross should be used, with a figure of the Crucified."[44] Although in the new *Roman Missal* of Pope Paul VI (1970) this latter stipulation was removed from the rubrics, with both the *Missal* and the 1985 *Caeremoniale Episcoporum* only using the term *crux* in this regard,[45] the 1985 edition of the *De Benedictionibus*, an official book of blessings forming part of the *Rituale Romanum* (which governs various rites such as baptismal ceremonies and the consecration of new churches) states that it is particularly "fitting" that crosses with the image of the body of Jesus crucified affixed to the wood be used for public veneration in churches.[46] Thus the crucifix remains the preferred form of *crux* in the judgment of the Church, and indeed, there are sound pastoral reasons for continuing this time-honored tradition.[47]

By the twelfth century another feature had been introduced into the Good Friday veneration at Rome: the ceremonial unveiling of the cross.[48] The practice existed elsewhere as early as the ninth century (appearing in the Gallican *Roman Ordo 31* [Andrieu]);[49] one of the oldest examples of it can be found in the *Ordo* of Abbot Ratold of Corbie (France), from a tenth-century manuscript (*Paris Bibl. Nationale ms. Latin #12052*).[50] The Veneration of the Cross was held in the evening, when after the general intercessions two deacons would station themselves either in the sacristy (*sacrarium*) or behind the altar, and then intone the refrain of the *Improperia*, "My people, what have I done to you?" Following this, the first of three Reproaches chanted by the deacons, two priests standing before a veiled cross in the sanctuary would answer with the *Trisagion*:

> *Holy is God! Holy and strong!*
> *Holy immortal One, have mercy on us!*

At this point the cross was brought several steps forward. Then the deacons chanted the second Reproach, to which the two priests once more responded with the *Trisagion*; the cross was now advanced a second time. Following the third Reproach and *Trisagion*, the cross was moved forward yet again and the veil around it removed. As the antiphon *Ecce lignum crucis* ("Behold the wood of the cross") was sung, the cross was lifted up; afterwards each of the clergy present would prostrate himself three times before it and venerate it.[51]

In medieval England there appeared an especially impressive form of the Good Friday veneration, known as the "Creeping to the Cross." A detailed account of this custom appears in an anonymous document written in 1593 describing the ceremonies of England's Durham Abbey Church as they existed earlier in the century, before the Protestant Reformation swept the country. During the Good Friday service a gold crucifix was placed on a velvet cushion and held by two of the oldest monks, who sat on their knees on either side of it. Then the Veneration of the Cross began:

> *. . . one of the said monks did rise and went a pretty way from it, sitting down upon his knees, with his shoes put off, very reverently did creep away upon his knees unto the said Cross, and most reverently did kiss it. And after him the other monk did so likewise, and then they did sit them down on every side of the said Cross, and holding it betwixt them, and after that the prior came forth of his stall, and did sit him down of his knees, with his shoes off, and in like sort did creep also unto the said Cross, and all the monks after him, one after another in the same order, and in the meantime all the whole quire singing a hymn.*[52]

The "Creeping to the Cross" was not confined to England. Saint Louis, King of France (1214-1270), also engaged in this practice, clothing himself in haircloth and then crawling on hands and knees to the cross.[53]

Following the Council of Trent (mid-sixteenth century) the veneration ceremony reached its fullest stage of development and remained relatively unchanged until the revisions of the Holy Week liturgy inaugurated in 1955. By consulting the rubrics of the *Roman Missal*, the *Caeremoniale Episcoporum* and the *Memoriale Rituum* in editions from the nineteenth and early twentieth centuries, we can construct an accurate picture of the Veneration of the Cross during this period.[54] At the conclusion of the general intercessions, the celebrant removes his black chasuble and then proceeds to the rear corner of the "epistle side" of the altar (the right side) where a deacon gives him a crucifix veiled in violet (or black) cloth.[55] Facing the people, the priest uncovers the top of the cross, elevates it, and chants the *Ecce lignum crucis*; the choir answers, *Venite adoremus*, as all (except the celebrant) genuflect. The celebrant advances to the front corner of the epistle side of the altar and uncovering the right arm of the crucifix together with the head of the corpus, raises it a second time (but higher than the first elevation) and sings in a higher tone of voice the *Ecce lignum crucis*; once more the choir responds, *Venite adoremus*. The priest moves to the center of the altar and after completely removing the violet veil from the crucifix he elevates it a third and final time, higher still, chanting the *Ecce lignum crucis* in an even higher tone. Following the response of *Venite adoremus*, the celebrant, still holding the cross aloft, proceeds down the altar steps; kneeling down, he lays the crucifix on a violet cushion before the altar. He rises, genuflects to the cross, and walks to a seat where he removes his shoes. Returning before the cross, he genuflects thrice, each time advancing several steps closer, after which he bends forward to kiss the crucifix. Upon rising, he genuflects once more and returns to his seat where he puts on his shoes. As the choir chants the *Improperia* the other members of the clergy and the faithful now come forward, two by two, to venerate the cross in the same manner (the laity were not required to remove their shoes, however).

In nineteenth-century Madrid, during Veneration of the Cross, the King of Spain would announce the pardon of a number of prisoners sentenced to death. When the king came forward to kiss the cross, the Cardinal-Archbishop of Toledo would give him a bundle of papers tied together with a black ribbon; these papers contained the names of those the king had decided to pardon. The archbishop would ask him if he wished to grant a pardon to these men; after removing the black ribbon, the king would return the papers to the archbishop and answer him: "I forgive them, as I hope God will forgive me."[56]

The celebration of Mass on Good Friday had been prohibited in both the East and West by the beginning of the fifth century.[57] Thus in Rome, as we have already seen, only the non-Eucharistic *synaxis* was originally held on this day. But eventually a special liturgical service was to arise that would give the faithful the opportunity to receive the holy Eucharist on Good Friday. Such a service may have existed as early as the fifth century in Antioch (then part of Syria),[58] and is known to have appeared in the Good Friday liturgy of Jerusalem sometime between the fifth century and the eighth,[59] but it is an entry for the year 645 in the *Chronicon Paschale*, a seventh-century Eastern document, that provides the first definite and specific record of a Communion service that would later come to be known as the Mass of the Presanctified.[60] There was no celebration of the Eucharistic sacrifice at this service; instead, Hosts consecrated at a previous Mass were given to the faithful. This Mass of the Presanctified, held on most of the weekdays of Lent in the East, soon turned up in the Good Friday liturgy of the West, where it is mentioned in the *Gelasian Sacramentary* (seventh century)[61] and in *Roman Ordo I* (eighth century). In the latter document we are told that during the ceremony of the Veneration of the Cross two priests entered the sacristy and placed the Eucharist reserved there into a paten, after which a subdeacon gave them a chalice of unconsecrated wine. Then the two priests took the Blessed Sacrament and the chalice of wine to the bare altar. Following the end of Veneration of the Cross the pope said three prayers: 1) *Oremus, Praeceptis salutaribus moniti* ("Let us pray.

Prompted by saving precepts. . . ."); 2) the *Pater Noster* (the Our Father); and 3) *Libera nos* ("Free us. . ."). In silence he would then put a fragment of the holy Eucharist into the unconsecrated wine, after which all of the clergy and laity received holy Communion. There was no singing during the Communion.[62]

In the twelfth century the Good Friday Communion rite in the papal liturgy began to acquire certain features from the Ordinary of the Mass said during the rest of the year, as reflected in a *Roman Pontifical* from this period.[63] These additions over the course of several centuries eventually gave the Mass of the Presanctified something of the appearance of a Mass without consecration. Likewise, as the reservation of the Blessed Sacrament following Mass on Holy Thursday grew increasingly elaborate during the Middle Ages, so too did the ceremony on Good Friday for bringing the holy Eucharist back to the altar for the Mass of the Presanctified. By the time of the *Roman Missal* of 1570, the whole rite had taken on a highly developed format. As Veneration of the Cross comes to an end, the candles at the altar are lighted, and a corporal is spread upon the *mensa* (the surface of the altar). The celebrant and other ministers go to the repository, preceded by a cross and lights; after a deacon opens the *capsula*, the celebrant censes the Sacrament, and taking the chalice containing the Host, returns in procession, carrying the Eucharist beneath a canopy, flanked by the deacon and a subdeacon, and accompanied by lights and incense, as Venantius Fortunatus' sixth-century hymn of the cross, *Vexilla Regis*, is sung. Upon reaching the altar the celebrant removes the single consecrated Host from the chalice and places It on the paten; the deacon and subdeacon pour unconsecrated wine and water into the chalice and leave it near the Host. At this point the celebrant censes both the holy Eucharist and the chalice of wine and water and says several prayers from the Ordinary of the Mass. Following these prayers he holds up the Host, after which he breaks It into three fragments, one of which he places in the chalice. The celebrant consumes the two other fragments of the Host, and then the fragment in the chalice together with the wine and water. He concludes the service with one final prayer from the Mass and then leaves the altar in silence.[64]

In the *Missale Mixtum* of Spain's Mozarabic Rite, issued in 1500, we encounter a particularly striking example of the Good Friday Eucharistic procession, in which all the clergy and laity participate. A black cross, lights, and a burning *thurible* lead the cortege, which proceeds in silence to the *monumentum* (the repository), the celebrant vested in a black chasuble and the deacon and subdeacon accompanying him in black dalmatics. Upon reaching their destination, the celebrant ascends the steps to the *monumentum* together with the two lords to whom the keys to the repository's *capsa* (the special tabernacle enclosing the Eucharist) had been entrusted on the previous day. When the *capsa* is opened the celebrant takes some of the incense that had been placed in this tabernacle on Holy Thursday and puts it into the *thurible*, with which he then censes the holy Eucharist. After showing the Host in the chalice to the two lords, he leaves the *monumentum* and brings the Blessed Sacrament in procession back to the main altar. Over the holy Eucharist a silk canopy is borne by four or six of the lords of the city; before It the black cross, candles, *thurible*, and incense are carried, and as on Holy Thursday green branches are strewn in Its path. In the middle of the procession, between the canons and the sextons, a black banner is borne by a sexton vested in a white superhumeral. Upon reaching the high altar, the celebrant continues with the Mass of the Presanctified in a manner similar to that found in the *Roman Missal* of 1570, as presented above.[65]

With the issuance of the revised Ordo of Holy Week in 1955 the Church returned to the austere, uncomplicated format of the Mass of the Presanctified as it was originally celebrated, along the lines of the Good Friday Communion rite of the seventh-century *Gelasian Sacramentary*.[66] A description of the current Liturgy of the Eucharist for Good Friday will be provided in due course.

Our earliest record of the Mass of the Presanctified in Rome (in the *Gelasian Sacramentary*) indicates that originally all of the faithful received holy Communion at this service.[67] However, the eighth-century *Roman Ordo 23* (Andrieu) tells us that such was not the case at the papal Good Friday service, during which neither the pope nor anyone else received the Sacrament; nonetheless, the people were allowed to do so at services held in the other churches of Rome.[68] The practice of a general Communion on Good Friday spread across the West, appearing in the *Romano-Germanic Pontifical*[69] and in the monastic constitutions of England[70] and France[71] during the tenth and eleventh centuries. Yet the custom subsequently entered into a decline. With the promulgation of the *Roman Missal* of 1570 Communion during the Mass of the Presanctified was thenceforth limited to the celebrant alone,[72] a decision that was to be further reinforced in 1622 when the Congregation of Sacred Rites specifically forbade a general Communion on Good Friday.[73] But when the restored liturgy of Holy Week was promulgated in 1955, the Church returned to her more ancient practice of making the Sacrament available to all her children on this solemn day, that they might be more intimately united with their crucified Redeemer on the very afternoon He consummated His sacrifice.[74]

Having now examined separately the three components of the Liturgy of the Passion — the *synaxis*, the Veneration of the Cross, and the Mass of the Presanctified — it seems appropriate at this point to present one nineteenth-century example of the Good Friday liturgy as a whole, set in the city where the events this liturgy commemorates actually took place, Jerusalem.[75]

The service at the Church of the Holy Sepulchre would begin at seven o'clock in the morning in the Chapel of Calvary, which had become densely crowded with the kneeling figures of the faithful. In conformity with the solemnity of the occasion, everything was draped in black. As was customary elsewhere, the passion of Saint John was delivered by three clerics:

> *The voice of the priest who chanted the words of Jesus was gentle and sad, and so like what we may imagine to have been that of our Lord, as to become painful and oppressive. When the ejaculation, consummatum est ["It is consummated"], had been made, the first chanter went to the place where the cross had been set up on which Jesus died, and kneeling there, in a low voice uttered the words, et inclinato capite, tradidit spiritum ["And bowing his head, he gave up the ghost"].*[76]

Later in the service, the patriarch would unveil the crucifix to begin the Veneration of the Cross:

> *Then commences that portion of the office which none can ever forget who have witnessed it at Rome; how much less at Jerusalem, in the very spot which witnessed the actual throes and death-agony of the Man-God, and the woes of His Blessed Mother! One by one the worshipers rise and prostrate themselves in adoration three times, kissing the feet of their Lord, while the wail of the Reproaches rises and falls and reverberates through the sacred shrine. The Crux fidelis and Pange lingua are taken up by the choir. . . .*

The Mass of the Presanctified followed:

> *. . . the mournful ceremony over, the candles on the altar are lighted,*

*illuminating the many upturned and weeping faces, and the priests go
in procession to the chapel below to bring back the Blessed Sacrament,
which has been deposited in the Holy Sepulchre the preceding day,
while the glorious hymn Vexilla Regis is sung by the whole congregation. . . . It is impossible to exaggerate the effect of this office on this
spot, or the sense of utter desolation which falls upon the soul when all
is over. It is an approach to Mary's sorrow, and a shadow of it; but to
one who has not felt it, it cannot be explained. We have read of the
Crucifixion all our lives, and have tried in our various degrees to realize
it; but here we see it, as it were, with our bodily eyes, which help out
our weak faith. . . .*[77]

The Liturgy of the Passion Today

Having now examined the history of today's liturgy, let us turn
our attention to the Liturgy of the Passion in its current form.[78] As three
o'clock approaches, the faithful quietly fill the church; the hour of our
Lord's death draws near. Suddenly, and without any entrance hymn,
the celebrant and a deacon enter the sanctuary dressed in red vestments;
as the rest of the congregation kneels they prostrate themselves before
the altar, remaining thus for several moments. Upon rising the celebrant
says the opening prayer:

*Lord,
by shedding his blood for us,
your Son, Jesus Christ,
established the paschal mystery.
In your goodness, make us holy
and watch over us always.
We ask this through Christ our Lord.*

The Liturgy of the Word follows immediately, beginning with
a reading from the prophet Isaiah (52:13-53:12) which describes the
Suffering Servant and prophesies the passion:

*Therefore I will give him his portion among the great,
and he shall divide the spoils with the mighty,
Because he surrendered himself to death
and was counted among the wicked;*

[241]

And he shall take away the sins of many,
and win pardon for their offenses.

[Is 53:12; NAB]

While on the cross our Lord quoted from two of the Psalms, the 22nd and the 31st. The latter of these serves as the responsorial psalm for this afternoon's liturgy (Ps 31:2, 6, 12-13, 15-17, 25):

Into your hands I commend my spirit;
you will redeem me, O Lord, O faithful God.

For all my foes I am an object of reproach,
a laughingstock to my neighbors, and a dread to my friends;
they who see me abroad flee from me.
I am forgotten like the unremembered dead;
I am like a dish that is broken.

[Ps 31:6, 12-13; NAB]

The second reading, from the Letter to the Hebrews (4:14-16; 5:7-9), emphasizes the fruits of the passion won for us by Christ our High Priest, who though He was Divine humbled Himself to share in our human nature:

We have a great high priest who has passed through the heavens, Jesus, the Son of God; let us hold fast to our profession of faith. For we do not have a high priest who is unable to sympathize with our weakness, but one who was tempted in every way that we are, yet never sinned. So let us confidently approach the throne of grace to receive mercy and favor and to find help in time of need.

[Heb 4:14-16; NAB]

Just before the gospel we hear the antiphon *Christus factus est*, with which we are already familiar from its use during *Tenebrae*:

Christ became obedient for us even to death,
dying on the cross.
Therefore God raised him on high
and gave him the name above all other names.

Three lecterns are brought into the sanctuary and set before the altar by the acolytes. Then three deacons come to the lecterns to begin the passion of our Lord according to Saint John (18:1-19:42). Following a centuries' old tradition, the passion is chanted, with the parts divided among the three deacons as on Palm Sunday (see chapter II). One chants the narrative, while a second, with a deep bass voice, chants the words of Christ; the third, with an alto voice, chants the other dialogue. The passion continues uninterrupted until these words:

> *When Jesus took the wine, he said, "Now it is finished." Then he bowed his head, and delivered over his spirit."*
>
> [Jn 19:30; NAB]

All immediately kneel and pause for several moments in silence.

The deacon assigned the narrative parts completes the chanting of the passion, after which the celebrant gives a homily on the themes of this holiest of Fridays.

The General Intercessions

The celebrant now leads the faithful in the general intercessions, consisting of ten petitions for the needs of the Church and of the world. We pray for:

1) The Church.
2) The pope.
3) The clergy and laity.
4) Those preparing for Baptism.
5) The unity of Christians.
6) The Jewish people.
7) Those who do not believe in Christ.
8) Those who do not believe in God.
9) All in public office.
10) Those in special need.

Each petition begins with an invitation to prayer:

> *Let us pray
> for the Jewish people,
> the first to hear the word of God,
> that they may continue to grow*

in the love of his name
and in faithfulness to his covenant.

The deacon now invites the congregation to pause for silent prayer:

Let us kneel.

A few moments later the deacon says,

Let us stand.

After all rise, the celebrant says a prayer from the *Roman Missal* for the intention:

Almighty and eternal God,
long ago you gave your promise
to Abraham and his posterity.
Listen to your Church as we pray
that the people you first made your own
may arrive at the fullness of redemption.
We ask this through Christ our Lord.
Amen.

The Veneration of the Cross

For blessed is the wood
by which righteousness comes.

[Wis 14:7]

The *Roman Missal* of Pope Paul VI provides two alternative formats for the Veneration of the Cross. The cross may either be brought to the altar wrapped in a red cloth, and there unveiled in three stages by the celebrant, or it may be carried without a veil in a three-stage procession through the church. Here we will present a version of the veneration that combines both forms.

The celebrant goes to the door of the church and at the appointed moment reappears, bearing a crucifix veiled in red cloth. Two acolytes with lit tapers accompany him. Proceeding with measured steps into

Pope John Paul II, Veneration of the Cross. *"For blessed is the wood by which righteousness comes" (Wis 14:7).*

the church, the celebrant stops a short distance from the entrance and removes one part of the red pall, revealing the top of the crucifix; holding the cross aloft, he proclaims:

This is the wood of the cross,
on which hung the Savior of the world.

The congregation responds:

Come, let us worship.

All now kneel in a moment of silent veneration. The celebrant proceeds once more, going forward until he is about halfway to the altar. He now unveils the right arm of the crucifix, again lifting it up and repeating the invitation:

This is the wood of the cross. . . .

Come, let us worship.

Again all kneel in silence. Now the celebrant completes his journey to the altar, stopping at the entrance to the sanctuary. He turns toward the congregation and having completely unveiled the cross, lifts it up a third time:

This is the wood of the cross. . . .

Come, let us worship.

Two acolytes then take the crucifix and hold it erect between them at the edge of the sanctuary; on each side is placed a lit candle. The first to venerate the cross is the celebrant; he is followed by the other members of the clergy. Each approaches the cross, genuflects before it, and then kisses the feet of the Crucified. The laity come forward to do likewise as the *Improperia* — the Reproaches — are sung:

My people, what have I done to you?
How have I offended you? Answer me!

I led you out of Egypt, from slavery to freedom,

but you led your Savior to the cross.

Holy is God! Holy and strong!
Holy immortal One, have mercy on us!

For forty years I led you safely through the desert.
I fed you with manna from heaven
and brought you to a land of plenty;
but you led your Savior to the cross.

What more could I have done for you?
I planted you as my fairest vine,
but you yielded only bitterness:
when I was thirsty you gave me vinegar to drink,
and you pierced your Savior with a lance.

For your sake I scourged your captors and their first-born sons,
but you brought your scourges down on me.

I led you from slavery to freedom
and drowned your captors in the sea,
but you handed me over to your high priests.

I opened the sea before you,
but you opened my side with a spear.

I led you on your way in a pillar of cloud,
but you led me to Pilate's court.

I bore you up with manna in the desert,
but you struck me down and scourged me.

I gave you saving water from the rock,
but you gave me gall and vinegar to drink.

For you I struck down the kings of Canaan,
but you struck my head with a reed.

I gave you a royal scepter,
but you gave me a crown of thorns.

I raised you to the height of majesty,
but you have raised me high on a cross.

My people, what have I done to you?
How have I offended you? Answer me!

[Reproaches of Good Friday]

Loudly sing your hymns,
O all ye ends of the earth,
when ye behold men venerating
that wood whereon Christ was fastened,
and whereby Satan received his wound.

The life-giving cross is this day exposed:
let us, then, with joy and fear,
venerate the cross of our Lord,
that we may receive the Holy Ghost.

O life-giving cross,
my tongue and heart tremble with fear,
as I draw nigh to touch thee,
for I see the divine Blood of my Lord
poured forth upon thee.

[Excerpts of Hymn from Greek Liturgy][79]

After all have individually venerated the cross, it is placed near the altar, between two candles, with a burning censer before it.

We adore your cross, O Lord;
we praise and glorify your holy resurrection.
For behold, by reason of that wood,
joy has come into all the world.

[Crucem tuam][80]

Dark nails they drove through me;
on me are still the scars,
Wide wounds of malice,
nor revenge durst I one of them.
Us both they besmeared;
all with blood was I wet

From that Man's side shed
when His spirit forth He sent.

[The Dream of the Rood][81]

. . . the Cross of the Lord, an instrument of torture . . . is become glorious in the might of the Crucified. The multitude raged against one man; Christ had compassion on all men. What was inflicted through cruelty was suffered by majesty: so that in the permitting of the evil deed, the purpose of the eternal will might be accomplished.

[Pope Saint Leo the Great][82]

Mass of the Presanctified

Following Veneration of the Cross, the previously stripped altar is now covered with a cloth in order to make ready for the Communion rite. The deacon leaves the chapel and goes to the repository, where he removes the ciborium from the *capsa*, and wrapping it in the ends of a humeral veil around his shoulders, carries it back into the church, flanked by two acolytes with burning tapers. The Blessed Sacrament is borne to the altar in total silence. The deacon places the ciborium on the *mensa* (surface of the altar) and uncovers it, the acolytes setting down their candles nearby. The celebrant, having left his place, genuflects, approaches the altar and invites the faithful to say the Our Father with him. This is followed by the usual prayer and response from the Ordinary of the Mass:

Priest: "Deliver us, Lord, from every evil. . . ."

People: "For the kingdom, the power, and the glory are yours, now and for ever."

The sign of peace and *Agnus Dei* (Lamb of God) that ordinarily follow these prayers during Mass are omitted. The priest quietly recites his private prayer of preparation ("Lord Jesus Christ, with faith in your love and mercy. . . ."), after which he genuflects; elevating one of the Hosts over the ciborium, he says:

This is the Lamb of God who takes away the sins of the world. Happy are those who are called to his supper.

The congregation responds:

Lord, I am not worthy to receive you, but only say the word and I shall be healed.

The celebrant consumes the Host; holy Communion is now given to the faithful, as an appropriate hymn is sung:

Ah, holy Jesus, how hast thou offended,
That man to judge thee hath in hate pretended?
By foes derided, by thine own rejected,
O most afflicted.

Who was the guilty? Who brought this upon thee?
Alas, my treason, Jesus, hath undone thee.
'Twas I, Lord Jesus, I it was denied thee:
I crucified thee.

Lo, the good Shepherd, for the sheep is offered;
The slave hath sinned, and the Son hath suffered;
For man's atonement, while he nothing heedeth,
God intercedeth.

Therefore, kind Jesus, since I cannot pay thee,
I do adore thee, and will ever pray thee,
Think on thy pity and thy love unswerving,
Not my deserving.

[Ah, Holy Jesus, vs. 1-3, 5][83]

As the people make their thanksgiving following holy Communion, the remaining Hosts are quietly carried out of the church in a ciborium and taken to a suitable place for reservation until the Mass of the Easter Vigil.

Finally, the celebrant rises and says a concluding prayer:

Let us pray.
Almighty and eternal God,
you have restored us to life
by the triumphant death
and resurrection of Christ.

Continue this healing work within us.
May we who participate in this mystery
never cease to serve you.
We ask this through Christ our Lord. Amen.

Extending his hands toward the faithful, the celebrant then blesses them in these words:

Lord,
send down your abundant blessing
upon your people who have devoutly
recalled the death of your Son
in the sure hope of the resurrection.
Grant them pardon; bring them comfort.
May their faith grow stronger
and their eternal salvation be assured.
We ask this through Christ our Lord.
Amen.

The liturgy ended, all depart in silence. Afterwards the altar is stripped. The crucifix is left in the sanctuary for the veneration of the faithful.

The *Platsenitsia*: Good Friday in the Byzantine Rite

In the Byzantine Rite, there is on Good Friday no Communion service (Mass of the Presanctified) or liturgical veneration of the cross. Instead, the afternoon of this day is marked by the solemn public recitation of Vespers (Evening Prayer) from the Divine Office; the service is somewhat analogous to the Roman Rite's *Tenebrae*, but the former is characterized by two distinctive features. In the course of the Byzantine Vespers service a gospel harmony of the passion is read, consisting of excerpts from three of the four Evangelists (Mt 27:1-38; Lk 23:39-44; Mt 27:39-54; Jn 19:31-37; Mt 27:55-62).[84] In addition, there is a special ceremony that the Ukrainians and other Slavs of the Byzantine Rite call the *Platsenitsia* (Winding Sheet),[85] in which the death of our Lord is commemorated with a cloth known as the *Epitaphios*, a large shroudlike tapestry with the image of Christ laid in death shown on it. To determine the origin of this practice we must first look at the earlier

changes in the Byzantine Good Friday liturgy that preceded the introduction of the *Epitaphios*.

As we have seen already in chapter I, the Good Friday liturgy
of fourth-century Jerusalem as described by the pilgrim Egeria was
quite complex, with a total of six different services for this day, beginning with an all-night vigil, followed by veneration of the cross in the
morning, a Scripture service at midday, and a Vespers service at three;
the day ended with a reading of one of the gospel accounts of the
entombment of Christ, after which a second vigil began before the holy
sepulchre. All of these rites, except for the second vigil, likewise appear
in the Jerusalem liturgy of the early fifth century as found in the
Armenian Lectionary,[86] but we begin to see significant changes during
the period of the fifth to eighth centuries in a later Jerusalem book, the
Georgian Lectionary. There is no longer any mention of a service for the
veneration of the cross, and the reading in the evening of the gospel
account of the entombment appears to have been merged with Vespers,
during which there were lections from the Book of Wisdom (2:12-18),
the Prophet Isaiah (57:1-21) and the Lamentations of Jeremiah (Lam
3:52-66). The gospel, formerly from Saint Matthew (27:57-61) in the
Armenian Lectionary, was now taken from Saint John (19:38-42), a passage that speaks of Joseph of Arimathea and Nicodemus preparing our
Lord's body for burial. These readings were followed by two new
additions to the Good Friday liturgy; according to the rubrics of the
Lectionary, a deacon "washes the cross," after which those present
"share the Eucharist," that is, holy Communion is given to the faithful.[87]
No further details are provided, but it is obvious that the latter was a
Mass of the Presanctified similar to that still celebrated in the West on
this day, while the former seems to have constituted a symbolic burial
rite,[88] meant to evoke the image of Christ's body being washed before
entombment; it is likely that the "cross" washed was a relic of the true
cross itself. By the tenth century, however, both the "washing of the
cross" and the Mass of the Presanctified had disappeared from the
Good Friday liturgy of the holy city, for neither are to be found in the
Typicon of the Anastasis, which dates from this later period. There are,
nonetheless, two ceremonies at the end of the day's liturgy which may
represent faint echoes of the *Georgian Lectionary's* earlier practices. In
association with Vespers there was a rite for the blessing of the "holy
leaven," a bread (*not* the Eucharist) that was then distributed to the
people; afterwards a number of monks kept watch through the night in
the Anastasis (the church enclosing the holy sepulchre), apparently in

commemoration of the entombment.[89] Of course, we should point out that there was much in the Good Friday liturgy of Jerusalem that underwent little or no significant change over the years from the fifth century until the tenth; thus the selection of Old and New Testament readings for the midday Scripture service as given in the *Armenian Lectionary* (a listing of which was provided earlier in our discussion of the West's extraliturgical *Tre Ore* observance) was retained with few modifications in the *Georgian Lectionary* and in the *Typicon of the Anastasis*, although the ordering and length of the gospel lections did evolve somewhat (Mt 27:1-32, Mk 15:1-32, Lk 22:66-23:49, and Jn 18:28-19:37 in the *Typicon*).

At Constantinople, the medieval capital of the Byzantine Empire, the liturgy of Good Friday was always far more austere than that of Jerusalem; nothing comparable to Jerusalem's lengthy midday Scripture service can be found in the *Typicon of the Great Church*, a liturgical book of Constantinople dating from the ninth to tenth centuries, nor is there any evidence in this text of a Friday night vigil or of symbolic burial rites.[90] However, the Old Testament readings and Epistle for Vespers (Ex 33:11-23, Job 42:12-17, Is 52:13-54:1, 1 Cor 1:18-2:2) are, with only one minor exception, identical to those specified in the *Typicon of the Anastasis*, and are no different from those used to this very day in the Byzantine Rite;[91] even the Vesperal gospel selection at Constantinople (Mt 27:1-38, Lk 23:39-43, Mt 27:39-54, Jn 19:31-37, Mt 27:55-61 — virtually that of the current Byzantine liturgy) is related to that of tenth-century Jerusalem (Mt 27:1-61), for the same verses from Saint Matthew were used in both cities, the only difference being the "insertion" of passages from Saint Luke and Saint John in the case of Constantinople. The *Typicon of the Great Church* also mentions that the Mass of the Presanctified followed Vespers, as in the *Georgian Lectionary*; but this feature did not endure, for by the beginning of the thirteenth century the Communion Rite on Good Friday had disappeared from the Byzantine liturgy.[92]

Veneration of the cross on Good Friday existed in Constantinople during the seventh century, as observed by the Frankish Bishop Arculf and recorded by the Irish monk Saint Adamnan in his work *De Locis Sanctis*. Adamnan writes that Constantinople possessed both the horizontal beam of the true cross and two portions of the vertical beam; these were kept in a chest at the Church of Santa Sophia. Veneration began on Holy Thursday with the Emperor and the soldiers each coming forward to kiss the relic exposed on an altar; on Good Friday the women of the city did likewise. On Holy Saturday the patriarch, together with the clergy, venerated the cross.[93] By the tenth century, however, this veneration is no longer mentioned as part of the Holy Week liturgy in the Byzantine capital; the rite had been assigned a separate feast of its own during the fourth Week of Lent.[94] In its place there appeared a ceremony for venerating the "Holy Lance" (the lance that pierced our Lord's side on the cross) which was conducted at the Basilica of Santa Sophia both on Holy Thursday and Good Friday, beginning at dawn and continuing until midday, according to the *Typicon of the Great Church;*[95] this practice is also found in the *De Cerimoniis Aulae Byzantinae,* a ceremonial book of the Emperor Constantine VII Porphyrogenitus (tenth century with some later interpolations).[96] A portion of the lance's blade had been brought to Constantinople in the early part of the seventh century; the rest of the lance is thought to have arrived there by the tenth century.[97] But eventually the Holy Week veneration of the lance likewise disappeared from the Eastern liturgy. It is likely that the *troparion* (refrain) "Noble Joseph," which originated as part of the East's Divine Office for Good Friday and Holy Saturday, together with the mystagogical interpretation accorded the *aer,* one of the cloths used in the Byzantine Eucharistic liturgy, provided the basis for the one form of Byzantine Good Friday veneration that has survived to the present day — the ceremony of the *Epitaphios.* The *aer* is a cloth brought to the altar during the "Great Entrance," the offertory procession of the Byzantine Liturgy of the Eucharist; it is used to veil the chalice together with the *discos* (the paten holding the unconsecrated altar bread). In the tradition of mystagogic interpretation, the *aer* came to be seen as symbolic of the stone that sealed our Lord's tomb; a related cloth, the *eiliton,* which was placed under the chalice, was seen to represent the Burial Shroud of Christ.[98] During the thirteenth century, embroidered liturgical cloths and vestments began to appear in the Byzantine Rite,[99] and it was not long before the *aer* underwent this change. By the early fourteenth century, *aers* embroidered with an image of Christ asleep in death were introduced,[100] thus giving visual expression to the burial symbolism that had been connected with the *aer* for centuries. During this very same period, the thirteenth to fourteenth centuries, the processions for carrying the gospel book following Vespers on Good Friday and at Matins on Holy Saturday gradually came to be interpreted as representing the funeral cortege of Christ. This trend seems to have originated in a monastic setting, and evidently stemmed from the chanting of the *troparion* known as "Noble Joseph,"[101] which had already been inserted into the Divine Office for Good Friday (and Matins of Holy Saturday), at least in Jerusalem, by the tenth century:[102]

Noble Joseph took your immaculate body from the wood of the cross, anointed it with fragrant ointments, wrapped it in pure linen, and placed it in a new tomb.[103]

By the fourteenth century the gospel book in this procession was being wrapped in an *aer* and carried on the shoulder of a priest.[104] Eventually a new name arose for the *aer* — *Epitaphios* — appearing in the fifteenth-century writings of the Archbishop Symeon of Thessalonika.[105] But it is not until the sixteenth century, in a Slavic Typicon, that we find a description of the *Epitaphios* procession as it exists today — in which the *Epitaphios* is borne above the gospel book as if it were a canopy.[106]

The introduction of a "burial procession" into the Byzantine Divine Office of Good Friday may also have been inspired by the veneration accorded another of the relics kept in Constantinople: the Shroud of Christ. In a letter the Eastern Emperor Constantine VII Porphyrogenitus sent to his troops near Tarsus in the year 958, we find mention of "the *sindon* which God wore" — evidently the earliest surviving reference to the presence of the burial linens of Christ in the Byzantine capital.[107] At the beginning of the thirteenth century a French soldier named Robert de Clari, who was in Constantinople in A.D. 1203, recorded seeing at the Church of Saint Mary of Blachernae "the *sydoine* [shroud] in which Our Lord had been wrapped, which stood up strait every Friday so that the *figure* of Our Lord could be plainly seen there."[108] It is clear from these words that the Shroud had some sort of image of Christ on it, and indeed this reference would help to explain a cryptic passage dating from before 1130 (an interpolation in a much older sermon of Pope Saint Stephen III) which describes the display on Good Friday of an image of Christ, "at the ninth hour [three in the afternoon] visible in his full manhood, in which form the Son of God went to his Passion when he bore for our sins the suffering of the cross."[109] These two passages suggest that a ceremony for displaying the Shroud of Christ was being conducted every Friday and/or on Good Friday during the twelfth and early thirteenth centuries in Constantinople. It seems plausible that this veneration of the original Shroud (which may have been the same cloth that is now known as the

Shroud of Turin[110]) could have inspired the subsequent use on Good Friday of *aers* embroidered with the image of Christ in death.

The earliest surviving examples of the *Epitaphios* date from the late thirteenth or early fourteenth centuries.[111] One of the finest of these early *Epitaphioi* is kept in the Museum of the Serbian Orthodox Church in Belgrade, Yugoslavia; the "shroud," embroidered with gold thread on a dark red background, and with borders consisting of little crosses, depicts Christ in death, flanked on each side by rows of angels.[112] The *Epitaphioi* have ranged in size from 1 x 1.5 meters to 1.5 x 2.5 meters. Over time there was a trend toward ever larger *Epitaphioi* with increasingly elaborate burial imagery.[113] Originally only the image of Christ was depicted, but with time other figures were added to the Deposition scene: first the Blessed Virgin Mary, then Joseph of Arimathea. Later Mary Magdalene, Nicodemus, and the "Myrrh-Bearing Women" were added.[114]

In the current Byzantine liturgy the *Epitaphios* and the gospel book are laid on the altar at the beginning of Good Friday Vespers (around four o'clock). After the readings, as the Office concludes, the celebrant censes the cloth three times, then takes the gospel book into his hands and begins a procession around the altar and out of the sanctuary as the concelebrating priests take up the *Epitaphios* and accompany him, carrying it above him like a canopy. They continue to an "altar-like table" representing the holy sepulchre, on which the *Epitaphios* is now laid; the gospel book is then placed on the cloth. Again the celebrant censes the *Epitaphios*, afterwards sprinkling rose water and strewing flowers on it. Each of the clergy and the faithful come forward, first prostrating twice before the cloth, after which they kiss the image of Christ and the gospel book. Each worshiper is given a flower, and then a third and final prostration is made.[115]

In Czarist Russia the *Epitaphios* would be placed with a "silver coffin bearing a cross" in the middle of the church, amidst flowers and lights. The people would each come forward on their knees to kiss the cross and venerate the *Epitaphios*.[116]

In Egypt's Coptic Rite a service analogous to the *Platsenitsia* is held late in the day on Good Friday. As early as the fourteenth century the wrapping of a cross "in a cloth in figure of the shrouding of the body of Our Savior" and the sprinkling of "fragrant plants and roses" in commemoration of the embalming is mentioned in a Coptic book, Abu'l Barakat's *The Lamp of the Darkness*.[117] In the current rite the senior priest wraps an icon of the burial of Christ (or one of the crucifixion) in a veil of white linen, and laying a cross upon the wrapped image, places it on the southwest corner of the altar. He then strews roses and myrrh on or around the shrouded icon, after which he puts over it a second cloth known as the *Prospherein*. The priest sets two lighted candlesticks on the altar, one to the north and the other to the south of the icon; these lights symbolize the two angels in the tomb of our Lord. The clergy begin the recital of the Psalms, and upon reaching verse five of the third Psalm, "I lie down and sleep," they descend from the sanctuary, after which a curtain of red or white material is drawn before the sanctuary door.[118]

Good Friday in the Maronite Rite

In the Church's Syro-Maronite Rite, found mostly in Lebanon, Syria, Egypt, and Cyprus, Good Friday is known as "the Sorrowful Friday"; the liturgy for this day contains a number of remarkable features, as is evident in Father Peter Sfeir's account of Holy Week among the Maronite Catholics of Lebanon (1928). The more dramatic aspects of the ceremonies here described had in large part been introduced into the Maronite liturgy by the seventeenth century,[119] with some elements probably borrowed from an extraliturgical service conducted by the Franciscans each year at the Church of the Holy Sepulchre in Jerusalem (see chapter IX).[120] At this time of the year in Lebanon the air is filled with such a fragrance that no other season can compare with it. The land, even in rocky areas, is clothed with fresh grass and splendidly varied flowers. On the morning of Good Friday, the people lay aside all their normal occupations and go into the fields and gardens around their villages, barefooted in a spirit of self-denial, there to search for flowers. After collecting a large supply, they return to their homes and fashion bouquets, one for each member of the family. Then at a certain hour the church bell is rung, in a peculiar manner suited to "the spirit of the day," calling the people to the Good Friday service about to begin. In the church, a wooden crucifix covered with a transparent veil rests upon a rich cloth laid on the first step of the sanctuary, outside the altar rail. As each person enters he approaches the crucifix, prostrates himself before it, and kisses the wounded feet of Christ. On the cloth he leaves his bouquet of flowers and then, after a short prayer, proceeds to his place in the church. Soon the Crucified is surrounded with flowers, covering the whole cloth.

Atop the stripped altar is another cross, a large wooden one draped in a thin black veil. On either side of it is a candle stand with an unlit taper. These two candles symbolize the two thieves with whom our Lord was crucified; both are unlit, since at first both thieves joined in the mockery of Christ on the cross:

> And the robbers who were crucified with him also reviled him in the same way.
>
> [Mt 27:44]

A corpus made for this service is mounted on the wooden cross; the arms can be moved, and the nails and crown of thorns are removable.

The rite begins with several hymns followed by the reading of the gospel account of the passion. When the passage relating the conversion of one of the two thieves (Lk 23:39-43) is read, the candle to the right of the large crucifix is lit, signifying the reclamation of his soul. The left candle remains unlit.

As the verse relating the death of Christ is read, the black veil is stripped from the large crucifix on the altar. Wearing a surplice, black cope, and stole, the celebrant and two attendants now kneel down at the bottom step of the altar. The former chants a prayer concerning the removal of the crown of thorns while the two attendants step forward and reverently take the crown from our Lord's head, laying it on a tray brought by an acolyte. Similarly, nails are removed from the wounded hands and the arms lowered down to each side after another relevant prayer is said; the nails are likewise put on a tray. With a final prayer two more nails are removed from the feet; the attendants then give the corpus to the celebrant.

Assuming the role of pallbearers, four priests or pious laymen and an attendant go to the flower-covered cloth at the foot of the sanctuary, and after removing the crucifix on it, lift the cloth to their shoulders and lay it on a stretcher. They now bring it before the celebrant, who reverently lays the corpus of the Crucified upon this "bed of flowers."

A procession forms, led by acolytes and members of the clergy carrying lighted tapers. Then comes the celebrant, who continuously censes the "coffin of flowers" borne by the pallbearers directly behind him. The attendants follow, carrying the trays that hold the nails and crown of thorns. Behind them a choir and some of the faithful walk, chanting a Syro-Maronite hymn of the passion, *Ya shaabie wa saabie:*

O my people, my friends,
where is your oath of fidelity,
the payment of your love's debt?
Where is your submission?
Like a homicide, an enemy,
you have delivered me to ill-treatment,
and naked between thieves you have crucified me.

What have I done to deserve that?
Who are my accusers,
and what are the proofs
of the sentence pronounced against me?
Do you recall no longer
my acts of charity and generosity?
How many of your sick
who were incurable have I healed?

O you, who see my sorrows,
contemplate my sufferings,
and hear my mother's weeping,
have you ever seen anyone
who has suffered so much as I,
anyone who has drunk of my chalice
or tasted of its bitterness?

O Mary, my mother,
your lamentations increase my sorrows;
for compassion's sake leave me.
Why, my Father, hast Thou forsaken me?
My tortures have choked me
and my flesh has been torn!

The incomparable beauty of the cortege, set to the haunting strains of this Oriental chant, move many of the faithful to tears. So extraordinary is the service that even large numbers of Moslems attend. There is a belief among the Islamic women that if during the procession those who are childless get the opportunity to pass beneath the "Coffin of Christ," God will grant their prayers for a child. For this reason quite a number of these anxious women stand praying in the path of the cortege. Many of them afterwards assert that God did indeed answer their supplication by sending them a baby; nor do they neglect to show their gratitude, for they invariably return to the church with their little ones and there kiss the altar step, say a prayer, and leave a donation.

Under the right side altar a "tomb" has been readied. When the procession reaches it the "coffin of flowers" is put into the sepulchre; the celebrant censes the figure of the Crucified and then draws a curtain across the door of the tomb, setting a lighted oil lamp in front of it. He and the rest of the clergy and attendants kneel, bow three times, and pray: "O Christ, Who has been crucified for us, have mercy on us." A beautiful fragrance of fresh flowers and incense lingers about the sepulchre, reminiscent of the aloes and myrrh with which the Body of Christ was prepared for burial on that first Good Friday.[121]

Endnotes

1. Father John H. Miller, CSC, "The History and Spirit of Holy Week," *American Ecclesiastical Review*, April 1957, p. 229.
2. Ibid.
3. Ibid.
4. Father Herman Schmidt, SJ, *Hebdomada Sancta: Fontes Historici, Commentarius Historicus*, 1957, Vol. II, pp. 778-779. For text of *Ordo 23* see *Les Ordines Romani du Haut Moyen Age: III: Les Textes (Ordines XIV-XXXIV)* (Etudes et Documents, Vol. 24), Michel Andrieu, ed., 1961, p. 271.
5. Congregation for Divine Worship, *Circular Letter Concerning the Preparation and Celebration of the Easter Feasts*, Feb 20, 1988, #65, in *L'Osservatore Romano*, Feb 29, 1988, p. 17.
6. Dom Germain Morin, "Le plus ancien *Comes* de l'Eglise Romaine," *Revue Benedictine*, Vol. 27 (1910), p. 54; Dom G. Morin, "Liturgie et basiliques de Rome au milieu du VII siecle: D'apres les Listes d'Evangiles de Wurzburg," *Revue Benedictine*, Vol. 28 (1911), p. 304.
7. Reverend John Tyrer, *Historical Survey of Holy Week: Its Services and Ceremonial* (Alcuin Club Collections #29), 1932, p. 123.
8. See chapter X, pp. 306.
9. See chapter II, pp. 56-57.
10. Father Herbert Thurston, SJ, *Lent and Holy Week*, 1904, p. 232; the selection of Saint Matthew's gospel is mentioned by Tyrer, p. 122.
11. R. H. Connolly, "Liturgical Prayers of Intercession: I: The Good

Friday Orationes Solemnes," *Journal of Theological Studies*, 1920, pp. 219-221.

12. Ibid., pp. 221-223.
13. *Gelasian Sacramentary* in *Patrologia Latina*, Vol. 74, col. 1103c-1105c; Paduan in *Le Sacramentaire Gregorien: Ses principales formes d'apres les plus anciens manuscrits: I* (Spicilegium Friburgense, Vol. 16), Jean Deshusses, ed., 2nd ed., 1979, pp. 630-631.
14. Translation from Tyrer, p. 124 (footnote).
15. G. G. Willis, "The Solemn Prayers of Good Friday," *Essays in Early Liturgy* (Alcuin Club Collections, #46), 1964, p. 41.
16. ". . . in view of the introduction of certain changes in the Order of Holy Week, it has seemed well to modify a phrase here and there in the solemn prayers for Good Friday so that they may be more in accord with the mind and decrees of Vatican Council II regarding ecumenism" (Congregation of Sacred Rites, *Quamplures Episcopi*, 7 March 1965, in *Documents on the Liturgy, 1963-1979: Conciliar, Papal and Curial Texts*, International Commission on English in the Liturgy, 1982, p. 1186).
17. Connolly, p. 225.
18. *The Hours of the Divine Office in English and Latin*, Liturgical Press, 1964, Vol. II, p. 148.
19. Tyrer, p. 133.
20. *Patrologia Latina*, Vol. 74, col. 1105d.
21. Andrieu, *Les Ordines*, pp. 270-272.
22. *Patrologia Latina*, Vol. 78, col. 954b.
23. Jerome Gassner, OSB, "The 'Reproaches,' " *Homiletic and Pastoral Review*, Feb 1946, pp. 324, 325-327.
24. Ibid., p. 323.
25. Ibid., p. 324.
26. *Patrologia Latina*, Vol. 72, col. 89c-90a.
27. *Le Pontifical Romain au Moyen Age: Tome I: Le Pontifical Romain du XII siecle* (Studi e Testi, Vol. 86), Michel Andrieu, ed., 1938, p. 236.
28. T. P. Gilmartin, "Good Friday," *Catholic Encyclopedia*, 1907, Vol. 6, p. 644.
29. Schmidt, Vol. II, p. 794.
30. Ibid., Vol. II, p. 796; I.-H. Dalmais, "L'Adoration de la Croix," *La Maison-Dieu*, Vol. 45, 1956, p. 81.
31. Schmidt, Vol. II, p. 795; for texts of Good Friday *troparia* specified in *Georgian Lectionary* see Adolf Rucker, "Die Adoratio Crucis am Karfreitag in Den Orientalishen Riten," *Miscellanea Liturgica in*

Honorem L. Cuniberti Mohlberg (Biblio "Ephemerides Liturgicae," #22), Vol. I, pp. 383-387.

32. Tyrer, p. 131.

33. Text in *Missale Romanum: Mediolani, 1474: Vol. I: Text* (Henry Bradshaw Society, Vol. 17), Robert Lippe, ed., 1899, pp. 170-171.

34. *De Ecclesiasticis Officiis*, Liber I, Caput XIV, quoted in Tyrer, p. 129.

35. Text in *Missale Romanum: Mediolani, 1474: Vol. II: A Collation with Other Editions Printed Before 1570* (Henry Bradshaw Society, Vol. 33), Robert Lippe, ed., 1907, p. 79.

36. *The Monastic Constitutions of Lanfranc*, David Knowles, ed./tr., pp. 40-41.

37. Ibid.

38. *Ordinarium Canonicorum Regularium S. Laudi Rotomagensis*, in *Patrologia Latina*, Vol. 147, col. 174a, c, d.

39. Father Herbert Thurston, SJ, "Cross," *Catholic Encyclopedia*, 1907, Vol. 4, p. 533.

40. *The Ordinal and Customary of the Benedictine Nuns of Barking Abbey* (Henry Bradshaw Society, Vol. 65), J. B. J. Tolhurst, ed., 1927, Vol. I, p. 99.

41. *Patrologia Latina*, Vol. 85, col. 430a, 431b.

42. Liber II, Caput XXV, #23, p. 253 (1902 printing).

43. Titulus V, Caput II, ii, #5, p. 46 (1862 printing).

44. *The English-Latin Sacramentary*, Benziger Brothers, 1966, p. 99.

45. *Missale Romanum*, Typis Polyglottis Vaticanis, 1970, "Feria VI in Passione Domini," #14-#20, pp. 256-258; *Caeremoniale Episcoporum*, Typis Polyglottis Vaticanis, 1985, Caput X, #315, #321-#324, pp. 91, 93-94.

46. *Rituale Romanum: De Benedictionibus*, Typis Polyglottis Vaticanis, 1985, Caput XXVIII ("Ordo Benedictionis Novae Crucis Publicae Venerationi Exhibendae"), #961, #962, p. 364.

47. In an age when crucifixion is a long-forgotten form of execution, an empty cross runs the risk of becoming an ambiguous symbol; but the crucifix confronts us with the "scandal of the cross" in its fullest measure. See Albert F. Kaiser, CPPS, "The Historical Backgrounds and Theology of *Mediator Dei*: Part I: Backgrounds," *American Ecclesiastical Review*, Dec 1953, p. 378.

48. It appears in the rubrics of the *Roman Pontifical* of the twelfth century (Andrieu, *Le Pontifical*, p. 236).

49. Andrieu, *Les Ordines*, p. 498.

50. For the dating of this document cited repeatedly by Dom Menard in his "Notae et observationes in librum sacramentorum sancti

Gregorii papae I" (reprinted in *Patrologia Latina*, Vol. 78), see Cyrille Vogel, *The Medieval Liturgy: An Introduction to the Sources*, p. 229, and Aime-Georges Martimort, *La Documentation liturgique de Dom Edmund Martene* (Studi e Testi, #279), 1978, p. 97.

51. O. B. Hardison, *Christian Rite and Christian Drama in the Middle Ages*, pp. 131-132 (for Latin text see commentary of Dom Menard in *Patrologia Latina*, Vol. 78, col. 332d-333a). Translation of *Trisagion* and *Improperia* refrain from *The Vatican II Sunday Missal*, Daughters of St. Paul, p. 406.

52. Spelling modernized; original text quoted in Karl Young, *The Drama of the Medieval Church*, 1933, Vol. I, pp. 137-138.

53. Father Herbert Thurston, SJ, *Lent and Holy Week*, 1904, p. 358.

54. *Missale Romanum* (1942 edition), Benziger Brothers, 1952, "Feria Sexta in Parasceve," p. 183 (English tr. of rubrics in *Holy Week: Containing the Offices of Holy Week from the Roman Breviary and Missal*, John Murphy & Co., n.d. [ca. 1860], pp. 109-110); *Caeremoniale Episcoporum* (1886 edition), Liber II, Caput XXV, #3, #22-#27, pp. 248-249, 253-254; *Memoriale Rituum* (1853 edition), Titulus V, Caput I, Caput II, ii, #1-#17, pp. 43, 46-48.

55. The color of the cloth is not specified in the 1853 *Memoriale Rituum*, but it is given in the 1920 edition (Title V, chapter I, in *The Ritual for Small Churches: A Translation of the Memoriale Rituum*, Father Bartholomew Eustace, ed., 1935, p. 61).

56. Alquien, pp. 853-854.

57. Tyrer, pp. 118-119, 137-138.

58. Mario Righetti, *Manuale Di Storia Liturgica*, 1950, Vol. II, p. 179 (footnote).

59. See p. 252 of this chapter.

60. Tyrer, p. 134. For original text see *Patrologia Graeca*, Vol. 92, col. 989a-b, 990a-b.

61. *Patrologia Latina*, Vol. 74, col. 1105c, d.

62. Ibid., Vol. 78, col. 954a-c (summarized in Tyrer, p. 135).

63. Miller, p. 231; for relevant text of twelfth-century *Roman Pontifical*, see Andrieu, *Le Pontifical*, p. 237.

64. Lippe, Vol. II, pp. 81-83 (summarized in Tyrer, pp. 135-136).

65. *Patrologia Latina*, Vol. 85, col. 418c, 432b-436a; English translation in Hardison, pp. 134-135.

66. J. D. Crichton, *The Liturgy of Holy Week*, 1983, p. 59.

67. *Patrologia Latina*, Vol. 74, col. 1105d.

68. Andrieu, *Les Ordines*, p. 272.

69. *Le Pontifical Romano-Germanique du Dixieme Siecle: Le Texte: II* (Studi e Testi, Vol. 227), Cyrille Vogel and Reinhard Elze, eds., 1963, p. 93.

70. *Regularis Concordia: The Monastic Agreement of the Monks and Nuns of the English Nation* (Medieval Classics), Dom Thomas Symons, tr., p. 45.

71. *Ordinarium Canonicorum Regularium* of John of Avranches (eleventh century) in *Patrologia Latina*, Vol. 147, col. 175a-b; *Consuetudines Cluniacenses* of Udalric (eleventh century) in ibid., Vol. 149, col. 662a-b.

72. Lippe, Vol. II, p. 83.

73. Tyrer, p. 140.

74. *Instruction on the Correct Use of the Restored Ordo of Holy Week*, Nov 16, 1955, Section I, #2c, in *American Ecclesiastical Review*, Jan 1956, p. 57.

75. Based upon two accounts from the 1860s: "Good Friday at Jerusalem," *The Month*, Vol. IV, Jan-June 1866, pp. 350-351; "Holy Week in Jerusalem," *The Catholic World*, Vol. VII, April-Sep 1868, p. 79.

76. *The Catholic World*, p. 79.

77. *The Month*, pp. 350-351.

78. Liturgical texts from *The Vatican II Sunday Missal*, pp. 386-410, and *Lectionary for Mass*, Catholic Book Pub. Co., 1970, pp. 89-93.

79. Abbot Guéranger, OSB, *The Liturgical Year*, 1952, Vol. 6, pp. 140-141.

80. Antiphon for Good Friday, tr. in *Roman Missal* (1960 ed.), Benziger Bros., 1964, p. 193.

81. Excerpt, *The Catholic Anthology: The World's Great Catholic Poetry*, Thomas Walsh, ed., 1943, p. 32.

82. Sermon 62 (*"De passione Domini XI"*), V, *The Sunday Sermons of the Great Fathers*, M. F. Toal, ed., 1958, Vol. II, p. 183.

83. Text of Johann Heermann, tr. by Robert Bridges, in *The Yattendon Hymnal*, Oxford University Press.

84. D. Pochin Mould, "Byzantine Holy Week," *Doctrine and Life*, Vol. 14, March 1964, p. 180.

85. Father Francis X. Weiser, SJ, *The Easter Book*, 1954, pp. 119-120.

86. John Wilkinson, *Egeria's Travels*, 1971, pp. 267-269.

87. Rubrics of *Georgian Lectionary* in Theodor Kluge and Anton Baumstark, "Quadragesima und Karwoche Jerusalems im siebten Jahrhundert," *Oriens Christianus*, Vol. 5, new series (1915), pp. 225-229.

88. Kenneth Stevenson refers to this rite as a symbolic "burial of the cross" ("The Ceremonies of Light: Their Shape and Function in the

Paschal Vigil Liturgy," *Ephemerides Liturgicae*, 1985, p. 175).

89. *Analekta Hierosolymitikes Stachyologias*, A. Papadopoulos-Kerameus, ed., 1894 (rpt. 1963), Vol. II, pp. 147-162.

90. Rubrics in *Le Typicon de la Grande Eglise: Tome II: Le Cycle des Fetes mobiles* (Orientalia Christiana Analecta #166), Juan Mateos, ed., 1963, pp. 78-83.

91. Current readings listed in I.-H. Dalmais, "Le *Triduum Sacrum* dans la liturgie Byzantine," *La Maison Dieu*, 1955, Vol. 41, p. 125. In the *Typicon of the Anastasis* the Isaiah lection is one verse shorter (52:13-53:12 — as in the current Liturgy of the Passion in the Roman Rite).

92. Mateos, p. 83 (note).

93. *De Locis Sanctis*, III, iii, in *Corpus Christianorum, Series Latina: CLXXV: Itineraria et Alia Geographia*, pp. 228-229; also Daphne Pochin Mould, "Holy Cross Day," *Doctrine and Life*, Sep 1963, p. 459.

94. Gerard Bonnet, "Le Mystere de la Croix dans le Careme Orthodoxe" (Part One), *Irenikon*, 1979, Vol. 52, pp. 44-45.

95. Mateos, pp. 72-73, 78-79.

96. *Patrologia Graeca*, Vol. 112, col. 421a-424a.

97. Father Herbert Thurston, SJ, "Lance, The Holy," *Catholic Encyclopedia*, 1907, Vol. 8, p. 773.

98. Father Robert Taft, SJ, *The Great Entrance: A History of the Transfer of Gifts and other Preanaphoral Rites of the Liturgy of Saint John Chrysostom* (Orientalia Christiana Analecta #200), 1978, pp. 210, 216-217, 244.

99. Ibid., p. 216.

100. Ibid.

101. Ibid., pp. 217-218.

102. Thus it appears in the *Typicon of the Anastasis* (Papadopoulos-Kerameus, Vol. II, pp. 161, 162).

103. Hans Joachim Schulz, *The Byzantine Liturgy: Symbolic Structure and faith Expression*, 1986, p. 19.

104. Taft, pp. 217-218.

105. *De Sacra Liturgia*, chapter 96, in *Patrologia Graeca*, Vol. 155, col. 288a.

106. "Trebnik Cod. Moscow Synod 377," cited in Taft, p. 218.

107. Ian Wilson, *Holy Faces, Secret Places: An Amazing Quest for the Face of Jesus*, 1991, p. 153.

108. Ian Wilson, *The Shroud of Turin: The Burial Cloth of Jesus Christ?*, 1979, p. 95.

109. Ibid., p. 162.

110. The results of the Carbon-14 tests on the Shroud of Turin, dating the cloth to the period A.D. 1260-1390, have not resolved the question

of the Shroud's authenticity as a relic of the passion. There is a considerable mass of scientific and archaeological data that contradicts the Carbon-14 dating. See John P. Jackson, "The Radiocarbon Date and How the Image was Formed on the Shroud," and John Tyrer, "Textile Questions that Remain Following the Carbon Dating Test," both in *Shroud Spectrum International*, Sep-Dec 1988, pp. 2-12 and 13-15 respectively; regarding the historical questions that remain see Ian Wilson, *Holy Faces*, pp. 5-13, 130-181.

111. John Beckwith, *Early Christian and Byzantine Art* (The Pelican History of Art), 1970, pp. 156-157.

112. Ian Wilson, *The Mysterious Shroud*, 1986, pp. 114, 116-117; Wilson, *The Shroud of Turin*, p. 161.

113. Taft, p. 210.

114. Ibid., p. 216.

115. Mould, p. 180; A. Verheul, "Le Mystere du Samedi Saint," *Questions Liturgiques*, 1984, pp. 33-34.

116. Weiser, p. 120.

117. Dom Emmanual Lanne, OSB, "Textes et rites de la liturgie Pascale dans l'ancienne Eglise Copte," *L'Orient Syrien*, Vol. 6, 1961, p. 296. The *Lamp* was written before 1328 (Lanne, p. 279).

118. O. Hadji-Burmester, "Rites and Ceremonies of the Coptic Church: Part XI: Holy Week Services and Ceremonies," *Eastern Churches Quarterly*, Autumn 1956, pp. 329, 333-335.

119. Rucker, pp. 402-403.

120. Solange Corbin, *La Deposition liturgique du Christ au Vendredi Saint: Sa Place dans l'histoire des rites et du theatre religieux*, p. 245.

121. Father Peter Sfeir, "Holy Week Customs in Syria," *The Catholic Mind*, April 22, 1928, pp. 148-152; passion hymn text in Father P. Sfeir, "From Other Lands: Good Friday and Easter in the Syrian Church," *Orate Fratres*, Vol. 7, April 15, 1933, p. 268.

IX

Sunset on Good Friday

By oppression and judgment he was taken away;
and as for his generation, who considered
that he was cut off out of the land of the living,
stricken for the transgression of my people?
And they made his grave with the wicked
and with a rich man in his death,
although he had done no violence,
and there was no deceit in his mouth.

[Is 53:8-9]

The Entombment of Christ

And when evening had come, since it was the day of Preparation,
that is, the day before the sabbath, Joseph of Arimathea, a respected
member of the council, who was also himself looking for the kingdom
of God, took courage and went to Pilate, and asked for the body of Jesus.

[Mk 15:42-43]

FOLLOWING THE LITURGY OF the Passion there are no further liturgical services in the Roman Rite on Good Friday. Yet the desire to commemorate the concluding scenes of the passion has resulted in the development of a variety of devotional exercises focusing upon the death and burial of our Savior.[1] These devotions build upon the themes of the Liturgy of the Passion, and help the faithful to continue their reflections upon the events of this solemn day. In the West the earliest records of such customs, dating from the tenth century, describe an extraliturgical Good Friday rite known as the *Depositio*, the "Deposition," in which the burial of Christ is symbolically reenacted by the placing of a cross, crucifix, or image of Christ laid in death and/or the holy Eucharist into an enclosure representing the holy sepulchre. As previously noted, there was during an earlier period in Jerusalem a symbolic "washing" of the cross in commemoration of the Burial of Christ, according to the *Georgian Lectionary*, thought to contain practices from the fifth to eighth centuries.[2] Even in Egeria's time (fourth century) Jerusalem observed a watch at the holy sepulchre on the night of Good Friday (although Egeria does not specifically mention any Deposition rite). It is possible that pilgrims returning from the Holy Land carried the idea of a Good Friday Deposition to the West; in any event, by the tenth century the *Depositio* had appeared both in Germany and in England.[3] During the Middle Ages the ceremony spread throughout northern and central Europe; in his two-volume work *The Drama of the Medieval Church*, Karl Young cites examples of the *Depositio* from France, Belgium, Hungary, Austria, Switzerland, Czechoslovakia, Ireland, and northern Italy, as well as England and Germany.[4] It existed in Sweden and Norway as well.[5]

> *And he [Joseph] bought a linen shroud, and taking him down, wrapped him in the linen shroud. . . .*
>
> [Mk 15:46]

One of the very earliest examples of the *Depositio* is to be found in a document containing observances of English Benedictine monasteries during the tenth century, known as the *Regularis Concordia* of Saint Ethelwold.[6] On an empty section of the altar was placed "a representation as it were of a sepulchre, hung about with a curtain" ("a veil stretched upon a ring," according to Young[7]). Following Veneration of the Cross deacons would wrap the cross used for the preceding ceremony in a cloth symbolizing the burial shroud of Christ. While antiphons were chanted, the wrapped cross was borne to the "sepulchre" and there deposited, after which the antiphon *Sepulto Domino*, a responsory from the Divine Office for Holy Saturday, was chanted: *"The Lord having been buried, the sepulchre is sealed. . . ."* This antiphon was destined to reappear in virtually all other medieval versions of the *Depositio* ceremony. A watch was kept at the symbolic tomb of Christ from the conclusion of the *Depositio* until the "night of the Lord's Resurrection"; at least two brothers were always present at the sepulchre, chanting Psalms through the night.

> *Nicodemus also, who had at first come to him by night, came bringing a mixture of myrrh and aloes, about a hundred pounds' weight. They took the body of Jesus, and bound it in linen cloths with*

the spices, as is the burial custom of the Jews.

[Jn 19:39-40]

In the majority of medieval *Depositio* rites the object "buried" was a cross or crucifix. But there were many local variations in the details of the burial ceremony. At the Cathedral of Rouen, France (thirteenth century), the *Depositio* immediately followed Veneration of the Cross. In remembrance of the flow of blood and water from our Lord's side, the crucifix was washed with wine and water, then borne to the sepulchre and laid in it, where it was covered with a winding sheet and censed before the door of the sepulchre was closed.[8] At Moosburg in Germany (ca. 1500) the crucifix was wrapped both in linen cloths (*linteamina*) and in a shroud (*sudarium*), in conformity with the two separate burial cloths mentioned by Saint John (Jn 20:6-7).[9] At Andechs (Germany) and elsewhere the altar stone (that is, the *lapis*) was used for the purpose of closing the sepulchre in the manner of the stone rolled before the tomb in the gospels (Mt 27:60; Mk 15:46; Lk 24:2; Jn 20:1).[10] In Seckau, Austria (sixteenth century) the sepulchre was sealed with wax, an action undoubtedly derived from Saint Matthew's reference to the sealing of Christ's tomb by the Pharisees (Mt 27:66).[11]

Now in the place where he was crucified there was a garden, and in the garden a new tomb where no one had ever been laid. So because of the Jewish day of Preparation, as the tomb was close at hand, they laid Jesus there.

[Jn 19:41-42]

The "sepulchre" in which the cross was placed was usually a wooden or stone structure adorned with rich crimson, purple, or gold drapery. Candles were lit before these shrines, sometimes in large numbers; thus at the college church of Saint Edmund's in Salisbury, England, the sepulchre was surrounded by a hundred tapers.[12] In some cases statues of angels or of Roman soldiers were placed around the tomb. Another frequently used furnishing was that of an empty cross of wood, draped about with a winding sheet; such a feature was still common in the sepulchre scenes of northern Italy at the turn of the century.[13]

Down in yon forest there stands a hall:
cover'd all over with purple and pall:
In that hall there stands a bed:

cover'd all over with scarlet so red:

And in that bed there lieth a knight,
His wounds bleeding day and night.

At the bed-side there lies a stone:
Which the sweet Virgin Mary knelt upon:

Under that bed there runs a flood:
The one half runs water, the other runs blood. . . .
[*Down in Yon Forest,* Medieval English Carol][14]

Clergy and laity maintained a continuous watch before these sepulchres, beginning with the *Depositio* ceremony on Good Friday and continuing through Holy Saturday. The origin of this practice is thought to lie in the much more ancient belief of the early Christians that the Second Coming of our Lord at the end of the world would take place during the night before Easter Sunday. This belief lasted into the Middle Ages and thus prompted the mounting of a continuous watch.[15] Candles or lamps were kept burning before the "tomb" throughout the long vigil. In a number of cases watchers recited the Psalter (the Psalms) while at the Easter sepulchre. Students performed this function in the Bavarian city of Augsburg (1453); in Biberach (also in southern Germany) school children chanted the Psalms antiphonally while sitting beside the "tomb," according to an account from 1535.[16] In some places the custom of the sepulchre "watch" was continued into the present century. As late as 1938, a continuous watch was still being kept not only during the daylight hours but through the night as well in Schingiswalde (along the German-Czechoslovakian border near Dresden).[17] In Austria, an honor guard of army soldiers, arrayed in full parade uniform, with fixed bayonets and steel helmets, was customarily posted near the sepulchre, serving to atone for the irreverent Roman guards assigned to the original tomb of Christ. While keeping watch the Austrian soldiers would "take turns standing at 'present arms.' "[18]

Frequently the Eucharistic Species remaining after the Mass of the Presanctified or a third Host consecrated on Holy Thursday for reservation in the Easter sepulchre was the center of devotion in the medieval *Depositio* ceremony. This practice may have arisen from the necessity to reserve some Hosts following the general Communion on this day.[19] Sometimes the Blessed Sacrament was put into the sepulchre

[270]

together with a cross or crucifix; in other cases the Eucharist alone was deposited. In fact, the earliest recorded *Depositio* ceremony in the West, mentioned in a tenth-century biography of Saint Ulrich, a bishop of the German diocese of Augsburg, involved the "burial" of the holy Eucharist rather than a cross:

> On Good Friday . . . early in the morning, he [St. Ulrich] hastened to complete the Psalm service; and, when the holy mystery of God was completed, the people fed with the holy Corpus Christi, and the remainder buried in the customary manner, he finished the Psalm service while walking from church to church. . . . When the most delectable day of Easter arrived, he entered the church of St. Ambrose after prime, where he had placed the Corpus Christi on Good Friday, covering it with a stone. And there with a few clerks he celebrated the Mass of the Holy Trinity. When the Mass was completed, he took the Corpus Christi and the gospels [gospel book] with him, along with candles and incense. And . . . he proceeded to the church of St. John the Baptist.[20]

As is evident in the above example, the Blessed Sacrament was not only deposited in the sepulchre to commemorate the burial of Christ; it was also later brought forth from the "tomb" on Easter Sunday to commemorate the resurrection; the latter ceremony, known as the *Elevatio,* will be discussed at length in chapter XII.

The manner in which the Sacrament was carried in procession to the Easter sepulchre differed in certain respects from place to place. At the Monastery of Saint Blaise in Germany's Black Forest (fourteenth century) the Hosts reserved for the Viaticum of the sick, presumably in a pyx, were brought with candles and incense to the sepulchre, while the responsories *Agnus Dei Christus* and *Ecce quomodo moritur* from the Office of Matins for Holy Saturday were sung.[21] In Gran, Hungary (1580), a third Host consecrated on Holy Thursday for this ceremony was borne on a paten atop a chalice, covered with cloths; the holy Eucharist along with the chalice and paten were placed together in the sepulchre, which was then closed, sealed, and censed, as the responsories *Jerusalem, luge* (from Matins of Holy Saturday) and *Sepulto Domino* were chanted.[22] Sometimes a special vessel other than a chalice or pyx was used for the reservation of the Host in the Easter sepulchre. Thus at the Abbey of Durham, England (sixteenth century, pre-Reformation) the Eucharist was enclosed under crystal in the breast of a "finely gilded" image of Christ which was deposited in the Easter sepulchre along with a gold crucifix that had been used earlier for the Veneration of the Cross.[23]

In the sixteenth century the Eucharistic *Depositio* ceremony of Good Friday underwent a significant change. With the onslaught of the Protestant Reformation, belief in the real presence of Christ in the Eucharist was challenged in many places, particularly northern Europe. In response to this attack, there arose the desire to reaffirm and publicly confess faith in the holy Eucharist with particular fervor on Good Friday, the day on which the sacrifice of Calvary was consummated. Prior to this time the Eucharist had traditionally been placed within the Easter sepulchre on this day so as to represent the burial of Christ. But now a new custom was introduced; instead of concealing the Blessed Sacrament in the sepulchre, the Host was placed atop the sepulchre for public exposition, either in a chalice or in a veiled monstrance. The newly founded Society of Jesus (the Jesuits) was instrumental in the introduction of this practice in the Bavarian region of Germany during the latter part of the sixteenth century. In one of the earliest descriptions of these "Jesuit Easter Sepulchres," dating from 1580, we learn that in Munich the Blessed Sacrament was placed in a "hall" (presumably a chapel), the walls of which were decked with black tapestries. The sepulchre itself featured a statue of Christ resting in death; the Eucharist was mounted in a veiled monstrance above the tomb. The sepulchre was surrounded with numerous lit candelabras and lamps, as well as with statues of adoring angels and of various scenes from the passion. Father Paul Hoffaeus, the Jesuit Provincial of Bavaria, and Father Ferdinand Alber, the Rector of the Jesuit school known as the "Gymnasium," took turns delivering sermons to the faithful concerning the passion and death of our Lord, with funeral music played between the sermons.[24]

This manner of veiled exposition at the Easter sepulchre on Good Friday eventually spread throughout southern Germany, Austria, Poland, Hungary, Bohemia (western Czechoslovakia), and Slavonia (northern Yugoslavia) and continued into the present century.[25] Special rubrical directions were composed for the ceremony by the dioceses in these regions, such as are found in the *Salzburg Ritual* (Austria), which dates from 1686. According to this *Ritual*, a third Host was consecrated on Holy Thursday; at the end of the Mass of the Presanctified on Good Friday, the Host was carried by the celebrant in a veiled chalice to the Easter sepulchre (what is known as the *Heilige Grab* in Germany and Austria), where he inserted it into a monstrance that was covered with a white silk veil. A deacon then placed the veiled monstrance on a throne above the sepulchre; the Sacrament remained thus, adored by the faithful, until the evening, when it was taken out of the monstrance for the night and deposited in a tabernacle used for the reservation of the Viaticum of the sick. On Holy Saturday morning the Host was put back into the monstrance; once again the faithful came to keep watch at the sepulchre until this "exposition" concluded with a service commemorating the resurrection (the *Elevatio*).[26] The rite we have just described is fairly representative of this practice everywhere, but there were certain differences from one place to another. Thus in some dioceses the Host was inserted in the veiled monstrance at the high altar and then carried in it (rather than in a chalice) to the Easter sepulchre.[27]

The various diocesan rituals directed that the "exposition" rite of the Easter sepulchre was to be conducted in a manner consonant with the mournful atmosphere of Good Friday and Holy Saturday. For example, the candles or lamps placed about these Easter sepulchres were often dimmed with colored "Easter globes" (hollow glass globes), resulting in a subdued light more appropriate to the occasion.[28] Such was the usage in the German Diosese of Augsburg (ca. 1900):

> These are variously coloured glass globes about four inches in diameter, filled with water, which are arranged in rows one above another around the sepulchre, often to the number of many score, and are brilliantly illuminated by means of oil lamps placed behind them. In order to heighten the colour effect the water is mixed with chemicals and brilliant pigments. The church windows are also hung with black draperies in order to exclude the daylight.[29]

But above all, the veiling of the monstrance created an inherently different atmosphere from that usually associated with exposition of the Blessed Sacrament on Corpus Christi and other festive occasions. Indeed, this Good Friday custom did not really constitute exposition in the strict sense, for the Host was more or less concealed by the translucent veil covering the monstrance. In 1896 the Congregation of Sacred Rites issued a Decree (#3939 ad 3) permitting the continued observance of this rite in southern Germany and Austria, and thus it was retained in these regions into the present century. In an official commentary on its 1896 Decree, the Congregation of Sacred Rites acknowledged that it had prohibited Eucharistic versions of the Easter sepulchre in other places, but pointed out special circumstances justifying the practice in Austria and Germany. The Congregation also stressed that the bringing of the Blessed Sacrament to a "sepulchre" is not at all contrary to faith, as some had suggested, for while it is true that the impassible, risen Body of Christ is present in the holy Eucharist, it is likewise true that this Sacrament *re-presents* the passion and death of the Lord, as indicated in the words of consecration: ". . . this is my body which will be given up for you . . . this is the cup of my blood. . . . It will be shed for you and for all so that sins may be forgiven. . . ."[30] The reader may recall the words of Saint Paul in this regard, which are read at the evening Mass on Holy Thursday: "For as often as you eat this bread and drink the cup, you proclaim the Lord's death until he comes" (1 Cor 11:26). Following the Holy Week reforms of the 1950s the Archbishop of Vienna instructed his pastors to make certain changes regarding the procession of the *Depositio* rite, but authorized them to retain the veiled exposition and adoration of the Host if they chose to do so.[31]

The vast majority of medieval *Depositio* ceremonies of which we have record are from Germany, France, and England. Nevertheless, the rite was to become quite widespread in southern Europe in the centuries that followed. The *Depositio* seems to have been introduced into northern Italy at a relatively early date, for it is claimed that by the eleventh century both the Blessed Sacrament and a cross were being placed in a sepulchre in the Diocese of Milan.[32] We likewise know that a *Depositio* of the cross existed in Padua in the thirteenth century.[33] But these are isolated cases. It is not until the fifteenth century that we begin to find more numerous references to the *Depositio* in Italy; by this time the rite had spread as far south as Naples.[34] In Spain there is no surviving record of a *Depositio* earlier than the sixteenth century. Through the intervention of Saint Francis Borgia, and the granting of a papal privilege, a Eucharistic version of the *Depositio* was introduced at the Royal Monastery of Santa Clara in Gandia (near Valencia) by 1550; the Blessed Sacrament was adored in or at a sepulchre (*expuesto en el monumento*) from Good Friday until the morning of Easter Sunday.[35] There is likewise record of a Eucharistic *Depositio* dating from about the year 1604 conducted by the Discalced Carmelites of Madrid at their Monastery of Descalzadas Reales (where it has continued by special privilege up to the present century).[36] In Portugal, the *Depositio* appears to have entered the country from England in the fourteenth century, when King John I married the English princess Philippa of Lancaster, who brought her entourage and the liturgical practices of her native land to Lisbon; the ceremony is first mentioned explicitly in a description of Good Friday services in the Royal Chapel during the reign of her son King Duarte (1433-1438).[37] By 1561 Portuguese Jesuit missionaries had carried the *Depositio* to India; in an account of the missions of Japan for the year 1581, we learn that the Portuguese Jesuits arranged for the setting up of two sepulchres during Holy Week — the first, very richly adorned, for reposition on Holy Thursday; the second, veiled in black, for the *Depositio* on Good Friday.[38]

> *From afar came there*
> *some few eager ones,*
> *Nobly sought Him in solitude.*
> *As this I saw,*
> *smitten with sorrow,*
> *I must yet bow to the might of man,*
> *Humbly with tireless zeal.*
> *Then they took thence the almighty God,*
> *Lifted Him down from that terrible torment;*
> *there the armed ones left me abandoned,*
> *Wet with the welter,*
> *wounded with arrows.*
>
> [*The Dream of the Rood*][39]

The Deposition ceremonies of which we have thus far spoken, although extraliturgical in that they have never been incorporated into the official liturgy of Rome, nevertheless possess certain liturgical characteristics — the presence of the holy Eucharist in at least some cases, the selection of hymns and verses from the official liturgy (such as *Sepulto Domino*) and the supervision of the clergy (their participation necessitated in all cases of a Eucharistic *Depositio*).[40] Often enough such rites appeared in the official liturgical books of northern and central Europe, such as in the *Sarum* and *Hereford Missals* of medieval England.[41] But it is to Italy that we must look for the origins of a more dramatic and representational form of the *Depositio* which spread across southern Europe (and even into parts of northern Europe) at the end of the Middle Ages. These ceremonies feature a figure of the recumbent Christ (in some cases articulated so that it can be taken down from a cross at the beginning of the ceremony), which is carried in an outdoor stational procession conducted at a late hour of the day by confraternities of laymen; often other scenes from the passion (*tableaux*) are included in the cortege, depicted either with statues or with costumed participants (dressed as the Roman soldiers, the women who mourned at the tomb, among others). The absence of the Eucharist, the less prominent participation of the clergy, the prevalent and even supervisory role of lay confraternities, and the use of quasi-popular hymns (such as the Planctus, *Heu, Heu! Deus meus!*) as well as biblical verses other than those from the official liturgy all indicate the clearly extraliturgical character of such processions.[42] Unfortunately, the beginnings of this practice are veiled in obscurity, but various elements of it had made their appearance by the fifteenth century. Thus, the thirteenth-century *Depositio* of Padua in northern Italy includes the verse, *Domine, jube custodiri sepulchrum — habetis custodiam, ite et custodite sicut scitis* ("Sir, command the sepulchre to be guarded — you have a guard, go and guard it as you know"), a paraphrase of Matthew 27:63-65, and thus a very early example of the use of extraliturgical verses in this setting.[43] In an *Ordinal* of the Benedictine Convent of Barking, England, reflecting practices of the late fourteenth century, we find what is perhaps the earliest example of a *Depositio* in which the corpus of the crucifix from the Veneration of the Cross is detached from the cross by two clerics representing Joseph of Arimathea and Nicodemus, and then laid in a sepulchre.[44] Similar ceremonies existed at Florence (Italy)[45] and Prufening (Germany)[46] during the fifteenth century. In Vienna a seventeenth-century manuscript of a Good Friday Passion Play thought to have been instituted at least a hundred years earlier mentions a procession in Saint Stephan's Church with a corpus taken down from a large cross and carried on a bier to a sepulchre.[47] But in addition to such detachable, articulated images of the Crucified, some figures were sculpted only as entombment statues, portraying Christ resting in death. One of the earliest extant figures of this nature comes from Lucerne, Switzerland, and dates from the beginning of the fifteenth century. The posture of the statue, measuring thirty-nine inches in length, strikingly resembles that of the image on the Shroud of Turin.[48] A number of fifteenth-century references to "Representations" on Good Friday at the Castel Nuovo of Naples suggest that the *Depositio* rite conducted in this southern Italian city (identified as the *funzioni sacre del Sepolcro* in a 1457 account) was also of a highly representational nature.[49] Thus all such evidence seems to indicate that the Italian *Depositio* must have developed during the previous century, the fourteenth, apparently under the influence of three other Italian devotional practices — the Lauds, *Sacred Representations*, and the *Planctus*, which were made popular by the Franciscan Order.[50] There is reportedly a detailed account of a *Depositio* procession in the Archives of the Confraternity of Saint Stephen in Assisi dating from the year 1300; according to Tudor Edwards, a columnist for the English Catholic paper, *The Tablet* (writing in 1956), the current Good Friday procession in Assisi is nearly identical in every aspect to that described in 1300.[51] If this is indeed the case, then the ceremony at Assisi would be by far the oldest recorded version of the Italian *Depositio*, and would further confirm the role of the Franciscans in its development and dissemination.

On Good Friday a wood-carved statue of Christ in death, dating from the seventeenth century, is carried in a small procession from the Cathedral of Assisi to the lower church of the Basilica of Saint Francis, where it is "laid in state" before the altar that stands over the tomb of the Poverello. During the day, the people of Assisi come to pay their respects, venerating the life-size image of their Savior, which is shrouded with a thin black veil, and laid out on a gilded catafalque draped in black velvet.

Gradually the brightness of the afternoon sun wanes and twilight descends upon Assisi. In the streets outside, a procession featuring an image of Our Lady of Sorrows, with seven swords run through her heart, approaches the church. This procession is intended to act out a medieval legend that on the night of Good Friday the distraught Virgin Mother wandered in search of her dead Son.

Soon the Sorrowful Virgin arrives at the Basilica of Saint Francis. After Mother and Son are somberly reunited, the procession begins to make its way under the night sky back to the cathedral. At its head a drummer plays on a muffled drum; behind him, a crucifix is held aloft ahead of the clergy and the members of the confraternities, all of whom carry tall lit candles. They are followed by barefoot penitents, each shouldering a heavy wooden cross, and altar boys carrying the instruments of the passion (that is, representations of the crown of thorns, nails, spear, and so on). Finally the bier of Christ Crucified comes into view, followed by the bereaved Mother of God. Along the route, lined by the flickering light of candles on balconies and window ledges, the strains of the *Stabat Mater* and the *Miserere* waft through the quiet streets. As the catafalque passes, all cross themselves, while some are moved to tears.

Eventually the cortege returns to the cathedral, where the bishop, the clergy, and the laity once more honor the Crucified and His

Mother, bringing the ceremony to an end.[52]

A procession very similar to that of Assisi is held each year in the little village of Grassina in north central Italy (1917). It seems likely that the rite at Grassina is also quite old, considering that a cross with a detachable corpus was used in the nearby city of Florence as early as the fifteenth century. Shortly after sunset the hamlet suddenly falls silent; then, in the hush of the evening the words of the sixth-century hymn *Pange, lingua, gloriosi* begin to float across the countryside:

> *Lo, with gall His thirst He quenches*
> *Nails His tender flesh are rending.*
> *See, His side is opened now!*
> *Whence, to cleanse the whole creation*
> *Streams of blood and water flow.*

Leaving the church, the nighttime procession moves up one hill and down again, then across a small bridge to another hill on the other side. Countless lanterns dot the surrounding farmland and hilltops, as if to guide the holy funeral on its way. Among the marchers is a contingent of "Roman soldiers" on horseback, dressed in medieval armor. The haunting *Vexilla Regis* is now sung; in the blackness of the night the smoky orange light of torches illuminates the bier of Christ in death, which comes to a stop from time to time as peasants surge forward to kiss the waxen image. Little children are lifted up so that they, too, might press their lips to the wounded feet and side of the Crucified. Behind the bier are three women, the "Marys" who come to anoint our Lord's Body, dressed in white and carrying ointment and spices, with small bands of black crape about their sleeves. Further back in the cortege is a statue of the Sorrowful Virgin Mary, a handkerchief in her uplifted hand, "wan and pallid in the moonlight." The procession continues for another hour before finally returning to the village and the church from which it began.[53]

Good Friday processions of this nature were eventually introduced throughout Italy, as well as on the neighboring islands of Sardinia, Malta, and Sicily. Thus at San Filippo (1956) near Sicily's Mount Etna, the recumbent Christ is placed in an ornate glass-sided casket by a priest and borne down from a hilltop sanctuary by confraternity members in Arab costumes; it is brought to the mother church and watched through the night.[54] The Good Friday procession at Trapani (1962), on the northwest coast of the island, is characterized by its extraordinary number of tableaux — twenty in all. This "Procession of the Mysteries" seems to be at least four hundred years old, for the life-size wooden figures of the tableaux, carved by the local people, date from the sixteenth and seventeenth centuries. Each scene is carried by the men of a particular workers' guild; thus sailors carry the "First Fall of Christ" under the cross; bakers, the "Crowning with Thorns"; and masonry workers, the "Scourging at the Pillar"; while carpenters carry the "Crucifixion." Other scenes are borne on the shoulders of tailors, fruit vendors, fishermen, barrelmakers, and pastamakers, as well as men of a number of other professions. Spectators on the balconies lining the route scatter flower petals on the procession as it slowly passes through the streets of Trapani.[55]

It is thought that the Italian *Depositio* probably reached the southeast coast of France during the fifteenth century;[56] there are modern records of this ceremony in the French cities of Nice, Roquebrune, Breil, Menton, Sospel, Saorge, and Perpignan (the only example from southwest France).[57] Rites of this nature and evidently of comparable antiquity are found in the city-state of Monaco and on the Mediterranean island of Corsica. At both of the Corsican cities of Sartene and Porto-Vecchio (1931), mourners keep watch before the recumbent Christ, interred in a church, from Good Friday night until the morning of Easter Sunday.[58]

The Italian *Depositio* must have entered the Iberian Peninsula sometime during or before the sixteenth century, for it was at this time that in the Spanish city of Seville confraternities were being founded expressly for the purpose of conducting Holy Week processions.[59] The sculpting of statues of the passion in polychrome wood for use as tableaux (that is, *pasos*) in such processions flourished from the late sixteenth century through the first half of the seventeenth; it was in 1605 that the Spanish artist Gregorio Fernandez carved one of the most beautiful life-size figures of Christ resting in death, an image known as the *Cristo de El Pardo*, named after the Capuchin Monastery of El Pardo in Madrid, where it is now kept.[60] Good Friday *Depositio* processions (what the Spanish refer to as the *Santo Entierro*) eventually appeared in the Spanish cities of Seville, Cadiz, Malaga, Murcia, Alicante, Teruel, Madrid, Cuenca, Zamora, Valladolid, Huesca, Medina de Rioseco, Grenada, and Saint Martin de Unx, among others.[61] In Toledo (1909) the procession would consist of six tableaux, including an image of the Virgin of Sorrows, seated in front of the empty cross with her Son's Body, wrapped in a translucent lace veil, resting on her lap; on the flower-covered platform of the final tableau she kneels alone before the cross.[62] In Salamanca (early twentieth century), the *Santo Entierro* would follow a course through the cloisters of the city's world-famous university. As each of the *pasos* carried in the procession arrived at the western entrance, two of the university's doctors (who had kept watch before the repository on Holy Thursday), attired in full academic robes, would meet the *paso* there and escort it through the cloisters.[63]

The clergy play a prominent role in the *Depositio* at the Cathedral of Palma, on the Spanish island of Mallorca (1942), where as early as the fourteenth century the Italian custom of the *Planctus* had been introduced.[64] On Good Friday a life-size figure of Christ resting in death is placed in the sanctuary upon a sable bier. A transparent veil is draped over the Body; candles surround the bier, providing the only illumination; a large black cross of wood stands behind it, with a white strip of linen hung across its two arms. Thousands of kneeling figures gradually fill the church. The quiet is suddenly broken by the toll of a bell, upon which four men, clad in black, enter through a door on one side of the sanctuary; stepping before the bier they kneel to pray in silence for a brief interval. The men then rise, and lifting the bier to their shoulders, they proceed down the steps and out of the sanctuary, followed by the clergy, seminarians, and acolytes, all bearing lighted tapers. The procession heads to a side chapel where there is a white marble sarcophagus lying open before the altar. In it the Crucified is laid to rest; the clergy kneel down around the tomb and chant Psalm 130, the *De Profundis*, joined by the people.[65]

Tell of the loveliness of the garment of His Body that suffered, made beautiful by His Passion, made glorious by His Divinity, than which nothing can be more lovely, nothing more loved.
[Saint Gregory Nazianzen][66]

The Italian *Depositio* became quite common throughout the northern Spanish provinces of Navarra and Guipuzcoa.[67] An account dating from the beginning of the present century provides us with a detailed description of the "Descent from the Cross" held on Good Friday each year in one of the cities in this region, the Basque town of Fuenterrabia, located in the northeast corner of the country, close to the French border.[68] On this day the small round windows of Fuenterrabia's huge church are veiled with red silk, allowing only a dim light to filter inside. During the early afternoon the church begins to fill with villagers. The men bring very large four-sided candles, in readiness for the procession later on, the women, in black dresses with kerchiefs or mantillas covering their heads. In the subdued light is seen a huge crucifix erected in front of the high altar, with only the outline of the corpus on it discernible through the black curtain hung before it. Around the cross are figures of Our Lady of Sorrows, Saint John, and the Magdalene. As midafternoon approaches, a reverential silence pervades the place, now crowded with kneeling figures. Then the clock strikes three. Suddenly the sound of muffled trumpets is heard emanating from the west end of the church; as the trumpets play a somber march, a number of men dressed as Roman soldiers enter through the west door and separate into two columns, each slowly marching up a different side aisle. Upon reaching the sanctuary, they come together again to form a semicircle around the large cross erected there. As soon as the priest enters the pulpit to give a sermon for the occasion, the black curtain is pulled away, revealing the pallid Body of the Crucified amidst the darkness of the dimly lit church. Ascending a pair of ladders set against the back of the cross, two other priests in surplices reverently remove the crown of thorns and nails as the preacher relates how the Body of our Lord was taken down from the cross. The crown and nails are then "presented" to the statue of the Virgin of Sorrows standing nearby. Using a sling of white linen hung loosely about the crossbeam, the priests lower the corpus down to a group of four Capuchins stationed below, who in turn lay it to rest on a bier.

The people of Fuenterrabia now head out of the church as a procession forms. Thousands have come down from the Pyrenes mountain villages to the east and line the streets to see this cortege. At the head of the procession are several hundred men, walking in double file, followed by women and children dressed in white; then come the clergy and religious. The torch-like candles carried by all but the smallest participants form two long rows of light that slowly snake through the streets and byways. Statues are also borne in the procession, including the images of Saint Mary Magdalene and Our Lady of Dolors. Six Dominicans serve as pallbearers for the Crucified. After traversing the city the procession returns to the church from wence it came; here a watch is held in the late afternoon, followed in the evening by the interment of the recumbent Christ at a side altar.

It is difficult to ascertain when the Italian *Depositio* reached Portugal. Popular processions of this nature are known to have existed during the nineteenth century in the capitol of Lisbon.[69] A liturgical directory of this same city dating from 1738, composed by a secular priest for "the choirs and the cures of parishes," provides rubrics for conducting a *Depositio* procession in which four priests carry the figure of the recumbent Christ in a catafalque. The institution of the ceremony is attributed to the zeal and piety of "two canons of Vilar de Frades, of the Congregation of the Evangelist"; significantly the motherhouse of this congregation was located in Italy.[70] The latter is actually one of the more "liturgical" versions of the *Depositio*, with the prominent participation of the clergy and the use of verses from the liturgy; however it does include several elements of the more representational Italian *Depositio* and thus it constitutes something of a hybrid rite. In the Portuguese Diocese of Braga we find an even older hybrid ceremony, the only surviving example of a *Depositio* that combines the "burial" of the holy Eucharist with various features of the Italian *Depositio*. Indeed, the ceremony is believed to have originated in Italy; it existed in Venice during the first part of the sixteenth century,[71] from whence it seems to have been carried to Braga, appearing for the first time in the *Missale Bracarense* of 1558.[72] The practice has since been suppressed elsewhere, but has continued for four hundred years in the Diocese of Braga, which has a distinctive liturgical rite of its own (separate from but similar to the Roman Rite). As of the early 1960s this ceremony was still extant at the primatial church in Braga.[73] At the end of the Mass of the Presanctified, while the choir chants Vespers, a bier covered with a black and gold pall is brought forward and put on the altar. Then the celebrant places the Blessed Sacrament, enclosed in a chalice, in the bier. The Eucharist is censed, after which four priests, vested in albs and black chasubles, lift the bier from the altar and carry it, with a black canopy over it, in a slow procession around the cathedral. During this procession in which the participants cover their heads in mourning and carry candles, the planctus *Heu, heu, Domine, Salvator noster* ("Oh, Oh, Lord, our Savior"), with verses from the Lamentations of Jeremiah (Lam 5:3, 16, 15), is chanted. Exiting through the south door of the cathedral, the cortege follows a route along the main street and returns on a different avenue to the west door. Upon reentering the cathedral the procession continues to a separate chapel in the north transept, where on the previous night the Altar of Repose had been located; the entrance is veiled with a violet curtain. The bier is brought into the chapel, placed on the altar, and censed. After this the violet curtain is pulled back to reveal the stark scene within. At the top of a long flight of steps rests the bier with the holy Eucharist; at the bottom is a statue of Our Lady of Sorrows. The Eucharist will remain here until Easter Sunday.[74]

Never was earth adorned by a tomb which sheltered actual life, or rather by a tomb which proved to be a wedding chamber. For the one entombed was not liable to death, and he descended to the tomb to celebrate a marriage.

[Saint Proclus of Constantinople][75]

In Jerusalem, where the custom of a symbolic burial rite on Good Friday first arose, yet subsequently disappeared before the advent of the Crusades, a Eucharistic version of the Deposition was introduced sometime before (or in) the year 1552, but by 1617 this had been superseded by a non-Eucharistic *Depositio*, probably imported from Italy, featuring a crucifix with a detachable corpus.[76] Thereafter this rite, held in the evening in the Church of the Holy Sepulchre, evidently changed little over the centuries that followed, and appears to have been the source for very similar practices introduced into the Good Friday liturgies of several Eastern Rites.[77] A nineteenth-century description of the Jerusalem ceremony will suffice for our purposes. The service consists of a series of seven sermons, each delivered in a different language by a priest speaking in his native tongue. The first of these sermons is delivered in the Latin Chapel by an Italian priest. Following his talk a procession forms, headed by a Franciscan carrying a large crucifix and flanked by two acolytes. As the *Miserere* (Psalm 51) is sung, the procession moves to a station marking the site where the garments of our Lord were divided among the Roman soldiers; here the sermon is given in Greek. At the next station, associated with the mocking of Christ, the sermon is in another Eastern tongue. As the procession reaches Calvary, the crucifix is laid upon the spot where our Savior was nailed to the cross; a priest now preaches in German. Finally the crucifix is brought to the place where the cross stood nearly two thousand years ago. Following a sermon delivered in French, several priests remove the corpus from the cross and lay it on a sheet of fine linen, which is subsequently carried down the stairs to the "stone of unction," believed to be the stone on which our Lord's Body was anointed for burial. Here the patriarch sprinkles myrrh and rose water over the corpus; a Franciscan now preaches in Arabic. The figure of the Crucified is then borne in procession to the final station, the holy sepulchre, where it is laid to rest on the marble slab covering the tomb. After a final sermon in Spanish, the service comes to an end.[78]

If you are a Joseph of Arimathea, beg the Body from him who

Church of the Holy Sepulchre, Jerusalem. *". . . For the one entombed was not liable to death, and he descended to the tomb to celebrate a marriage" (Saint Proclus of Constantinople).*

crucified it . . . make yours that which cleanseth us from all sin. . . . If you are a Nicodemus, who worshipped God by night, anoint Him with spices for burial. . . .

[Saint Gregory Nazianzen][79]

The colonization of Latin America by Spain and Portugal carried the Italian *Depositio* to the New World. Eventually the practice took root in such countries as Mexico, Cuba, Guatemala, Peru, and Brazil; it is likewise found in India and the Philippines.[80] Immigrants from different lands have brought this custom to the United States as well. At Our Lady of Mt. Carmel Church, an Italian parish in New York City, the *Depositio* tradition has been maintained. After Stations of the Cross in the evening, a statue of Christ resting in death is borne in procession around the church; a priest in the cortege carries a relic of the true cross.

The high altar, Communion rails, and sanctuary are veiled in black. The altar serves as a "funeral bier" for the image of Christ in death, surrounded by candles.[81]

It should be noted that the Congregation of Sacred Rites has explicitly approved of the practice of placing statues of the recumbent Christ and of Our Lady of Sorrows in the church and their use in processions on Good Friday. Permission for the extraliturgical use of a statue of Mary wrapped in a black veil and of Christ in death was originally affirmed by the Congregation in a decree dating from 1744 (#2375 ad 4, issued March 21, 1744), and reiterated in another decision dating from 1831 (Decree #2682 ad 52, Nov 12, 1831).[82] In the Vatican's most recent document on Holy Week, promulgated in February of 1988, the placing of statues of this nature in Church is expressly permitted on Holy Saturday (thereby implicitly reaffirming the permission for their use following the Liturgy of the Passion on Good Friday).[83]

They laid Him, limb-weary, down,
stood at His body's head,
Looked they at heaven's Lord
the while He there lay,
Aweary for that
so much He had won them.
Then men of both hands began
building a sepulcher,
Shaped it of shining stone,
shut there the Vanquisher.
Began they a sorrow-song
for Him to sing,
At the dusk, desolate
for that they must depart,
Must leave the best of Lords,
leave Him there lonely.
We there a long while waited weeping,
Stood in our strength;
our stem they mounted,
the soldier band.
Cold was the corpse,
Christ's beautiful body.

[The Dream of the Rood][84]

Of course, in examining the historical development of such devotional exercises as the *Depositio* we mustn't lose sight of the ultimate intent of these rites. In her short story, *At the Bier of the Crucified*, written at the turn of the century and set in the Italian village of Branciano (near Sorrento), Anna Sprague McDonald provides a particularly moving account of a Deposition procession and the impact it had on one who watched it. Her story tells of a parish priest named Padre Antonio and one of the souls entrusted to his care, Assunta, a teenage girl with a beautiful voice who sang the *Stabat Mater* each year during the Good Friday *Depositio* procession. When the priest intervenes to save her from spiritual disaster, she angrily turns against him and turns away from God. Once more Holy Week arrives, and on Holy Thursday he pleads with Assunta to return to God and join in the *Stabat Mater* on Good Friday. With a heart full of bitterness, she adamantly refuses. The following night Padre Antonio spends praying for her at the Altar of Repose. Then Good Friday comes:

> The church bell announced that it was three o'clock, the hour at which, long years ago, the Redeemer had rendered up His spirit. At this moment the burial procession set forth. The pious village folk bore an image of the Crucified from the little church to a chapel on the mountain side. There it was to lie entombed in memory of how the real body had rested in Arimathean Joseph's sepulchre. The cortege was to pass 'Vanni Arelli's. All the household, except Assunta, had gone to follow in the procession. She had determined to stand defiantly in the doorway while the villagers went by, knowing that nothing could more wound Padre Antonio.
>
> At last, in the distance, Assunta heard Chopin's funeral march, wonderfully played, albeit the musicians were but simple peasant lads. The band passed on. Then came the procession proper, headed by the most prominent citizen of Branciano. He wore the robe of the Misericordiae Brotherhood, which shrouds the wearer completely, leaving only the eyes uncovered. For centuries, in this sure disguise, prince and peasant alike have wrought noble deeds of mercy or repentance. The leader of Branciano's procession bore aloft the standard of the King — a golden crucifix. Surrounding this gleamed lighted tapers, carried by others of the Brethren. Then, three by three, came the remaining men of the village, all wearing the society's long, black robe. They went by slowly and reverently. Assunta watched them disdainfully. Not even the sight of the emblems

carried had power to soften her angry heart. For, in each row of three, those on the outside carried candles, but in the centre, the post of honor, some emblem of the awful sufferings of the Crucified was borne. On rich cushions rested the pillar stained with His royal blood, the crown of thorns, the nails, the spear, even the cock which crew after the triple betrayal of the Lord.

All these and many more went by; yet still Assunta stood scornfully upright in the Arelli doorway. Now came Padre Antonio, his old and spiritual face rapt and solemn with this commemoration of the burial of the Most High. After him the acolytes, some with candles like the Brethren; two with swinging censers of incense walked facing the bier. Under a magnificently embroidered canopy — the gift of some old-time prince — was borne the bier of the Crucified. Surrounded by burning tapers, strewn thickly with pallid lilies and fragrant roses, was a life-sized image of the dead Christ. It was startlingly realistic with bloody wound-prints and thorn-crowned head. The face was turned towards Assunta. As she gazed upon that tortured figure something in her proud heart gave way. It seemed as if that pierced hand were raised in a benediction which dispelled all anger and all bitterness, leaving only her old-time faith and love. Sobbing, she fell on her knees as the bier with its sorrowful burden passed on.

Back of the Crucified the village maidens bore a statue of His Mother, His first and greatest mourner. . . . In her [Assunta's] eyes, and in those of all the simple Branciano people, it was indeed the Blessed Mary, she who had so valorously stood at the foot of the cross.

Now came the rest of the village girls and women, singing the "Stabat Mater." Richer and clearer rose the hymn as a new voice [Assunta's] joined them. Far in front it reached the grey-haired shepherd, who humbly thanked the Crucified for the lost lamb which had come back.[85]

Let us now visit a sepulchre scene ourselves. It is around six o'clock in the evening. As we enter the church we find it veiled in darkness and absolute stillness. Our attention is drawn to the edge of the sanctuary where a stark scene is presented before us. The floor of the sanctuary in front of the altar is covered with a large white and green pall of the kind used to cover a casket during a funeral Mass; resting upon it is a sculpture of Christ asleep in death. His head rests to one side, the crown of thorns and nails lying near His wounded feet. Two sculpted angels keep watch, one near His head, the other at His feet.

The edges of the underlying pall are lined with lilies. The soft light of the setting sun, filtering through a stained-glass window at the rear of the church, gently illuminates the face of the King in death, His eyelids closed upon this world. The battle with sin and death is over. He has triumphed over the Enemy. The King now takes His rest.

> *He was a knight on the field of battle . . . the crown of thorns was His helmet, His scourged body was His armour; the pierced hands His gauntlets; His sword was the spear in His side, and His spurs were His pierced feet nailed to the cross. Behold how gloriously this knight is armed!*
>
> [Saint Catherine of Siena][86]

The rest of the sanctuary is barren. The altar cloths, the flowers, are all gone. The doors of the empty tabernacle hang wide open. The sanctuary is desolate, for the Church is grieving her slain Spouse.

> *Mary Magdalene and the other Mary were there, sitting opposite the sepulchre.*
>
> [Mt 27:61]

Into the Night: *Myrophores*

> *Thou, O Life,*
> *wast buried in a grave, O my Christ,*
> *and the armies of the Angels were shuddering,*
> *as they praised thy condescension and thy love.*
>
> *Meadows, hills, and mountains,*
> *and all nations of men, come today,*
> *lament, and cry bitterly*
> *with the Mother of your Savior and your Lord.*
>
> *Rise, O Lord Life-giver!*
> *Tearful and heart-broken,*
> *thy Holy Mother calls thee.*
>
> [Lamentations, Greek Liturgy][87]

In the Byzantine Rite the office of Matins (the first "canonical Hour" of the Divine Office) for Holy Saturday is held late at night on Good Friday and is called *Myrophores*; it commemorates the women bringing spices with which to anoint the Body of Jesus, and serves as a meditation on the entombment of Christ.[88] At this service all the worshipers have lit candles; the clergy and choir gather around the decorated stand on which the *Epitaphios* (Winding Sheet)[89] is placed and sing a chant consisting of verses from Psalm 118 alternating with composed verses such as the following:

> *O Life, how can you die,*
> *and how can you lie in the tomb?*
> *You have destroyed the kingdom of death*
> *and raised the dead from hell.*

> *Jesus, my Christ, king of all,*
> *what are you looking for in hell?*
> *Do you want to rescue mortal men?*

As in other services described earlier, the *Myrophores* includes a funeral procession. The *Epitaphios* is borne out of the church into the darkness of the night, followed by the congregation carrying lit tapers, as a solitary bell is rung. After the procession returns to the darkened church there are three readings, including Ezekiel's description of the vision he has of a strange valley (Ez 37:1-14):

> *The hand of the Lord was upon me, and he brought me out by the Spirit of the Lord, and set me down in the midst of the valley; it was full of bones. And he led me round among them; and behold, there were very many upon the valley; and lo, they were very dry.*
>
> [Ez 37:1-2]

But this vision of death ends with a prophecy of the resurrection:

> *Behold, I will open your graves, and raise you from your graves, O my people. . . .*
>
> [Ez 37:12]

The second reading is a combination of passages from Saint Paul's first Letter to the Corinthians (5:6-8) and from his Epistle to the

Galatians (3:13-14). In the latter passage Saint Paul refers to an injunction from the Book of Deuteronomy:

> *And if a man has committed a crime punishable by death and he is put to death, and you hang him on a tree, his body shall not remain all night upon the tree, but you shall bury him the same day, for a hanged man is accursed by God. . . .*
>
> [Dt 21:22-23]

Saint Paul applies these verses to our Lord, the innocent Lamb who was slain on a tree:

> *Christ redeemed us from the curse of the law, having become a curse for us — for it is written, "Cursed be every one who hangs on a tree" — that in Christ Jesus the blessing of Abraham might come upon the Gentiles, that we might receive the promise of the Spirit through faith.*
>
> [Gal 3:13-14]

Both the lection from Ezekiel and the two passages from the epistles of Saint Paul had already been assigned to Holy Saturday Matins by the tenth century, appearing in Jerusalem's *Typicon of the Anastasis*[90] and in Constantinople's *Typicon of the Great Church*.[91] The last of the three readings is Saint Matthew's gospel account of the stationing of Roman guards at the sepulchre (Mt 27:62-66), the same as that read in Jerusalem fifteen hundred years ago at dawn on Holy Saturday, according to the *Armenian Lectionary* (early fifth century).[92]

The *Soledades*

> *O daughter of my people,*
> *gird on sackcloth,*
> *and roll in ashes;*
> *make mourning as for an only son,*
> *most bitter lamentation. . . .*
>
> [Jer 6:26]

On this evening in Puerto Rico a procession known as the *Soledades* (the "Loneliness") is held. The custom commemorates the terrible loneliness of the Blessed Virgin Mary upon losing her Divine

[290]

Son; the people gather to "keep her company" in her suffering. Along the way of the procession every house is lit with candles.[93]

> She weeps bitterly in the night,
> tears on her cheeks. . . .
>
> [Lam 1:2]

In Tasco, Mexico (nineteenth century) a similar devotion was held late on this night in honor of Our Lady of Sorrows. Over two thousand women, dressed in black and carrying lit candles, would walk in complete silence as they accompanied an image of the bereaved Mother of God.[94] In the Mexican city of Puebla (1935), where this devotion was known as the *Pesame*, the procession would be conducted within the precincts of the seventeenth-century cathedral:

> All the candles were extinguished, and the only light was that of the immense tapers carried by young girls as they followed the priests in a long procession through the dim aisles of the church, a life-sized figure of the Virgin at their head. It was an effect that will long be remembered — those dark young faces glowing with devotion in the flickering candlelight, the majestic tread of the priests, the sorrowing figure of the afflicted Mother, and echo answering the chant of the "Mater Dolorosa" as it rose from hundreds of young voices.[95]

> Mother, whose heart is deep as the deep sea!
> What hast thou seen today, what hast thou done?
> What is this place of slaughter and of sculls?
> What day has this been, since the first ray broke,
> And all the Temple precincts woke, and stirred
> With bleatings of the lambs? What hours were those
> Till noon? — when from the Temple steps there rang
> The blast of trumpets, telling the Lamb was slain,
> And over thee was reared and fixed the Cross?
> What were those hours that passed — or were they years? —
> Here, — and thou standing by? Here didst thou stand;
> Until a great cry rent the earth apart,
> And in the Temple shook down right and left
> The columns, and the Veil was rent in the midst.
> In all the days was ever a day like this?
>
> ["Mater Desolata," Maria Monica][96]

"She weeps bitterly in the night,
tears on her cheeks. . ." (Lam 1:2).

Final Thoughts for Good Friday

What did you hear last night,
your head on His breast there?
It was Peter in the dark supper-room
Asking of John,
Who with Mary, His Mother, was just returned
From burying Him.

I heard His blood moving like an unborn child,
And His Heart crying.
I heard Him talking with His Father
And the Dove.
I heard an undertone as of the sea swinging, and a whispering
at its centre.
I listened, and all the sound
Was a murmuring of names.
I heard my own name beating in His Blood,
And yours, Peter,
And all of you.
And I heard Judas,
And the names of all that have been
Or shall be to the last day.
And it was His Blood was calling out these names,
And they possessed His Blood.

Did you hear my name?
Asked a woman who was sitting at His Mother's feet.
I heard your name, Mary of Magdala, and it was like a storm at sea
And the waves racing.
I heard Peter's name,
And the sea broke, I thought, and ran over the world.
You heard then the name of Mary, His Mother, Peter said
quietly, as he wept there kneeling.
I did, and it was like the singing of winds and they
moving over an ocean of stars, and every star like a
hushed child sleeping.

Again Peter —
What of Iscariot?

I heard the tide come in, and I felt the tide go out,
And I saw a dead man washed upon the shore.

And then John fell to weeping, and no one there could
comfort him but only Mary, the Mother of Jesus, and
he could tell them
No other word.

[Charles L. O'Donnell, CSC, *In the Upper Room*][97]

Endnotes

1. The four most important historical studies on the various rites commemorating the burial of Christ on Good Friday are those of the Congregation of Sacred Rites (Commentary in *Decreta Authentica Congregationis Sacrorum Rituum*, pub. Typographia Polyglotta, 1898-1901, Vol. IV, pp. 429-441), Karl Young (*The Drama of the Medieval Church*, 1933, Vol. I, pp. 112-148 and passim), Neil C. Brooks (*The Sepulchre of Christ in Art and Liturgy*, 1921, pp. 30-110) and Solange Corbin (*La Deposition liturgique du Christ au Vendredi Saint: Sa Place dans l'histoire des rites et du theatre religieux*, 1960). Those of the Congregation of Sacred Rites, Young, and Brooks discuss for the most part the practices of northern and central Europe; that of Corbin is the most comprehensive, with much material on the ceremonies of southern Europe.
2. See p. 252 previous chapter.
3. Young, Vol. I, pp. 121, 132-133.
4. For examples see ibid., Vol. I, pp. 112-148, 152-176, 553-565.
5. Corbin, pp. 50, 314.
6. Text in *Regularis Concordia: The Monastic Agreement of the Monks and Nuns of the English Nation* (Medieval Classics), Dom Thomas Symons, 1953, pp. 44-45.
7. Young, Vol. I, p. 133.
8. Ibid. , Vol. I, pp. 135-136.
9. Ibid. , Vol. I, pp. 140-142.
10. Ibid. , Vol. I, pp. 142, 556.
11. Father Joseph Jungmann, SJ, *Pastoral Liturgy*, 1962, p. 228 (footnote).
12. Archdale King, *Eucharistic Reservation in the Western Church*, 1965, p. 154.

13. Father H. Philibert Feasey, OSB, "The Easter Sepulchre" (Part II), *American Ecclesiastical Review*, Vol. 32, 1905, p. 474 (footnote).

14. Selected verses from two versions of this carol in P. Dearmer, R. Vaughan Williams, and M. Shaw, ed., *The Oxford Book of Carols*, 1928 (rpt. 1964), p. 134.

15. E. R. Yarham, "Medieval Easter Sepulchre," *Ave Maria*, April 4, 1942, p. 433.

16. Jungmann, pp. 229-230.

17. Ibid., p. 231 (footnote).

18. Reverend Francis Weiser, SJ, *The Easter Book*, 1954, p. 119; Father James Monks, SJ, *Great Catholic Festivals*, pp. 53-54.

19. Corbin, pp. 233-237.

20. O. B. Hardison, *Christian Rite and Christian Drama in the Middle Ages*, 1965, p. 136; Latin text in *Patrologia Latina*, Vol. 135, col. 1020b, d-1021a.

21. Young, Vol. I, pp. 112-114.

22. Ibid., Vol. I, pp. 123-124.

23. Ibid., Vol. I, pp. 137-139.

24. Commentary, *Decreta*, Vol. IV, pp. 433-434.

25. Ibid., Vol. IV, p. 435.

26. Ibid., Vol. IV, pp. 429-430.

27. Ibid., Vol. IV, p. 430.

28. Jungmann, pp. 233-234.

29. From a description by M. Raich (*Der Katholik*, March 1902, p. 261 seq.) as summarized in Father Herbert Thurston, SJ, *Lent and Holy Week*, 1904, p. 464.

30. Decree #3939 (Dec 15, 1896) in *Decreta*, Vol. III, pp. 323-324, and Commentary, *Decreta*, Vol. IV, pp. 436-439.

31. Corbin, p. 312.

32. King, p. 145.

33. Corbin, pp. 63, 114.

34. Ibid., pp. 63-64, 117, 257-258.

35. Richard Donovan, CSB, *The Liturgical Drama in Medieval Spain*, 1958, p. 139; *Decreta*, Vol. IV, p. 433.

36. Corbin, pp. 122-123, 313.

37. Ibid., pp. 132, 134-135, 259-260; King, p. 218.

38. Ibid., pp 147-148, 263-265.

39. Excerpt in *The Catholic Anthology: The World's Great Catholic Poetry*, Thomas Walsh, ed., 1943, p. 33.

40. Corbin, pp. 13, 23, 35-37, and passim.

41. The relevant rubrics of both the *Hereford Missal* and the late thirteenth-century edition of the *Sarum Missal* are cited in Edmund Bishop, *Liturgica Historica*, 1918, pp. 295-296.

42. Based upon Corbin's definition of what she classifies as the "popular deposition" (pp. 22-23, 39, 113, 119, and passim).

43. Ibid., pp. 114-115.

44. *The Ordinal and Customary of the Benedictine Nuns of Barking Abbey* (Henry Bradshaw Society, Vol. 65), J. B. J. Tolhurst, ed., 1927, Vol. I, p. 100; also Brooks, p. 39.

45. Corbin, pp. 115-116.

46. Young, Vol. I, pp. 157-158, 160-161.

47. Neil C. Brooks, "The *Sepulchrum Christi* and its Ceremonies in Late Mediaeval and Modern Times," *Journal of English and Germanic Philology*, 1928, Vol. 27, pp. 154-155.

48. Ian Wilson, *The Mysterious Shroud*, 1986, p. 73 (photograph).

49. Corbin, pp. 117, 257-258. Date of 1437 on p. 257 of Corbin is a misprint.

50. Ibid., p. 243.

51. Tudor Edwards, "As for Six Hundred Years: Easter in Assisi," *The Tablet*, March 31, 1956, p. 297.

52. Ibid.; Felix M. Kirsch, "Holy Week in Assisi," *Commonweal*, March 23, 1932, p. 576.

53. Barry Maguire, "The Funeral of Christ," *The Catholic World*, April 1917, pp. 60-63.

54. Vito Fiorenza, "Holy Week in Sicily," *Jubilee*, April 3, 1956, pp. 47-51.

55. Vito Fiorenza, "Faces of Holy Week," *Jubilee*, April 1962, pp. 6-15.

56. Corbin, p. 244.

57. Ibid., pp. 57-58, 80, 103-107.

58. Ibid., p. 105.

59. See chapter II, pp. 61-65.

60. "Fernandez (Gregorio)," *Enciclopedia Universal Ilustrada*, 1958 ed., Vol. 23, p. 756; photograph in Jose Ortiz Echague, *Espana Mystica*, 1964, Plate 174.

61. Corbin, pp. 123-128.

62. Ethel L. Urlin, *Festivals, Holy Days, & Saints' Days*, 1915 (rpt. 1971) pp. 69-71.

63. M. J. O'Doherty, "Holy Week in Spain," *Irish Ecclesiastical Record*, 1911, p. 360.

64. See chapter VI, pp. 187-188.

65. G. E. Karmany, "Holy Week Memories of Palma de Mallorca," *Ave Maria*, March 28, 1942, p. 402.

66. Oratio 45, "On the Holy Pasch II," XXV, *The Sunday Sermons of the Great Fathers*, M. F. Toal, ed., 1958, Vol. II, p. 259.

67. Corbin, p. 126.

68. The following is based upon Sara H. Dunn, "Good Friday in Fuenter-rabia," *The Month*, July 1903, pp. 68-72, with a few additional details from a more recent account in Corbin, p. 126.

69. Corbin, pp. 152-153, 284-285.

70. Ibid., pp. 141, 149, 271-272.

71. King, p. 219; Corbin, pp. 64, 117. A very detailed description of a Eucharistic *Depositio* with a bier appears in the *Liber Sacerdotalis* of Alberto Castellani (1523), and is reprinted in Young, Vol. I, pp. 125-130. H. Fulford Williams asserts that a procession of this kind also existed at Taormina, Sicily (H. F. Williams, "The Diocesan Rite of the Archdiocese of Braga," *Journal of Ecclesiastical History*, Vol. 4, 1953, p. 133). In 1632, and again in 1702, the Congregation of Sacred Rites suppressed the use in the Roman Rite of a bier in carrying the Sacrament to the sepulchre (Decrees #586, #2089 ad 1, *Decreta*, Vol. I, pp. 140, 462). This prohibition evidently did not apply to the Diocese of Braga, which has a distinctive rite of its own approved by the Holy See. In 1924 the Vatican implicitly approved of Braga retaining its *Depositio* when Pope Pius XI authorized a new edition of the *Missale Bracarensis* that included this ceremony (Williams, p. 128).

72. King, p. 218. For relevant text of 1558 *Missale* see Corbin, pp. 261-262.

73. In 1971 the Congregation for Divine Worship gave the diocese of Braga permission to maintain its distinctive liturgical rite, with certain modifications in virtue of the liturgical reforms of the Second Vatican Council. The author has not been able to determine whether these modifications included alteration or abolition of the Good Friday *Depositio* ceremony. See "Il rito Bracarense e la riforma liturgica," *Notitiae*, Vol. 8, 1972, pp. 145-150.

74. King, pp. 222-226; Williams, p. 133. For relevant texts of rubrics see Corbin, pp. 279-286.

75. Sermon 13, #1, *The Paschal Mystery: Ancient Liturgies and Patristic Texts* (Alba Patristic Library, Vol. 3), Andre Hamman, OFM, ed., 1969, p. 114.

76. Corbin, pp. 172-173.

77. See account of "Taking down from the Cross" in the Maronite Rite, provided earlier (pp. 257-260). In the Melkite Rite a corpus detached from the cross is laid upon an *Epitaphios* and then covered with a

translucent veil, after which the gospel book is placed upon it (I. H. Dalmais, OP, "Une Relique de l'antique liturgie de Jerusalem: L'-Office de l'ensevelissement du Christ au soir du Vendredi Saint," *L'Orient Syrien*, 1961, Vol. 6, pp. 445-446). A *Depositio* may have once existed in the Chaldean Rite (of Iraq, Iran, among others), perhaps as far back as the eleventh century, but there is no longer any ceremony of this nature in the Chaldean Good Friday liturgy (Alphonse Raes, SJ, "La Paix Pascale dans le Rite Chaldeen," *L'Orient Syrien*, Vol. 6, 1961, pp. 77-78, 79-80).

78. "Holy Week in Jerusalem," *The Catholic World*, Vol. 7, April-Sep 1868, pp. 80-81; Dr. A. Breen, *A Diary of My Life in the Holy Land*, 1906, p. 503.
79. Oratio 45, "On the Holy Pasch II," XXIV, in Toal, Vol. II, p. 259.
80. For examples from Mexico and Brazil, see Corbin, pp. 128-129, 156-158.
81. "Ancient Good Friday Rite to Be Revived," *Catholic New York*, March 16, 1989, p. 55. The parish is located in Manhattan (448 E. 116th St.).
82. *Decreta*, Vol. II, pp. 85, 236-237.
83. *Circular Letter Concerning the Preparation and Celebration of the Easter Feasts*, Feb 20, 1988, #74, in *L'Osservatore Romano*, Feb 29, 1988, p. 18.
84. Excerpt in Walsh, p. 33.
85. "At the Bier of the Crucified," *The Catholic World*, March 1901, pp. 723-725.
86. Letter 260, quoted in Johannes Jorgensen, *Saint Catherine of Siena*, 1938, pp. 257-258.
87. Stanzas I, III, from Holy Saturday Matins, in *Orthodox Prayer Book*, Bishop Fain Stylian Noli, ed., 1949, pp. 201-202, 204.
88. The following is based upon D. Pochin Mould, "Byzantine Holy Week," *Doctrine and Life*, XIV, March 1964, pp. 180-181, except where noted otherwise.
89. The *Epitaphios* is described in the previous chapter.
90. *Analekta Hierosolymitikes Stachyologias*, A. Papadopoulos-Kerameus, ed., 1894 (rpt. 1963), Vol. II, p. 177.
91. *Le Typicon de la Grande Eglise: Tome II: Le Cycle des Fetes mobiles* (Orientalia Christiana Analecta #166), Juan Mateos, ed., 1963, pp. 82-83.
92. John Wilkinson, *Egeria's Travels*, 1971, p. 270.
93. Cynthia Hettinger, "Faith of the Puerto Rican," *America*, April 16, 1960, p. 67.
94. J. V. Wilfrid Amor, "Holy Week at Tasco, Mexico," *The Month*, April 1885, pp. 515-516.

95. Arthemise Goertz, "Easter in Old Mexico," *Ave Maria*, April 20, 1935, pp. 483-484.

96. Excerpt, in *The Month*, April 1896, pp. 495-496.

97. *The Tree and the Master: An Anthology of Literature on the Cross of Christ*, Sister Mary Immaculate, CSC, ed., 1965, pp. 16-17.

$\overline{\text{X}}$

Holy Saturday

*And on the seventh day God finished his work which he had done,
and he rested on the seventh day. . .*

[Gen 2:2]

*For as Jonah was three days and three nights in the belly of the whale,
so will the Son of man be three days and three nights in the heart of
the earth.*

[Mt 12:40]

. . . on the sabbath day they rested, as the Law required.

[Lk 23:56; JB]

Tenebrae[1]

*O death, I will be thy death;
O grave, I will be thy destruction.*

[Antiphon, Old Office of Holy Saturday][2]

HOLY SATURDAY HAS ALWAYS been an "aliturgical" day. There has never been a Eucharistic liturgy, not even a Mass of the Presanctified, for Holy Saturday — although the gradual advancement of the timing of the Easter Vigil into the daylight hours and even the morning of Holy Saturday in later centuries tended to obscure this fact.[3] As far back as the first years of the fifth century, Pope Innocent I (A.D. 401-417) testifies that the Eucharist was not celebrated on this day in view of the Apostles who spent the day mourning the death of our Lord.[4] In more recent times (1955) the unique character of Holy Saturday was reiterated by the Congregation of Sacred Rites:

*This is the day of the most intense sorrow, the day on which the
Church tarries at the Lord's tomb, meditating about His passion and*

[300]

death. While the altar remains stripped, the Church abstains from the sacrifice of the Mass until, after the solemn vigil or the nocturnal wait for the Resurrection, there come the Easter joys, the abundance of which carries over to the days that follow.[5]

Today is the third and final day of *Tenebrae*, the one and only official act of worship assigned to Holy Saturday proper. The mood at the morning Office is a mixture of darkness and light, sorrow and hope. The Church as it were sits in silence by the tomb of her Divine Spouse. The opening hymn, sung to the melody of the sixth-century *Vexilla Regis*, reflects this pensive atmosphere:

> *Great silence reigns on earth this day!*
> *Great loneliness embraces all!*
> *For death has had its ruthless way,*
> *And caught the Lord and Love of all.*
>
> *But Jesus, gone to darkest hell,*
> *Has entered on the Sabbath Rest,*
> *In which He, with His Father still,*
> *Works mighty wonders for the blest.*
>
> *His body's vessel smashed apart,*
> *His Life and Love now flood the world*
> *And penetrating to its heart,*
> *Among all men whirl up and swirl.*
>
> *Thus in that darkness, Light shines out*
> *And men, from Adam to the last,*
> *Raise up their hands; in joy they shout:*
> *"Behold! the Lord, the First, the Last!"*
>
> *The bonds and gates of hell give way.*
> *A great procession comes to sight.*
> *Who leads them is Himself the Way*
> *Their goal — Himself, in God's full Light.*
>
> *O may we, Lord, who yet must die,*
> *Who pray awaiting the great Feast*
> *Of your arising from the dead*

Be joined with you in endless peace. Amen!
[*Great Silence Reigns on Earth Today!*]⁶

Until recent times *Tenebrae* for Holy Saturday, like *Tenebrae* for the two previous days, was held on the preceding evening. The atmosphere of this third and final *Tenebrae* service is evident in a description of the Office as it was held each year on the evening of Good Friday in the Italian lakeside village of Anguillara (north of Rome):

> *On the day of woe, the sky above the lake is lead; and the waves beneath it roll and toss like one in dull foreboding. Tenebrae — the hour of darkness draws near. The Victim pre-sanctified has been consumed. The Christ is not on His throne. The Holy of Holies is empty and its door stands ajar. The Temple of the Christ is in gloom, save for the little thorns of light on the pointed arch, near the denuded altar. And one by one these points of flame are gone as voices rise in lamentation. One light alone is left; and it goes out behind the empty altar. "Miserere — God, have mercy."*
>
> *In the dim silence comes a sudden clatter — the slap of closing books. All is finished; the dread hour has come — the time when the rocks were rent.*⁷

In the passage above we find a reference to another ancient custom associated with *Tenebrae* — the making of noise at the conclusion of the service. This peculiar practice was intended to symbolize the confusion of nature upon the death of Christ. *Tenebrae* on all three days used to end with this clamor; usually the priests or monks attending would rap their breviaries on the choir stalls, or a wooden clapper would be used.⁸ The making of "a little noise" (*strepitus aliquantulum*) was specifically mentioned in the rubrics of both the *Roman Breviary* and the *Caeremoniale Episcoporum*⁹ until the practice was suppressed following the Holy Week reforms of the 1950s.¹⁰

From time to time the people of later centuries have been given a vivid reminder by nature herself of what the "convulsion of nature" on that first Good Friday must have been like. Thus we read in a twentieth-century account of Holy Week in Guatemala that on one Good Friday, at three o'clock in the afternoon, an earthquake struck with a roar in the vicinity of the capital city, sending frightened residents into the streets.¹¹ The author of an account of Holy Week in Havana, Cuba, as she observed it there in March of 1869, tells of how nature provided a particularly dramatic setting for the celebration of Tenebrae on the afternoon of Good Friday:

> . . . a south wind was blowing, and great water-laden clouds were fast covering the sky; the heat was very oppressive, and soon heavy drops of rain began to fall. . . . I ran back to the cathedral. . . . The Tenebrae had just commenced, and I sat there and listened to the doleful lamentations of Jeremiah, and the wails of the holy women, mingling with the thunder-crashes and the noise of the pouring rain, which fell as it only falls within the tropics. It was a combination of sounds not easily to be forgotten.[12]

At this morning's *Tenebrae* service, the Office of Readings begins with Psalm 4, which brings to mind the peaceful repose of our Lord in the sepulchre reflected in the antiphon assigned to it:

> *In peace, I will lie down and sleep.*

This same theme is continued with Psalm 16 that follows:

> *I will bless the Lord who gives me counsel,*
> *who even at night directs my heart.*
> *I keep the Lord ever in my sight:*
> *since he is at my right hand, I shall stand firm.*
>
> *And so my heart rejoices, my soul is glad;*
> *even my body shall rest in safety.*
> *For you will not leave my soul among the dead,*
> *nor let your beloved know decay.*
>
> [Ps 16:7-10]

After this we hear Psalm 24, which was used on Palm Sunday as a meditation upon our Lord's triumphant entry into Jerusalem. Here it serves as a reflection on our Lord's victorious entry into Sheol to free the souls of the just:

> *O gates, lift high your heads;*
> *grow higher, ancient doors.*
> *Let him enter, the king of glory!*
>
> [Ps 24:7]

As on the previous two days, the Lamentations of Jeremiah today (Lam 3:22-30; 4:1-6; 5:1-11) speak of the bitter sufferings of the children of Jerusalem, but even here the theme of hope breaks through the darkness:

HETH.   *The steadfast love of the Lord never ceases, his mercies never come to an end;*

HETH.   *they are new every morning. . .*

TETH.   *It is good that one should wait quietly for the salvation of the Lord.*

TETH.   *It is good for a man that he bear the yoke in his youth.*

IOD.   *Let him sit alone in silence when he has laid it on him;*

IOD.   *let him put his mouth in the dust — there may yet be hope. . . .*

[Lam 3:22-23, 26-29]

Once more the first lection for the Office of Readings is taken from the Letter to the Hebrews (4:1-13):

. . . a sabbath rest still remains for the people of God. And he who enters into God's rest, rests from his own work as God did from his. Let us strive to enter into that rest, so that no one may fall, in imitation of the example of Israel's unbelief.

[Heb 4:9-11; NAB]

Today's second reading, from an ancient homily of Holy Saturday, captures the meaning of this day:

Something strange is happening — there is a great silence on earth today, a great silence and stillness. The whole earth keeps silence because the King is asleep. The earth trembled and is still because God has fallen asleep in the flesh and he has raised up all who have slept ever since the world began. God has died in the flesh and hell trembles with fear.

He has gone to search for our first parent, as for a lost sheep . . . he has gone to free from sorrow the captives Adam and Eve, he who is both God and the son of Eve. The Lord approached them bearing the cross, the weapon that had won him the victory. . . .

For your sake I, your God, became your son. . . . For the sake of you, who left a garden, I was betrayed to the Jews in a garden, and I was crucified in a garden.

See on my face the spittle I received in order to restore to you the life I once breathed into you. See there the marks of the blows I received in order to refashion your warped nature in my image. On my back see the marks of the scourging I endured to remove the burden of sin that weighs upon your back. See my hands, nailed firmly to a tree, for you who once wickedly stretched out your hand to a tree.

I slept on the cross and a sword pierced my side for you who slept in paradise and brought forth Eve from your side. My side has healed the pain in yours. . . . The sword that pierced me has sheathed the sword that was turned against you.

[Ancient Homily on Holy Saturday]

In the Office of Morning Prayer that follows the Office of Readings, we hear Psalm 64 and a canticle from Isaiah 38 (vs. 10-14, 17-20), both of which serve as further reflections on the passion of the Lord:

Hear my voice, O God, as I complain,
guard my life from dread of the foe.
Hide me from the band of the wicked,
from the throng of those who do evil.

They sharpen their tongues like swords;
they aim bitter words like arrows
to shoot at the innocent from ambush,
shooting suddenly and recklessly.

[Ps 64:1-4]

The antiphon for Psalm 64 repeats the motif of Holy Saturday:

Though sinless, the Lord has been put to death. The world is in mourning as for an only son.

[305]

The antiphon for the final Psalm (Ps 150) anticipates the joy that will come with the Easter Vigil tonight:

I was dead, but now I live for ever,
and I hold the keys of death and of hell.

As on the two previous days, Morning Prayer also includes a reading (Hos 5:15b-6:2), as well as the antiphon *Christus factus est* and the Canticle of Zechariah. The reading is of particular interest, with its succinct prophecy of the Easter Triduum (this same lection, with a few additional verses, used to be read at the Liturgy of the Passion on Good Friday):

"Come, let us return to Yahweh.
He has torn us to pieces,
but he will heal us;
he has struck us down,
but he will bandage our wounds;
after a day or two
he will bring us back to life,
on the third day he will raise us
and we shall live in his presence."

[Hos 6:1-2; NAB]

The *Redditio Symboli*

On the morning of Holy Saturday, the Church in Rome during the earlier centuries conducted a final preparatory rite for the catechumens who were to be baptized at the Easter Vigil. These candidates, who had only recently been taught the words of the Creed, were now required to recite this profession of faith before the bishop or his representative — hence the name, *Redditio Symboli* ("Return of the Creed").[13] In the East and in the Gallican and early Mozarabic Rites the *Redditio* was held on Holy Thursday instead. The Roman ceremony is described in the seventh-century *Gelasian* and *Gregorian* (Paduan) Sacramentaries, and a century later in the Hadrian edition of the latter, as well as in *Roman Ordo I*.[14] At about the third hour of the day (around nine o'clock in the morning) the candidates would arrive at the church and stand in order before the pope himself or the priest officiating, the men taking their place on the right, the women on the left. They repeat the words of the Creed in his presence, after which the pope (or priest) makes the sign of the cross on each of their foreheads, lays his hand on their heads, and says a prayer of exorcism. He then touches each catechumen's ears and nose with spittle and prays:

> Ephphatha, that is, be opened, for a sweet-smelling savour. But do thou, O devil, take to flight, for the judgment of God will draw nigh.

Anointing the shoulders and breast of each candidate with the Oil of Catechumens, he now asks them to renounce Satan and his works, after which he places his hand on their heads and recites the Creed. At the invitation of the archdeacon, the candidates kneel, engage in silent prayer, and upon rising say "Amen" in unison. Then the archdeacon tells them:

> Let the catechumens withdraw; if there be any catechumen (here), let him withdraw; let all catechumens go out.

The candidates return home to await their Baptism at the Easter Vigil, only hours away.

At the Tomb

> Next day, that is, after the day of Preparation, the chief priests and the Pharisees gathered before Pilate and said, "Sir, we remember how that impostor said, while he was still alive, 'After three days I will rise again.' Therefore order the sepulchre to be made secure until the third day, lest his disciples go and steal him away, and tell the people, 'He has risen from the dead,' and the last fraud will be worse than the first." Pilate said to them, "You have a guard of soldiers; go, make it as secure as you can." So they went and made the sepulchre secure by sealing the stone and setting a guard.
>
> [Mt 27:62-66]

> Rejoice not over me, O my enemy;
> when I fall, I shall rise;
> when I sit in darkness,
> the Lord will be a light to me.
> . . . . He will bring me forth to the light;

I shall behold his deliverance.

[Mic 7:8-9]

There is now a general consensus among modern scholars that the Church of the Holy Sepulchre does evidently mark the authentic site of Calvary and of the empty tomb.[15] From the time of the Emperor Hadrian (A.D. 117-138) until the beginning of the fourth century, the location was hidden under the terrace of a Roman temple. But in 326-327 the Emperor Constantine had the site cleared; underneath the rubble a single tomb was found, carved into the side of a slope.[16] The Church historian Eusebius, a contemporary of Constantine, tells us:

> . . . *as soon as the original surface of the ground, beneath the covering of earth, appeared, immediately, and contrary to all expectation, the venerable and hallowed monument of our Saviour's resurrection was discovered.*[17]

Constantine's architect Zenobius carved away the tomb's immediate surroundings, leaving only a free-standing shell of rock, which was then adorned with pillars. A courtyard was built around the sepulchre, bordered on three sides by a semicircular portico and on the fourth by an oblong basilica, the "Martyrium"; the site of Calvary was situated in one corner of the courtyard, close to the Martyrium. These structures were completed by A.D. 335.[18] Soon thereafter (by about 348) a rotunda was built over the holy sepulchre, thus forming a circular church, separate from the "Martyrium" basilica — what became known as the "Anastasis." It was similar in shape to the Moslem Dome of the Rock that now stands on the former site of the ancient Temple of Jerusalem.[19] A lantern-like cupola was at some point added to the top of the rock shell of the tomb; a porch was added to the entrance, as well as bronze doors.[20] In A.D. 614 Persian invaders destroyed much if not all of the Constantinian structures over and around the tomb and Calvary, but these were rebuilt by 626. Again in 1010 the Moslem El Hakim, Caliph of Egypt, totally destroyed the complex; once more the buildings were restored in 1048. Finally in 1130 the Crusaders put the whole site under one roof, thus forming the vast Church of the Holy Sepulchre with which we are familiar in our own day, albeit with numerous modifications and reconstructions over the last eight centuries. Even so, there are still some remains of Constantine's original work incorporated into the current building.[21]

As early as the year 820, a German chapel, the Michaelskapelle of Fulda, had been constructed in imitation of the rotunda of Jerusalem's Church of the Holy Sepulchre.[22] In the centuries that followed, representations of the holy sepulchre were built for innumerable churches throughout northern and central Europe, largely to serve as the focal point for the *Depositio* rite of Good Friday and for related ceremonies on Easter Sunday. These "Easter Sepulchres," designed to enclose the holy Eucharist and/or a cross or image of the Crucified, ranged from modest coffers to elaborate entombment scenes, often taking on distinctive forms in the various countries were the burial of Christ was symbolically commemorated, as we shall see.

In pre-Reformation England the Easter sepulchre played a prominent role in the observances of Good Friday and Holy Saturday. Generally located along the north wall of the *chancel* (the part of the church surrounding the main altar), these medieval English structures can be grouped into five different categories of design.[23] It is likely that the first of these to arise was the "walled recess," a small opening, usually arched, in the wall. Another much more elaborate type of sepulchre was the "vaulted enclosure"; these stone structures reflected an attempt to portray in a more realistic manner the holy sepulchre itself, an effort inspired by the Crusades and the military religious order of Knights Templars, who often built their churches to resemble the rotunda of Jerusalem's Church of the Holy Sepulchre, with a replica of the tomb of Christ in the middle.[24] One of the best examples of the "vaulted enclosure" can be found in Lincoln Cathedral. This sepulchre, dating from the thirteenth century, has the proportions of a life-size sarcophagus, surmounted by an ornate stone canopy supported by three gothic arches; the front panel of the sarcophagus is decorated with carved images of three Roman soldiers.[25] In some of the larger churches an entire chapel served as the Easter sepulchre, thus constituting a third category of entombment. A fourth kind of sepulchre was a portable painted wooden coffer, ornamented with gables and coping, that could be used both by itself and as a second inner chest for the three other varieties of sepulchre mentioned above. Unfortunately, during the Reformation virtually all of these wooden sepulchres were sold for profane purposes or destroyed; in Lincolnshire alone at least fifty sepulchres were lost.[26] One such wooden sepulchre, thought to date from the fourteenth century, is described as measuring twenty-one inches in height, forty-five inches in length, and fifteen inches in width. The front is decorated with three carved panels depicting the Deposition from the Cross, the resurrection, and the appearance of Christ to Saint Mary Magdalene. Side panels depict our Lord before Pilate and the carrying of the cross.[27]

The fifth manner of representing the sepulchre of Christ was to erect a wooden coffer over the actual tomb of a deceased benefactor in the church. Thus we find in the will of Thomas Lord Dacre, who died in 1531, the following request: "My body to be buried in the parish church of Hurst Monceaux, on the north side of the high altar. I will that a tomb be there made for placing the sepulchre of our Lord, with all fitting furniture thereto in honour of the most blessed sacrament; also I will that cl. [amount of money] be employed towards the lights about the said sepulchre, in wax-tapers of ten pounds weight each, to burn about it."[28] This latter request for votive candles at the Easter sepulchre on behalf of the deceased appears in many other wills; a particularly interesting bequest of this nature was made in 1529 by a parishioner in the Northamptonshire village of Naseby, who left all his hives of bees for the maintenance of both the rood and sepulchre lights.[29]

In order to understand the furnishings used to adorn the Easter sepulchre, particularly in medieval England, it is important to keep in mind that most of these accoutrements were imitations or borrowings from the furnishings employed at state funerals and the like. Thus in the case of portable wooden Easter sepulchres special frames were erected both to hold the coffer and to support various cloth hangings, as well as the numerous bleached-wax votive candles requested by the faithful. This frame was essentially equivalent to a medieval funeral hearse, a wooden structure that served as a bier for the coffin of the deceased and likewise supported candles and hangings.[30] The Easter sepulchre was sometimes separate from the frame holding the candles lit before it;[31] one would presume this to have been the case with permanent stone sepulchres. In addition, there was a "great Sepulchre Light," a massive candle up to thirty-six feet in height and weighing as much as eighty pounds, which burnt continuously before the sepulchre from Good Friday to Easter Sunday.[32] This practice, too, is comparable to the use of one exceptionally large candle amidst other smaller tapers at the funerals of men and women of prominence.[33]

In further imitation of medieval funeral customs, English Easter sepulchres were decked with hangings, canopies, palls, pennons, streamers, and curtains made from the finest materials, including cloth of gold, brocade, velvet, and silk, often donated by the faithful.[34] Thus we find mention of a "great cloth of tapestry work for to hang upon the wall behind the Sepulchre" in the records of the London parish of Saint Margaret Pattens (1470).[35] The church-wardens' accounts for another parish in Southwark (1485) list such items as a "little curtain of green silk for the head [door?] of the sepulchre," "blue curtains (to) draw before the sepulchre," and "stained cloths with [scenes of] the passion and the resurrection to hang about the sepulchre on Good Friday."[36]

In continental Europe, unlike England, the location of the Easter sepulchre within the church has varied considerably. In France the Easter sepulchre was usually located in the choir or chancel (in or immediately in front of the sanctuary); in Germany and Italy the nave was most commonly the setting. In some churches the sepulchre was situated in a side chapel; at Wurzburg and Treves (both in Germany) it was located in the crypt.[37] In certain cases during the Middle Ages the high altar itself was used for this purpose, thereby evoking the burial symbolism of the stripped altar within the context of the Easter Triduum; thus at Metz (France) the sepulchre was in the form of a veiled silver *capsa* placed on the high altar.[38] The receptacle for the Host or image to be "buried" was often a coffer (sometimes cloth-covered) in the shape of a coffin or sarcophagus; a large, ornately carved sepulchre of this nature, mounted on wheels, and dating from the 1470s, has been preserved in Hungary, and there are other extant examples from Switzerland, Germany, and Sweden.[39] A curtained enclosure, with an altar or coffer within, could also serve as the Easter sepulchre; in some instances a temporary wooden enclosure was evidently used instead. There were even churches with a special sepulchre chapel, designed more or less in imitation of the site of the Holy Sepulchre in Jerusalem, and containing a permanent entombment scene.[40] A particularly colorful description of continental practices dating from 1569 is provided by the Protestant Belgian writer, Philipp van Marnix (1538-1598; pseudonym: Isaac Rabbotenu):

> They made the grave in a high place in the church, where men must go up many steps, which are decked with black cloth from above to beneath, and upon every step standeth a silver candlestick with a wax candle burning in it, and there do walk soldiers in harness, as bright as Saint George, which keep the grave, till the Priests come and take him up.[41]

In medieval Germany we find a more representational form of sepulchre, the *Heilige Grab* ("Holy Grave"), featuring a figure of Christ resting in death laid out upon a sarcophagus, with several "Holy Women" (Saint Mary Magdalene, Mary Cleopas, and others) standing behind and an angel at each end, as well as sleeping Roman soldiers crouched along the front side of the monument.[42] These detailed permanent sepulchres appear to have become common in the fourteenth century, but at least some must have been introduced at an earlier date, for there are two older surviving examples of statues from such "Holy Graves," one a large stone effigy of the recumbent Christ from Maria-Modingen, thought to date from around 1230-1240, the other, a wood sculpture of a "Holy Woman" from Adelhausen, estimated to be of the late thirteenth century.[43] In some cases the figure of Christ was made with a cavity in the breast for the Deposition of the holy Eucharist therein.[44] "Portable" wooden sepulchres were also constructed which could be brought out for use during the Easter Triduum. These would consist of a box within which a figure of the recumbent Christ was laid; the figure was removable, thus facilitating Deposition rites involving the carrying of the figure itself to the tomb, and its subsequent removal on Easter Sunday in order to represent the resurrection. In some cases the holy women and angels, as well as two additional figures — the Blessed Virgin and Saint John — were portrayed in miniature with either statues or paintings on the inside of the sepulchre's lid.[45] There are surviving portable sepulchres with all these features from the convent of Lichtental (currently kept at the Badisches Landesmuseum of Karlsruhe, Germany) and at the Swiss convent of Maigrauge (near Fribourg).[46] On the lid of another rather large sepulchre of this nature from Barr, Switzerland, over five feet long and dating from the early sixteenth century, can be seen a painted image of the two angels holding up the burial shroud of Christ, a scene which was often reenacted in the Easter rites associated with these sepulchres.[47] Both the corpus and the coffin-shaped wooden box of a medieval Swedish portable sepulchre have been preserved in the Norse Museum of Upsala.[48]

From the late sixteenth century onward, the *Heilige Grab* in southern Germany took on the form of which we have already spoken — that of a figure of Christ resting in the tomb below an altar on top of which stands a veiled monstrance containing the holy Eucharist. In the larger churches of Munich (1937) these altars, usually situated in a side chapel, would be surrounded by a veritable garden of shrubs, plants, and flowers, including even a small pool and fountain, as well as statues of Roman guards and colored Easter globes which were suspended all about, reflecting the flickering light of oil lamps in the darkened surroundings. A cross is left in front of the *Heilige Grab* for the veneration of the faithful, who come to visit from Good Friday until the evening of Holy Saturday.[49] An earlier account from 1877 mentions that the Easter sepulchres of this city were also adorned with the instruments of the passion (the scourge, spear, crown of thorns) and in some cases with "groups of statuary representing typical scenes from the Old Law, for example Abraham's sacrifice of Isaac," as yet another reminder of how the New Covenant fulfilled the Old. At the city's cathedral the veiled monstrance was placed atop a massive multitiered *Heilige Grab* thirty feet high; another particularly beautiful sepulchre was set up in the open courtyard of a hospital where it could be seen by the patients from the windows of their wards.[50] Some idea of the devotion of the people of Austria to the custom of the *Heilige Grab* can be gleaned from the words of the famous Maria Augusta Trapp (1955):

> *Like the creche around Christmas time, so the Holy Sepulchre on Good Friday would be an object of pride for every parish, one parish trying to outdo the other. The people in Salzburg used to go around at Christmas time and in Holy Week to visit the Christ Child's crib and the Holy Sepulchre in all thirty-five churches of the town, comparing and criticizing. There would be literally hundreds of vigil lights surrounding the Body of Christ in the tomb of rock, which was almost hidden beneath masses of flowers. There would be a guard of honor, not only of the soldiers, but also of firemen in uniform and of war veterans with picturesque plumed hats. I still remember the atmosphere of holy awe stealing over my little heart when as a child I would make the rounds of churches. There in the Holy Sepulchre He would rest now, watched over by His faithful until Holy Saturday afternoon.[51]*

In other places as well as Austria, the Easter sepulchre has been "guarded" by uniformed watchers. Father H. Philibert Feasey, OSB, notes that in his time (1905), in the Italian village of Roccacaramanico (Abruzzi region) twenty-four young men representing the Roman soldiers, dressed in tunics with helmets and lances, would keep watch "day and night" before a statue of Christ resting in death which had been placed at the foot of the altar.[52]

In Poland the twentieth-century customs regarding the Easter sepulchre greatly resemble those instituted during the Counter-Reformation in Bavaria, and appear to be at least as old as the seventeenth century.[53] On Good Friday the sepulchre is erected, with a figure of Christ in the tomb, surrounded by flowers. To it (following Vespers) one of the Hosts consecrated on Holy Thursday is brought and placed in a monstrance; the faithful visit and mount a "guard of honor" from Good Friday until the morning of Easter Sunday.[54] Often the sepulchre is made to resemble a rocky cave — a "tomb which had been hewn out of the rock" (Mk 15:46), in some cases with statues of angels or Roman soldiers placed about it, as well as numerous candles.[55] Somewhat related to the Easter sepulchre is the unusual Polish custom of the "Prison of Christ" — a darkened, unadorned room (perhaps the sacristy) prepared on Wednesday of Holy Week and intended to represent the place wherein our Lord would have been imprisoned until the morning following His late night trial before the Sanhedrin. The Host from the Mass on Holy Thursday which is to be adored at the Easter sepulchre on Good Friday is sometimes reserved beforehand in this "Prison of Christ," where the faithful come to visit, thus responding in a unique way to Christ's words, "I was in prison and you came to me" (Mt 25:36).[56]

In Hungary, where the *Depositio* has existed since the fourteenth century, we find very much the same practice as in Poland — the recumbent Christ in a tomb below an altar decorated with candles and flowers, with the holy Eucharist in a monstrance above.[57] In Luxemburg a simpler and far more ancient form of Easter sepulchre still existed in at least one parish around the turn of the century, as described in an account published in 1932. Following the Good Friday liturgy, the crucifix used for the Veneration of the Cross was carried to a side altar and there deposited, with a large purple curtain drawn before it; from Good Friday through Holy Saturday the faithful would visit this primitive sepulchre, somewhat reminiscent of that described in the tenth-century *Regularis Concordia*.[58] The custom of the Easter sepulchre has also survived among the Lithuanian people despite fifty years of Communist oppression. In one of the *Chronicles of the Catholic Church in Lithuania* smuggled out of the country during the 1970s, there is mention of a group of the faithful "praying at a casket that symbolized the coffin of Christ" in their parish church in Mazeikiai during the pre-dawn hours on Holy Saturday, evidently keeping a night watch at the sepulchre.[59]

In France, sculptured depictions of the entombment of Christ were erected in many churches as permanent monuments during the fifteenth and sixteenth centuries.[60] The portrayal of this closing scene of the passion may have been inspired, at least in part, by the emergence in eastern France of the Shroud of Turin, with its forward and reverse images of Christ resting in death, during the second half of the fourteenth century.[61] The earliest of the French entombments for which a date has been established is that of Langres, originally sculpted for a chapel in the south cloister of the cathedral, and dating from 1419-1420.[62] There are other examples extant in Amiens and Reims in the north, Nevers and Poitiers in the central part of the country, and Arles and Avignon in the south; many more could be cited.[63] Among the finest are those of Pont-a-Mousson, L' Epine, Solesmes, Tonnerre, Chatillon-sur-Seine, and Saint Mihiel.[64] One of the most beautiful of the French Entombment scenes is that of Chaource (near Troyes), dating from 1515 and still in its original setting. The monument is located in a small, secluded, "cryptlike" chapel at the bottom of a short flight of steps in the Church of Saint John the Baptist. Nicodemus and Joseph of Arimathea are depicted arranging the Body of Christ for burial atop a sarcophagus as the Virgin Mary stands near, gazing fixedly at the lifeless face of her Son, while the young Apostle John, the Magdalene and two other holy women look on in stunned grief.[65]

> *Death has seized Our Lord Jesus Christ; but shall not keep its hold on Life. It swallowed Him; it swallowed Him, not knowing Him: but, with Him, it will give up many. Of His own will He is now held; tomorrow, He shall rise again, and hell shall be emptied. Yesterday, on the Cross, He darkened the sun's light, and behold in full day it was as night; today death has lost its dominion, suffering itself a kind of death. Yesterday the earth mourned, contemplating the evil hate of the Jews, and in sadness clothed itself in a garment of darkness. Today, the people that walked in darkness have seen a great light (Is. 9:2).*
>
> *Yesterday the earth trembled, as though it would dissolve, threatening to swallow those who dwelt in it; and the mountains were cleft asunder, the rocks were split, the Temple appeared as though naked, and as though it were a living being threw off its veil; seeking as it were to show by what had happened to itself that its holy places were no longer sacred to the Lord. They that suffered these things were lifeless, without mind. The elements mourned, as though it wanted little for them to dissolve in chaos, and bring disaster on the world, were it not that they could see the purpose of their Maker; namely, that of His own will He suffered.*
>
> [Saint Amphilochius of Iconium][66]

The Harrowing of Hell

"Truly, truly, I say to you, the hour is coming, and now is, when the dead will hear the voice of the Son of God, and those who hear will live."

[Jn 5:25]

The gospels do not provide us with any description of our Lord's descent into Sheol (following His death) to free the departed souls of the just who had awaited Him there since the fall of Adam; nonetheless, that such an event took place is an article of faith, and is included in the Apostles' Creed ("... was crucified, died and was buried. He descended into hell. . ."). Among the various non-scriptural, apocryphal writings of the early Church is a work known as the *Gospel of Nicodemus*, the second portion of which is identified as the *Descensus Christi ad Inferos* ("Descent of Christ to the Nether World"), and dates from the second or third century.[67] In it Hades (the Greek term for Sheol, the "abode of the dead") is personified; Satan comes to Hades and asks him to take hold of the Crucified when He enters, but Hades answers that he fears Christ's power. What follows is well worth quoting at length:

> *While Satan and Hades were speaking thus to one another, a loud voice like thunder sounded: Lift up your gates, O rulers, and be lifted up, O everlasting doors, and the King of glory shall come in (Ps. 24:7). When Hades heard this, he said to Satan: Go out, if you can, and withstand him. So Satan went out. Then Hades said to his demons: Make fast well and strongly the gates of brass and the bars of iron, and hold my locks, and stand upright and watch every point. For if he comes in, woe will seize us. When the forefathers heard that, they all began to mock him, saying: O all-devouring and insatiable one, open, that the King of glory may come in. The prophet David said: Do you not know, blind one, that when I lived in the world, I prophesied that word: Lift up your gates, O rulers? (Ps. 24:7). Isaiah said: I foresaw this by the Holy Spirit and wrote: The dead shall arise, and those who are in the tombs shall be raised up, and those who are under the earth shall rejoice (26:19). . . .
> Again the voice sounded: Lift up the gates. When Hades heard the voice the second time, he answered as if he did not know it and said: Who is this King of glory? The angels of the Lord said: The Lord*

strong and mighty, the Lord mighty in battle (Ps. 24:8). And imme-diately at this answer the gates of brass were broken in pieces and the bars of iron were crushed and all the dead who were bound were loosed from their chains, and we with them. And the King of glory entered in . . . and all the dark places of Hades were illumined.

Hades at once cried out: We are defeated, woe to us. But who are you, who have such authority and power? And who are you, who without sin have come here, you who appear small and can do great things, who are humble and exalted, slave and master, soldier and king, and have authority over the dead and the living? You were nailed to the cross, and laid in the sepulchre, and now you have become free and have destroyed all our power. Are you Jesus, of whom the chief ruler Satan said to us that through the cross and death you would inherit the whole world? Then the King of glory seized the chief ruler Satan by the head and handed him over to the angels, saying: Bind with iron fetters his hands and his feet and his neck and his mouth. Then he gave him to Hades and said: Take him and hold him fast until my second coming.[68]

This apocryphal account of the event appears to have served as a source for ceremonial quasi-dramatic "reenactments" of the Descent into Sheol that were introduced into the rites of the Easter Triduum during the Middle Ages. In a ninth-century portion of the English *Book of Cerne* there appears what may be the earliest text of just such a dramatization of the "Harrowing of Hell"; the text itself may originally date from the eighth century.[69] Extraliturgical ceremonies of this nature later appeared elsewhere in Europe; Karl Young provides examples of this rite from Germany, Switzerland, and Ireland, as well as from England.[70]

A particularly striking instance of the ceremonial "Harrowing of Hell" appeared at the Monastery of Barking in England during the second half of the fourteenth century. All the members of this community of women religious, assuming the role of the souls of the patriarchs waiting in Sheol, would be "imprisoned" in the chapel of Saint Mary Magdalene behind closed doors. A priest representing Christ would then stand before the entrance and intone three times the antiphon, *Tollite portas* ("Lift up your gates. . . ."), after which the door was thrown open, and all the nuns, carrying palms and candles, would come out of the chapel in a joyful procession to the Easter sepulchre.[71] Although practices of this nature were usually conducted in the early morning hours of Easter Sunday as part of another rite, the *Elevatio*, which commemorated the resurrection (see chapter XII), the subject matter of the "Harrowing of Hell" belongs more appropriately to Holy Saturday, as is evident in the current Breviary's Office of Readings for this day (in particular, the Second Reading); in fact the Congregation for Divine Worship's 1988 *Circular Letter* on Holy Week expressly permits the placing of an image of the "descent into hell" in churches on Holy Saturday.[72]

The Restoration of Holy Saturday

In its 1955 reforms of the Holy Week liturgy, the Church had intended to restore Holy Saturday to its ancient status as a day of watching at the Lord's tomb. Unfortunately, it seems that this day has in many cases remained in the minds of the faithful nothing more than a day to get ready for the Easter celebrations; all too often its penitential character has been virtually ignored. But the celebration of *Tenebrae* on Holy Saturday morning in local parishes would help to give this day a more distinctive character. Likewise, the extraliturgical devotion of the Easter sepulchre would also serve to establish in the minds of the faithful the true nature of Holy Saturday, as has been suggested by the Jesuit scholar Father Francis Weiser (1958)[73] and more recently by Ambroise Verheul (1984), who proposes the placing "in our churches, between the time of the office of Good Friday and of the Paschal Vigil, a memorial in remembrance of the repose of Christ in the Tomb or of His descent to the Underworld," and notes the presence of analogous but fully liturgical ceremonies in the Byzantine Rite.[74] In its 1988 document on the Easter feasts, the Congregation for Divine Worship attempts to restore the "forgotten day" of the Easter Triduum by encouraging both the celebration of *Tenebrae* and the use of devotional practices commemorating the Entombment of Christ:

> *On Holy Saturday the Church is as it were at the Lord's tomb, meditating on his passion and death, and on his descent into hell, and awaiting his resurrection with prayer and fasting. It is highly recommended that on this day the Office of Readings and Morning Prayer be celebrated with the participation of the people (cf. n. 40). Where this cannot be done, there should be some celebration of the Word of God, or some act of devotion suited to the mystery celebrated on this day.*

The image of Christ crucified or lying in the tomb, or the descent into hell, which mystery Holy Saturday recalls, as also an image of the Sorrowful Virgin Mary can be placed in the church for the veneration of the faithful.[75]

A Final Thought for Holy Saturday

We give glory to you, Lord, who raised up your cross to span the jaws of death like a bridge by which souls might pass from the region of the dead to the land of the living. . . . Your murderers sowed your living body in the earth as farmers sow grain, but it sprang up and yielded an abundant harvest of men raised from the dead.

[Saint Ephraem][76]

Endnotes

1. Liturgical texts from *The Office of Readings*, Daughters of St. Paul, 1983, pp. 480-484, and *Christian Prayer: The Liturgy of the Hours*, Liturgical Press, 1976, pp. 366-370, unless noted otherwise.
2. Lauds in *The Roman Breviary*, John, Marquess of Bute, tr., 1908, Vol II, p. 384.
3. See discussion of timing for Easter Vigil in chapter XI, pp. 323-324.
4. Epistle 25, Caput 4, in *Patrologia Latina*, Vol. 20, col. 555b-556a, cited in Father John H. Miller, CSC, "The History and Spirit of Holy Week," *American Ecclesiastical Review*, April 1957, p. 232.
5. *Instruction on the Correct Use of the Restored Ordo of Holy Week*, Nov 16, 1955, Section 1, #2d, in *American Ecclesiastical Review*, Jan 1956, p. 57.
6. Text from Saint Meinrad Archabbey (Saint Meinrad, Indiana), 1972; original composition, based upon "Ancient Homily on Holy Saturday" from Office of Readings for Holy Saturday.
7. Ernest Wiley, "Easter Comes to Anguillara," *Sign*, April 1935, p. 567.
8. Father Francis X. Weiser, SJ, *The Easter Book*, 1954, p. 102.
9. *Brevarium Romanum: Pars Verna* (1861 ed.), "Feria quinta in Coena Domini: Ad Matutinum," p. 218; *Caeremoniale Episcoporum* (1886 ed.), 1902, Liber II, Caput XXII, #15, p. 238.
10. "Questions and Answers: Tenebrae," *Clergy Review*, March 1958, p. 170.

11. Lucie Hickman and Katherine Willis, "Holy Week in Guatemala," *Commonweal*, April 3, 1942, p. 589.

12. "The Holy Week of 1869 in Havana"(Part Two), *The Catholic World*, May 1870, p. 213.

13. The following is based upon Reverend John Tyrer, *Historical Survey of Holy Week: Its Services and Ceremonial* (Alcuin Club Collections #29), 1929, pp. 84-85, 144-145.

14. For original texts see *Patrologia Latina*, Vol. 74, col.1105d-1106c (*Gelasian*), Vol. 78, col. 954c-955b (*Roman Ordo I*); *Gregorian* texts in *Le Sacramentaire Gregorien: Ses principales formes d'apres les plus anciens manuscrits: I* (Spicilegium Friburgense, Vol. 16), Jean Deshusses, ed., 2nd ed., 1979, pp. 182-183 (Hadrian), 631 (Paduan).

15. Kenneth John Conant, "The Original Buildings at the Holy Sepulchre in Jerusalem," *Speculum*, Jan 1956, p. 2.

16. Ibid., pp. 2-3.

17. Neil C. Brooks, *The Sepulchre of Christ in Art and Liturgy*, 1921, p. 9.

18. Conant, pp. 3, 16-17 (Plate IIIc), and Brooks, pp. 9-10.

19. Brooks, p. 10, and Conant, pp. 5, 16-17 (Plate IIId).

20. Conant, pp. 3-5.

21. Brooks, pp. 11-12.

22. Ibid., p. 88.

23. Reverend O. Bussy, "The Easter Sepulchre," *The Clergy Review*, April 1936, pp. 289-291.

24. Ibid., p. 291, and Ian Wilson, *The Shroud of Turin*, 1979, p. 187.

25. Archdale King, *Eucharistic Reservation in the Western Church*, 1965, Plate 11.

26. Father H. Philibert Feasey, OSB, "The Easter Sepulchre" (Part I), *American Ecclesiastical Review*, April 1905, pp. 352-353; Bussy, p. 290.

27. Ibid., p. 353.

28. Bussy, p. 291.

29. Feasey (Part II), May 1905, p. 484.

30. Ibid., p. 471.

31. See example in ibid., pp. 471-472.

32. Bussy, p. 294.

33. Feasey (Part II), p. 485.

34. Ibid., pp. 472-478.

35. Ibid., p. 473 (spelling modernized).

36. Ibid., pp. 473, 476 (spelling modernized).

37. Brooks, pp. 53-54, 56-58.

38. Ibid., pp. 54, 61.

39. Ibid., pp. 62-63, plus Figures 16, 17; see also p. 312 of the present volume. The Hungarian Sepulchre (approximately nine feet long, three feet wide and nine feet high), from Garamszentbenedek, is presently kept in a museum of the Basilica of Esztergom. See Olivier Bernier, "A Glittering Hungarian Treasury," *New York Times*, March 21, 1993, Travel Section, p. 29.

40. Brooks, pp. 63-66.

41. Ibid., p. 69. This text is from a 1579 English translation (spelling modernized).

42. William H. Forsyth, *The Entombment of Christ: French Sculptures of the Fifteenth and Sixteenth Centuries*, 1970, p. 13.

43. Ibid., p. 15.

44. Brooks, pp. 38, 88, and Forsyth, p. 14.

45. Forsyth, pp. 16-17.

46. Ibid., p. 17, plus Figure 12.

47. Ian Wilson, *The Mysterious Shroud*, 1986, pp. 74-76 (illus. on pp. 74, 75).

48. Brooks, p. 63 plus Figure 17.

49. John Murray, "Quaint Easter Customs," *The Month*, Vol. 169, April 1937, p. 333.

50. "Holy Week in Munich," *Ave Maria*, Vol. 13 (1877), pp. 202-203, 216-217.

51. *Around the Year with the Trapp Family*, 1955, p. 127.

52. Feasey (Part I), p. 344 (footnote).

53. Solange Corbin, *La Deposition Liturgique du Christ au Vendredi Saint*, 1960, pp. 20-21.

54. Ibid., pp. 109-110, 256-257.

55. For example see "Easter in 'Little Poland' Buffalo," *Sign*, April 1953, p. 60 (photograph).

56. Corbin, p. 110 (footnote).

57. Ibid., p. 111.

58. "Communications: Some Peculiar Liturgical Customs," *Orate Fratres*, March 19, 1932, p. 236. For ceremony in *Regularis Concordia*, see previous chapter (pp. 268-269).

59. *The Chronicle of the Catholic Church in Lithuania*, Nijole Grazulis, ed., 1981, p. 174.

60. Forsyth, passim; the relationship of these monuments with the *Depositio* rites of Good Friday is unknown. In Italy an art form similar to the French entombment likewise arose during the fifteenth century — the *Mortorio* — a group of figures, typically in terra cotta, gathered around the Body of Christ resting in death and

usually laid upon the ground, rather than on a sarcophagus (Forsyth, pp. 138-139).

61. Wilson, *The Shroud of Turin*, pp. 191-210, 212; Forsyth, p. 63.

62. Forsyth, pp. 25-28.

63. Ibid., Figures 205-206 (Amiens), 259-260 (Reims), 119 (Nevers), 219-220 (Poitiers), 110 (Arles), 109 (Avignon).

64. Ibid., Figures 14-16 (Pont-a-Mousson), 61-62 (L'Epine), 120-128 (Solesmes), 88-92 (Tonnerre), 251-252, 254-258 (Chatillon-sur-Seine), 266 and 268 (Saint-Mihiel).

65. Ibid., pp. 52-54, plus Figures 65, 67-68, 70-71.

66. *Oratio V* ("For Holy Saturday"), #1; *The Sunday Sermons of the Great Fathers*, M. F. Toal, ed., 1958, Vol. II, pp. 191-192.

67. Karl Young, *The Drama of the Medieval Church*, 1933, Vol. I, p. 149.

68. *New Testament Apocrypha*, Edgar Hennecke and Wilhelm Schneemelcher, eds., 1963, Vol. I, pp. 473-474.

69. David N. Dumville, "Liturgical Drama and Panegyric Responsory from the Eighth Century? A Re-examination of the Origin and Contents of the Ninth-Century Section of the Book of Cerne," *Journal of Theological Studies*, Oct 1972, pp. 374, 381-382, 387-388.

70. Young, Vol. I, pp. 152-177.

71. *The Ordinal and Customary of the Benedictine Nuns of Barking Abbey* (Henry Bradshaw Society, Vol. 65), J. B. J. Tolhurst, ed., 1927, Vol. I, pp. 107-108, quoted and summarized in Young, Vol. I, pp. 164-167.

72. Congregation for Divine Worship, *Circular Letter Concerning the Preparation and Celebration of the Easter Feasts*, Feb 20, 1988, #74, in *L'Osservatore Romano*, Feb 29, 1988, p. 18.

73. *Handbook of Christian Feasts and Customs: The Year of the Lord in Liturgy and Folklore*, 1958, p. 202.

74. "Le Mystere du Samedi Saint," *Questions Liturgiques*, 1984, p. 38.

75. Congregation for Divine Worship, #73, #74, p. 18.

76. "*Sermo de Domino nostro*," *The Office of Readings*, Friday, Third Week of Easter, p. 554.

XI

The Easter Vigil

O Night brighter than day;
O Night brighter than the sun;
O Night whiter than snow;
O Night more brilliant than torches;
O Night more delightful than paradise;
O Night which knows not darkness;
O Night which has banished sleep;
O Night which has taught us to join vigil with angels;
O Night terror of demons;
O Night most desirable in the year;
O Night of torchbearing
  of the bridegroom in the Church;
O Night mother of the newly baptized;
O Night when the devil slept and was stripped;
O Night in which the Inheritor brought the beneficiaries
  into their inheritance;
An inheritance without end.

[Asterius of Amasea][1]

FROM THE EARLIEST DAYS of the Church's history, the Easter Vigil has been considered the single most important liturgical celebration of the year. The paschal liturgy consists of four basic elements: 1) the Service of Light; 2) the Liturgy of the Word; 3) the Liturgy of Baptism; 4) the Liturgy of the Eucharist. Each of these elements will be dealt with separately below. The Easter Vigil originated as a *nocturnal* liturgy that began no earlier than sunset on Holy Saturday and continued past midnight, sometimes lasting until dawn on Easter Sunday. One of the earliest references to this celebration appears in an apocryphal work of the East known as the *Epistula Apostolorum,* dating from the period A.D. 140-160, which speaks of the vigil as taking place during the night until after midnight.[2] Saint Augustine (354-430) and Saint Paulinus of Nola (353-431) among others testify to its *nocturnal* character as well.[3]

It was especially on the night before Easter Sunday that the Christians of the early Church thought our Lord would return in glory at the end of the world. Of particular significance was the hour of midnight, in virtue of the Bridegroom's arrival at this hour in the parable of the ten virgins (Mt 25:1-13); thus according to Saint Jerome (343-420) the faithful "held fast to a tradition of apostolic origin that during the Easter Vigil no one was to leave before midnight, for all awaited the coming of Christ."[4]

As late as the seventh century the *Gelasian Sacramentary* identifies the Eucharistic liturgy of the vigil as a *Missam in nocte* ("Mass in
the night").[5] But the situation soon started to change.[6] Thus in the
eighth-century *Roman Ordo I* the time given for the beginning of the
service is the *hora nona* ("ninth hour") — three in the afternoon on Holy
Saturday.[7] In another eighth-century source, *Roman Ordo 23* (Andrieu),
the vigil begins even earlier — at the seventh hour, that is, one o'clock;[8]
this same time also appears in the tenth-century liturgical work *De
Divinis Officiis* (mistakenly attributed to Alcuin).[9] By the twelfth century
the time had been advanced to midday in *Roman Ordines 11* and *12*;[10] a
Roman Pontifical also from this period indicates that the vigil could
begin either at noon or at eleven in the morning (*hora . . . quinta vel
sexta*),[11] the latter time a harbinger of what would eventually happen by
the end of the Middle Ages. Although as late as the fourteenth century
the hour given for beginning the vigil was still midday in *Roman Ordo
14*,[12] the tendency to advance the time of the Easter Vigil nonetheless
continued. With the issuance of the *Missale Romanum* of Pope Saint Pius
V in 1570, the assignment of this liturgy to the early morning of Holy
Saturday became obligatory in the Roman Rite.[13] Such remained the
case until 1951, when the Holy See gave the bishops of the world
permission to return the Easter Vigil to its original *nocturnal* setting in
their dioceses on a one-year experimental basis.[14] In 1952 this arrangement was extended for three more years;[15] then in 1955 the assignment
of the Easter Vigil to the night between Holy Saturday and Easter
Sunday was made permanent and universal with the issuance of the
revised Ordo for Holy Week.[16]

The Service of Light

The Service of Light, that is, the lighting of illuminating flames
with which the Easter Vigil begins, is one of the most beautiful and
memorable elements of the Easter liturgy. It presents us with powerful
imagery of the Risen Christ as the Light of the World shattering the
darkness of the long night of sin and death. While the image of light is
simple enough in itself, the Service of Light involves several different
uses of illumination that over time came to be drawn into a unified
whole. There was the use of light at all Christian vigils that took on
special significance at the Easter Vigil. Illumination was also associated
with the administration of Baptism, which was originally reserved for

the Easter Vigil. There was the singling out of one candle above all the other lights of this night as the paschal candle. And later there was the use of a bonfire with which to start the service and from which the paschal candle was lighted. There was also the distribution of the paschal flame to candles held by the faithful.

The Service of Light is rooted in very ancient practices; to discover the origins of this rite we must go back to the Old Testament. In the Book of Exodus, among the instructions concerning the tent housing the Ark of the Covenant and the services of worship to be conducted there, we find two passages that make reference to the use of light and incense in the evening:

> *And you shall command the people of Israel that they bring to you pure beaten olive oil for the light, that a lamp may be set up to burn continually. In the tent of meeting, outside the veil . . . Aaron and his sons shall tend it from evening to morning before the Lord.*
>
> [Ex 27:20-21]

And in another place:

> *You shall make an altar to burn incense upon. . .*
> *And Aaron shall burn fragrant incense on it . . . and when*
> *Aaron sets up the lamps in the evening, he shall burn it, a perpetual*
> *incense before the Lord throughout your generations.*
>
> [Ex 30:1, 7-8]

The early Christians continued the Jewish practice of lighting the lamps in the evening at the end of the Sabbath and made it the opening rite of their service, the *Lucernarium*, a vigil that consisted of Scripture readings alternating with Psalms and which concluded with the celebration of Mass. An all-night *Lucernarium* may have been held on various occasions throughout the year, perhaps on a weekly basis (scholars are currently uncertain on this point),[17] but it was on the actual anniversary of Easter that the service became what Saint Augustine termed "the mother of all the sacred vigils";[18] the lighting of lamps with which the vigil began readily came to symbolize the resurrection of Christ.

We have confirmation in the writings of the early Christian historian Eusebius that lights were already being used at the Easter Vigil in the third century.[19] Eusebius also mentions that in fourth-century

Milan (Italy) the Emperor Constantine "transformed the night of the sacred vigil into the brilliance of day, by lighting throughout the whole city pillars of wax, while burning lamps illuminated every part, so that this mystic vigil was rendered brighter than the brightest daylight" (*De Vita Constantini*, IV, 22).[20] No doubt this spectacle must have been especially meaningful for the Christians of that time, when the light of Christ had finally prevailed over the darkness of paganism after two and a half centuries of terrible persecutions. There is reason to believe that in other places as well as Milan the illumination of this night took on extraordinary dimensions, for Saint Gregory of Nyssa, also of the fourth century but living in Cappadocia (now part of south central Turkey), speaks of the Easter Vigil in terms of "radiant light which links the splendour of the burning lamps to the morning rays of the sun, and makes one long uninterrupted day without any break of darkness" (*In Sanctum Pascha, Oratio IV*).[21] Even in our own century, bonfires would be set ablaze on the mountain tops of Alpine Austria following sunset on Holy Saturday evening to usher in the "most blessed of all nights, chosen by God to see Christ rising from the dead" (*Exultet*).[22]

> *On that day there shall be neither cold nor frost. And there shall be*
> *continuous day (it is known to the Lord), not day and not night, for at*
> *evening time there shall be light.*
>
> [Zech 14:6-7]

From the very earliest centuries the Sacrament of Baptism has been administered during the Easter Vigil. There are indications in Saint Justin's *Dialogue with Trypho* of this being the case already in the first half of the second century.[23] And since even in apostolic times the concept of illumination was associated with this sacrament, it was only logical that a single "paschal candle" should eventually emerge as a symbol of Christ in the midst of the many other lights of the newly baptized shining on this night. Such a "paschal candle" would also have been viewed as the New Testament symbolic counterpart of the pillar of fire that led the people of Israel through the night in the course of their deliverance from Egypt. The particular light that was used to illuminate the sacred texts as they were being read at the Easter Vigil would naturally have taken on a certain preeminence over the other lamps burning during the liturgy, and hence most probably developed into what we now know as the "paschal candle."[24]

Wake up from your sleep
rise from the dead,
and Christ will shine on you.

[Eph 5:14; JB]

Around the year 378 we find the first reference to the practice of blessing a paschal candle at the Easter Vigil in a letter of Saint Jerome (Epistle 28, *Ad Praesidium*).[25] From the fifth century onwards there are numerous references to this blessing throughout the Christian West from Spain to Italy, yet it is generally claimed that there is no definite evidence of it becoming part of the Roman liturgy until the twelfth century. However, as early as the fifth or sixth century, Rome was authorizing the blessing of the paschal candle in its suburban churches.[26] There is reason to believe that by the early eighth century the paschal candle had begun to appear in Rome itself, for the famous English scholar Saint Bede (673-735) mentions in his work *De Temporum Ratione* (chapter 47) that the practice of inscribing dates on these candles could be found in Rome in his own day.[27] And as will be seen below, even the papal Church of Saint John Lateran was making use of a special flame (albeit not a paschal candle per se) for lighting the candles at the Easter Vigil by the middle of the eighth century.

Your sun shall no more go down,
nor your moon withdraw itself;
for the Lord will be your everlasting light,
and your days of mourning shall be ended.

[Is 60:20]

Over the centuries the paschal candle has been lighted in one of three ways: by flint, by sunlight, or by lighting with a flame previously hidden on Holy Thursday or Good Friday. We find the use of sunlight to spark the paschal fire in ninth-century Germany and other Teutonic lands; from a biography of Saint Ulrich, bishop of the German city of Augsburg (tenth century), we learn that the glass lenses used to focus the sunlight for this sacred purpose were treated with great reverence, and were even carried in processions. This method of starting the paschal flame could also be found in England in Anglo-Saxon times.[28] Eighth-century Rome provides an example of another way of lighting the paschal fire. In a letter of Pope Zacharias (741-752) to Saint Boniface, there is a description of the lighting of three large vessels filled with oil taken from all the lamps of the Lateran Basilica. The oil vessels would be filled and lit at the Chrism Mass on Holy Thursday and put in a corner of the church, where they remained burning but in some sense "hidden" during the course of the triduum, suggesting the death and burial of Christ. At the Easter Vigil these three flames were used to ignite all the other lights.[29] But the most common means employed to light the Easter fire down through the centuries has been the striking of a flint. This practice, which serves to evoke the image of Christ as the Rock, is evidently first mentioned in a homily of Pope Leo IV from the middle of the ninth century, and has continued to the present day.[30]

Early references to the paschal candle from Milan (Italy) and Spain mention that a cross was "painted" onto the paschal candle by anointing it with chrism. In place of this practice there later arose the custom of engraving a cross in the wax of the candle; in other cases, the anointing with chrism was replaced by the signing of the cross over the paschal light with a second lit candle.[31] The custom of inserting five grains of incense in the form of a cross into the side of the candle dates back to the tenth century or earlier. It is mentioned in a volume from England, the *Pontifical of Egbert*, named after an eighth-century Archbishop of York; the passage referring to the blessing and insertion of incense is thought to have been written in the tenth century.[32] These five grains have traditionally been seen as symbolic of the five wounds of Christ retained in His risen, glorified Body. Still another interesting practice connected with the paschal candle is that of dating it, either by directly inscribing the year on the wax or by mounting a plate with this information onto the candle; we have already seen that such a usage evidently existed in Rome in Saint Bede's time. Paschal candles are still dated in our own day. In some cases additional calendar information has been put onto the candles, such as dates of movable feasts. A seventeenth-century paschal candle in Rouen, France bore forty-eight different pieces of chronological data, including the number of years since the creation of the world, as well as the year in which the cathedral was dedicated.[33] The custom of inscribing on the wax the first and last letters of the Greek alphabet, an action undoubtedly inspired by a verse from the Book of Revelation (" 'I am the Alpha and the Omega'. . ." [Rev 1:8]), is at least seven hundred years old, appearing in the *Roman Pontifical* of the twelfth century.[34]

In an account of parish life among the Catholics of China published in 1942, we learn that the paschal candle was prepared by the village candle maker, who would begin to fashion it quite some time before Easter. The product of his diligent efforts was a finely molded and carved paschal candle, colorfully decorated with appropriate symbols, together with a chart that listed the names of all the parishioners and which also explained the symbolism of this meticulously crafted pillar of wax.[35]

During the Middle Ages, paschal candles more often than not were made with a square cross-section, rather than the cylindrical shape we are familiar with in our own day. Perfumes were mixed into the wax of the paschal candle in order to produce a fragrant scent as the taper burned, reminiscent of the spices the holy women brought to our Lord's sepulchre.[36]

The large size of the paschal candle necessitated the use of a smaller, more portable taper that could be carried in procession from the place where the Easter fire was kindled to the sanctuary within which the actual paschal candle stood. This arrangement is evident in the directions for the Easter Vigil found in the eleventh century *Constitutions* of Lanfranc:

> *The sacristan shall go first, carrying the staff on which he shall bring back the blessed fire. . . . When the fire is blessed the priest shall sprinkle it with holy water . . . and incense the fire. Then the candle shall be lighted and carried on the staff by the sacristan. A candle shall also be lighted in a lantern, so that if by chance the blessed candle is extinguished in the procession it may be relighted thence; this lantern shall be carried by one of the masters of the children.*[37]

The "staff" mentioned in the passage above for carrying the new fire in procession to the paschal candle was to be used in vigil services for centuries to come. A particularly significant detail in this account is the lantern that served as a precautionary measure in the event that the single candle on the staff should suddenly be extinguished by a gust of wind or some other unforeseen accident. Indeed, this problem of "losing" the Easter fire seems to have been instrumental in the subsequent introduction (by the twelfth century) of two additional candles on the processional candle staff, resulting in a "triple candle," although this form could also be thought of as symbolic of the Trinity as well as the three days in the tomb.[38] It should be noted that there was a much earlier precedent for the use of a "triple candle" at the Easter Vigil. One of three surviving manuscripts of the *Armenian Lectionary* (early fifth century) specifies the lighting of three candles at the beginning of the service in Jerusalem's Church of the Holy Sepulchre (the "Anastasis").[39] Three centuries later, we again encounter the use of three flames in Pope Zacharias' letter to Saint Boniface, to which we have already referred. Unfortunately, it is not possible to say whether these two earlier isolated examples of a threefold Easter light were in any way influential in the later appearance of the "triple candle."

Both the triple candle and the lantern were incorporated into the official liturgical books of the Roman Rite, the triple candle appearing by the twelfth century in a *Roman Pontifical*.[40] In the 1920 edition of the *Memoriale Rituum* (first issued by Pope Benedict XIII in 1725) the triple candle is described as a "reed furnished with three candles at the top." It calls for a "lantern with extinguished candle . . . or a single candle" to be lit from the initial fire outside the principal door of the church. As soon as the celebrant and assistants enter the church, the first of the three candles on the reed is lit from this lantern or "single candle." All kneel and the celebrant, who bears the reed, says (or sings), *Lumen Christi* ("Light of Christ"). The other clerics present or the choir answer with *Deo gratias* ("Thanks be to God"). Upon rising, the celebrant and assistants proceed; the two remaining candles on the reed are successively lit in the middle of the church and on the front steps of the altar, each time with the same ceremony. The "lantern" is now extinguished, after which the celebrant gives the still lit triple candle to an assistant. On the gospel side of the altar is the paschal candle itself, mounted in a candle stand where it was placed before the service began. Shortly afterwards, during the singing of the hymn known as the *Exultet*, the paschal candle is lit from the triple candle. The reed is then set on a stand for it on the gospel side of the altar.[41] This rather complicated "Service of Light" was considerably simplified with the reform of the Easter Vigil in 1951; both the triple candle and the lantern were eliminated, but the threefold proclamation of *Lumen Christi* with its response *Deo gratias*, a feature introduced by the time of the twelfth-century *Roman Pontifical*,[42] has been retained as we shall see shortly.

The paschal candle has sometimes assumed enormous proportions. According to *Roman Ordo 7*, one of the oldest extant *ordines* (perhaps dating from the second half of the seventh century),[43] two candles were used for the liturgy of the Easter Vigil, each of which was of the "stature of a man."[44] The pre-Reformation *Sarum Missal* (England, 1526) speaks of the paschal candle being thirty-six feet high.[45] At two other medieval English cathedrals, those of Westminster and Canterbury, the paschal taper weighed 300 pounds. So great was the height of the paschal candles used at Norwich and Durham that in each of these English churches a special aperture had to be made in the high vaulted ceiling in order to provide an outlet for the smoke and forestall the hazard of fire.[46] An account of the Easter Vigil in the Cathedral of Seville, Spain from the beginning of the nineteenth century describes a candle twenty-seven feet high (not counting its marble pedestal) and weighing 1500 pounds (three quarters of a ton!). The candle could only be lit by climbing a mast mounted with steps that led to a railed platform at its top.[47]

The use of a bonfire to begin the Service of Light at the Easter Vigil can be traced to Saint Patrick (fifth century), who introduced the practice in Ireland to replace the old pagan springtime fire rites. Eventually the custom spread across Europe and towards the end of the ninth century was incorporated into the official liturgy of the Church in the West.[48] The faithful appreciated the significance of the "Easter fire," and consequently desired to sanctify their everyday lives with it. Thus in many countries the custom arose of extinguishing all fires in the home early on Holy Saturday morning, that they might be replaced with the new fire of Easter. Everything from the vigil lights kept before holy images to the hearth that warmed the house received the freshly kindled flame.[49] As early as the eleventh century we read in the monastic *Constitutions* of Lanfranc:

> *The blessed fire that remains in the cloister shall be collected by the cellarer's servants, and from this fire all the hearths in all the household offices, which had previously been extinguished, shall be rekindled.*[50]

Such customs have continued into the present century. In the Alpine regions of central Europe the father of the family extinguishes the vigil lamp before the family crucifix around three o'clock on Good Friday, after which he puts out the fireplace by pouring water on it; no fires are allowed again until the celebration of the resurrection begins.[51] In the Carniola region of northern Yugoslavia (1933) the boys in each family had the job of carrying home the Easter fire every year on Holy Saturday. They would go to the village church, bringing with them a mushroom-like forest growth that burned slowly when ignited and thus was ideally suited to transporting a flame from one place to another; the boys waited in line to light these makeshift torches from the newly kindled Easter fire that the parish priest blessed at the opening of the Easter Vigil. They then ran off with their torches before the flames burned down to their fingers. Awaiting them at home, their parents readied the fireplace, which was rekindled with the new Easter fire when the boys arrived.[52]

The concept of the faithful wishing to bring the Easter fire into their homes touches upon one further aspect of the Service of Light: the "sharing of light," the passing of the flame from the newly lit paschal candle to candles held by the faithful. We find an early example of this custom in the *Liber Ordinum*, a liturgical book of Spain's Mozarabic Rite containing practices of the fifth to seventh centuries. The clergy would gather with the bishop in the sacristy, where the paschal candle was then lit from a lamp that in turn had been kindled with flint. After the bishop blessed both the paschal candle and the lamp, the rest of the clergy lit their candles from the paschal taper. The door of the sacristy, until now tightly shut, was suddenly thrown open. A deacon then carried the paschal candle out of the sacristy, after which the people kindled their candles with the flame from it.[53] In the East a similar custom was observed at Jerusalem's Church of the Holy Sepulchre; indeed, the custom of passing the flame to the candles of the faithful appears to have originated in Jerusalem itself, where it is mentioned explicitly for the first time in one of the manuscripts of the *Armenian Lectionary*, dating from the early fifth century.[54]

In the earliest reference to the paschal candle, that of Saint Jerome in his letter *Ad Praesidium* (Epistle 28 — ca. 378), we likewise find the first mention of a special composition known as the *Exultet*, a song of praise and rejoicing that arose as a formula for blessing the paschal taper. From Saint Jerome's time until the present, the singing of the *Exultet* has been assigned to a deacon (when available). Originally the words of the *Exultet* varied from place to place, but only one version of it is now in use — one attributed to Saint Ambrose.[55] In the Middle Ages scrolls inscribed with the words of the *Exultet* were lavishly illuminated (decorated) in such a way that as the reader unrolled the scroll and the completed portion fell to the ground, his listeners could see instructive illustrations on it that helped them to understand the Latin text. Father Herbert Thurston, SJ (1856-1939), described one of these scrolls in the keeping of the British Museum (as of 1896); it consists of a strip of vellum or parchment approximately eleven inches wide and over twenty-two feet in length, fastened to a wooden roller at one end. The vellum is inscribed with Lombardic alphabetical characters; at intervals the text is interrupted by a colorful illustration that appears upside-down in relation to the text. The pictures are reversed this way so that they will appear right-side-up to the congregation as the vellum is unrolled by the reader. There are a total of fourteen such illustrations in the scroll, ranging in subject matter from the fall of Adam and the crossing of the Red Sea to the descent of Christ into Sheol and His appearance to Mary Magdalene following the resurrection.[56]

As mentioned in chapter II, the procession of palms on the first day of Holy Week had its counterpart in one of the feasts of Jewish antiquity, the Feast of Tabernacles. This same Jewish feast had two other elements that correspond to two aspects of tonight's Easter Vigil. On each of the seven days of the Feast of Tabernacles water would be drawn from the Pool of Siloe in Jerusalem. On the last day of the festival this action was performed in a particularly solemn manner. A Levite would go to the pool and fill a golden bowl with water from it; returning to the temple, he would then mix wine into the water and pour it out over the altar of holocausts, as the people went in joyful procession around the altar. One can easily recognize a prefiguring of Baptism in this ceremony, and indeed our Lord Himself chose the last day of the Feast of Tabernacles to use the image of water in speaking of the Holy Spirit:

> "If any one thirst, let him come to me and drink.
> He who believes in me, as the scripture has said,
> 'Out of his heart shall flow rivers of living water.' "
>
> [Jn 7:37-38]

The imagery of water as well as light is an integral part of the Easter Vigil, as will be seen later. But a second aspect of this ancient Jewish feast is of more direct relevance to our current topic, the Service of Light. On the evening of the last day of the Feast of Tabernacles the city of Jerusalem was illuminated with four tremendous candelabra; it was on the day following this festive lighting that our Lord announced:

> "I am the light of the world; he who follows me will not walk in darkness, but will have the light of life."
>
> [Jn 8:12]

Our Lord's own words, spoken at the end of the Feast of Tabernacles, thus provide the basis for the symbolism of light at the Easter Vigil. We see these words fulfilled in the Service of Light, as the faithful, with lighted candles, follow in procession the paschal candle which represents "Christ our light."[57]

The Service of Light Today

Thou leader kind,
whose word called forth the radiant light,
Who by set bounds dividest night and day,
When the sun set, in gloom rose chaos on our sight:
Give back, O Christ, Thy light, Thy servants pray.

Although, with countless stars
and with the silvery tint
Of lunar lamp, thou dost the heavens dye,
Yet dost thou teach us how, by sudden stroke of flint,
The rock-born seed of light to vivify.

Lest man forget the hope for man of heavenly light,
That in Christ's body lies a hidden thing;
Who willed to be called the steadfast Rock of might,
Whence by our little sparks our race should spring.

[*Inventor Rutili*, refrain and vs. 1, 2][58]

Let us now witness the Easter Vigil ourselves.[59] It is well past sunset on the night of Holy Saturday. During the day, the faithful have had the opportunity to quietly reflect on the mystery of our Lord's repose in the tomb. No doubt this must have been a day of terrible grief for the Apostles, for they knew not what was so soon to follow. The brutal reality of Good Friday was still engraved in their hearts, nor could they forget their own pathetic desertion of Him who had loved them unto the end. But their grief was to be turned into joy, as He promised them at the Last Supper. This night we too are to share in that joy.

The faithful gather quietly in the porticoes along the perimeter of a courtyard adjacent to the church. Each holds a small unlit wax taper. In the middle of the courtyard, just in front of a statue of the Blessed Virgin Mary, is a stand with a small, pyramid-shaped pile of wood on top of it. All lights have been put out, leaving everything shrouded in the darkness and stillness of night. The celebrant appears and proceeds to the center of the courtyard, accompanied by the other priests con-celebrating with him, one of whom carries the unlit paschal candle in his hands. As they approach an acolyte ignites the wood; the flame is small at first, but soon begins to envelope the wooden pile and grows into a large orange tongue of fire reaching several feet in height. The celebrant begins the service with the usual greeting and then addresses the people in these words:

Dear friends in Christ,
on this most holy night,
when our Lord Jesus Christ passed from death to life,
the Church invites her children throughout the world
to come together in vigil and prayer.
This is the passover of the Lord:
if we honor the memory of his death and resurrection
by hearing his word and celebrating his mysteries,
then we may be confident
that we shall share his victory over death
and live with him for ever in God.

Then he blesses the paschal fire:

Let us pray.
Father,
we share in the light of your glory
through your Son, the light of the world.
Make this new fire + holy,
and inflame us with new hope.
Purify our minds by this Easter celebration
and bring us one day to the feast of eternal light.
We ask this through Christ our Lord.
Amen.

The celebrant takes a stylus and makes a number of incisions in the wax of the still unlit paschal candle. Tracing the vertical beam of a cross in the side of the candle he says:

Christ yesterday and today

Then he traces the horizontal cross beam, saying:

the beginning and the end

After this, he inscribes the Greek letter "Alpha" above the top of the cross, pronouncing the letter:

Alpha

Below the cross he carves the Greek letter "Omega," and says:

and Omega

He now inscribes the year on the candle; the first two digits are carved on either side of the vertical cross beam above the horizontal beam, the second two digits on either side below the horizontal beam. While doing this he says:

all time belongs to him	*(first digit)*
and all the ages	*(second digit)*
to him be glory and power	*(third digit)*
through every age for ever. Amen.	*(fourth digit)*

Having finished the inscriptions, he proceeds to insert five grains of incense into the side of the candle where he traced the cross. He puts a grain at each end of the vertical and horizontal beams of the cross; the fifth grain is inserted where the beams meet. As he adds the grains to the candle he says:

By his holy	*(first grain, top)*
and glorious wounds	*(second grain, middle)*
may Christ our Lord	*(third grain, bottom)*
guard us	*(fourth grain, left)*
and keep us. Amen.	*(fifth grain, right)*

The celebrant puts a wick to the still burning paschal fire and lights the paschal candle with it, saying:

May the light of Christ, rising in glory,
dispel the darkness of our hearts and minds.

A deacon[60] now takes the candle, goes to the edge of the court-yard and steps onto the portico, where he holds it aloft, singing in a triumphant strain:

Christ our light.

Pope John Paul II inscribing the paschal candle. *"Christ yesterday and today, the beginning and the end, Alpha and Omega. . . ."*

The faithful sing in response:

Thanks be to God.

The deacon leads the congregation in a silent procession to the threshold of the totally darkened church, where once again he stops and lifts up the paschal candle, chanting:

Christ our light.

Once more the people answer:

Thanks be to God.

The acolytes now begin to light the candles of the faithful from the flame of the paschal candle; quickly the light is spread from one person to another. All quietly take their place in the church, filling it with the dim illumination of hundreds of little dots of light. The stained-glass windows are dark, bringing to mind the darkness Christ came to dispel. The deacon continues to the front of the sanctuary; turning towards the people, he raises up the paschal candle a third and final time:

Christ our light.

Thanks be to God.

The candle is then mounted on an ornate stand in the center aisle of the church, a short distance from the sanctuary. On a lectern close to the candle stand is placed a book containing the words of the *Exultet*. Several of the lights in the church are now turned on in order to provide sufficient light for the readings to follow. The candle and book are censed, after which the deacon begins the jubilant chanting of the *Exultet*:

> *Rejoice, heavenly powers! Sing, choirs of angels!*
> *Exult, all creation around God's throne!*
> *Jesus Christ, our King, is risen!*
> *Sound the trumpet of salvation!*
>
> *Rejoice, O earth, in shining splendor,*
> *radiant in the brightness of your King!*

Christ has conquered! Glory fills you!
Darkness vanishes for ever!

Rejoice, O Mother Church! Exult in glory!
The risen Savior shines upon you!

Let this place resound with joy,
echoing the mighty song of all God's people!

My dearest friends, standing with me in this holy light,
join me in asking God for mercy,
that he may give his unworthy minister
grace to sing his Easter praises.

After a brief series of versicles in which the deacon invites the congregation to lift their hearts to God and give Him thanks, to which the people respond (the same versicles and responses as those used just before the Preface in every Mass), he continues with the *Exultet*:

It is truly right
that with full hearts and minds and voices
we should praise the unseen God,
the all-powerful Father,
and his only Son, our Lord Jesus Christ.
For Christ has ransomed us with his blood,
and paid for us the price of Adam's sin
to our eternal Father!

This is our passover feast,
when Christ, the true Lamb, is slain,
whose blood consecrates the homes of all believers.

This is the night when first you saved our fathers:
you freed the people of Israel from their slavery
and led them dry-shod through the sea.

This is the night when the pillar of fire
destroyed the darkness of sin!

This is the night when Christians everywhere,

washed clean of sin
and freed from all defilement,
are restored to grace and grow together in holiness.

This is the night when Jesus Christ
broke the chains of death
and rose triumphant from the grave.

What good would life have been to us,
had Christ not come as our Redeemer?

Father, how wonderful your care for us!
How boundless your merciful love!
To ransom a slave
you gave away your Son.

O happy fault, O necessary sin of Adam,
which gained for us so great a Redeemer!

Most blessed of all nights, chosen by God
to see Christ rising from the dead!
Of this night scripture says:
"The night will be as clear as day:
it will become my light, my joy."
The power of this holy night
dispels all evil, washes guilt away,
restores lost innocence, brings mourners joy;
it casts out hatred, brings us peace,
and humbles earthly pride.

Night truly blessed when heaven is wedded to earth
and man is reconciled with God!

Therefore, heavenly Father, in the joy of this night,
receive our evening sacrifice of praise,
your Church's solemn offering.

Accept this Easter Candle,
a flame divided but undimmed,
a pillar of fire that glows to the honor of God.

Let it mingle with the lights of heaven
and continue bravely burning
to dispel the darkness of this night!

May the Morning Star which never sets
find this flame still burning:
Christ, that Morning Star, who came back from the dead,
and shed his peaceful light on all mankind,
your Son who lives and reigns for ever and ever. Amen.

At the conclusion of the *Exultet* all extinguish their candles and sit as the Liturgy of the Word begins. Only the paschal candle remains lit "to dispel the darkness of this night."

The Liturgy of the Word

Our earliest records of the Easter Vigil allow us to form a sketchy picture of how this service was conducted prior to the fourth century. The feature for which there is the most ancient testimony is the use of Scripture readings; the vigil was an all-night event, the first portion of which was taken up with a series of twelve readings from the Old Testament, together with appropriate Psalms and prayers.[61] What were these scriptural selections, and why were they chosen? Father Herbert Thurston, SJ, saw these readings as "intended to open the minds and hearts of the whole assembly to the new creation typified in the Easter mystery."[62] This theme is evident in the very first of the readings at the vigil — the account of creation in the Book of Genesis — which foreshadows God's "new creation," the redemption of the world. Also selected were the accounts of Noah and the Great Flood, and of the passage of the Israelites through the Red Sea, each of which prefigures the role of water in Baptism, the Sacrament of Christian initiation. Likewise, the paschal themes of the death and resurrection of Christ conspicuously recur time and again in the early Church's selection of readings for this night. Thus we find included the Genesis account of God's testing of Abraham with regard to the sacrifice of his son Isaac. The Exodus account of the first Passover would bring before the minds of the faithful the image of the unblemished Lamb that was slain. A reading from the Book of Jonah, describing Jonah's three-day sojourn in the belly of the whale, provides a prefiguration that our Lord expressly applies to Himself in the gospels. Then there is the description from the Book of Daniel of the three young men who survive King Nebuchadnezzar's fiery furnace, as well as an account from the Book of Ezekiel telling of the prophet's vision of a valley full of dry bones that are afterwards clothed with flesh and restored to life.[63]

Originally, as stated above, twelve "lessons," that is, Old Testament Scripture readings, were heard during the Easter Vigil; early sources from Jerusalem (fifth century), Luxeuil (France — seventh century) and Silos (Spain — tenth century) all indicate this number.[64] Although the seventh century *Gelasian Sacramentary* specifies almost as many readings (ten),[65] it is evident that by this time the number had been reduced to four in the papal liturgy, according to both the Paduan (seventh century) and Hadrian (eighth century) editions of the *Gregorian Sacramentary*.[66] But eventually the lessons were increased again to twelve under the influence of the Germans, who became the powerful rulers of Charlemagne's Holy Roman Empire during the tenth century.[67] This number, appearing in the *Roman Pontifical* of the twelfth century,[68] was retained in the *Roman Missal* of 1570 (see Table below)

Table

The System of Twelve Old Testament Readings at the Easter Vigil: A Comparison[69]

Fifth century Jerusalem: *Armenian Lectionary*	Sixteenth century Rome: *Roman Missal* of 1570
Gen 1:1-3:24	Gen 1:1-2:2
Gen 22:1-18	Gen 5:31, 6:1-7, 13-22, 7:6, 11-14, 18-24, 8:1-3, 6-12, 15-21
Ex 12:1-24	Gen 22:1-19
Jonah 1:1-4:11	Ex 14:24-15:1
Ex 14:24-15:21	Is 54:17-55:11
Is 60:1-13	Bar 3:9-38
Job 38:1-28	Ez 37:1-14
2 Kgs 2:1-22	Is 4:1-6
Jer 31:31-34	Ex 12:1-11
Josh 1:1-9	Jonah 3:1-10
Ez 37:1-14	Dt 31:22-30
Dan 3:1-35a, 35-51	Dan 3:1-24

and remained the norm in the Western liturgy until the revision of the rites of the Easter Vigil in 1951, when the total was once more reduced to four.[70] However, with the issuance of the *Roman Missal* of Pope Paul VI in 1970, the number was raised to seven; up to four of these readings may be omitted for pastoral reasons, but the reading from Exodus must always be used.[71] In its 1988 *Circular Letter* on the Easter Feasts the Congregation for Divine Worship stressed that wherever possible "all the readings should be read in order that the character of the Easter Vigil, which demands the time necessary, be respected at all costs."[72]

The current selection of readings for the Easter vigil includes three of the Old Testament passages specifically mentioned earlier — the creation, the test of Abraham, and the passage through the Red Sea. At least two of the four other selections in the modern liturgy — the readings from the Book of Baruch and from chapter 55 of the Book of Isaiah — are found listed for the Easter Vigil in liturgical books from the early centuries of the Church. The two others — from chapter 36 of Ezekiel, and chapter 54 of Isaiah — both appear in the Old Testament in close proximity to readings used in the Easter Vigils of the early Church (Ezekiel 37 and Isaiah 55). The overall selection of Scripture passages in the current liturgy reflects the same thematic content of the early vigils: the "new creation" of redemption, the regenerative power of Baptism, and the unfolding of the Paschal Mystery. In rearranging the selection of readings, the Church has certainly not dispensed with the vivid paschal image of the Passover Lamb; the reading from the Book of Exodus concerning this has simply been shifted to the beginning of the Easter Triduum, where it is used as the first reading at the Mass of the Lord's Supper.

The reader may wonder why the theme of Baptism tonight is so predominant, almost on a level with the theme of the resurrection itself on this, the anniversary of the resurrection. The answer lies in the fact that on this night the Church rejoices not only in the great act of redemption itself — the passion, death, and resurrection of our Lord — but in what that act of redemption has wrought — the birth of all her children into the life of grace. Remember that the whole sacramental life of the Church flows from the wounded side of Christ. And it is in Baptism that Christ lays claim to us and makes us irrevocably His. The relationship between Baptism and Easter will be further explored in our discussion of the Liturgy of Baptism later on.

In the current liturgy, as in the ancient Easter Vigil, the first of the readings heard tonight is the Genesis account of God's creation of the world and of mankind (Gen 1:1-2:2):

In the beginning, when God created the heavens and the earth, the earth was a formless wasteland, and darkness covered the abyss, while a mighty wind swept over the waters.

Then God said, "Let there be light," and there was light. God saw how good the light was. God then separated the light from the darkness. . . . Thus evening came, and morning followed — the first day. . . .

Then God said: "Let us make man in our image. . . ."

[Gen 1:1-4, 5, 26; NAB]

The first responsorial psalm (Ps 104:1-2, 5-6, 10, 12-14, 24, 35) praises God for the wonders of His creation:

How manifold are your works, O Lord!
In wisdom you have wrought them all —
the earth is full of your creatures.
Bless the Lord, O my soul! Alleluia.

[Ps 104:24, 35; NAB]

The prayer said by the celebrant following the first reading and responsorial psalm highlights the relationship between the creation of the world and the redemption:

Almighty and eternal God, you created all things in wonderful beauty and order. Help us now to perceive how still more wonderful is the new creation by which in the fullness of time you redeemed your people through the sacrifice of our passover, Jesus Christ, who lives and reigns for ever and ever. Amen.

[Prayer following First Reading]

In the second reading (Gen 22:1-18) the sacrifice of our Lord on the wood of the cross is prefigured in Abraham's willingness to sacrifice even his own son in obedience to God:

When they came to the place of which God had told him, Abraham built an altar there and arranged the wood on it. Next he tied up his son Isaac, and put him on top of the wood on the altar. Then he reached out and took the knife to slaughter his son. But the Lord's messenger called to him from heaven, "Abraham, Abraham!" "Yes, Lord," he answered. "Do not lay your hand on the boy," said the messenger. "Do not do the least thing to him. I know now how devoted you are to God, since you did not withhold from me your own beloved son."

[Gen 22:9-12; NAB]

The responsorial psalm following this lection is Psalm 16 (vs. 5, 8-11), which is also used during the Office of Readings (as part of *Tenebrae*) on Holy Saturday morning. The third reading (Ex 14:15-15:1) relates the passage of the Israelites through the Red Sea:

The Lord said to Moses, "Why are you crying out to me? Tell the Israelites to go forward. And you, lift up your staff and, with hand outstretched over the sea, split the sea in two, that the Israelites may pass through it on dry land. But I will make the Egyptians so obstinate that they will go in after them. Then I will receive glory through Pharaoh and all his army, his chariots and charioteers. The Egyptians shall know that I am the Lord, when I receive glory through Pharaoh and his chariots and charioteers."

The angel of God, who had been leading Israel's camp, now moved and went around behind them. The column of cloud also, leaving the front, took up its place behind them, so that it came between the camp of the Egyptians and that of Israel. But the cloud now became dark. . . . Then Moses stretched out his hand over the sea, and the Lord swept the sea with a strong east wind throughout the night and so turned it into dry land. When the water was thus divided, the Israelites marched into the midst of the sea on dry land, with the water like a wall to their right and to their left.

The Egyptians followed in pursuit. . . . In the night watch just before dawn the Lord cast through the column of the fiery cloud upon the Egyptian force a glance that threw it into a panic; and he so clogged their chariot wheels that they could hardly drive. With that the Egyptians sounded the retreat before Israel, because the Lord was fighting for them against the Egyptians.

Then the Lord told Moses, "Stretch out your hand over the sea. . . ." The Egyptians were fleeing head on toward the sea, when the Lord hurled them into its midst. . . . Not a single one of them escaped. . . . When Israel saw the Egyptians lying dead on the seashore and beheld the great power that the Lord had shown against the Egyptians, they feared the Lord and believed in him and in his servant Moses.

[Ex 14:15-28, 30-31; NAB]

The responsorial psalm is actually a continuation of the above reading from Exodus 14-15 (Ex 15:1-6, 17-18). Moses and the Israelites sing in gratitude for their deliverance, praising the wonders of God's power:

My strength and my courage is the Lord,
and he has been my savior. . . .
Your right hand, O Lord,
magnificent in power,
your right hand, O Lord,
has shattered the enemy.

[Ex 15:2, 6; NAB]

The fourth reading, from the prophet Isaiah (54:5-14), uses beautiful nuptial imagery to describe God's love for the people He has redeemed:

He who has become your husband is your Maker;
his name is the Lord of hosts;
Your redeemer is the Holy One of Israel,
called God of all the earth.
The Lord calls you back,
like a wife forsaken and grieved in spirit,
A wife married in youth and then cast off,
says your God.
For a brief moment I abandoned you,
but with great tenderness I will take you back.
In an outburst of wrath, for a moment
I hid my face from you;
But with enduring love I take pity on you,
says the Lord, your redeemer.
This is for me like the days of Noah,
when I swore that the waters of Noah
should never again deluge the earth;
So I have sworn not to be angry with you,
or to rebuke you.
Though the mountains leave their place
and the hills be shaken,
My love shall never leave you
nor my covenant of peace be shaken,
says the Lord, who has mercy on you.

[Is 54:5-10; NAB]

The responsorial psalm following the fourth reading (Ps 30: 2, 4-6, 11-13) brings to mind our Lord's victory over sin and death in the resurrection:

I will extol you, O Lord, for you drew me clear
and did not let my enemies rejoice over me.
O Lord, you brought me up from the nether world;
you preserved me from among those going
down into the pit.

At nightfall, weeping enters in,
but with the dawn, rejoicing.

[Ps 30:2, 4, 6]

In the fifth reading (Is 55:1-11) our Lord invites all to "come to the water" — the waters of Baptism and of sanctifying grace; He promises spiritual nourishment — a promise fulfilled in the holy Eucharist. Then a theme from the beginning of Lent, that "now is the acceptable time," reappears; our Lord reminds us that now is the time to seek Him. The efficacy and fecundity of God's word is also stressed.

Thus says the Lord:
All you who are thirsty,
come to the water! . . .
Heed me, and you shall eat well,
you shall delight in rich fare.
Come to me heedfully,
listen, that you may have life. . . .
Seek the Lord while he may be found,
call him while he is near. . . .
For my thoughts are not your thoughts,
nor are your ways my ways, says the Lord. . . .
For just as from the heavens
the rain and snow come down
And do not return there
till they have watered the earth,
making it fertile and fruitful,
Giving seed to him who sows
and bread to him who eats,
So shall my word be

that goes forth from my mouth;
It shall not return to me void,
but shall do my will,
achieving the end for which I sent it.

[Is 55:1, 2-3, 6, 8, 10-11; NAB]

The responsorial psalm that follows the fifth reading likewise employs the imagery of water (Is 12:2-3, 4-6):

God indeed is my savior;
I am confident and unafraid.
My strength and my courage is the Lord,
and he has been my savior.
With joy you will draw water
at the fountain of salvation.

[Is 12:2-3; NAB]

The sixth reading (Bar 3:9-15, 32-4:4) exhorts us to seek wisdom, the "book of the precepts of God":

Hear, O Israel, the commandments of life:
listen, and know prudence! . . .
Who has found the place of wisdom,
who has entered into her treasuries? . . .
She is the book of the precepts of God,
the law that endures forever;
All who cling to her will live,
but those will die who forsake her. . . .
Blessed are we, O Israel;
for what pleases God is known to us!

[Bar 3:9, 15; 4:1, 4; NAB]

In the responsorial psalm (Ps 19:8-11) following the sixth reading, the commandments of God are seen not as an oppressive burden but as the key to true freedom and happiness:

The law of the Lord is perfect,
refreshing the soul. . . .
The precepts of the Lord are right,
rejoicing the heart;

The command of the Lord is clear,
enlightening the eye.
The fear of the Lord is pure,
enduring forever;
The ordinances of the Lord are true,
all of them just.

[Ps 19:8-10; NAB]

In tonight's seventh and final reading from the Old Testament (Ez 36:16-28) God speaks to us His children with paternal love, promising the cleansing and transformation of our hearts achieved by the passion, death, and resurrection of His Son:

. . . I will take you away from among the nations, gather you from all the foreign lands, and bring you back to your own land. I will sprinkle clean water upon you to cleanse you from all your impurities, and from all your idols I will cleanse you. I will give you a new heart and place a new spirit within you, taking from your bodies your stony hearts and giving you natural hearts . . . you shall be my people, and I will be your God.

[Ez 36:24-26, 28; NAB]

The responsorial psalm (Ps 42:3, 5;43:3-4) focuses upon the soul's thirst for God, a thirst that leaves the soul restless until it finds God:

Like a deer that longs for running streams,
my soul longs for you, my God.

[Antiphon]

Athirst is my soul for God, the living God.
When shall I go and behold the face of God?

Then will I go in to the altar of God,
the God of my gladness and joy. . . .

[Ps 42:3; 43:4; NAB]

The *Gloria*

The *Gloria*, a hymn of praise to God incorporated into the Mass on most Sundays and all feasts and solemnities, is believed to be of ancient origin; indeed, the opening verse is based upon the words of the angels to the shepherds in Bethlehem: "Glory to God in the highest, and on earth peace among men with whom he is pleased!" (Lk 2:14). The earliest surviving reference to the *Gloria* as a distinct composition, with several verses quoted, appears in a work of Saint Athanasius entitled *De Virginitate*, written in the fourth century;[73] a complete text of this hymn (albeit differing somewhat from the current version) is provided in the *Apostolic Constitutions*, an eastern document composed around A.D. 400.[74] But it is not until the sixth century that the *Gloria* is mentioned as part of the Roman Mass in the *Liber Pontificalis*.[75] Pope Symmachus (died 514) permitted the *Gloria* to be sung on Sundays,[76] and thus we may presume from this that the *Gloria* had entered the Easter liturgy by the time of his pontificate. It explicitly appears in the Easter Vigil of the seventh century *Gelasian Sacramentary*, which stipulates that the bishop is to say the *Gloria* following the Baptism of the catechumens.[77] The eighth-century Hadrian edition of the *Gregorian Sacramentary* specifies that only on Easter were ordinary priests granted the privilege of chanting the *Gloria;* bishops were permitted to do so on other occasions.[78] By the twelfth century the *Gloria* had become a part of all Masses of a jubilant nature.[79]

For centuries the intoning of the *Gloria* at the Easter Vigil has been marked by special actions that serve to emphasize the transition from the preparatory portion of the Easter Vigil, with its numerous lessons from the Old Testament, to the full joy of the resurrection proclaimed in the gospel and celebrated in the Mass. The most important of these symbolic actions is the "return" of the bells, the ringing of bells that have remained silent since the *Gloria* on Holy Thursday. We know from *Roman Ordo I* that the silencing of bells during the triduum already existed by the eighth century.[80] The tenth-century *Regularis Concordia* (England) is more explicit in regard to the Easter Vigil: It states that all the bells are to be rung when the *Gloria* begins.[81] By the fifteenth century this ringing during the *Gloria* had entered the Roman liturgy, appearing both in *Roman Ordo 15*[82] and in the *Missale Romanum* of 1474;[83] it was retained in the *Roman Missal* of 1570.[84] Another practice associated with the *Gloria* (albeit not a universal one) is the dramatic unveiling of the high altar. This custom is at least fourteen hundred years old; it is described in the ancient Spanish liturgical book known as the *Liber Ordinum*, dating from the fifth to seventh centuries. For the Vigil a veil would be put up to conceal the candles on the altar. During the service a cleric secretly entered the sanctuary and lit all of the altar tapers; the veil would then be suddenly lifted, revealing the lighted candles.[85] This unveiling formed part of the Service of Light with which the vigil began; but centuries later, in the Mozarabic Rite's *Missale Mixtum* of 1500, we find that the unveiling of the altar had been transferred to a different portion of the liturgy, having become directly associated with the intoning of the *Gloria* along with the ringing of the bells; the *Missale* specifies the removal of a black frontal from the altar, revealing gold altar cloths.[86]

In nineteenth-century Seville (Spain) the Easter Vigil would begin in a somber atmosphere, with a large black veil draped from the ceiling down to the floor, thus concealing the altar. But when the priest intoned the *Gloria*, the scene was suddenly transformed; immediately there was a volley of cannon fire, at which moment the black curtain was drawn back, revealing the high altar decked in white and ablaze in "light, gold and flowers." The pipe organ would pour forth a grand rush of sound, as a thousand silver bells pealed and the choir continued the *Gloria*.[87]

The custom of "unveiling" at the *Gloria* has been practiced in other places, such as Germany. The following is from a description (ca. 1930) of the Easter Vigil at the German Abbey of Maria Laach; the vigil was held each year in the abbey's 800-year-old basilica:

> The ceremony proceeds; we are at the Gloria which the Pontifex has intoned. The purple curtains which had previously shrouded the high altar roll back, seemingly of their own accord, and there on high, surrounded with fresh spring flowers, shines forth the gleaming crux gemmata, a worthy symbol of the Resurrection. The bells peal forth, the organ resounds through the Basilica. What a moment! One's thoughts are too deep for words. . . . It is indeed wonderful to experience this. The silver cross shining forth; the church flooded with light; the altar covered with white flowers; the sanctuary, choir and nave embellished likewise with flowers and floral decorations; the sacred ministers high up in the sanctuary; the cowled monks in the choir; the crowd of the faithful — all combine to produce an unforgettable effect. . . . The joyful Easter Gloria gives vent to our feelings; but that moment before the Gloria will never be forgotten.[88]

Although the unveiling of the altar is not mentioned by the *Roman Missal* (neither is it prohibited), the ringing of the bells is expressly permitted in the new *Missal* of Pope Paul VI, as it has been in the past:

> *After the last reading from the Old Testament with its responsory and prayer, the altar candles are lighted, and the priest intones the Gloria, which is taken up by all present. The church bells are rung, according to local custom.*[89]

The Congregation of Sacred Rites' second decree regarding the restoration of the Easter Vigil to its original nighttime setting (issued in 1952) adds a significant annotation to these directions:

> *. . . in places where there are a number of churches, the bells of all churches in that place should be rung together at the time the bells of the mother church or principal church begin their peals, namely when the hymn [the Gloria] is intoned in the latter. This applies whether the sacred services are celebrated in all churches at the same time or whether at different times.*[90]

Such a simultaneous ringing of all the church bells serves as a beautiful expression of the Church's unity in Christ, and gives moving testimony to all our non-Catholic brothers and sisters of our faith in the resurrection.

The Epistle and the Gospel

Until recently, the epistle assigned for this night's liturgy was from the third chapter of Saint Paul's Letter to the Colossians (vs. 1-4); this selection is found in the oldest surviving Roman lectionary, the *Capitulary of Wurzburg*, dating from the seventh or early eighth centuries; it is also mentioned in *Roman Ordo 30A* (Andrieu — eighth century).[91] This reading has since been transferred to morning Mass on Easter Sunday, and in its place a passage from the sixth chapter of the same Apostle's Letter to the Romans is used (vs. 3-11). The latter is the very same passage that was read at the Easter Vigil in tenth-century Constantinople,[92] and it has remained in the Byzantine liturgy down to the present day. In it Saint Paul tells us that through Baptism we share in the Paschal Mystery:

Are you not aware that we who were baptized into Christ Jesus were baptized into his death? Through baptism into his death we were buried with him, so that, just as Christ was raised from the dead by the glory of the Father, we too might live a new life. . . . If we have died with Christ, we believe that we are also to live with him. We know that Christ, once raised from the dead, will never die again; death has no more power over him.

[Rom 6:3-4, 8-9; NAB]

The responsorial psalm (Ps 118:1-2, 16, 17, 22-23) contains one of the most famous scriptural images of the Risen Christ: that of the "Cornerstone":

I shall not die, but live,
and declare the works of the Lord.
The stone which the builders rejected
has become the cornerstone.
By the Lord has this been done;
It is wonderful in our eyes.

[Ps 118:17, 22-23; NAB]

Just before the gospel, the *Alleluia*, which is omitted from the Roman liturgy throughout Lent, is chanted with the gospel verse for the first time in almost seven weeks, thus heralding the resurrection. The Hebrew word *Alleluia* is derived from two other Hebrew terms, *hallelu* — "praise," and *Jah*, a shortened form of the word *Jahve* — "God." It is generally thought that the *Alleluia* was first inserted into the Mass of the Roman Rite in the fourth century by Pope Damasus (pontificate A.D. 368-384) in imitation of the liturgy of Jerusalem, where such was already the practice.[93] The use of the *Alleluia* in the West was subsequently limited to Easter, but in the fifth century this restriction was loosened to permit the *Alleluia* throughout the Easter season.[94] Finally Pope Saint Gregory I (pontificate 590-604) expanded its use in the liturgy to include most of the liturgical year; only during the nine weeks from "Septuagesima Sunday" until Easter was the *Alleluia* excluded.[95] This provision remained the norm in the West until 1970, when the period without the *Alleluia* was reduced somewhat to the six and one half weeks from Ash Wednesday until Easter.[96]

For centuries the gospel of the Easter Vigil has been Saint Matthew's account of the women discovering the empty tomb (Mt

28:1-7); this selection appears in the *Capitulary of Wurzburg* cited earlier, as well as in the ninth-century *Roman Ordo 32* (Andrieu).[97] In the East Saint Matthew's account was in use by the fifth century, appearing in the liturgy of Jerusalem as found in the *Armenian Lectionary*.[98] In the modern Roman liturgy (as of 1970) a three-year cycle is used, with Matthew (28:1-10) read in the first year, while in the second and third years Saint Mark's (16:1-8) and Saint Luke's (24:1-12) accounts of the same episode are used respectively. Passages from all three accounts appear below, together with some appropriate verses from the Old Testament. Please note that the gospels specifically mention the names of four women who came to the tomb on Easter morning: Saint Mary Magdalene, "from whom he [the Lord] had cast out seven demons" (Mk 16:9); Mary the mother of the Apostle Saint James "the Less" (who was a relative of our Lord); Salome, wife of Zebedee and mother of the Apostles Saint John and Saint James "the Greater"; and Joanna, the wife of Chusa (steward of King Herod). Saint Mark tells us that the first three of these came together. The gospels do not indicate at what point Joanna joined them; she is mentioned by Saint Luke. It is evident from Saint John's gospel account that upon finding the empty tomb Mary Magdalene was so grief-stricken that she left her companions and ran to the house where Saint Peter and Saint John were staying. Thus when our Lord showed Himself to the women after the angels had spoken to them, Mary Magdalene was not with them. She too was to have the privilege of seeing Him on Easter morning, but this was to happen when she returned to the tomb by herself, crushed by the thought that not only had the Lord been struck down and borne away from her on Good Friday, but that now she could not even honor Him in death with the spices she had brought. Yet her sorrow would be turned to joy. We will leave Saint John's account of Mary Magdalene's meeting with the Lord for the next chapter; let us return here to the dawn of that first Easter morning:

> *And when the sabbath was past, Mary Magdalene, and Mary the mother of James, and Salome, bought spices, so that they might go and anoint him. And very early on the first day of the week they went to the tomb when the sun had risen. And they were saying to one another, "Who will roll away the stone for us from the door of the tomb?"*
>
> [Mk 16:1-3]

> *I will turn their mourning into joy,*

[355]

I will comfort them, and give
them gladness for sorrow.

[Jer 31:13]

And behold, there was a great earthquake; for an angel
of the Lord descended from heaven and came and rolled
back the stone, and sat upon it. His appearance was
like lightning, and his raiment white as snow. And for
fear of him the guards trembled and became like dead men.

[Mt 28:2-4]

When thou didst terrible things
which we looked not for,
thou camest down,
the mountains quaked at thy presence.

[Is 64:3]

And looking up, they [the women] saw that the stone
was rolled back; for it was very large.

[Mk 16:4]

But the angel said to the women, "Do not be afraid; for I know that
you seek Jesus who was crucified. He is not here; for he has risen, as he
said. Come, see the place where he lay."

[Mt 28:5-6]

We have escaped as a bird
from the snare of the fowlers;
the snare is broken,
and we have escaped!

[Ps 124:7]

. . . when they went in they did not find the body. While they were
perplexed about this, behold, two men stood by them in dazzling apparel;
and as they were frightened and bowed their faces to the ground, the men
said to them, "Why do you seek the living among the dead?"

[Lk 24:3-5]

I will extol thee, O Lord,
for thou hast drawn me up,

and hast not let my foes rejoice over me. . . .
O Lord, thou hast brought up my soul from Sheol,
restored me to life from among those
gone down to the Pit.

[Ps 30:1, 3]

"He is not here, but has risen. Remember how he told you, while he
was still in Galilee, that the Son of man must be delivered into the
hands of sinful men, and be crucified, and on the third day rise." And
they remembered his words. . . .

[Lk 24:5-8]

"But go, tell his disciples and Peter that he is going before you to
Galilee; there you will see him, as he told you."

[Mk 16:7]

He that goes forth weeping,
bearing the seed for sowing,
shall come home with shouts of joy,
bringing his sheaves with him.

[Ps 126:6]

So they departed quickly from the tomb with fear and great joy, and
ran to tell his disciples. And behold, Jesus met them and said, "Hail!"
And they came up and took hold of his feet and worshiped him. Then
Jesus said to them, "Do not be afraid; go and tell my brethren to go to
Galilee, and there they will see me."

[Mt 28:8-10]

I give thanks to thee, O Lord my God,
with my whole heart,
and I will glorify thy name for ever.
For great is thy steadfast love toward me;
thou hast delivered my soul
from the depths of Sheol.

[Ps 86:12-13]

While they were going, behold, some of the guard went into the city
and told the chief priests all that had taken place. And when they had
assembled with the elders and taken counsel, they gave a sum of money

to the soldiers and said, "Tell people, 'His disciples came by night and stole him away while we were asleep.' And if this comes to the governor's ears, we will satisfy him and keep you out of trouble." So they took the money and did as they were directed; and this story has been spread among the Jews to this day.

[Mt 28:11-15]

The Homily

The celebrant now gives a homily reflecting the themes of this night's liturgy, as has been done for centuries. There are surviving examples of Easter Vigil sermons by such monumental figures in the Church's history as Saint Augustine, Saint John Chrysostom, Saint Leo the Great, and Saint Bede, to name but a few.

In the darkness completely enveloping this Basilica of St. Peter, there resounded three times the deacon's words as a prophetic announcement of the paschal vigil: Lumen Christi!

Little by little the surroundings were lit up to express the significance of this night after the sabbath, approaching dawn.

Let us all enter into this night, still overwhelmed by yesterday's events, the death of Jesus of Nazareth and his burial not far from the Cross of Calvary. Let us proceed, as those two disciples on the road from Jerusalem to Emmaus (cf. Lk 24:13 f.).

The Church approaches us, as that stranger approached the disciples and walked with them towards Emmaus, and reveals to us her inspired teaching in a series of readings.

She shows God's eternal design which develops throughout human history beginning with creation, through the call of Abraham and consequently of his descendants. Patriarchs, prophets, and events speak; together they lead us finally to the Event of Easter night.

This is the light which illuminates the entire past; it reveals the profound significance of all the Old Testament books, and of all the readings of this Liturgy.

[Pope John Paul II][99]

The Liturgy of Baptism

The conferring of the Sacrament of Baptism has been linked with the celebration of the Easter Vigil from the very earliest times. The reader may recall that in the epistle at this night's vigil, mentioned previously, Saint Paul says that "we who were baptized into Christ Jesus were baptized into his death" (Rom 6:3). Thus from apostolic times Baptism has been most intimately associated with the death and resurrection of Christ; the annual commemoration of the Paschal Mystery would then have seemed the most appropriate time for the initiation of new Christians, as suggested by Tertullian in his early third-century treatise on Baptism:

> *Easter affords a more than usually solemn day for baptism; when, withal, the Lord's passion, in which we are baptized, was completed.*[100]

Although Baptism could also be administered on other occasions, such as Pentecost or the Feast of the Epiphany, Easter came to be seen both in the West and in the East as the most suitable time of all for this Sacrament, as explained by Saint Basil (A.D. 329-379) in his *Protreptic on Holy Baptism*:

> *. . . any time is suitable for obtaining salvation through baptism, be it day or night, or a precise hour, or the briefest moment. But assuredly that time should be considered most appropriate which is closest in spirit to it. What could be more akin to baptism than the day of the Pasch? For that day commemorates the Resurrection, and baptism makes the resurrection possible for us. Let us receive the grace of the resurrection on the day of the Resurrection.*[101]

Saint John Chrysostom (347-407) also treats of the relationship between Baptism and the resurrection in the celebration of Easter:

> *Why did our fathers ordain this feast at this time? Our King has now conquered in the war against the barbarians. And all the demons are barbarians, and more savage than barbarians. Now He has destroyed sin, now He has put down death and has subjected the devil, He has taken His captives.*
> *And so it is that on this day we celebrate the memory of those victories, and on this account our fathers ordained that the King's gifts be*

distributed at this time, for this is the custom of conquerors. . . .
. . . our fathers ordained the celebration of this season first in
order to remind you of the Master by the season of His victory, and
then that there might be, in the triumphal celebration, some who are
wearing shining robes and who are about to receive a reward from
the King.[102]

One of the earliest accounts of a baptismal rite at the Easter Vigil is found in the *Apostolic Tradition*, written by Saint Hippolytus around A.D. 215. The Baptism ceremony began at the time of "cockcrow" (3:00 in the morning) following an all-night vigil of readings and instructions. The candidates first renounced Satan and committed themselves to Christ; then came the actual Baptism, during which they were immersed in the blessed water of the font three times. Prior to each immersion they would profess their faith in the three Persons of the Blessed Trinity. Following this a priest anointed the newly baptized with oil, after which the bishop conferred the Sacrament of Confirmation upon them. The newly baptized then attended Mass and received holy Communion for the first time in their lives.[103]

By the beginning of the fourth century a detailed picture of the administration of Baptism at the Easter Vigil begins to emerge.[104] In Eastern countries the Baptism ceremony commenced with the renunciation of Satan. Each candidate would face the west and extend his hand, reciting these words:

I renounce thee, Satan, thy works, thy pomps, and all thy worship.[105]

The west was seen as the region of darkness, whereas the east was associated with the coming of Christ, the Light of the world. Having renounced Satan, the candidates now turned to the east and said the Creed. They then disrobed and entered the baptistry, where they were anointed with exorcised oil from head to foot. Modesty was respected in that the women candidates received this anointing from "deaconesses," that is, women commissioned to serve the Christian community in this and other nonordained roles. In the West the renunciation of Satan and recitation of the Creed took place during a separate ceremony earlier on Holy Saturday, as we have already seen (in chapter X). In both Latin and Eastern countries the actual Baptism itself, preceded by one final tripartite profession of faith, almost universally took the form of a threefold immersion in the font (in Spain there was only one immersion). In France, northern Italy, and Ireland the feet of the newly baptized were also washed.

In both Western and Eastern rites the newly baptized, upon emerging from the font, would be clothed in white garments, which symbolized their new life of grace. The origin of this image can be traced back to Saint Paul:

> *For as many of you as were baptized into Christ have put on Christ.*
> [Gal 3:27]

In disrobing before Baptism the candidates took off the "old man" enslaved by sin. Now they put on the "new man," with white robes that presage the eternal beatitude of the just,[106] evoking an image from the Book of Revelation:

> *After this I looked, and behold, a great multitude which no man could number, from every nation, from all tribes and peoples and tongues, standing before the throne and before the Lamb, clothed in white robes, with palm branches in their hands. . . . "These are they who have come out of the great tribulation; they have washed their robes and made them white in the blood of the Lamb."*
> [Rev 7:9, 14]

The newly baptized immediately received the Sacrament of Confirmation, which was administered by a bishop, but in the East by a priest if no bishop was present. In the Confirmation ceremony the bishop (or priest) laid his hands on the head of each candidate and using his thumb signed them on the forehead with chrism. During the Vigil Mass that followed, the newly baptized received a third Sacrament this night — the holy Eucharist. Additionally, in some places such as Rome and Alexandria (Egypt) a special drink consisting of a mixture of milk and honey was blessed prior to the end of the Canon (Eucharistic Prayer); following holy Communion it was given to each of the newly baptized.

> *. . . I have come down to deliver them out of the hand of the Egyptians, and to bring them up out of that land to a good and broad land, a land flowing with milk and honey. . . .*
> [Ex 3:8]

The current Liturgy of Baptism at the Easter Vigil begins with the recital of the Litany of the Saints; this is followed by the blessing of the font, and then by the actual Baptism of the candidates. It concludes with the renewal of the baptismal promises of all present at the vigil. Each of these elements will be discussed separately below.

The Litany

The Litany in this night's Easter Vigil can be traced at least as far back as the *Gelasian Sacramentary* (seventh century).[107] Originally the Litany was sung as the bishop made his way to the baptismal font, which was located in a baptistry apart from the church; this prayer served as a devotion for the faithful that filled the interval during which the bishop blessed the font and baptized the catechumens. It also served as a suitable prelude to the Eucharistic liturgy with which the vigil reached its climax and with which it ended.[108]

The Litany used for the Easter Vigil is a "Litany of Saints," the oldest of all the litanies; in it twenty-six different saints are invoked by name (the names of other canonized saints may be added, if need be):

> *Saint Peter and Saint Paul — pray for us*
> *Saint Andrew — pray for us*
> *Saint John — pray for us*
> *Saint Mary Magdalene — pray for us*

It also contains a series of petitions:

> *From every sin — Lord, save your people*
> *From everlasting death — Lord, save your people*
> *By your coming as man — Lord, save your people*
> *By your death and rising to new life — Lord, save your people*

In the current *Roman Missal*, the litany is included in the vigil if there are candidates to be baptized (or if the baptismal font is to be blessed); if not, it is omitted. It is sung by two cantors as all remain standing and respond to each invocation. If there is to be a somewhat lengthy procession of candidates to the baptistry, it is sung during this procession, at the head of which the paschal candle is carried. The clergy follow behind the candidates.

The Blessing of the Font

Here is born a noble people for heaven.
The Spirit gives them life in the fecund waters.
Sinner, descend into the sacred font
to be washed from your sins:
You go down old and return renewed in youth. . . .
In the waters Mother Church gives birth;
She remains a virgin in her fecundity,
Delivering to the world by virtue of the Spirit.
If you wish to be pure, wash yourself in those waters.
They wash away every sin — original or personal.
This is the source of life which washes the whole world.
It springs from the wounded side of Christ. . . .
[Inscription on baptistry, Church of Saint John Lateran, Rome][109]

The blessing of the baptismal font was already a part of the Liturgy of Baptism in the third century, as attested to by Saint Cyprian (died A.D. 258): "But the water must first be cleansed and hallowed by the priest [that is, the bishop], that by its baptism it may be able to wash away the sins of the man who is baptized."[110] Another third-century source, the *Apostolic Tradition* of Saint Hippolytus, also refers to the practice within the context of the Easter Vigil.[111] The words of blessing have been accompanied by various gestures and actions over the centuries. In the Hadrian edition of the *Gregorian Sacramentary* (eighth century) the celebrant was instructed to make the sign of the cross four times over the water during the prayer of blessing and to breathe three times upon it.[112] *Roman Ordo I* (eighth century) prescribed that the celebrant divide the water crosswise with his hand three times; then, after mixing chrism into the blessed water, he would sprinkle the faithful with it. Some of this water the people took home for their own use.[113] The addition of chrism to the baptismal waters is also mentioned in another, older, Roman document — *Roman Ordo 7* (Andrieu's *Ordo 11* — ca. 650-700).[114] In the later Middle Ages the practice of adding oil as well as chrism to the water was introduced.[115]

In the current *Roman Missal* the celebrant is instructed to lower the bottom end of the paschal candle into the water in the font just before the end of the blessing. An action of this nature is first mentioned as a facet of the Roman Rite during the eighth century (in Andrieu's *Roman Ordo 23*);[116] it serves as a reminder that the waters of Baptism derive their efficacy from the passion, death, and resurrection of Christ as symbolized by the paschal candle.

Water is blessed at the vigil even if there are no candidates for Baptism; in the latter case the following shorter prayer of blessing is said:

> *. . . Lord our God,*
> *this night your people keep prayerful vigil.*
> *Be with us as we recall the wonder of our creation*
> *and the greater wonder of our redemption.*
> *Bless this water: it makes the seed to grow,*
> *it refreshes us and makes us clean.*
> *You have made of it a servant of your loving kindness:*
> *through water you set your people free,*
> *and quenched their thirst in the desert.*
> *With water the prophets announced a new covenant*
> *that you would make with man.*
> *By water, made holy by Christ in the Jordan,*
> *you made our sinful nature new*
> *in the bath that gives rebirth.*
> *Let this water remind us of our baptism;*
> *let us share the joys of our brothers*
> *who are baptized this Easter.*
> *We ask this through Christ our Lord. Amen.*

The longer prayer of blessing (used when Baptism is to be administered or the baptismal font is to be blessed at the vigil) ends with the celebrant dipping the bottom of the paschal candle into the water and saying:

> *We ask you, Father, with your Son*
> *to send the Holy Spirit upon the waters of this font.*

With the candle still in the water, he continues:

> *May all who are buried with Christ*
> *in the death of baptism*
> *rise also with him to newness of life.*
> *We ask this through Christ our Lord. Amen.*

The celebrant now draws the candle out of the water as the people sing:

Springs of water, bless the Lord.
Give him glory and praise for ever.

Those to Be Baptized

If there are candidates who are to be baptized[117] at this night's vigil, they are now questioned by the celebrant, who asks them to renounce Satan and profess their faith in Christ and in His Church. The formula for this questioning is the same as that given below in the section entitled, "Renewal of Baptismal Promises." For infants that are to be baptized, these questions are answered on their behalf by their parents and godparents. The actual Baptism follows immediately. Each adult candidate steps forward to the font and leans over it as the priest pours water[118] over the candidate's head three times and says:

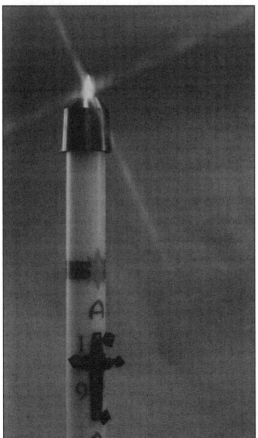

May all who are buried with Christ in the death of baptism rise also with him to newness of life.

(John Zierten)

[Baptismal name], I baptize you in the name of the Father, and of the Son, and of the Holy Spirit.

In the case of an infant, the mother (or father) holds the child over the font as he or she is baptized.

Each of the newly baptized is given a white garment to symbolize their "baptismal robes" with which Christ has clothed them. Each is also given a candle lighted from the paschal candle, symbolizing their new life in Christ. If any of the newly baptized are adults, they now receive the Sacrament of Confirmation, provided a bishop or a priest with the faculty to administer this sacrament is present. If "for some special reason"[119] the baptized are to be confirmed on a later occasion instead (as is the case with infants), they are anointed with chrism prior to receiving their white garments.

Every year at the Vatican Pope John Paul II celebrates the Easter Vigil in Saint Peter's Basilica; during the Liturgy of Baptism he confers the Sacrament of Christian Initiation on a large number of catechumens from many different nations. At the 1988 Easter Vigil the Holy Father baptized twenty-seven men and women from eleven countries: seven from Korea, four from the Cape Verde Islands, three from Vietnam, three from Japan, three from Italy, two from Germany, and one each from India, Indonesia, Peru, Hungary, and the United States.[120]

I see that your gathering is brighter than usual today and the Church is rejoicing over her children. A loving mother rejoices when she sees her children surrounding her; she exults and is borne along on the wings of her joy. So, too, that spiritual mother, the Church, looks on her children, rejoices, and is glad when she sees herself as a fertile field lush and green with this spiritual crop. Consider, my beloved, the excess of her love. See how many children this spiritual mother has brought forth suddenly and in a single night!

[Saint John Chrysostom][121]

Renewal of Baptismal Promises

The restored rite of the Easter Vigil of 1951 included a totally new element: the renewal of the baptismal promises of all present at the Vigil. This addition lends itself so well to the whole thematic content of the Easter Vigil that one is only surprised that the practice was not introduced long ago. For on this night we rejoice not only in the new life of grace conferred on those who are baptized during the vigil, but we also give thanks to God for the "glorious grace which he freely bestowed on us in the Beloved" (Eph 1:6) — that He has made us all His adopted sons and daughters in this great Sacrament of Baptism. It is also well to be reminded of our obligations to God on this night when we celebrate the victory over sin and death that His Son has won for us.

The renewal ceremony follows the Baptisms of any candidates present, or, when there is no one to be baptized, immediately follows the blessing of the water. After all have relit their candles from the flame of the paschal candle, the celebrant addresses the faithful as follows:

> *Dear friends,*
> *through the paschal mystery*
> *we have been buried with Christ in baptism,*
> *so that we may rise with him to a new life.*
> *Now that we have completed our lenten observance,*
> *let us renew the promises we made in baptism*
> *when we rejected Satan and his works,*
> *and promised to serve God faithfully*
> *in his holy Catholic Church.*

The celebrant now poses a series of questions (the same asked of every candidate for Baptism), to which the congregation answers, "I do":

Do you reject Satan?	*I do.*
And all his works?	*I do.*
And all his empty promises?	*I do.*
Do you believe in God, the Father almighty,	
creator of heaven and earth?	*I do.*
Do you believe in Jesus Christ, his only Son,	
our Lord, who was born of the Virgin Mary,	
was crucified, died, and was buried,	
rose from the dead,	
and is now seated at the right hand of the Father?	*I do.*
Do you believe in the Holy Spirit,	
the holy Catholic Church, the communion of saints,	
the forgiveness of sins, the resurrection of the body,	
and life everlasting?	*I do.*

After a concluding prayer the celebrant sprinkles the faithful with the newly blessed water, during which an appropriate hymn is sung. Following the sprinkling, all extinguish their candles; this brings the Liturgy of Baptism to a close.

The Liturgy of the Eucharist

The Easter Vigil leads into the celebration of the Vigil Mass. As far back as the early second century (and probably earlier) this Eucharistic liturgy was already considered the most important rite of the paschal season and of the whole liturgical year.[122] By the time of Tertullian (late second century / early third century) attendance at the Easter Vigil and its concluding Mass was obligatory for all the faithful. The Vigil Mass has undergone very little change over the centuries; it follows the format of the ancient Sunday morning Masses which came at the end of the Saturday night vigils of the first three centuries.[123]

As the offertory begins, two acolytes light six tall candlesticks on the old high altar directly behind the main altar. After the gifts have been brought to the altar, the Offertory prayers are said over the unconsecrated bread and wine; following this the celebrant censes the gifts and the main altar. He gives the *thurible* to a deacon, who censes the celebrant and afterwards those concelebrating. The deacon then proceeds to the front of the sanctuary; the congregation having risen, he now censes them also.[124]

> *Let my prayer be counted*
> *as incense before thee,*
> *and the lifting up of my hands*
> *as an evening sacrifice!*

[Ps 141:2]

The Eucharistic Prayer this night begins with a preface that speaks of the passion, death, and resurrection of our Lord as a single mystery — the Paschal Mystery:

> *We praise you with greater joy than ever*
> *on this Easter night,*
> *when Christ became our paschal sacrifice.*
> *He is the true Lamb who took away*

the sins of the world.
By dying he destroyed our death;
by rising he restored our life.

As on Holy Thursday, the Church deems the selection of Eucharistic Prayer I as "particularly apt" for tonight's liturgy. The Roman Canon is provided with two special insertions for the Mass of the Easter Vigil (and for the other Masses of the Easter Octave), the first of which reminds us of the great event we are commemorating:

In union with the whole Church
we celebrate that night
when Jesus Christ, our Lord,
rose from the dead in his human body.

These insertions have been part of the Easter Vigil for at least thirteen hundred years, for they can both be found as far back as the seventh century in the *Gelasian Sacramentary* as well as in the Paduan edition of the *Gregorian Sacramentary*.[125] The second insertion touches on the other dominant theme of the Easter liturgy — Baptism — and mentions those in our midst who through this Sacrament are fully participating in the Eucharistic sacrifice for the first time:

Father, accept this offering
from your whole family
and from those born into the new life
of water and the Holy Spirit,
with all their sins forgiven.

From the earliest times the Church has always considered the reception of holy Communion in the Easter season, and in particular on Easter itself, of the utmost importance. The matter was codified for the universal Church in the year 1215, when the Fourth Lateran Council decreed that all the baptized were obligated to receive holy Communion at Easter under pain of severe ecclesiastical penalties, that is, a life-long denial of admittance into churches and of Christian burial.[126] In 1440 Pope Eugenius IV modified this Church law in his apostolic constitution *Digna fide* so that the faithful could fulfill their obligation of an Easter Communion on any day from Palm Sunday until "Low Sunday," that is, the first Sunday after Easter, thus providing a period of fifteen days.[127] The obligation to receive holy Communion at least once a year is still enjoined upon the faithful by the current Code of Canon Law, although the time span within which this obligation (known as the "Easter Duty" or "Paschal Precept") may be satisfied has been broadened considerably. Canon 920 states:

> #1 Once admitted to the blessed Eucharist, each of the faithful is obliged to receive holy communion at least once a year.
> #2 This precept must be fulfilled during paschal time, unless for a good reason it is fulfilled at another time during the year.[128]

A special indult of the Sacred Congregation for the Propagation of the Faith issued on October 16, 1830, gave the bishops of the United States authority to extend the period for the fulfillment of the "Easter Duty" from the first Sunday of Lent to Trinity Sunday (the Sunday after Pentecost) inclusive;[129] under the present Canon Law this indult remains in effect,[130] and thus the faithful of America have a total of fourteen weeks during which they may receive their Easter Communion.

At tonight's holy Communion, we share in the joy of the Apostles as we, like them, are reunited with our risen Savior, filled with hope by His promise: ". . . he who eats my flesh and drinks my blood has eternal life, and I will raise him up at the last day" (Jn 6:54).

> And as the vine tree planted in the earth will in due time yield fruit, and a grain of wheat falling to the ground, and there perishing, will rise again, multiplied by the Spirit of God that sustains all things, then through the Wisdom of God goes on to serve the needs of man, and, receiving the word of God, they both become the Eucharist, Which is the Body and Blood of Christ, so also our bodies, which are nourished by It, are placed in the earth, and dissolve there, shall in due time rise again, the Word of God bestowing on them an awakening unto the glory of God the Father Who freely clothes this mortal body with immortality, and gives to this corruptible flesh incorruptibility. . . .
>
> [Saint Irenaeus][131]

Following holy Communion, as the faithful make their thanksgiving, the Blessed Sacrament is returned to the Tabernacle, which has been empty since Holy Thursday. The red sanctuary lamp is lit once more and hoisted up on the cord from which it is suspended before the tabernacle. Two more lit candles are left on either side, serving as a further reminder that the Lord has been returned to us.

The choir and organ combine to fill the church with the triumphant sound of the recessional hymn, as an acolyte brings out the processional cross and takes his place before the altar. The celebrant and concelebrants now follow him and the other acolytes in procession down the central aisle. The cross, held aloft in the brightly lit church, passes us at a measured pace as all sing *Jesus Christ is Risen Today*:

> *Jesus Christ is ris'n today, Alleluia!*
> *Our triumphant holy day, Alleluia!*
> *Who did once upon the cross, Alleluia!*
> *Suffer to redeem our loss, Alleluia!*
>
> *Hymns of praise then let us sing, Alleluia!*
> *Unto Christ, our heav'nly King, Alleluia!*
> *Who endured the cross and grave, Alleluia!*
> *Sinners to redeem and save, Alleluia!*
>
> *But the pains which he endured, Alleluia!*
> *Our salvation have procured, Alleluia!*
> *Now he rules eternal King, Alleluia!*
> *Where the angels ever sing, Alleluia!*
>
> [vs. 1-3][132]

> *What have we seen? A light like a cloud of fire of the candles burning during the night. All night our ears have resounded with psalms, hymns and spiritual chants; it was like a river of joy running through our ears to our soul and filling us with blessed hopes.*
> [Saint Gregory of Nyssa][133]

The Easter Vigil in the Byzantine Rite

As in the West, the Easter Vigil in the Byzantine Rite[134] is rooted in ancient liturgical practices dating back to the fourth century and earlier. But in the East two cities in particular were to play pivotal roles in the development of the Byzantine liturgy: Jerusalem and Constantinople. The earlier stages of this development were dominated by the influence of Jerusalem, the city where the Church was born, but by the end of the seventh century, Constantinople (modern-day Istanbul,

Turkey), the capital of the Byzantine Empire, had begun to exert a powerful influence throughout the East that eventually spread to Jerusalem itself.[135] In the modern Greek liturgy we see elements of both these traditions intermingled.

The *Armenian Lectionary* is among the oldest surviving texts of the liturgy of Jerusalem, dating from the early fifth century; although Egeria's pilgrimage account is slightly older, the latter does not provide much information concerning the Easter Vigil. The *Armenian Lectionary* is far more helpful in this regard. Services began with a gathering in the *Anastasis*, the church built directly over the site of the holy sepulchre; the bishop chanted Psalm 113, after which (either in the *Anastasis* or in the *Martyrium*, an adjoining church) at least one lamp was lit. The later of two existing manuscripts of this document indicates that three lights were initially kindled, perhaps a subsequent development with Trinitarian symbolism. It appears likely that the flame was taken from a lamp that was maintained at all times within the tomb itself. The *Lectionary* does say that the fire was spread among candles held by each of the faithful, a practice that has only recently entered the Roman Rite (in 1951). Following this distribution of light, the Vigil proper commenced immediately with the chanting of Psalm 118.[136]

According to the *Georgian Lectionary*, a later document reflecting the Jerusalem liturgy from the fifth century through the eighth, the Service of Light began with the preparation of three *thuribles*, followed by a series of three processions around the Church of the holy sepulchre (the *Anastasis*), during each of which a Psalm was chanted. After returning to the step of the altar, the clergy exchanged the sign of peace; then the "new candle" was blessed, from which others were lit and distributed to the faithful. The doors were now opened after which Psalm 141 and the hymn *Phos hilaron* were sung. The beginning of the Vigil proper followed as the clergy entered the sanctuary during the chanting of Psalm 147.[137]

The source of the flame for the "new candle" is not specified in the *Georgian Lectionary*, but presumably it was still being lit from the lamp kept burning in the holy sepulchre. However, an important change in this aspect of the Service of Light in Jerusalem appears to have taken place by the close of the ninth century. In the *Itinerarium* of Bernhardus Monachus, an account of a pilgrimage to the Holy Land thought to date from about 870, the source of the Easter fire is attributed to an angel who enters the holy sepulchre and kindles the flame.[138] This attribution of the fire to a miraculous origin is repeated in a number of other accounts from the tenth, eleventh, and twelfth centuries;[139] even a

Moslem who visited the Holy City in 926 mentions it:

> *The Christians assemble for this festival from out all lands. For on it the fire from heaven doth descend among them, and they kindle therefrom the candles . . . the fire is produced by a clever artifice, which is kept a great secret.*[140]

The most important liturgical work describing the Jerusalem Easter liturgy at this stage of its development is the *Typicon of the Anastasis* (*Hagios Stauros 43*), a manuscript dating from 1122 but probably reflecting tenth-century usage. In it we find that the Service of Light was no longer held at the very beginning of the Easter Vigil; instead it was conducted following the Old Testament readings. First, the holy sepulchre as well as the site of Golgotha and several other shrines were each censed three times. Then the patriarch of Jerusalem would prostrate himself nine times (in three triple prostrations) before the holy sepulchre, and upon entering it, engaged in three more triple prostrations. The door to the tomb having been shut, the patriarch prays for forgiveness of his own sins and those of the people, while the *Kyrie eleison* ("Lord, have mercy") is chanted. Finally he reemerges with the new Easter fire, which is subsequently passed to the candles of all the faithful.[141] Several other interesting details of the ceremony can be gleaned from the various pilgrim accounts of the "holy fire." Arethas, a Metropolitan of the Cappadocian city of Caesarea (in what is now eastern Turkey), writing in the early tenth century, mentions that there was a preliminary sealing of the doors of the holy sepulchre by the Moslem Emir of Jerusalem, who evidently served as an objective witness to the miracle. Arethas also mentions that all the lights in the Holy City were extinguished, undoubtedly in anticipation of the coming of the new Easter flame. Both Arethas and Bernhardus (ca. 870) testify that the people brought the Easter fire home with them in order to kindle their own lamps.[142]

The Jerusalem ceremony of the Easter fire has continued to the present day; it is now conducted by the Greek Orthodox Patriarch. In the days of the Russian czars prior to World War I, the flame was carried from Jerusalem and taken by boat to the Ukrainian city of Odessa, from which it was then spread throughout Russia.[143]

Both the *Armenian Lectionary* (early fifth century) and the *Georgian Lectionary* (fifth to eighth centuries) list twelve Old Testament lections for the Easter Vigil.[144] The epistle and gospel in both of these books are from the first Letter to the Corinthians (15:1-11) and chapter 28 of Saint Matthew (vs. 1-20) respectively;[145] the latter of these is nearly identical to that used in the West for at least twelve hundred years. The *Typicon of the Anastasis* (tenth century) contains fifteen Old Testament readings,[146] the same number found in the current Byzantine liturgy. This larger number of lections appears to have originated in Byzantium's capital, Constantinople. According to the *Typicon of the Great Church*, a liturgical document of Constantinople dating from the ninth to tenth centuries, the selection of Old Testament readings during the Easter Vigil in the Basilica of Santa Sophia was as follows:[147]

1) Gen 1:1-5	9) Is 61:10-62:5
2) Is 60:1-16	10) Gen 22:1-18
3) Ex 12:1-11	11) Is 61:1-10
4) Jonah 1:1-4:11	12) 2 Kings 4:8-37
5) Josh 5:10-15	13) Is 63:11-64:4
6) Ex 13:20-14:31	14) Jer 31:31-34
7) Zeph 3:8-15	15) Dan 3:1-51
8) 1 Kings 17:8-24	

The Easter liturgy of Constantinople, although considerably less elaborate than that of Jerusalem, nonetheless featured a number of distinctive practices, as described in the *Typicon of the Great Church* and in a later manuscript of the tenth to eleventh centuries (Codex A 104 of the Royal Library of Dresden). At noon on Holy Saturday, the emperor comes to the basilica and changes the altar cloths; then the patriarch censes the edifice. In the evening, during the Easter Vigil, the patriarch leaves the church to baptize the catechumens while the Old Testament lessons are read. When the Baptisms are completed, he returns in procession, dressed in white vestments. If the Old Testament readings are not yet finished, all of the remaining readings except the last (from the Book of Daniel) are omitted. A rug is laid at the threshold of the central doors of Santa Sophia; upon arriving, the patriarch prostrates himself on the rug three times, and then makes the sign of the cross with a candle. He enters the basilica with the gospel book; twelve other bishops enter through the side doors. Following the epistle, which reflects the theme of Baptism (Rom 6:3-11), the eighth verse of Psalm 82 is chanted in place of the *Alleluia* that normally precedes the gospel: "Arise, O God, judge the earth; for to thee belong all the nations!" Meanwhile a plain cloth covering the altar is removed, revealing a golden altar cloth underneath. The theme of the resurrection now emerges in full as Saint Matthew's gospel account of the empty tomb (Mt 28:1-20) is read.[148]

Over the centuries the Byzantine Rite's observance of the Easter Vigil has been shifted from the night between Holy Saturday and Easter Sunday to the early morning of Holy Saturday, as had happened with the vigil in the Roman Rite. But while the Roman Rite vigil has since been restored to its original time of celebration on the night of Holy Saturday, the Byzantine vigil is still held on the preceding morning. This liturgy resembles the Roman vigil in several important respects.[149] As in the tenth-century vigil of Constantinople, there are fifteen Scripture readings from the Old Testament, comparable to the seven Old Testament readings in the current *Roman Missal*. The epistle that follows is from chapter 6 of Saint Paul's Letter to the Romans (vs. 3-11), as in medieval Constantinople and in the current Western liturgy. The gospel reading, Saint Matthew's account of the women finding the empty tomb, is that used in the first year of the Roman Rite's three-year cycle of readings. During the service there is a dramatic transformation from mourning to joy, analogous to the customs surrounding the beginning of the *Gloria* in the Roman Rite. The clergy exchange their dark-colored vestments for gold ones; the black cloths on the icon stands are replaced with white cloths. Handfuls of green branches are strewn about the church, symbolizing new life in Christ. And as in the Western Rite, the vigil comes to its climax with the celebration of Mass.

A second vigil has been added to the Byzantine liturgy for the nighttime hours leading into Easter Sunday. It begins toward midnight in the darkened church, where branches still lie scattered across the floor and garlands of greenery hang from the roof. The clergy, vested in white, enter and remove the *Epitaphios*, the symbolic burial shroud, that has been in the sanctuary since Good Friday. After taking away the shroud, they reenter and start a procession out of the church, carrying icons and gospel books. The people join them, carrying lighted candles into the night air outside, while the church bells are rung jubilantly. The doors of the church are closed behind them. The procession continues and eventually returns, stopping before the church door. Here the chief celebrant sings:

Christ is risen from the dead. By death he conquered death, and to those in the grave he granted life.[150]

The choir responds in the same words. Then the celebrant makes the sign of the cross on the door; it is opened, revealing an interior now filled with light. All reenter the church for Easter Matins (the first prayers of the day in the Divine Office), followed by the celebration of

Mass, with the gospel reading from chapter 1 of Saint John (vs. 1-17):

In the beginning was the Word. . . . In him was life, and the life was the light of men. The light shines in the darkness, and the darkness has not overcome it.

[Jn 1:1,4-5]

The gospel is read several times over, each time in a different language, beginning with the ancient tongues, such as Hebrew and Greek, and ending with the vernacular. Following Mass an Easter icon as well as a loaf of decorated Easter bread is left on the same stand that previously held the *Epitaphios* of Good Friday.

O death, where is thy victory?
O death, where is thy sting?

[1 Cor 15:55]

A Final Thought for the Night of the Resurrection

Yesterday the Lamb was slain, and the doorposts sprinkled with His Blood; while Egypt mourned for her firstborn. But the Destroying Angel and his sacrificial knife, fearful and terrifying, passed over us (Ex. 12): for we were protected by the Precious Blood. This day we have wholly departed from Egypt, and from Pharaoh its cruel tyrant, and his oppressive overseers. . . .

Yesterday I was crucified with Christ; today I am glorified with Him. Yesterday I died with Him; today I am given life with Him. Yesterday I was buried with Him; today I rise again with Him.

[Saint Gregory Nazianzen][151]

Endnotes

1. "Homily 19 on psalm 5," *The Paschal Mystery: Ancient Liturgies and Patristic Texts* (Alba Patristic Library, Vol. 3), Andre Hamman, OFM, ed., 1969, pp. 109-110.
2. Father John Miller, CSC, "The History and Spirit of Holy Week," *American Ecclesiastical Review*, April 1957, pp. 235-236.

3. Ibid., p. 236.

4. Ibid., p. 235.

5. *Patrologia Latina*, Vol. 74, col. 1112b.

6. The discussion of the timing of the Easter Vigil that follows is based upon Father Josef Jungmann, SJ, "Die Vorverlegung der Ostervigil seit dem christlichen Altertum," *Liturgisches Jahrbuch*, 1951, Vol. 1, pp. 51-53.

7. Ibid., Vol. 78, col. 955b.

8. *Les Ordines Romani du Haut Moyen Age: III: Les Textes (Ordines XIV-XXXIV)* (Etudes et Documents, Vol. 24), Michel Andrieu, 1961, p. 272.

9. *Patrologia Latina*, Vol. 101, col. 1216b.

10. Ibid., Vol. 78, col. 1041c, 1076c, respectively.

11. *Le Pontifical Romain au Moyen-Age: Tome I:Le Pontifical Romain du XII Siecle* (Studi e Testi, Vol. 86), Michel Andrieu, ed., 1938, p. 238.

12. *Patrologia Latina*, Vol. 78, col. 1218a-b.

13. Miller, pp. 236-237. For relevant rubric see *Missale Romanum* (1942 edition), Benziger Brothers, 1952, "Rubricae generales," XV, #2, p. xxx.

14. *Decree of the Congregation of Sacred Rites Restoring the Solemn Easter Vigil*, Feb 9, 1951, in *American Ecclesiastical Review*, March 1952, pp. 181-182.

15. Decree of the Congregation of Sacred Rites, Jan 11, 1952, *American Ecclesiastical Review*, April 1952, pp. 299-300.

16. *Maxima redemptionis*, Congregation of Sacred Rites, Nov 16, 1955, Section II, #9, in *American Ecclesiastical Review*, Jan 1956, pp. 54-55.

17. Liturgists once spoke convincingly of a weekly all-night vigil ending with Sunday Mass in the early Church, but more recent studies have questioned whether there is sufficient evidence that such a rigorous practice would have been conducted so frequently. See Thomas J. Talley, "History and Eschatology in the Primitive Pascha," *Worship*, April 1973, p. 215; also Father Joseph Jungmann, SJ, *Pastoral Liturgy*, pp. 105-107.

18. Sermon 219, *The Sunday Sermons of the Great Fathers*, M. F. Toal, ed., 1958, Vol. II, p. 193.

19. Reverend John Tyrer, *Historical Survey of Holy Week: Its Services and Ceremonial* (Alcuin Club Collections #29), 1932, p. 148.

20. Father Oswald Bussy, "The Great Paschal," *Clergy Review*, Vol. 22, 1942, p. 205.

21. Ibid.

22. Father Francis X. Weiser, SJ, *Handbook of Christian Feasts and Customs:*

The Year of the Lord in Liturgy and Folklore, 1958, p. 208.

23. Father Herbert Thurston, SJ, "The Exultet and the Paschal Candle," *The Month*, April 1896, p. 508.

24. David Baier, OFM, "The Liturgy of the Paschal Candle," *Homiletic and Pastoral Review*, April 1933, p. 702; Thurston, pp. 508-509.

25. Cardinal Ildefonso Schuster, *The Sacramentary: Historical and Liturgical Notes on the Roman Missal*, Vol. II, 1925, p. 250.

26. Baier, p. 703.

27. Thurston, p. 517 (relevant text of Saint Bede in *Patrologia Latina*, Vol. 90, col. 425a).

28. Daniel Rock, *The Church of Our Fathers*, 1903-1904, Vol. 3, Part II, pp. 97-98; Vol. 4, p. 107.

29. Monsignor L. Duchesne, *Christian Worship: Its Origin and Evolution*, p. 251; for burial symbolism of this practice see Father Herbert Thurston, SJ, "Easter Sepulchre or Altar of Repose?," *The Month*, April 1903, pp. 407-408.

30. Thurston, "The Exultet," p. 511.

31. Baier, pp. 704-705.

32. Thurston, pp. 516-517.

33. Baier, p. 705.

34. Andrieu, *Le Pontifical*, pp. 240-241.

35. Father Charles Meeus, "China's New Order," *Orate Fratres*, March 22, 1942, pp. 229-230.

36. Bussy, p. 209.

37. *The Monastic Constitutions of Lanfranc*, David Knowles, tr./ed., 1951, pp. 43-44.

38. Bussy, p. 205.

39. Gabriel Bertoniere, *The Historical Development of the Easter Vigil and Related Services in the Greek Church* (Orientalia Christiana Analecta 193), 1972, pp. 29-32.

40. Andrieu, *Le Pontifical*, p. 239.

41. *Memoriale Rituum*, Title VI, chapter 1, 2, Sections 1, 2, in *The Ritual for Small Churches*, Reverend Bartholomew Eustace, tr., 1935, pp. 85-86, 88-92.

42. Andrieu, *Le Pontifical*, pp. 239-240.

43. This dating is proposed by Cyrille Vogel, *The Medieval Liturgy: An Introduction to the Sources*, William G. Storey and Niols Krogh Rasmussen, OP, tr./rev., 1986, p. 165 (*Roman Ordo 7* is classified by Andrieu as *Roman Ordo 11* — hence Vogel identifies it as such).

44. *Patrologia Latina*, Vol. 78, col. 999a.

45. *The Sarum Missal in English*, Frederick Warren, tr., 1911, Part I, p. 265.

46. Bussy, pp. 207-208.

47. Thurston, p. 518.

48. Weiser, pp. 215-216.

49. Ibid., p. 217.

50. *The Monastic Constitutions of Lanfranc*, p. 44.

51. Maria Augusta Trapp, *Around the Year with the Trapp Family*, 1955, p. 134.

52. John Scholar, "Living with the Liturgy," *Orate Fratres*, March 18, 1933, pp. 208-209.

53. Kenneth Stevenson, "The Ceremonies of Light: Their Shape and Function in the Paschal Vigil Liturgy," *Ephemerides Liturgicae*, 1985, pp. 179, 184; Latin text quoted in H. Leclercq, "Paques," *Dictionnaire d'archeologie chretienne et de liturgie*, ed. F. Cabrol and H. Leclercq, 1907-1953, Volume 13, Part II, col. 1567-1568.

54. Bertoniere, p. 32.

55. W. J. O'Shea, "Easter Vigil," *New Catholic Encyclopedia*, 1967, Vol. 5, p. 11.

56. Thurston, pp. 502-505.

57. Jerome Gassner, OSB, "Rising with Christ: The Blessing of the Baptismal Font," *Homiletic and Pastoral Review*, April 1949, p. 534.

58. *The Sarum Missal in English*, Part I, p. 269.

59. Liturgical texts from *The Vatican II Sunday Missal*, Daughters of St. Paul, 1974, pp. 412-454, and *Lectionary for Mass*, Catholic Book Publishing Co., 1970, pp. 93-102.

60. If there is no deacon, the celebrant takes the paschal candle (*Roman Missal*, "Easter Vigil," #14).

61. Father Josef Jungmann, SJ, "Introduction," K. Becker, *O Truly Blessed Night: A Study of the Theology of the Easter Vigil*, p. 9.

62. Father Herbert Thurston, SJ, *Lent and Holy Week*, 1904, p. 427.

63. Jungmann (in Becker), pp. 9-10.

64. Anton Baumstark, *Comparative Liturgy*, 1958, pp. 167-168. For Jerusalem see discussion of *Armenian Lectionary* in this chapter (pp. 372, 373 and Table on p. 343). For Luxeuil see *Lectionary of Luxeuil* in *Patrologia Latina*, Vol. 72, col. 194c-196a. For Silos see list of lections from *Liber Comicus* in G. Godu, "Epitres," *Dictionnaire d'archeologie chretienne et de liturgie*, F. Cabrol and H. Leclercq, ed., 1907-1953, Vol. 5, Part I, col. 266.

65. *Patrologia Latina*, Vol. 74, col. 1108b-1109d.

66. Texts in *Le Sacramentaire Gregorien: Ses principales formes d'apres les*

plus anciens manuscrits: I (Spicilegium Friburgense, Vol. 16), Jean Deshussses, ed., 2nd ed., 1979, pp. 183-184 (Hadrian), 631 (Paduan).

67. Baumstark, p. 168. Regarding the Holy Roman Empire see Philip Hughes, *A Popular History of the Catholic Church*, 1947 (rpt. 1962), p. 102.

68. Andrieu, *Le Pontifical*, p. 241.

69. Lections in *Armenian Lectionary* from John Wilkinson, *Egeria's Travels*, 1971, p. 276; lections in 1570 *Roman Missal* from *Missale Romanum: Mediolani, 1474* (Henry Bradshaw Society, Vols. 17 and 33), Robert Lippe, ed., 1899 and 1907, Vol. I, pp. 177-189, Vol. II, pp. 86-89.

70. Sacred Congregation of Rites, *Decretum: De solemni vigilia paschali instauranda*, Feb 9, 1951, "Rubricae Sabbato Sancto Servandae," Titulus II, Caput IV, #17, in *Ephemerides Liturgicae*, Vol. 65, 1951, Fasc. 1 — Supplementum, p. 6.

71. *Roman Missal*, "Easter Vigil," #20, #21.

72. *Circular Letter Concerning the Preparation and Celebration of the Easter Feasts*, Feb 20, 1988, #85, *L'Osservatore Romano*, Feb 29, 1988, p. 18.

73. Pius Parsch, *The Liturgy of the Mass*, 1950, p. 99.

74. Ibid., pp. 99-101.

75. Ibid., pp. 101-102.

76. Ibid., p. 102.

77. *Patrologia Latina*, Vol. 74, col. 1112b.

78. Deshusses, p. 85.

79. Parsch, p. 102.

80. See chapter V, pp. 102 of this volume.

81. *Regularis Concordia: The Monastic Agreement of the Monks and Nuns of the English Nation* (Medieval Classics), Dom Thomas Symons, tr., 1953, p. 48.

82. *Patrologia Latina*, Vol. 78, col. 1325a.

83. Lippe, Vol. I, p. 193.

84. Ibid., Vol. II, p. 96.

85. O. B. Hardison, *Christian Rite and Christian Drama in the Middle Ages*, 1965, p. 158; Latin text in Leclercq, col. 1567.

86. *Patrologia Latina*, Vol. 85, col. 470a, b.

87. Alquien, "Holy Week in Spain," *The Catholic World*, March 1894, p. 847.

88. Aloysius Carruth, OSB, "Holy Week and Easter at Maria Laach," *Orate Fratres*, March 1933, pp. 199, 201.

89. *Roman Missal*, "Easter Vigil," #31 (*The Vatican II Sunday Missal*, p. 441).

90. Decree of Jan 11, 1952, #22, in *American Ecclesiastical Review*, April 1952, p. 303.

91. *Capitulary* in Dom Germain Morin, "Le plus ancien *Comes* de l'Eglise Romaine," *Revue Benedictine*, Vol. 27, 1910, p. 55; *Ordo 30A* in Andrieu, *Les Ordines*, p. 457.

92. Bertoniere, p. 137.

93. W. G. Weakland, "Alleluia," *New Catholic Encyclopedia*, 1967, Vol. I, pp. 321-322.

94. Ibid., p. 322.

95. Weiser, pp. 157, 167 (footnote).

96. *General Instruction on the Roman Missal*, 26 March 1970, chapter II,#37, in *Vatican Council II: The Conciliar and Post Conciliar Documents*, Austin Flannery, OP, ed., 1975, p. 172.

97. *Capitulary* in Dom Germain Morin, "Liturgie et Basiliques de Rome au Milieu du VII Siecle: D'apres les Listes d'Evangiles de Wurzburg," *Revue Benedictine*, Vol. 28, 1911, p. 304; *Ordo 32* in Andrieu, *Les Ordines*, p. 523.

98. Bertoniere, pp. 66-67.

99. Homily at Easter Vigil, April 2, 1988, #1-#3, in *L'Osservatore Romano*, April 18, 1988, p. 6.

100. "Treatise on Baptism," #19, in *Baptism: Ancient Liturgies and Patristic Texts* (Alba Patristic Library, Vol. 2), Andre Hamman, OFM, ed., 1967, p. 47.

101. Hamman, *Baptism*, p. 76.

102. "Tenth Baptismal Instruction," #5-#6, #7, in *Saint John Chrysostom: Baptismal Instructions* (Ancient Christian Writers, #31), Paul W. Harkins, tr., 1963, p. 150.

103. J. D. Crichton, *The Liturgy of Holy Week*, 1983, p. 71.

104. The following synopsis of fourth-century practices is based upon Duchesne, pp. 312-315, 329-333, except where noted otherwise.

105. Ibid., p. 329.

106. Father Jean Danielou, SJ, *The Bible and the Liturgy* (University of Notre Dame Liturgical Studies, Vol. 3), 1956, pp. 49-53.

107. *Patrologia Latina*, Vol. 74, col. 1110a.

108. Tyrer, p. 160.

109. Hamman, *Baptism*, pp. 16-17.

110. Tyrer, p. 162.

111. *Apostolic Tradition*, in ibid.

112. Deshusses, pp. 185-188 (summarized by Tyrer, p. 163).

113. *Patrologia Latina*, Vol. 78, col. 956c (Tyrer, p. 163).

114. Ibid., Vol. 78, col. 999b.

115. Gassner, p. 531.

116. Schuster, Vol. II, p. 306; text of *Ordo 23* in Andrieu, *Les Ordines*, p. 273.

117. Description of current baptismal rite based upon Congregation for Divine Worship, *Christian Initiation of Adults*, Decree of Jan 6, 1972, #208-#231, and *Baptism for Children*, Decree of May 5, 1969, #5, #53-#66, both in *The Rites of the Catholic Church*, International Commission on English in the Liturgy, tr., 1976, pp. 94-104 and 189, 204-210, respectively.

118. Baptism by immersion of the head or even the entire body is also permitted, provided that "decency and decorum" are observed. See *Christian Initiation of Adults*, #220 (*The Rites*, p. 100).

119. Ibid., #224, p. 101.

120. "Catechumens from Eleven Countries," *L'Osservatore Romano*, April 18, 1988, p. 6.

121. "Fourth Baptismal Instruction," #1, in Harkins, p. 66.

122. Tyrer, p. 169.

123. Schuster, Vol. II, p. 308.

124. The rubrics of the incensation rite here described appear in the current edition of the *Caeremoniale Episcoporum* (1985), #96 and #149, pp. 34 and 47 respectively.

125. *Gelasian* text in *Patrologia Latina*, Vol. 74, col. 1113b; Paduan text in Deshusses, p. 631.

126. Thurston, p. 448.

127. Ibid., p. 453 (footnote).

128. Book IV, Part I, Title III, chapter 1, in *The Code of Canon Law: In English Translation*, Canon Law Society of Great Britian and Ireland, 1983, p. 168.

129. Father Connell Clinton, *The Paschal Precept: An Historical Synopsis and Commentary* (CUA Canon Law Studies, No. 73), 1932, p. 75.

130. Commentary for Canon 920 in *The Code of Canon Law: A Text and Commentary*, James Coriden, Thomas Green, and Donald Heintschel, eds., 1985, p. 655.

131. Saint Irenaeus, Bishop and Martyr, *Against Heresies*, Book 5, chapter 2, in *The Sunday Sermons of the Great Fathers*, Vol. III, p. 114.

132. *Christian Prayer: The Liturgy of the Hours*, Liturgical Press, 1976, Hymn #118.

133. *In Sanctum Pascha*, Oratio IV, *The Paschal Mystery*, p. 96.

134. The following discussion of the history of the Byzantine Easter Vigil

is based upon Father Gabriel Bertoniere's definitive volume on the subject (except where noted otherwise). For the relevant texts of the original documents see J. Wilkinson, ed., *Egeria's Travels*, 1971, pp. 270, 276 (*Armenian Lectionary*); T. Kluge and A. Baumstark, "Quadragesima und Karwoche Jerusalems im siebten Jahrhundert," *Oriens Christianus*, Vol. 5, n.s., 1915, pp. 230-233 (*Georgian Lectionary*); A. Papadopoulos-Kerameus, ed., *Analekta Hierosolymitikes Stachyologias*, 1894 (rpt. 1963), Vol. II, pp. 179-189 (*Typicon of the Anastasis*); J. Mateos, ed., *Le Typicon de la Grande Eglise: Tome II*, 1963, pp. 84-91 (*Typicon of the Great Church*).

135. Bertoniere, pp. 14-15.

136. Ibid., pp. 29-33, 59.

137. Ibid., pp. 25-26, 33-36, 59.

138. Ibid., pp. 40, 46.

139. Ibid., pp. 40-47.

140. Ibid., p. 41.

141. Ibid., pp. 37-40, 49, 55; Baumstark, pp. 146-147.

142. Bertoniere, pp. 40-41, 47-48.

143. Father Francis X. Weiser, SJ, *The Easter Book*, pp. 138-139.

144. Bertoniere, p. 59; for listing of readings in *Armenian Lectionary* see Table on p. 343 of the present volume.

145. Ibid., pp. 66-67.

146. Ibid., p. 61.

147. Ibid., Charts C-1, C-2, C-3.

148. Ibid., pp. 119, 121-124, 126, 132-134, 137-139, plus Charts C-1 thru C-6.

149. The following is based upon D. Pochin Mould, "Byzantine Holy Week," *Doctrine and Life*, March 1964, pp. 181-183, and Mary Sullivan, "A Byzantine Holy Week," *Sign*, April 1982, p. 16.

150. Sullivan, p. 16.

151. "On the Holy Pasch," #3-#4, *The Sunday Sermons of the Great Fathers*, Vol. II, p. 220.

XII

Easter Sunday

On the horizon of all of us, pilgrims with Christ through faith, through his saving death, the truth about him, the Living One, is revealed at dawn on the day of the resurrection.

[Pope John Paul II][1]

"I am the Alpha and the Omega," says the Lord God, who is and who was and who is to come, the Almighty.

[Rev 1:8]

Mass on Easter Morning[2]

This day seems brighter than others to me. The sun shines brighter on the world, the stars and all the elements rejoice. At the death of Christ they had ceased to shed their light and had gone into hiding. They could not look on their creator crucified. But now that this is his day of victory, after his resurrection from the dead, they perform their proper task attending upon him by their own brightness. . . .

[Saint Jerome][3]

Fear not, I am the first and the last, and the living one; I died, and behold I am alive for evermore, and I have the keys of Death and Hades.

[Rev 1:17-18]

WHILE IT CAN JUSTLY be said that the Mass of the Easter Vigil is *the* first and foremost liturgical celebration of the resurrection, none-theless the celebration of Mass on the morning of Easter Sunday still retains an exalted place in the paschal season. This latter liturgy had been introduced by the seventh century, appearing both in the *Gelasian Sacramentary* and in the Paduan edition of the *Gregorian Sacramentary*.[4] For many centuries the attention now focused upon the vigil liturgy was accorded to the Sunday morning Mass as a result of the gradual

"I am the Alpha and the Omega," says the Lord God, who is and who was and who is to come, the Almighty (Rev 1:8).

transfer of the vigil to the morning hours of Holy Saturday. This tendency of previous generations to focus upon the Easter Sunday morning Mass was not all that much out of step with the liturgy of the early Church, for our most primitive sources indicate that at the ancient Easter Vigils the length of the Scripture readings, together with the time needed to administer Baptism and Confirmation to numerous candidates, delayed the celebration of Mass until three o'clock in the morning or even later. Thus it could be said that the Easter Masses of the early Church were held in the morning, almost at daybreak. The revision of the liturgy of Holy Week during the 1950s rightfully restored the Easter Vigil to its original primal position in the commemoration of the Paschal Mystery, yet in doing this, the Church recommended that the Eucharistic portion of the Easter Vigil ought not to *begin* until about midnight.[5] The morning Mass has neither been suppressed nor stripped of its solemnity; in the piazza before Saint Peter's Basilica in Rome the Holy Father continues to celebrate this Mass each year with tens of thousands in attendance. Thus Easter morning has retained its sacred character, for it is on this morning that the empty tomb of our Lord was discovered.

In the current liturgy the first reading of the morning Mass is from the Acts of the Apostles (10:34, 37-43). The Church presents to us Saint Peter's proclamation of the gospel to the Gentiles of Caesarea gathered in the house of the centurion Cornelius:

> *"I take it you know what has been reported all over Judea about Jesus of Nazareth. . . . We are witnesses to all that he did in the land of the Jews and in Jerusalem. They killed him finally, 'hanging him on a tree,' only to have God raise him up on the third day and grant that he be seen, not by all, but only by such witnesses as had been chosen beforehand by God — by us who ate and drank with him after he rose from the dead. . . . To him all the prophets testify, saying that everyone who believes in him has forgiveness of sins through his name."*
>
> [Acts 10:37, 39-41, 43; NAB]

The responsorial psalm is the same as that preceding the gospel at the Easter Vigil (Ps 118:1-2, 16-17, 22-23). The antiphon, however, is different:

> *This is the day the Lord has made; let us rejoice and be glad.*

The second reading, from Saint Paul's Letter to the Colossians (3:1-4), reminds us that our true and lasting joy is not to be found in the things of earth but in those of Heaven, won for us by our crucified and Risen Savior:

> *Since you have been raised up in company with Christ, set your heart on what pertains to higher realms where Christ is seated at God's right hand. Be intent on things above rather than on things of earth. After all, you have died! Your life is hidden now with Christ in God. When Christ our life appears, then you shall appear with him in glory.*
>
> [Col 3:1-4; NAB]

The *Lectionary* also offers as an alternative to the above reading a passage from the first Letter of Saint Paul to the Corinthians (1 Cor 5:6-8). The earliest extant Roman lectionary — the *Capitulary of Wurzburg* (seventh to early eighth centuries) — specifies essentially this same lection (1 Cor 5:7-8),[6] which remained the only epistle for the

Easter Sunday liturgy up until 1970; thus for at least twelve hundred years these words have been part of the morning Mass:

> . . . *Christ our Passover has been sacrificed. Let us celebrate the feast not with the old yeast, that of corruption and wickedness, but with the unleavened bread of sincerity and truth.*

[1 Cor 5:7-8; NAB]

The Sequence

In the Easter Sunday liturgy there appears an example of a special liturgical composition known as the "sequence." The origin of sequences will be discussed later; suffice it to say at this point that the *Victimae paschali* ("To the Paschal Victim") — the sequence assigned to Easter Sunday and the seven other days of the Easter Octave — is 900 years old. It is recited or sung following the second reading, before the *Alleluia* of the gospel:

> *Christians, to the Paschal Victim*
> *Offer your thankful praises!*
> *A Lamb the sheep redeems: Christ,*
> *who only is sinless,*
> *Reconciles sinners to the Father.*
> *Death and life have contended in that combat stupendous:*
> *The Prince of life, who died, reigns immortal.*
> *Speak, Mary, declaring*
> *What you saw, wayfaring.*
> *"The tomb of Christ, who is living,*
> *The glory of Jesus' resurrection;*
> *Bright angels attesting,*
> *The shroud and napkin resting.*
> *Yes, Christ my hope is arisen:*
> *To Galilee he goes before you."*
> *Christ indeed from death is risen,*
> *our new life obtaining.*
> *Have mercy, victor King, ever reigning!*
> *Amen. Alleluia.*

The Gospel

Prior to the promulgation of the *Roman Missal* of Pope Paul VI in 1970, the account of the resurrection from the gospel of Saint Mark (Mk 16:1-7) was read at the Easter morning Mass; as with the reading from the first Letter to the Corinthians, this selection can likewise be traced all the way back to the *Capitulary of Wurzburg*.[7] Saint Mark's account is now part of the three-year cycle of gospel readings for the Easter Vigil; the gospel passage currently assigned to Easter morning is that of Saint Peter and Saint John's visit to the empty tomb (Jn 20:1-9). Here we will present verses from this passage together with Saint John's subsequent account of Christ appearing to Saint Mary Magdalene:[8]

It was very early on the first day of the week and still dark, when Mary of Magdala came to the tomb.

[Jn 20:1; JB]

I arose to open to my beloved, and my hands dripped with myrrh, my fingers with liquid myrrh. . . .

[Sg 5:5]

She saw that the stone had been moved away from the tomb. . . .

[Jn 20:1; JB]

I opened to my beloved, but my beloved had turned and gone. . . . I sought him, but found him not; I called him, but he gave no answer.

[Sg 5:6]

She . . . came running to Simon Peter and the other disciple, the one Jesus loved. "They have taken the Lord out of the tomb," she said, "and we don't know where they have put him."

[Jn 20:1-2; JB]

Whither has your beloved turned, that we may seek him with you?

[Sg 6:1]

So Peter set out with the other disciple to go to the tomb.

[Jn 20:3; JB]

Arise, shine; for your light has come, and the glory of the Lord has risen upon you.

[Is 60:1]

They ran together, but the other disciple . . . reached the tomb first; he bent down and saw the linen cloths lying on the ground, but did not go in. Simon Peter who was following now came up, went right into the tomb, saw the linen cloths on the ground, and also the cloth that had been over his head; this was not with the linen cloths but rolled up in a place by itself.

[Jn 20:4-7; JB]

And they will say, "This land that was desolate has become like the garden of Eden. . . ."

[Ez 36:35]

Then the other disciple who reached the tomb first also went in; he saw and he believed. Till this moment they had failed to understand the teaching of scripture, that he must rise from the dead. The disciples then went home again.

[Jn 20:8-10; JB]

Behold, I will open your graves, and raise you from your graves, O my people; and I will bring you home into the land of Israel. And you shall know that I am the Lord, when I open your graves, and raise you from your graves, O my people.

[Ez 37:12-13]

Meanwhile Mary stayed outside near the tomb, weeping. Then, still weeping, she stooped to look inside. . . .

[Jn 20:11; JB]

"Blessed are those who mourn, for they shall be comforted."

[Mt 5:4]

. . . she . . . saw two angels in white sitting where the body of Jesus had been, one at the head, the other at the feet. They said, "Woman, why are you weeping?" "They have taken my Lord away," she replied, "and I don't know where they have put him."

[Jn 20:11-13; JB]

". . . her sins, which are many, are forgiven, for she loved much. . . ."

[Lk 7:47]

As she said this she turned around and saw Jesus standing there, though she did not recognize him. Jesus said, "Woman, why are you weeping? Who are you looking for?"

[Jn 20:14-15; JB]

Have you seen him whom my soul loves?

[Sg 3:3]

Supposing him to be the gardener, she said, "Sir, if you have taken him away, tell me where you have put him, and I will go and remove him." Jesus said, "Mary!"

[Jn 20:15-16; JB]

The voice of my beloved!

[Sg 2:8]

She knew him then and said to him in Hebrew, "Rabbuni!" —which means Master.

[Jn 20:16; JB]

. . . I found him whom my soul loves. I held him, and would not let him go. . . .

[Sg 3:4]

Jesus said to her, "Do not cling to me, because I have not yet ascended to the Father. But go and find the brothers, and tell them: I am ascending to my Father and your Father, to my God and your God."

[Jn 20:17; JB]

She then went to those who had been his companions, and who were mourning and in tears, and told them.

[Mk 16:10; JB]

How beautiful upon the mountains are the feet of him who brings good tidings . . . who says to Zion, "Your God reigns."

[Is 52:7]

So Mary of Magdala went and told the disciples that she had seen the Lord and that he had said these things to her.

[Jn 20:18; JB]

But they did not believe her when they heard her say that he was alive and that she had seen him.

[Mk 16:11; JB]

. . . these words seemed to them an idle tale. . . .

[Lk 24:11]

Following the gospel and the homily, the Renewal of Baptismal Promises as found in the liturgy of the Easter Vigil (see chapter XI, pp. 366-367) takes the place of the Creed. Mass continues in the usual manner; however, if Eucharistic Prayer I is selected, the two insertions used with the Roman Canon at the Easter Vigil are again utilized in this morning's liturgy. As far back as the seventh century, the *Gelasian* and *Gregorian* (Paduan) Sacramentaries stipulated these insertions for both the vigil *and* the morning Mass.[9]

Easter Morning Mass in Saint Peter's Square

Perhaps nowhere is the liturgy of Easter morning celebrated with greater splendor than in Saint Peter's Square[10] in Rome; pilgrims from all over the world attend this Mass at which Pope John Paul II is the principal celebrant. According to an account from 1987, the liturgy begins at ten-thirty in the morning; bright spring sunlight fills the square, which has been adorned by Dutch florists with innumerable flowers and plants, including tulips, narcissus, hyacinths, anemoni, geraniums, violets, azalias, and rododendrums, as well as young conifer and birch trees. The Mass begins with the Latin hymn *Surrexit Dominus vere*, sung by the Vatican's Sistine Choir; two other choirs from Belgium and Germany are also present for this day's liturgy. One of the Scripture passages is read in German, another in English; the gospel is proclaimed in Italian, the language of Rome. Following the Holy Father's homily, the intercessions (that is, the "Prayer of the Faithful") are read in French, German, English, Spanish, Italian, and Polish. For the consecration the Holy Father uses the same chalice with which Pope Pius IX celebrated Mass on the morning that he solemnly proclaimed the Dogma of the Immaculate Conception in 1854.

At noon, following the Mass, Pope John Paul II enters the central balcony of Saint Peter's Basilica to deliver his annual Easter message and blessing to the world, known as the *Urbi et Orbi* ("To the City and to the World"). It is broadcast via television to forty-five different countries around the globe: fourteen in Europe, eight in Africa, eighteen in the Americas, four in Asia, and one in Oceania (the Pacific). The Holy Father concludes his message by giving his Easter greetings in fifty-one different languages, including Singalese (the tongue of Sri Lanka) and Cambodian. Following these greetings the pope imparts his solemn apostolic blessing upon all present and all watching him around the world.

> *Most fittingly does the world rejoice, with great gladness, upon this day; for with Christ returning from the dead the hope of resurrection has everywhere been awakened in the hearts of men. For it is but right that when the Lord of creation triumphs, the creatures He has made should also rejoice. This day the heavens rejoice, for now at length they see the earth, defiled by sin, made clean in the Blood of the Lord. The multitudes of the hosts of heaven rejoice, for their king has overthrown in battle the hosts of the prince of evil. The sun rejoices, and now with unceasing thankfulness holds back by its joyful beams that woeful darkness that overshadowed it as Christ was dying. And together with them we too above all others must rejoice, for whom the Only-Begotten Son of God, Who also is True God, clothed Himself in our flesh, that through that flesh He might come to the Cross, by the Cross suffer death, and through death despoil the kingdom of hell. Should we not rejoice: we whose sins the mystery of this new sacrament has taken away, to whom heaven is given, paradise restored?*
>
> [Saint Maximus, Bishop][11]

The *Elevatio*

In our description of Good Friday observances we examined a medieval ceremony known as the *Depositio*, in which a cross, crucifix, or other image of Christ in death and/or the Blessed Sacrament were symbolically entombed. In many places this Good Friday ceremony had its appropriate counterpart on Easter Sunday — the *Elevatio* (Elevation). Early in the morning the Blessed Sacrament or the crucifix (or some other image of Christ) would be ceremoniously brought forth from the sepulchre in commemoration of the resurrection. In some cases, when the object "buried" on Good Friday was an image of Christ Crucified, the image would be quietly replaced with another one more suited to the mystery of the resurrection before the *Elevatio* began.

During the fifteenth century just such an *Elevatio* was conducted at the Monastery of Prufening, Germany. On Good Friday the corpus of the crucifix used in the veneration ceremony was removed from the cross and put into the sepulchre together with a Sacred Particle of the holy Eucharist remaining from the Mass of the Presanctified. Both were wrapped in cloths representing the burial cloths of Christ; the sepulchre where they were placed was located at an altar and consisted of a "box surrounded by curtains," around which five lamps burned through the night. Prior to the *Elevatio* service on Easter morning, an image referred to in the original Latin text as the *Ymaginem Dominice Resurreccionis* was put into the sepulchre; most likely this was an image of Christ holding in His hand a cross with an attached banner, or some other emblem of the resurrection (just such a figure is mentioned in the rubrics of a sixteenth-century *Elevatio* from Halle, Germany[12]). In the *Elevatio* rite the abbot, accompanied by a chaplain, would first come before the curtain of the sepulchre and intone the recitation of Psalms 57 and 139. The two then entered within the curtain; standing before the altar the abbot sprinkled holy water over the "sarcophagus" containing the Blessed Sacrament and censed it, afterwards doing the same over the interred "image of the Crucified." Taking the vessel holding the holy Eucharist out of the sarcophagus, the abbot now began a procession from the sepulchre, while the chaplain took and carried the *Ymaginem Dominice Resurreccionis*, which was brought to and placed on a second altar; here the abbot gave Benediction, making the sign of the cross with the Sacrament. The Eucharist was then borne to a third altar, where Benediction was repeated before the Sacred Particle was placed in a tabernacle. Afterwards all the bells were rung. Only the *Ymaginem Crucifixi* was left in the sepulchre, to be quietly removed later.[13]

Another example (1965) of the *Elevatio* is provided by the special rite of Braga, Portugal;[14] Braga's medieval *Depositio* ceremony, in which the Blessed Sacrament is carried in a bier to a sepulchre on Good Friday, was described earlier.[15] On the morning of Easter Sunday, at the primatial church, the archbishop goes in procession to the sepulchre accompanied by deacons and two canons; ahead of them are carried the primatial cross, candles, and incense. At the north chapel, which has served as the sepulchre since Good Friday, the black pall on the bier holding the Blessed Sacrament has been replaced prior to this morning's service with a pall of cloth of gold; the statue of Our Lady of Sorrows has been removed as well. When the procession arrives, the holy Eucharist is removed from the bier and put into a monstrance as the ceremony of the *Elevatio* begins. The archbishop censes the Sacrament and then, taking the monstrance into his hands, carries our Lord in triumphant procession around the cathedral, underneath a cloth of gold canopy held by two canons. Two more canons carry a bare wooden cross covered with a veil of white gauze. Along the way the *Regina caeli* ("Queen of heaven, rejoice") is sung repeatedly. The procession heads to the Chapel of the Blessed Sacrament in the south transept, where Benediction is given before the Eucharist is put into the tabernacle. The archbishop and those accompanying him now proceed to the choir to make ready for Mass as the famous Easter hymn *O filii et filiae* ("Ye Sons and Daughters") is sung:

Alleluia, alleluia, alleluia.

Ye sons and daughters, let us sing!
The King of heav'n, the glorious King,
O'er death today rose triumphing. Alleluia!

That Easter morn, at break of day,
The faithful women went their way
To seek the tomb where Jesus lay. Alleluia!

An angel clad in white they see,
Who sat, and spoke unto the three,
"Your Lord doth go to Galilee." Alleluia!

On this most holy day of days,
To God your hearts and voices raise,
In laud and jubilee and praise. Alleluia!

[refrain and vs. 1-4][16]

The gradual advancement of the Easter Vigil into the morning hours of Holy Saturday during later centuries eventually led to a corresponding shift in the timing of the *Elevatio* rite in some places. Thus in Vienna, Austria (pre-1951), during the evening on Holy Saturday, the Blessed Sacrament would be carried in procession from the Easter sepulchre to an outdoor square as bells were rung and a band played. At the square a battalion of four thousand soldiers in full parade uniform with white gloves await the arrival of the Blessed Sacrament, which is heralded by the sounding of a trumpet. The troops now "present arms," all dropping down on one knee in unison and saluting. The Eucharist is then borne back into the church, where Benediction is given and the *Regina Caeli* sung. Finally, upon the sounding of a bugle at the square, the soldiers salute one final time before heading back to their army post, accompanied by the band.[17]

The reader may recall the description provided earlier of the Easter sepulchre at a parish in Luxemburg (turn of the century).[18] An *Elevatio* ceremony was likewise observed on Easter Sunday in this same parish. At four o'clock on Easter morning, after the first bell tolled, the parish priests, robed in fine vestments and accompanied by acolytes, would proceed to the sepulchre (the side altar veiled behind a large purple curtain to which the crucifix had been brought on Good Friday). After saying a part of the Divine Office, the priests withdraw the purple curtain and take up the crucifix from the altar. The people now join the priests in a procession that wends its way out of the church and around it three times; along the route the first decade of the "Glorious Mysteries" of the Rosary is recited repeatedly. Each time the procession reaches the main door of the church, the priests engage in a symbolic act that we have already seen used in Palm Sunday processions; knocking upon the closed door with the crossbeam of the crucifix, they sing the words from Psalm 24:

> *Lift up your heads, O gates!*
> *and be lifted up, O ancient doors!*
> *that the King of glory may come in.*
>
> [Ps 24:7]

A choir within the church responds, "Who is the King of glory?" (Ps 24:8). The procession then continues on without "answering" the choir, but when the priests perform this ceremony a third and final time, they respond to the choir with the words, "The Lord of hosts, he is the King of glory!" (Ps 24:10). Suddenly the doors are thrown open, and in imitation of the Easter morning earthquake mentioned by Saint Matthew (Mt 28:2) a roar shakes the church as the organ breaks out in a thunder of sound. Pausing in the back of the church, the priests begin the *Te Deum*:

O God, we praise you,
and acknowledge you
to be the supreme Lord.
Everlasting Father,
all the earth worships you. . . .[19]

The choir joins in the singing of this ancient hymn of thanksgiving, while the clergy heads for the main altar. A deacon then places the crucifix on the gospel side of the sanctuary; following the *Te Deum* the priests withdraw to the sacristy to prepare for Easter Mass.[20]

Easter in the Maronite and Syro-Malabar Rites

In Lebanon (1928) the beautiful observances of Good Friday in the Maronite Rite (described earlier) have a fitting sequel in the Easter Mass which begins at midnight on Easter Sunday. Following the Introit and a series of lessons, prayers, and hymns, the celebrant, accompanied by acolytes and attendants with lighted candles, proceeds to the sepulchre where the corpus of the Crucified had been lain to rest on Good Friday. He censes the tomb and, alternating with the choir, chants three times:

O Christ, who has risen from amongst the dead, have mercy on us!

Assuming the part of the angel (mentioned in Saint Matthew's gospel account) who rolled back the stone from the sepulchre, a deacon withdraws the curtain from the door of the tomb. Prior to this service the corpus within has already been reattached to a cross; the celebrant now lifts the crucifix from the "coffin of flowers," after which a white veil is put over the top of it. He carries the crucifix in procession through the church as another priest continually censes it and the choir sings the "Hymn of the Resurrection." Following this, the celebrant confers four blessings with the crucifix, one for each point of the compass (north, south, east, and west). Afterwards he puts the cross cloaked in its white veil on the altar, and continues with the celebration of Mass. At the end of the Eucharistic liturgy he takes the crucifix into his hands once more so that the faithful can come forward to kiss it. A second priest gives each of the people a few of the flowers that had been placed in the sepulchre during the "burial" on Good Friday. The veiled crucifix will be left on the altar for the rest of Easter Sunday.[21]

> *. . . your robes are all fragrant with myrrh and aloes. . . .*
>
> [Ps 45:8]

In India there is a tradition that our Lord rose from the dead at three o'clock in the morning, and thus the Easter liturgy in the Indian churches of the Syro-Malabar Rite begins at this hour on Easter Sunday. In the Great Church of Saint Thomas in North Parur (1947), located along the southwest coast of India, the people fill the large edifice to overflowing. As the church falls silent, the parish priest and his assistant enter and proceed to the front step of the sanctuary, which is veiled by a double curtain. The two priests intone the *Alleluia* in a native Indian chant that is then taken up by a choir and a band of drums, flutes, wood-winds, and stringed instruments in the back of the church. After the *Alleluia* has been chanted three times, the curtain before the altar is withdrawn to reveal a sepulchre with walls of black cloth set up in the middle of the sanctuary. With the lights out, a spotlight is directed upon the tomb, from which a statue of Christ triumphant over death is made to slowly rise. The statue is then placed beside the sepulchre; the band starts up once more as fireworks are set off outside. A procession forms and moves out into the streets, in which the parish priest carries the image of the Risen Savior; the band and hundreds of the faithful participate, bringing paraffin lamps and every church statue and banner they can lay their hands on. Finally, after much celebration they return to the church for Easter Mass.[22]

The Visit to the Empty Sepulchre

Closely related to the *Depositio* and *Elevatio* rites of the Middle Ages is another extraliturgical ceremony, the *Visitatio Sepulchri* (Visitation of the Sepulchre),[23] in which the discovery of the empty tomb on the first Easter morning is symbolically reenacted. This custom appears to have stemmed from the introduction into the liturgy of the "trope" — what Karl Young defines as a "verbal amplification of a passage in the authorized liturgy,"[24] that is, a formula added to, and elaborating upon, the official text of the Mass. We see an example of this in the optional formulas used in conjunction with the *Kyrie eleison* ("Lord, have mercy") in the current *Roman Missal*. In the late ninth or early tenth centuries, a trope appeared for the Introit (the Entrance Rite) of the Easter Sunday Mass that has come to be known as the *Quem quaeritis* ("Whom do you seek"); this trope in its original form consisted of three lines of dialogue between the women who came to our Lord's tomb and the angels stationed at the empty sepulchre:

Whom do you seek in the Tomb, Christians?

Jesus of Nazareth who was crucified, O inhabitants of Heaven.

He is not here, He has risen just as He had foretold; go, announce that He has risen from the Tomb.[25]

This trope is thought to have originated at the Monastery of Saint Gall in Switzerland; the author was probably an Irish monk of Saint Gall's named Tutilo, for the above text of the *Quem quaeritis* was found in a tenth-century manuscript together with two other tropes known to have been written by him.[26]

The *Quem quaeritis* provided the nucleus for the subsequent development of the *Visitatio Sepulchri* when this trope was moved from the Mass to the end of Matins (the first "Hour" of the Divine Office) on Easter morning, immediately preceding the singing of the *Te Deum*.[27] It is in the tenth-century that we find the earliest surviving examples of the *Visitatio Sepulchri*, but like the Good Friday *Depositio* ceremony, there are hints that the custom may go back even earlier.[28] In the Byzantine East an extraliturgical dramatization of the holy women's visit to the tomb already existed at Jerusalem by the tenth century; it is described in the *Typicon of the Anastasis*.[29] The women to play this role, known as the *myrophoroi*, first come to the holy sepulchre with the patriarch and clergy at eight o'clock on the morning of Holy Saturday. Entering the tomb, they clean and prepare the lamps inside it. Hours later, after the liturgy of the Easter Vigil, they return to the holy sepulchre with ointment and incense in symbolic imitation of the women who came to anoint our Lord's Body. Afterwards, the patriarch enters the tomb, then reemerges, at which point the women fall down at his feet, thus recreating the scene described in Matthew 28:9:

And behold, Jesus met them and said, "Hail!" And they came up and took hold of his feet and worshiped him.

In the West, one of the oldest descriptions of the *Visitatio Sepulchri* is to be found in England's tenth-century *Regularis Concordia* of Saint Ethelwold, the same work cited previously as containing the earliest complete text of the Good Friday *Depositio* ceremony. The sepulchre, "hung about with a curtain," is located on an otherwise empty section of the altar. On the morning of Easter Sunday, as Matins draws to an end, a cleric in an alb "stealthily" makes his way to the sepulchre, where he seats himself with a palm in his hand, assuming the role of the angel mentioned in Saint Matthew's gospel account of the resurrection. Clothed in copes and carrying *thuribles*, three other clerics, assuming the parts of the holy women, approach the sepulchre slowly, "as though searching for something." Engaging them in the *Quem quaeritus* dialogue ("Whom do you seek?," and so on) the "angel" tells them of the resurrection, upon which the "Marys" turn to the chorus and proclaim the news of Christ's triumph. The angel addresses the three a second time, drawing open the curtain of the sepulchre and pointing out the empty "shroud" in which the cross buried there on Good Friday had been wrapped, the cross having been removed before the *Visitatio*. The "Marys" now put down the *thuribles* they were carrying and take into their hands the symbolic linen shroud, holding it up for the other clerics present as once more they announce the resurrection. The service ends with the prior intoning the *Te Deum* as all the bells toll in jubilant celebration.[30]

The subsequent evolution of the *Visitatio Sepulchri* was influenced by another kind of trope — the "sequence" — which arose in association with the singing of the final *a* of the *Alleluia* in the first part of the Mass. Unlike other tropes, sequences were sufficiently developed to stand on their own when removed from their original liturgical setting.[31] Just such a sequence appeared in the eleventh century, known as the *Victimae paschali*. Thought to have been composed by a priest named Wipo, the *Victimae paschali* provided added dramatic material for the dialogue and action of the *Visitatio* in many places.[32] As seen earlier, this sequence is still recited prior to the gospel during the morning Mass on Easter Sunday, as well as on each of the succeeding days of the Easter Octave.

Like the *Depositio* and *Elevatio* ceremonies the *Visitatio Sepulchri* spread throughout northern and central Europe during the Middle Ages, growing more elaborate with the passage of time. One significant development was the addition of the visit of the Apostles Peter and John to the tomb. A good example of this can be found in a fourteenth-century *Visitatio* from the collegiate church of the canons and cannonesses of Essen, Germany. At Essen the sepulchre was in the form of a chest or shrine enclosed within a tent that had been set up before a side altar on a "raised passage," that is, a gallery, at the western end of the church. Two canons played the part of the two angels at the tomb mentioned in Saint Luke's and Saint John's gospel accounts. In most versions of the *Visitatio* clerics assumed the role of the "Marys," but at Essen women were employed: three canonesses would make their way to the sepulchre by traveling along the gallery lining the south side of the church. Following the usual conversation between the Marys and the angels, during which the women peer into the tent asking, "Where is Jesus?," and afterwards proclaim His resurrection, two more canons, one older (in the role of Peter) and the other younger (as John), approach the sepulchre by rushing along the gallery lining the north side of the church. The younger canon arrives first but waits for the older cleric to go into the tent before he himself enters. The angels lift up and display the burial cloth, after which one of the two Apostles makes his way to the organ loft and three times chants, "Christ the Lord has risen." The congregation responds, "Thanks be to God."[33]

At the Church of Saint John the Evangelist in Dublin, Ireland (fourteenth century), the text of the *Visitatio Sepulchri* specified distinctive costumes for the two Apostles who came to the tomb. Both were barefooted; Saint John wore a white tunic and carried a palm, while Saint Peter was clothed in a red tunic and carried keys, symbolizing the authority our Lord invested him with.[34]

In two versions of the *Visitatio Sepulchri* from Prague, Czechoslovakia (thirteenth and fourteenth centuries respectively), the "play" begins with a scene depicting the Marys purchasing ointments from an *unguentarius*, a seller of spices; this episode is based upon the first verse of chapter 16 of the gospel of Saint Mark:

> And when the sabbath was past, Mary Magdalene, and Mary the mother of James, and Salome, bought spices, so that they might go and anoint him.

This scene was probably acted out at a side altar away from the place of the sepulchre itself; indeed, the text of a *Visitatio* from Toul, France (thirteenth century) specifies that the Marys first went to a side altar to receive their vessels before proceeding to the sepulchre.[35]

Still another important addition to the action of the *Visitatio Sepulchri* was the inclusion of a scene depicting Mary Magdalene's meeting with the Risen Christ near the tomb. An example of this can be found in the fourteenth-century *Visitatio* of the nuns' Abbey of Barking, England. With motherly care the abbess herself dresses the three nuns chosen to play the women who discover the empty tomb. Upon entering the choir section of the church, the women sing a lament of several verses; meanwhile a cleric wearing a white stole and assuming the role of an angel awaits them at the sepulchre, seated on top of a stone beside the door of the tomb. The women engage in the usual dialogue with this first angel and then enter the sepulchre, where Mary Magdalene picks up the burial cloth. There another cleric playing the second angel speaks with the Magdalene, but to no avail; she laments the loss of her Lord. Then, on the left side of the altar Christ appears (probably played by a priest — the text does not say); He asks the distraught Magdalene, "Woman, why weepest thou? Whom seekest thou?," to which she responds, "Sir, if thou hast taken him hence, tell me where. . . ." He answers, "Mary!" Recognizing Him, she prostrates herself at His feet and says, "Rabboni!" After Christ withdraws, Mary Magdalene goes to the two other women and describes what has just happened. As she is doing this, Christ appears once again, this time at the right side of the altar. All three women prostrate themselves before Him, grasping and kissing His feet. Following this scene the women engage in a dialogue with the clergy, who represent the disciples. Mary Magdalene offers the "burial cloth" to them that they might kiss it. The *Visitatio* concludes with the Magdalene and the choir singing the antiphon *Christus Resurgens*.[36]

Although still a thriving custom at the beginning of the sixteenth century, the Visitatio had largely disappeared by the year 1600. In a few places though, it managed to survive into the first half of the eighteenth century; such was the case in Cologne (Germany), in Angers (France), and at Saint Mark's Cathedral in Venice.[37] Nonetheless, the legacy of the *Visitatio* is still with us; it is widely believed by scholars that the *Visitatio* exercised a decisive role in the subsequent development of Western Drama, serving as yet another example of the lasting heritage of medieval Christian culture.

The Risen Christ Greets His Mother

Come then, my love,
my lovely one come.
For see, winter is past,

the rains are over and gone.
The flowers appear on the earth.
The season of glad songs has come,
the cooing of the turtledove is heard
in our land.
The fig tree is forming its first figs
and the blossoming vines give out their fragrance.
Come then, my love,
my lovely one, come.

[Sg 2:10-13; JB]

In our discussion of Good Friday we saw that the sorrows of the Blessed Virgin Mary figure prominently in the devotions of the faithful. It is only natural, therefore, that on Easter Sunday the joy of the Blessed Mother at the resurrection of her Son should likewise be commemorated. Beginning on Easter Sunday and throughout the Easter Season the Church herself asks her children to replace the *Angelus* (a Marian prayer said three times each day during the rest of the year) with the jubilant *Regina caeli*:

Queen of heaven, rejoice. Alleluia.
For He, whom thou wast made worthy to bear. Alleluia.
Hath risen, as He said. Alleluia.
Pray for us to our God. Alleluia.
Rejoice and be glad, O Virgin Mary. Alleluia.
For the Lord hath risen indeed. Alleluia.[38]

In many countries the faithful have found beautiful childlike ways to express their joy at the reunion of Mary with her Divine Son. Usually the "Meeting" is reenacted with statues. In the town of Submona, located in the Abruzzi region of central Italy (1915), an outdoor altar would be erected for Easter morning under one of the arches of an aqueduct that ran by the market place. On this altar a statue of the risen Christ was set; statues of the local patron saints were then borne out of the different churches of Submona and carried around the outdoor altar. Subsequently all these saints were hurriedly taken to the "Church of the Tomba," where there was a statue of the Blessed Mother. Having come to "tell" the Virgin Mary that her Son has risen from the dead, the "saints" would then "bring" her to meet Him.[39]

In Puerto Rico (1960), where the "Meeting" is known as the

Encuentro, the Blessed Sacrament, rather than a statue, is borne out of the church, accompanied by the men of the parish. They proceed around the block; meanwhile, the women set out in the opposite direction, accompanying a statue of the Blessed Virgin Mary robed in a black mantle. When they meet, Mary "bows" three times before her Divine Son in the Holy Eucharist; the black mantle falls from her shoulders, unveiling garments of blue and white. Our Lord and His Mother now joyfully return together to the church.[40]

> *Listen, daughter, pay careful attention:*
> *forget your nation and your ancestral home,*
> *then the king will fall in love with your beauty.*
> *He is your master now, bow down to him.*
>
> [Ps 45:10-11; JB]

In the Philippines (1972), the "Meeting" is reenacted late at night. Two processions leave the local parish church at around half past three on Easter morning. One features an image of the Risen Christ carried on a float decorated with lights and flowers. The people in this procession are jubilant, as a band with them plays joyful music. But those in the other walk slowly, as if in mourning, as they accompany an image of the Blessed Virgin Mary veiled in a heavy black cloth.

> *. . . you are sad now, but I shall see you again, and your hearts will*
> *be full of joy, and that joy no one will take from you.*
>
> [Jn 16:22; JB]

The two processions follow different routes through the town and are joined by additional people as they move towards their common destination, the *Pasalubong* (Meeting Place). Here is erected a large four-way arch illuminated with lights and decked with flowers and hangings. At the top of the structure is a sizable flower-shaped ornament that faces downwards. When the Marian procession arrives, the Blessed Mother comes to a stop directly underneath this "flower." Then her Risen Son appears with the first procession and is brought face to face with her. Controlled by an operator hidden at the top of the archway, the artificial flower opens, from which an image of a dove emerges; it descends and with its feet lifts the black veil from Mary. Reunited, the Risen Christ and His Mother are carried back to the church amidst universal rejoicing.[41]

And Mary said:
"My soul proclaims the greatness of the Lord
and my spirit exults in God my saviour;
because he has looked upon his lowly handmaid.
. . . the Almighty has done great things for me."

[Lk 1:46-49; JB]

The Road to Emmaus and the Cenacle: Points for Meditation

The reader may wish to spend some time on the afternoon of Easter Sunday in reflection upon our Lord's appearance to the two disciples on the road to Emmaus (Lk 24:13-35); in fact, the current *Lectionary* specifies that this particular passage may be used as the gospel reading at any afternoon Masses on this day.[42] Likewise the gospel accounts of our Lord's appearance to the eleven Apostles on the evening of the first Easter Sunday (Lk 24:36-47; Jn 20:19-23; Mk 15:14) provide a most suitable source of meditation with which to conclude our celebration of Holy Week and the Easter Triduum.

Then he said to them, "These are my words which I spoke to you, while I was still with you, that everything written about me in the law of Moses and the prophets and the psalms must be fulfilled." Then he opened their minds to understand the scriptures, and said to them, "Thus it is written, that the Christ should suffer and on the third day rise from the dead. . . ."

[Lk 24:44-46]

A Final Thought for Easter Sunday

Then I saw a new heaven and a new earth. . . . I saw the holy city, and the new Jerusalem, coming down from God out of heaven, as beautiful as a bride all dressed for her husband. Then I heard a loud voice call from the throne, "You see this city? Here God lives among men. He will make his home among them. . . . He will wipe away all tears from their eyes; there will be no more death, and no more mourning or sadness."

[Rev 21:1-4; JB]

Endnotes

1. Homily, Easter Vigil, March 25, 1989, #6, *L'Osservatore Romano*, April 3, 1989, p. 8.

2. Liturgical texts from *Lectionary for Mass, Catholic Book Publishing Co.,* 1970, pp. 103-104, except where noted otherwise. PLEASE NOTE: "The faithful who go to Communion at the Mass of the Easter Vigil . . . may also receive Communion again in the second Mass of Easter. . ." (Congregation of Sacred Rites, Instruction of Sep 26, 1964, #60, cited in "Summary of Holy Week Changes," Bishops' Committee on the Liturgy Newsletter, Vol. 4, March 1968, p. 124).

3. "The Gates of Heaven," #1, in *The Paschal Mystery: Ancient Liturgies and Patristic Texts* (Alba Patristic Library, Vol. 3), Andre Hamman, OFM, ed., 1969, p. 142.

4. *Gelasian Sacramentary* in *Patrologia Latina*, Vol. 74, col. 1113c-1114b; Paduan text in *Le Sacramentaire Gregorien: Ses principales formes d'apres les plus anciens manuscripts: I* (Spicilegium Friburgense, Vol. 16), ed. Jean Deshusses, 2nd ed., 1979, p. 632.

5. *Maxima redemptionis*, Nov 16, 1955, #9, in *American Ecclesiastical Review*, Jan 1956, pp. 54-55.

6. Dom Germain Morin, "Le plus ancien *Comes* de l'Eglise Romaine," *Revue Benedictine*, Vol. 27, 1910, p. 55.

7. Dom Germain Morin, "Liturgie et basiliques de Rome au milieu du VII Siecle: D'apres les Listes d'Evangiles de Wurzburg," *Revue Benedictine*, Vol. 28, 1911, p. 304.

8. The Scripture passages that follow are from the *Jerusalem Bible: Reader's Edition* (passages marked with the letters "JB") and *Revised Standard Version of the Bible*, Catholic Edition (those not marked).

9. *Gelasian* text in *Patrologia Latina*, Vol. 74, col. 1113b, 1114a; Paduan text in Deshusses, pp. 631, 632.

10. Based upon *L'Attivita Della Santa Sede, Nel 1987*, Libreria Editrice Vaticana, pp. 314-316.

11. Sermon 39, in *The Sunday Sermons of the Great Fathers*, M. F. Toal, ed., 1958, Vol. II, pp. 239-240.

12. Neil C. Brooks, *The Sepulchre of Christ in Art and Liturgy*, 1921, p. 102.

13. Karl Young, *The Drama of the Medieval Church*, 1933, Vol. I, pp. 157-161.

14. Archdale King, *Eucharistic Reservation in the Western Church*, 1965, pp. 226-227.
15. For Braga's *Depositio* see chapter IX, p. 282.
16. *Christian Prayer: The Liturgy of the Hours*, Liturgical Press, 1976, Hymn #119.
17. Father James Monks, SJ, *Great Catholic Festivals*, 1951, p. 58.
18. See chapter X, p. 314.
19. Text of *Te Deum* in *Enchiridion of Indulgences: Norms and Grants*, William T. Barry, CSSR, tr., 1969, p. 72.
20. "Communications: Some Peculiar Liturgical Customs," *Orate Fratres*, March 19, 1932, pp. 236-237.
21. Reverend Peter Sfeir, "Holy Week Customs in Syria," *The Catholic Mind*, April 22, 1928, pp. 152-153.
22. Dominic de Turville, "A Short Survey of the Christians of South India and Their Rites, with an Account of the Easter Celebration at North Parur, Northern Travancore," *Eastern Churches Quarterly*, Vol. VII, Oct-Dec 1947, pp. 219-220.
23. Karl Young provides an in-depth analysis of the "*Visitatio Sepulchri*" in chapters 7-13 of his *Drama of the Medieval Church*, Vol. I, pp. 201-410. The following is based largely upon Young's findings.
24. Ibid., Vol. I, p. 178.
25. Ibid., Vol. I, pp. 201, 204-205; text of *Quem quaeritis* is author's own translation of Latin text on p. 201 of Young.
26. Ibid., Vol. I, pp. 204-205.
27. Ibid., Vol. I, pp. 231-232.
28. O. B. Hardison, *Christian Rite and Christian Drama in the Middle Ages*, 1965, pp. 309, 181. Hardison questions Young's conclusions regarding the origins of the "*Quem quaeritis*" and "*Visitatio Sepulchri*" (pp. 178-219).
29. Gabriel Bertoniere, *The Historical Development of the Easter Vigil and Related Services in the Greek Church* (Orientalia Christiana Analecta 193), 1972, pp. 50-51.
30. *Regularis Concordia: The Monastic Agreement of the Monks and Nuns of the English Nation* (Medieval Classics), Dom Thomas Symons, tr., 1953, pp. 49-50.
31. Young, Vol. I, pp. 182-183, 188.
32. Ibid., Vol. I, pp. 273-274.
33. Ibid., Vol. I, pp. 333-335.
34. Ibid., Vol. I, pp. 347-350.
35. Ibid., Vol. I, pp. 265-266, 402-407.

36. Ibid., Vol. I, pp. 381-385; original text also in *The Ordinal and Customary of the Benedictine Nuns of Barking Abbey* (Henry Bradshaw Society, Vol. 65), J. B. J. Tolhurst, ed., 1927, Vol. I, pp. 108-109.

37. Brooks, p. 49.

38. Text in *Key of Heaven: A Complete Manual of Prayers and Catholic Devotions*, Reverend J. M. Lelen, 1961, pp. 40-41.

39. Ethel Urlin, *Festivals, Holy Days & Saints' Days*, 1915 (rpt. 1971), p. 76.

40. Cynthia Hettinger, "Faith of the Puerto Rican," *America*, April 16, 1960, p. 67.

41. Sister Maria del Rey, "Pageant of the Cross," *Sign*, March 1972, pp. 14-15.

42. *Lectionary for Mass*, p. 104, #43.

Epilogue

If we have died with him,
then we shall live with him.
If we hold firm,
then we shall reign with him.

[2 Tm 2:11-12: JB]

WE HAVE NOW COME to the end of our journey through the mysteries of Holy Week. Yet Easter Sunday is really not an end — it is but the beginning of a whole season of paschal joy — fifty days of rejoicing in our new life in Christ. This joy the Church carries in her heart throughout the year, commemorating the resurrection every Sunday — indeed, she celebrates it each day in the Holy Eucharist. But neither does she ever forget the cross. How could she? The mystery of Good Friday is forever inscribed upon the hands, feet, and side of her Risen Spouse. And in the Eucharist she daily participates in her Savior's sacrifice on Calvary. Thus the weeks pass — with Advent and Christmas the Church will begin the liturgical year anew, remembering the first coming of the Messiah while anxiously anticipating His Second Coming. After a short interval of Ordinary Time, Ash Wednesday will return again, when on the foreheads of the faithful will be placed the ashes of last year's Palm Sunday branches. And soon enough we will find ourselves on the threshold of Holy Week once more.

We call the week great, not because it has a greater number of hours — other weeks having many more hours, after all — nor because it has more days, there being the same number of days in this and the other weeks, of course. So why do we call this week great? Because in it many ineffable good things come our way: in it protracted war is concluded, death is eliminated, curses are lifted, the devil's tyranny is relaxed, his pomps are despoiled, the reconciliation of God and man is achieved, heaven is made accessible, human beings are brought to resemble angels, those things which were at odds are united, the wall is laid low, the bar removed, the God of peace having brought peace to things on high and things on earth. This, then, is the reason we call the week great, because in it the Lord lavished on us such a plethora of gifts. This is the reason many people intensify their fasting as well as their sacred watching and vigils, and practice almsgiving, thus showing by their behavior the regard they have for the week. After all, since the Lord in this week has regaled us with such great goods, how are we too not obliged to demonstrate our reverence and regard as far as we can?

[Saint John Chrysostom][1]

Endnotes

1. Homily 30, #2, in *Saint John Chrysostom: Homilies on Genesis 18-45* (The Fathers of the Church, Vol. 82), Robert C. Hill, tr., 1990, p. 221.

Bibliography

Alquien. "Holy Week in Spain." *The Catholic World*, 58 (March 1894), pp. 840-854.

Alston, G. Cyprian. "Way of the Cross." *Catholic Encyclopedia*. 1907 ed. Vol. 15, pp. 569-571.

Amor, J. V. "Holy Week in Tasco, Mexico." *The Month*, 53 (April 1885), pp. 512-517.

"Ancient Good Friday Rite to be Revived." *Catholic New York*, March 16, 1989, p. 55.

Andrieu, Michel. *Les Ordines Romani du Haut Moyen Age: III: Les Textes (Ordines XIV-XXXIV)*. Etudes et Documents, Vol. 24. Louvain: Spicilegium Sacrum Lovaniense, 1961.

_____. *Le Pontifical Romain au Moyen-Age: Tome I:Le Pontifical Romain du XII siecle*. Studi e Testi, Vol. 86. Vatican City: Biblioteca Apostolica Vaticana, 1938.

Andujar, Claudia. "Holy Week in Seville." *Jubilee*, 7 (April 1960), pp. 8-15.

Anson, Peter F. *Churches: Their Plan and Furnishing*. Milwaukee: Bruce Publishing Co., 1948.

"Answers to Questions: Holy Thursday Repository or Sepulchre." *American Ecclesiastical Review*, 114 (April 1946), pp. 299-300.

"Answers to Questions: The Repository on Holy Thursday." *American Ecclesiastical Review*, 120 (June 1949), pp. 509-510.

Arranz, M., SJ. "Les Sacrements de l'ancien Euchologe Constantinopolitain." *Orientalia Christiana Periodica*, 48 (1982), pp. 284-335.

Baedeker, Karl. *Baedeker's Southern Italy and Sicily*. Leipzig, Germany: Karl Baedeker, 1930.

Baier, David, OFM. "The Liturgy of the Paschal Candle," *Homiletic and Pastoral Review*, 33 (April 1933), pp. 702-709.

Barry, William T., CSSR, tr. *Enchiridion of Indulgences: Norms and Grants*. New York: Catholic Book Publishing Co., 1969.

Batiffol, Pierre. *History of the Roman Breviary*. London: Longmans, Green & Co., 1912.

Baumstark, Anton. "Das Leydener griechisch-arabische Perikopenbuch fur die Kar-und Osterwoche." *Oriens Christianus*, new series, 4 (1914-1915), pp. 39-58.

_____. "La Solemnite des Palmes dans l'ancienne et la nouvelle Rome." *Irenikon*, 13 (Jan-Feb 1936), pp. 3-24.

_____. *Comparative Liturgy*. Revised by Bernard Botte, OSB; English edition by F. L. Cross. Westminster, Maryland: Newman Press, 1958.

Beckwith, John. *Early Christian and Byzantine Art*. Baltimore, Maryland: Penguin Books, 1970.

Beevers, John, tr. *The Autobiography of Saint Thérèse of Lisieux: The Story of a Soul*. Garden City, New York: Image Books, Doubleday, Co., Inc., 1957.

Benziger Brothers, ed. *The English-Latin Sacramentary*. New York: Benziger Brothers, 1966.

Bernier, Olivier. "A Glittering Hungarian Treasury." *New York Times*, March 21, 1993, Travel Section, pp. 16, 29.

Bertoniere, Gabriel. *The Historical Development of the Easter Vigil and Related Services in the Greek Church*. Orientalia Christiana Analecta, No. 193. Rome: Pont. Institutum Studiorum Orientalum, 1972.

Beyenka, Sister Mary Melchior, OP, tr. *Saint Ambrose: Letters*. Fathers of the Church, Vol. 26. New York: Fathers of the Church, Inc., 1954.

Bishop, Edmund. *Liturgica Historica: Papers on the Liturgy and Religious Life of the Western Church*. London: Oxford University Press, 1918.

Bonnet, Gerard. "Le Mysterie de la Croix dans le Careme Orthodoxe" (Part One), *Irenikon*, 52 (1979), pp. 34-53.

Bougaud, Right Reverend E. *Life of Saint Margaret Mary Alacoque*. New York: Benziger Brothers, 1920.

Breen, Dr. A. *A Diary of my Life in the Holy Land*. Rochester, New York: John P. Smith Printing Co., 1906.

Brevarium Romanum: Pars Verna. Mechelen, Belgium: H. Dessain, 1861.

Bridges, Robert. *Yattendon Hymnal*. New York: Oxford University Press, 1899.

Brooks, Neil C. *The Sepulchre of Christ in Art and Liturgy*. University of Illinois Studies in Language and Literature, Vol. 7, No. 2. Urbana, Illinois: University of Illinois, 1921.

_____. "The *Sepulchrum Christi* and its Ceremonies in Late Mediaeval and Modern Times." *Journal of English and Germanic Philology*, 27 (1928), pp. 147-161.

Broun, Heywood. "Good Friday in Venezuela." *Catholic Digest*, 5 (April 1941), pp. 99-100.

Buettner, Bonnie. "The Good Friday Scene in Chretien de Troyes' 'Perceval' ." *Traditio*, 36 (1980), pp. 415-426.

Bussy, Father Oswald. "The Easter Sepulchre." *The Clergy Review*, 11 (April 1936), pp. 287-295.

_____. "The Great Paschal." *The Clergy Review*, 22 (May 1942), pp. 203-210.

Cabrol, Right Reverend Abbot, OSB. *The Books of the Latin Liturgy*. Benedictines of Stanbrook, tr. Catholic Library of Religious Knowledge, Vol. 22. London: Sands & Co.; St. Louis, Missouri: B. Herder Book Co., 1932.

Camm, Dom Bede, OSB. "A Good Friday in Rome." *Ave Maria*, 68 (April 3, 1909), pp. 417-424.

Canon Law Society of Great Britain and Ireland, ed. *The Code of Canon Law: In English Translation*. London: Collins Liturgical Publications; Grand Rapids, Michigan: William B. Eerdmans Publishing Co., 1983.

Carruth, Aloysius, OSB. "Holy Week and Easter at Maria Laach." *Orate Fratres*, 7 (March 1933), pp. 199-203.

Cavanaugh, William Thomas, CP. *The Reservation of the Blessed Sacrament*. Catholic University of America Canon Law Studies, No. 40. Washington, D.C.: Catholic University of America, 1927.

Caeremoniale Episcoporum (1886 edition). Regensburg, Germany: Friderici Pustet, S. Sedis Apost. et S. Rit. Congr. Typogr., 1902.

Caeremoniale Episcoporum. Vatican City: Typis Polyglottis Vaticanis, 1985.

Chavasse, Antoine. "A Rome, le Jeudi-Saint, au VII siecle, d'apres un vieil Ordo." *Revue d'Histoire Ecclesiastique*, 50 (1955), pp. 21-35.

Church Pension Fund, ed. *The Hymnal of the Protestant Episcopal Church in the United States of America*. New York: The Church Pension Fund, 1943.

Clinton, Father Connell. *The Paschal Precept: An Historical Synopsis and Commentary*. Catholic University of America Canon Law Studies, No. 73. Washington, D.C.: Catholic University of America, 1932.

"Communications: Some Peculiar Liturgical Customs." *Orate Fratres*, 6 (March 19, 1932), pp. 236-237.

Conant, Kenneth John. "The Original Buildings at the Holy Sepulchre in Jerusalem." *Speculum*, 31 (Jan 1956), pp. 1-48.

Congregation for Divine Worship. *Circular Letter Concerning the Preparation and Celebration of the Easter Feasts*, 20 Feb 1988. *L'Osservatore Romano* (English edition), Feb 29,

1988, pp. 15-19. Latin text in *Notitiae*, Feb 1988, pp. 81-107.

Congregation of Sacred Rites. *Decreta Authentica Congregationis Sacrorum Rituum*. 5 vols. Rome: Typographia Polyglotta, 1898-1901.

_____, *Decretum: De solemni vigilia paschali in stauranda. Ephemerides Liturgicae*, 65 (1951), Fasc. 1 — Supplementum.

_____, *Decree of the Congregation of Sacred Rites Restoring the Solemn Easter Vigil*. 9 Feb 1951. *American Ecclesiastical Review*, 126 (March 1952), pp. 181-182.

_____, Decree of 11 Jan 1952. *American Ecclesiastical Review*, 126 (April 1952), pp. 299-307.

_____, *Maxima redemptionis*, 16 Nov 1955. *American Ecclesiastical Review*, 134 (Jan 1956), pp. 51-55.

_____, *Instruction on the Correct Use of the Restored Ordo of Holy Week*, 16 Nov 1955. *American Ecclesiastical Review*, 134 (Jan 1956), pp. 55-62.

Connolly, R. H. "Liturgical Prayers of Intercession: I: The Good Friday Orationes Solemnes." *Journal of Theological Studies*, 21 (April 1920), pp. 219-232.

Corbett, P. B. "Regula Magistri." *New Catholic Encyclopedia*. 1967 ed. Vol. 12, p. 208.

Corbin, Solange. *La Deposition liturgique du Christ au Vendredi Saint: Sa Place dans l'histoire des rites et du theatre religieux*. Collection Portugaise. Paris: Societe d'Editions 'Les Belles Lettres', 1960.

Coriden, James, Thomas Green and Donald Heintschel, eds. *The Code of Canon Law: A Text and Commentary*. New York: Paulist Press, 1985.

Corpus Christianorum, Series Latina: CLXXV: Itineraria et Alia Geographia. Turnhout, Belgium: Typographi Brepols Editores Pontificii, 1965.

Crichton, J. D. *The Liturgy of Holy Week*. Dublin: Veritas Publications, 1983.

Curtin, Right Reverend Monsignor Richard B., et al., eds. *The Catholic Hymnal and Service Book*. Pew Edition. New York: Benziger Editions, Inc., 1966.

Dalmais, I.-H., OP. "Le Triduum Sacrum dans la liturgie Byzantine." *La Maison-Dieu*, 41 (1955), pp. 118-127.

_____, "L'Adoration de la Croix." *La Maison-Dieu*, 45 (1956), pp. 76-86.

_____, "Une Relique de l'antique liturgie de Jerusalem: L'Office de l'ensevelissement du Christ au soir du Vendredi Saint." *L'Orient Syrien*, 6 (1961), pp. 441-451.

Danielou, Father Jean, SJ. *The Bible and the Liturgy*. University of Notre Dame Liturgical Studies, Vol. 3. Notre Dame, Indiana: University of Notre Dame Press, 1956.

Daughters of St. Paul, ed. *Vatican II Sunday Missal*. Boston: Saint Paul Editions, Daughters of St. Paul, 1974.

_____, ed. *Vatican II Weekday Missal*. Boston: Saint Paul Editions, Daughters of St. Paul, 1974.

_____, ed. *The Office of Readings: According to the Roman Rite*. Boston: Saint Paul Editions, Daughters of St. Paul, 1983.

Dearmer, Percy, Ralph Vaughan Williams and Martin Shaw, ed. *The Oxford Book of Carols*. 1928; rpt. London: Oxford University Press, 1964.

Debidour, Victor-Henry. *Christian Sculpture*. Twentieth Century Encyclopedia of Catholicism, Vol. 122. New York: Hawthorn Books, 1968.

De Herdt, P. J. B. *Sacrae Liturgiae Praxis Juxta Ritum Romanum*. 3 vols. Louvain: Josephus Vanlinthout, 1894.

Del Rey, Maria, Sister. "Pageant of the Cross." *Sign*, 51 (March 1972), pp. 12-15.

Deshusses, Jean, ed. *Le Sacramentaire Gregorien: Ses Principales Formes d'apres les plus anciens manuscrits: I*. Spicilegium Friburgense, Vol. 16. 2nd ed. Fribourg, Switzerland: Editions Universitaires Fribourg Suisse, 1979.

De Turville, D. "A Short Survey of the Christians of South India and Their Rites, with an Account of the Easter Celebration at North Parur, Northern Travancore." *Eastern*

Churches Quarterly, 7 (Oct-Dec 1947), pp. 214-221.

Division of Christian Education of the National Council of Churches of Christ in the USA. *Revised Standard Version of the Bible*, Catholic Edition. New York: 1971.

Dmitrievskij, Aleksei A. *Opisanie liturgitseskich rukopisej*. Vol. I. Kiev, 1895; rpt. Hildesheim, Germany: Georg Olms Verlagsbuchhandlung, 1965.

Donatien, Dom, OSB. "Holy Week in a Flemish Abbey." *Orate Fratres*, 8 (March 24, 1934), pp. 211-215.

Donovan, Richard, CSB. *The Liturgical Drama in Medieval Spain*. Toronto: Pontifical Institute of Medieval Studies, 1958.

Duchesne, Monsignor L. *Christian Worship: Its Origin and Evolution*. M. L. McClure, tr. London: Society for Promoting Christian Knowledge, 1904.

Dumville, David N. "Liturgical Drama and Panegyric Responsory from the Eighth Century? A Re-examination of the Origin and Contents of the Ninth-Century Section of the Book of Cerne." *Journal of Theological studies*, 23 (Oct 1972), pp. 374-406.

Dunn, Sara H. "Good Friday in Fuenterrabia." *The Month*, 102 (July 1903), pp. 68-72.

"Easter in 'Little Poland' Buffalo." *Sign*, 32 (April 1953), pp. 60-61.

Echague, Jose Ortiz. *Espana Mistica*. Madrid: Biblao, 1964.

Edwards, Robert. *The Montecassino Passion and the Poetics of Medieval Drama*. Berkeley: University of California Press, 1977.

Edwards, Tudor. "As for Six Hundred Years: Easter in Assisi." *The Tablet*, March 31, 1956, p. 297.

Eustace, Father Bartholomew, ed. *The Ritual for Small Churches*. New York: Joseph F. Wagner, Inc., 1935.

Faber, Father Frederick William. *Hymns*. American ed. Baltimore: Murphy & Co., 1880

Feasey, Father H. Philibert, OSB. "Palm Sundays." *American Ecclesiastical Review*, 38 (April 1908), pp. 361-381.

_____. "The Easter Sepulchre." *American Ecclesiastical Review*, 32 (1905), pp. 337-355 (Part I), pp. 468-499 (Part II).

"Fernandez (Gregorio)." *Enciclopedia Universal Ilustrada*. 1958 ed. Vol. 23, pp. 756-760.

Fiorenza, Vito. "Holy Week in Sicily." *Jubilee*, 3 (April 1956), pp. 47-53.

_____. "Faces of Holy Week," *Jubilee*, 9 (April 1962), pp. 6-15.

Fischer, Max. "Holy Week in Seville." *Commonweal*, 21 (April 19, 1935), pp. 704-705.

Flannery, Austin, OP, ed. *Vatican Council II: The Conciliar and Post Conciliar Documents*. Northport, New York: Costello Publishing Co., 1975.

_____, ed. *Vatican Council II: More Postconciliar Documents*. Vatican Collection, Vol. II. Northport, New York: Costello Publishing Co., 1982.

Forsyth, William H. *The Entombment of Christ: French Sculptures of the Fifteenth and Sixteenth Centuries*. Cambridge, Massachusetts: Harvard University Press, 1970.

"From our Notebook: Spain." *The Tablet*, April 11, 1953, p. 304.

Garrigou-Lagrange, Reginold. *The Love of God and the Cross of Jesus*. 2 Vols. St. Louis, Missouri: B. Herder Book Co., 1951.

Gassner, Jerome, OSB. "The 'Reproaches.' " *Homiletic and Pastoral Review*, 46 (Feb 1946), pp. 323-332.

_____. "Rising with Christ: The Blessing of the Baptismal Font." *Homiletic and Pastoral Review*, 49 (April 1949), pp. 529-538.

Gilmartin, T. P. "Good Friday." *Catholic Encyclopedia*. 1907 ed. Vol. 6, pp. 643-645.

Gingras, George E., trans. *Egeria: Diary of a Pilgrimage*. Ancient Christian Writers, No. 38. New York: Newman Press, 1970.

Goar, Jacobus. *Euchologion sive Rituale Graecorum*. Venice, 1730; rpt. Graz, Austria: Akademische Druck-und Verlagsanstalt, 1960.

Godu, G. "Epitres." *Dictionnaire d'archeologie chretienne et de liturgie.* Ed. Dom Fernand Cabrol and Dom Henri Leclercq. Paris: Libraire Letouzey et Ane, 1922, Vol. 5, Part I, col. 245-344.

Goertz, Arthemise. "Easter in Old Mexico." *Ave Maria*, new series, 41 (April 20, 1935), pp. 481-485.

"Good Friday in Jerusalem." *The Month*, 4 (1866), pp. 346-356.

Goodier, Most Reverend Alban, SJ. *The Passion and Death of Our Lord Jesus Christ*. n.d.; rpt. Boston: Saint Paul Editions, Daughters of St. Paul, n.d.

_____. *The Risen Jesus: Meditations.* New York: P. J. Kenedy & Sons, 1949.

Graf, Ernest, OSB. "The Washing of Feet on Maundy Thursday." *Homiletic and Pastoral Review*, 45 (Feb 1945), pp. 347-351.

Grazulis, Nijole, ed. *Chronicle of the Catholic Church in Lithuania: Underground Journal of Human Rights Violations.* Vol. 1. Chicago: Loyola University Press; Society for the Publication of the Chronicle of the Catholic Church in Lithuania, Inc., 1981.

Guéranger, Abbot, OSB. *The Liturgical Year: Vol. 6: Passiontide and Holy Week.* Westminster, Maryland: Newman Press, 1952.

Gy, P. M., OP. "Les Origines liturgiques du lavement des pieds." *La Maison-Dieu*, 49 (1957), pp. 50-53.

Hadji-Burmester, O. "Rites and Ceremonies of the Coptic Church: Part XI: Holy Week Services and Ceremonies." *Eastern Churches Quarterly*, 11 (Autumn 1956), pp. 321-335.

Hamman, Andre, OFM, ed. *Baptism: Ancient Liturgies and Patristic Texts.* Alba Patristic Library, Vol. 2. Staten Island, New York: Alba House, 1967.

_____, ed. *The Paschal Mystery: Ancient Liturgies and Patristic Texts.* Alba Patristic Library, Vol. 3. Staten Island, New York: Alba House, 1969.

Hardison, O. B., Jr. *Christian Rite and Christian Drama in the Middle Ages.* Baltimore, Maryland: John Hopkins Press, 1965.

Hardon, Father John A., SJ. *Christianity in the Twentieth Century.* Garden City, New York: Image Books/Doubleday & Co., Inc., 1972.

_____. *Modern Catholic Dictionary.* Garden City, New York: Doubleday & Co., Inc., 1980.

Harkins, Paul W., tr., *Saint John Chrysostom: Baptismal Instructions.* Ancient Christian Writers, No. 31. Westminster, Maryland: Newman Press; London: Longmans, Green and Co., 1963.

Hennecke, Edgar, and Wilhelm Schneemelcher, ed. *New Testament Apocrypha.* 2 vols. Philadelphia: The Westminster Press, 1963.

Hettinger, Cynthia. "Faith of the Puerto Rican." *America*, 103 (April 16, 1960), pp. 66-67.

Heuser, H. J. "Tenebrae and the New Light of the Holy Fire." *American Ecclesiastical Review*, 36 (March 1907), pp. 225-231.

Hickman, Lucie, and Katherine Willis. "Holy Week in Guatemala." *Commonweal*, 35 (April 3, 1942), pp. 587-589.

Hill, Robert C., tr. *Saint John Chrysostom: Homilies on Genesis 18-45.* Fathers of the Church, Vol. 82. Washington, D.C.: Catholic University of America Press, 1990.

Holweck, Frederick G. "Easter." *Catholic Encyclopedia.* 1907 ed. Vol. 5, pp. 224-228.

The Holy Bible: Douay Rheims Version. Baltimore, Maryland, 1899; rpt. Rockford, Illinois: Tan Books and Publishers, 1971.

Holy Week: Containing the Offices of Holy Week, from the Roman Breviary and Missal with the Chants in Modern Notation. n.p.: John Murphy & Co., n.d. (ca. 1860).

"Holy Week in Jerusalem." *The Catholic World*, 7 (1868), pp. 77-81.

"Holy Week in Munich." *Ave Maria*, 13 (1877), pp. 168-170,182-185, 201-203, 215-217, 233-235.

Homan, Helen. *Letters to the Martyrs*. New York: David McKay Co., Inc., 1951.

Horgan, A. D. "The Grail in Wolfram's *Parzival*." *Medieval Studies*, 36 (1974), pp. 354-381.

Hughes, Reverend Philip. *A Popular History of the Catholic Church*. Macmillan Paperbacks ed. New York: Macmillan Publishing Co., Inc., 1962.

"Il Rito Bracarense e la Riforma Liturgica." *Notitiae*, 8 (1972), pp. 145-150.

International Committee on English in the Liturgy, tr. *The Rites of the Catholic Church as Revised by the Second Vatican Ecumenical Council*. New York: Pueblo Publishing Co., 1976.

_____. *Documents on the Liturgy, 1963-1979: Conciliar, Papal and Curial Texts*. Collegeville, Minnesota: The Liturgical Press, 1982.

Jacobs, Jay, et al., ed. *The Horizon Book of Great Cathedrals*. New York: American Heritage Publishing Co., Inc./Bonanza Books, 1984.

John, Marquess of Bute, KT, tr. *The Roman Breviary*. 4 vols. London: William Blackwood and Sons, 1908. English translation.

John Paul II, Pope. *Pope John Paul II: Daily Meditations*. Valeria Caprioglio et al., eds. Sherbrooke, Canada: Editions Paulines, 1985.

_____. "Homily at Chrism Mass," 31 March 1988. *L'Osservatore Romano*, April 11, 1988, p. 11.

_____. "Homily During Easter Vigil," 2 April 1988. *L'Osservatore Romano*, April 18, 1988, p. 6.

_____. "Pope's Homily at Easter Vigil," 25 March 1989. *L'Osservatore Romano*, April 3, 1989, p. 8.

_____. "Participation in the Paschal Mystery" (Talk at General Audience), 27 March 1991. *L'Osservatore Romano*, April 2, 1991, 11.

_____. "Penance in the Ecclesial Community" (Talk at General Audience), 15 April 1992. *L'Osservatore Romano*, April 22, 1992, p. 7.

_____. Homily at Mass of the Lord's Supper, 14 April 1993. *L'Osservatore Romano*, April 14, 1993, p. 2.

Jones, Alexander, ed. *The Jerusalem Bible: Reader's Edition*. Garden City, New York: Doubleday, Co., Inc., 1968.

Jorgensen, Johannes. *Saint Catherine of Siena*. New York: Longmans, Green and Co., 1938.

Jungmann, Father Josef Andreas, SJ. *The Mass of the Roman Rite: Its Origins and Development*. 2 Vols. Reverend Francis A. Brunner, CSSR, tr. New York: Benziger Brothers, Inc., 1951 (Vol.I), 1955 (Vol. II).

_____. "Die Vorverlegung der Ostervigil seit dem christlichen Altertum." *Liturgisches Jahrbuch*, 1 (1951), pp. 48-54.

_____. "Die Andacht der Viervig Stunden und das Heilige Grab." *Liturgisches Jahrbuch*, 2 (1952) pp. 184-198 (English translation in Jungmann, 1962, pp. 223-238).

_____. "Introduction." In Karl Becker, *O Truly Blessed Night: A Study of the Theology of the Easter Vigil*. St. Louis, Missouri: Pie Decime Press, 1956, pp. 5-19.

_____. *Pastoral Liturgy*. New York: Herder and Herder, 1962.

Kaiser, Albert F., CPPS. "The Historical Backgrounds and Theology of *Mediator Dei*: Part I: Backgrounds." *American Ecclesiastical Review*, 129 (Dec 1953), pp. 368-378.

Karmany, G. E. "Holy Week Memories of Palma de Mallorca." *Ave Maria*, new series, 55 (March 28, 1942), pp. 399-402.

Kavanaugh, Kieran, OCD, and Otilio Rodriguez, OCD, tr. *The Collected Works of Saint Teresa of Avila*. Vol. I. Washington, D.C.: ICS Publications, Institute of Carmelite Studies, 1976.

Kazhdan, Alexander, et al., eds. *The Oxford Dictionary of Byzantium*. 3 vols. New York: Oxford University Press, 1991.

Kelly, Leo A. "Hearse." *Catholic Encyclopedia*. 1907 ed. Vol. 7, pp. 162-163.

King, Archdale A. *Liturgies of the Past*. Milwaukee: Bruce Publishing Co., 1959.

_____. *Eucharistic Reservation in the Western Church*. London: A.R. Mowbray & Co. Ltd., 1965.

King, N. Q. *The Emperor Theodosius and the Establishment of Christianity*. The Library of History and Doctrine. Philadelphia: The Westminster Press, 1960.

Kirsch, Felix. "Holy Week in Assisi." *Commonweal*, 15 (March 23, 1932), p. 576.

Kluge, Theodor, and Anton Baumstark. "Quadragesima und Karwoche Jerusalems im siebten Jahrhundert," *Oriens Christianus*, new series, 5 (1915), pp. 201-233.

Knowles, David, tr./ed. *The Monastic Constitutions of Lanfranc*. New York: Oxford University Press, 1951.

La Civita, Michael J. L. "Easter: An Orthodox Perspective," *Catholic Near East*, 17 (April 1991), pp. 26-29.

Landon, H.C. Robbins, Jacket Notes. *The Seven Last Words* (original version). By Franz Joseph Haydn. Cond. Neville Marriner, Academy of Saint Martin-in-the-Fields. Angel, S-37480, 1978.

Lane, Most Reverend Raymond, MM, ed. *Stone in the King's Highway: Selections from the Writings of Bishop Francis Xavier Ford (1892-1952)*. New York: McMullen Books, 1953.

Lanne, Dom Emmanuel, OSB. "Textes et rites de la liturgie Pascale dans l'ancienne Eglise Copte." *L'Orient Syrien*, 6 (1961), pp. 279-300.

Lasance, Father F. X., and Father Francis Augustine Walsh, OCD, eds. *The New Roman Missal: In Latin and English*. New York: Benziger Brothers, Inc., 1946.

L'Attivita della Santa Sede, Nel 1981. Vatican City: Libraria Editrice Vaticana, 1982.

L'Attivita della Santa Sede, Nel 1987. Vatican City: Libraria Editrice Vaticana, 1988.

L'Attivita della Santa Sede, Nel 1988. Vatican City: Libraria Editrice Vaticana, 1989.

Laverty, Maura. "Holy Week in Seville." *Ave Maria*, new series, 33 (March 14, 1931), pp. 333-335.

Lawlor, Hugh Jackson, ed. *The Rosslyn Missal*. Henry Bradshaw Society, Vol. 15. London: Henry Bradshaw Society, 1899.

Leclercq, Dom Henri. "Lavement de la Tete, des Mains, des Pieds." *Dictionnaire d'archeologie chretienne et de liturgie*. Ed. Dom Fernand Cabrol and Dom H. Leclercq. Paris: Libraire Letouzey et Ane, 1929, Vol. 8, Part 2, col. 2002-2009.

_____. "Paques." *Dictionnaire d'archeologie chretienne et de liturgie*. Ed. Dom Fernand Cabrol and Dom H. Leclercq. Paris: Libraire Letouzey et Ane, 1937, Vol. 13, Part II, col. 1521-1574.

Lectionary for Mass. New York: Catholic Book Publishing Co., 1970.

Legg, John Wickham. *Notes on the History of the Liturgical Colours*. London: John S. Leslie, 1882.

_____. *Missale ad Usum Ecclesie Westmonasteriensis*. Vol. I. Henry Bradshaw Society, Vol. I. London: Henry Bradshaw Society, 1891.

_____. *Essays Liturgical and Historical*. Studies in Church History. London: Society for Promoting Christian Knowledge, 1917.

Lelen, Reverend J. M, ed. *Key of Heaven: A Complete Manual of Prayers and Catholic Devotions*. New York: Catholic Book Publishing Co., 1961.

Lippe, Robert, ed. *Missale Romanum: Mediolani, 1474: Vol. I: Text*. Henry Bradshaw Society, Vol. 17. London: Henry Bradshaw Society, 1899.

_____. *Missale Romanum: Mediolani, 1474: Vol. II: A Collation with Other Editions Printed Before 1570*. Henry Bradshaw Society, Vol. 33. London: Henry Bradshaw Society, 1907.

Lipsmeyer, Elizabeth. "The *Liber Ordinarius* by Konrad Von Mure and Palm Sunday Observance in Thirteenth-Century Zurich." *Manuscripta*, 32 (1988), pp. 139-145.

Liturgical Press, ed. *Christian Prayer: The Liturgy of the Hours*. Collegeville, Minnesota: The Liturgical Press, 1976.

_____. *The Hours of the Divine Office in English and Latin: Vol. Two: Passion Sunday to August*, Collegeville, Minnesota: The Liturgical Press, 1964.

Lockton, W. *The Treatment of the Remains at the Eucharist After Holy Communion And the Time of the Ablutions*. London: Cambridge University Press (New York: The Macmillan Co.), 1920.

Low, Josef, CSSR. "The New Holy Week Liturgy: A Pastoral Opportunity." *Worship*, 30 (Jan 1956), pp. 94-113.

Maguire, Barry. "The Funeral of Christ." *The Catholic World*, 105 (April 1917), pp. 59-63.

Mallardo, Domenico. "La Pasqua e la Settimana Maggiore a Napoli dal Secolo val XIV." *Ephemerides Liturgicae*, 66 (1952), pp. 3-36.

Martimort, Aime-Georges. *La Documentation liturgique de Dom Edmund Martene*. Studi e Testi, No. 279. Vatican City: Biblioteca Apostolica Vaticana, 1978.

Mary Immaculate, Sister, CSC, ed. *The Tree and the Master: An Anthology of Literature on the Cross of Christ*. New York: Random House, 1965.

Mateos, Juan, ed. *Le Typicon de la Grand Eglise: Tome II: Le Cycle des Fetes mobiles*. Orientalia Christiana Analecta, No. 166. Rome: Pont. Institutum Orientalium Studiorum, 1963.

Mauriac, Francois. *The Eucharist: The Mystery of Holy Thursday*. Marie-Louise Dufrenoy, tr. New York: David McKay Co., Inc., 1944.

Maximilian, Prince of Saxony. *Praelectiones de Liturgiis Orientalibus: Tomus Primus*. Freiburg, Germany: Herder, 1908.

Mazza, Enrico. *The Eucharistic Prayers of the Roman Rite*. New York: Pueblo Publishing Co., Inc., 1986.

McCauley, Leo P., SJ, and Anthony A. Stephenson, tr. *The Works of Saint Cyril of Jerusalem*. Vol. 2. The Fathers of the Church, Vol. 64. Washington, D.C.: Catholic University of America Press, 1970.

McDonald, Anna Sprague. "At the Bier of the Crucified." *The Catholic World*, 72 (March 1901), pp. 717-726.

McManus, Frederick R., JCD, ed. *The Rites of Holy Week*. Paterson, New Jersey: Saint Anthony Guild Press, 1957.

Meeus, Father Charles. "China's New Order." *Orate Fratres*, 16 (March 22, 1942), pp. 228-232.

Memoriale Rituum (1853 edition). Regensburg, Germany: Georgii Josephi Manz, 1862.

Mercenier, R. P. E. *La Priere des Eglises de Rite Byzantin: II: Les Fetes: II: L'Acathiste, la Quinzaine de Paques, l'Ascension et la Pentecote*. Chevetogne, Belgium: Monastere de Chevetogne, 1948.

Migne, J.-P., ed. *Patrologia Graeca*. 161 vols. Paris: Garnier Fratres, 1857-1865.

_____. *Patrologia Latina*. 221 vols. Paris: Garnier Fratres, 1878-1890.

Miller, John, CSC. "The History and Spirit of Holy Week." *American Ecclesiastical Review*, 136 (April 1957), pp. 217-241.

Missale Romanum (1942 edition). Boston: Benziger Brothers, Inc., 1952.

Missale Romanum (edition of Pope Paul VI). Vatican City: Typis Polyglottis Vaticanis, 1970.

Monica, Maria. "Maria Desolata." *The Month*, 86 (April 1896), pp. 495-501.

Monks, Father James L., SJ. *Great Catholic Festivals*. "Great Religious Festivals" Series. New York: Henry Schuman, Inc., 1951.

More, Saint Thomas. *The Complete Works of Thomas More: Vol. 13: Treatise on the Passion, Treatise on the Blessed Body, Instructions and Prayers*. Garry E. Haupt, ed. New Haven, Connecticut: Yale University Press, 1976.

_____. *The Complete Works of Thomas More: Vol. 14: De Tristitia Christi, Part I: The Valencia Manuscript: Facsimiles, Transcription and Translation*. Clarence H. Miller, ed./tr. New Haven, Connecticut: Yale University Press, 1976.

Morin, Dom Germain. "Le plus ancien *Comes* de l'Eglise Romaine." *Revue Benedictine*, 27 (1910), pp. 41-74.

_____. "Liturgie et basiliques de Rome du milieu du VII siecle: D'apres les Listes d'Evangiles de Wurzburg." *Revue Benedictine*, 28 (1911), pp. 296-330.

Mould, Daphne Pochin. "Holy Cross Day." *Doctrine and Life*, 13 (Sep 1963), pp. 458-462.

_____. "Byzantine Holy Week." *Doctrine and Life*, 14 (March 1964), pp. 177-183.

Murray, John. "Quaint Easter Customs." *The Month*, 169 (April 1937), pp. 333-340.

National Conference of Catholic Bishops. "Summary of Holy Week Changes." *Bishops' Committee on the Liturgy Newsletter*, 4 (March 1968), p. 124.

_____. "The Celebration of the Sacraments During the Easter Triduum." *Bishops' Committee on the Liturgy Newsletter*, 14 (Jan 1978), p. 97.

Nesbitt, M. "Old-Time Holy Week and Easter Customs." *American Ecclesiastical Review*, 44 (April 1911), pp. 395-407.

Newman, John Henry Cardinal. *Discourses Addressed to Mixed Congregations*. London: Longmans, Green, and Co., 1909 (originally published 1849).

Nilles, Nicolaus, SJ. *Kalendarium Manuale Utriusque Ecclesiae Orientalis et Occidentalis*. Vol. 2. Innsbruck, 1897; rpt. Gregg International Publishers Limited, England, 1971.

Nocent, Adrian, OSB. *The Liturgical Year*. 4 Vols. Matthew O'Connell, tr. Collegeville, Minnesota: The Liturgical Press, 1977.

Noli, Bishop Fain Stylian, ed. *Orthodox Prayer Book*. Boston, Massachusetts: Albanian Orthodox Church in America, 1949.

Norris, Herbert. *Church Vestments: Their Origin and Development*. London: J.M. Dent & Sons, Ltd., 1949.

O'Doherty, M. J. "Holy Week in Spain." *Irish Ecclesiastical Record*, 4th ser., 29 (1911), pp. 355-362.

Ojeda, Juan Angel Onate. *El Santo Grial: Su historia, su culto y sus destinos*. Valencia, Spain: Tipografia Moderna, 1952.

O'Reilly, E. Boyle. *Heroic Spain*. New York: Duffield and Co., 1910.

O'Shea, W. J., "Easter Vigil." *New Catholic Encyclopedia*. 1967 ed. Vol. 5, pp. 9-13.

Palmer, Gretta. *God's Underground in Asia*. New York: Appleton-Century-Crofts, Inc., 1953.

Papadopoulos-Kerameus, A., ed. *Analekta Hierosolymitikes Stachyologias*. Vol. 2. Saint Petersburg, Russia, 1894; rpt. Brussels: Culture et Civilisation, 1963.

Parenti, Stefano. "Nota sull'impiego del Termine: 'Proskomide' nell'Euchologio Barberini 336 (VIII sec.)." *Ephemerides Liturgicae*, 103 (1989), pp. 406-417.

Parsch, Pius. *The Church's Year of Grace*. 2nd ed. Vol. 2. Reverend William G. Heidt, OSB, tr. Popular Liturgical Library. Collegeville, Minnesota: The Liturgical Press, 1953.

_____. *The Liturgy of the Mass*. Reverend Frederic C. Eckhoff, tr. St. Louis, Missouri: B. Herder Book Co., 1950.

Paschale Mysterium: Holy Week. Gregorian Chant I. Jacket Notes. Cond. Konrad Ruhland, Capella Antiqua Munich and Choralschola. Pro Arte, PALX-1004, 1981.

Pontificale Romanum Summorum Pontificum (edition of Pope Benedict XIV). 3 Vols. Mechelen, Belgium: Summi Pontificis, S. Congregationis De Propaganda Fide et Archiep. Mechl. Typographus, 1872-1873.

Pax, Wolfgang. *In the Footsteps of Jesus*. Tel-Aviv, Israel: Nateev and Steimatzky/Leon Amiel Publisher, 1970.

Pius XII, Pope. *Encyclical Letter of Pope Pius XII on the Sacred Liturgy: Mediator Dei* (20

Nov 1947). Vatican Library translation. Boston: Saint Paul Editions, Daughters of St. Paul, n.d.

"Questions and Answers: Tenebrae." *The Clergy Review*, 43 (March 1958), p. 170.

Raes, Alphonse, SJ. "La Paix Pascale dans le Rite Chaldeen." *L'Orient Syrien*, 6 (1961), pp. 67-80.

Revised Rites of Holy Week. New York: Catholic Book Publishing Co., 1971.

Rhodes, Dennis R. "The Service of the Washing of Feet on Holy Thursday: An Historical and Theological Investigation." Diss. Saint Vladimir's Orthodox Theological Seminary, 1977.

Righetti, Mario. *Manuale di Storia Liturgica*. 4 vols. Milan: Editrice Ancora, 1950.

Rios, Romanus, OSB. "The Great Antiphon of the *Triduum Domini*." *The Clergy Review*, 23 (April 1943), pp. 155-162.

Rituale Romanum: De Benedictionibus. Vatican City: Typis Polyglottis Vaticanis, 1985.

Robinson, Philip. "From Our Notebook: Jesus Del Gran Poder." *The Tablet*, April 1, 1961, p. 303.

Rock, Daniel. *The Church of Our Fathers*. 4 vols. London: John Hodges, 1903-1904.

Rojo, Casiano. "The Gregorian Antiphonary of Silos and the Melody of the Spanish Lamentations." *Speculum*, 5 (July 1930), pp. 306-324.

Roman Missal (1960 ed.). New York: Benziger Bros., 1964.

Rucker, Adolf. "Die Adoratio Crucis am Karfreitag in Den Orientalishen Riten." *Miscellanea Liturgica in Honorem L. Cuniberti Mohlberg*. Vol. I. Biblio "Ephemerides Liturgicae," No. 22. Rome: Edizioni Liturgiche, 1948, pp. 379-406.

Salter, Lionel, tr. Libretto. *Parsifal*. By Richard Wagner. With Peter Hofmann, Dunja Vejzovic, Kurt Moll, and Jose van Dam. Cond. Herbert Von Karajan, Berlin Philharmonic, and Chor der Deutchen Oper Berlin. Deutche Grammophon, 2741-002, 1981.

Salzer, Anselm. "Passion Plays." *Catholic Encyclopedia*. 1907 ed. Vol. 11, p. 533.

Schmidt, Father Herman, SJ. *Hebdomada Sancta*. Two vols. Rome: Herder, 1957.

Schoff, Philip, and Henry Wace, ed. *A Select Library of Nicene and Post-Nicene Fathers of the Christian Church, Second Series: Vol. IV: Saint Athanasius: Select Works and Letters*. 1891; rpt. Grand Rapids, Michigan: William B. Eerdmans Publishing Co., 1971.

Scholar, John. "Living with the Liturgy." *Orate Fratres*, 7 (March 18, 1933), pp. 204-210.

Schulz, Hans Joachim. *The Byzantine Liturgy: Symbolic Structure and Faith Expression*. Matthew J. O'Connell, tr. New York: Pueblo Publishing Co., Inc., 1986.

Schuster, Cardinal Ildefonso. *The Sacramentary: Historical and Liturgical Notes on the Roman Missal*. Vol. II. New York: Benziger Brothers, 1925.

Scribner, R. W. "Ritual and Popular Religion in Catholic Germany at the Time of the Reformation." *Journal of Ecclesiastical History*, 35 (Jan 1984), pp. 47-77.

"Semana Santa." *Enciclopedia Universal Ilustrada*. 1927 ed. Vol. 55, pp. 85-95.

"Seville." *The Catholic World*, 24 (Oct 1876), pp. 13-27.

Sfeir, Father Peter F. "Holy Week Customs in Syria." *The Catholic Mind*, 26 (April 22, 1928), pp. 141-154.

_____. "From Other Lands: Good Friday and Easter in the Syrian Church." *Orate Fratres*, 7 (April 15, 1933), pp. 266-271.

"Some Non-Believers on Easter in Rome." *The Catholic World*, 41 (April 1885), pp. 120-126.

Stehle, Reverend Aurelius, OSB, ed. *Manual of Episcopal Ceremonies*. Beatty, Pennsylvania: Saint Vincent Seminary, 1914.

Steinmueller, Father John E., and Kathryn Sullivan, RSCJ. *Catholic Biblical Encyclopedia*. 2 vols. New York: Joseph F. Wagner, Inc., 1959.

Stevenson, Kenneth. "The Ceremonies of Light: Their Shape and Function in the Paschal

Vigil Liturgy." *Ephemerides Liturgicae*, 99 (1985), pp. 170-185.

Sullivan, Mary. "A Byzantine Holy Week." *Sign*, 61 (April 1982), pp. 14-16.

Symons, Dom Thomas, tr. *Regularis Concordia: The Monastic Agreement of the Monks and Nuns of the English Nation*. Medieval Classics. New York: Oxford University Press, 1953.

Taft, Robert F., SJ. *The Great Entrance: A History of the Transfer of Gifts and other Preanphoral Rites of the Liturgy of Saint John Chrysostom*. Orientalia Christiana Analecta, No. 200. Rome: Pont. Institutum Orientalium Studiorum, 1978.

Talley, Thomas J. "History and Eschatology in the Primitive Pascha." *Worship*, 47 (1973), pp. 212-221.

_____. *The Origins of the Liturgical Year*. New York: Pueblo Publishing Co., Inc., 1986.

"The Holy Week of 1869 in Havana." *The Catholic World*, 11 (April 1870), pp. 58-69 (Part I), (May 1870), pp. 212-220 (Part II).

"The Lay-Brotherhoods of Seville." *The Month*, 77 (April 1893), pp. 491-500.

The Passion Play at Oberammergau, 1930: The Complete English Texts of the Play. London: Ernest Benn Limited; Munich: Carl Aug. Seyfried & Co., (1930).

Therese, Sister M. *I Sing of a Maiden: The Mary Book of Verse*. New York: Macmillan Company, 1947.

Thurston, Father Herbert, SJ. "Archdeacon Farrar on the Observance of Good Friday." *The Month*, 84 (May 1895), pp. 86-105.

_____. "Palms." *The Month*, 86 (March 1896), pp. 372-387.

_____. "The Exultet and the Paschal Candle." *The Month*, 86 (April 1896), pp. 502-518.

_____. "The Devotion of the 'Three Hours'." *The Month*, 93 (March 1899), pp. 249-262.

_____. "Easter Sepulchre, or Altar of Repose?" *The Month*, 101 (April 1903), pp. 404-414.

_____. *Lent and Holy Week*. London: Longmans, Green and Co., 1904.

_____. "The Blessed Sacrament and the Holy Grail." *The Month*, 110 (Dec 1907), pp. 617-632.

_____. "Cross: III: The Cross and Crucifix in Liturgy." *Catholic Encyclopedia*. 1907 ed. Vol. 4, pp. 533-539.

_____. "Holy Week." *Catholic Encyclopedia*. 1907 ed. Vol. 7, pp. 434-438.

_____. "Lance, The Holy." *Catholic Encyclopedia*. 1907 ed. Vol. 8, pp. 773-774.

_____. "Lent." *Catholic Encyclopedia*. 1907 ed. Vol. 9, pp. 152-154.

_____. "Tenebrae." *Catholic Encyclopedia*. 1907 ed. Vol. 14, p. 506.

Toal, M. F., tr./ed. *Sunday Sermons of the Great Fathers*. 4 Vols. Chicago: Henry Regnery Co.; London: Longmans, Green and Co. Ltd., 1958.

Tolhurst, J. B. J., ed. *The Ordinal and Customary of the Benedictine Nuns of Barking Abbey*. Vol. I. Henry Bradshaw Society, Vol. 65. London: Henry Bradshaw Society, 1927.

Trapp, Maria Augusta. *Around the Year with the Trapp Family*. New York: Pantheon Books, Inc., 1955.

Trochu, Abbe Francis. *The Cure of Ars: Saint Jean-Marie-Baptiste Vianney (1786-1859)*. London, 1927; rpt. Rockford, Illinois: Tan Books and Publishers, Inc., 1977.

Tyrer, Reverend John Walton. *Historical Survey of Holy Week: Its Services and Ceremonial*. Alcuin Club Collections, No. 29. London: Oxford University Press, 1932.

Urlin, Ethel. *Festivals, Holy Days, & Saints' Days*. London, 1915; rpt. Ann Arbor, Michigan: Gryphon Books, 1971.

Verheul, Ambroise. "Le Mysterie du Samedi Sant." *Questions Liturgiques*, 65 (1984), pp. 19-38.

Viale, Eugene. "Le Reposoir du Jeudi Saint." *La Maison-Dieu*, 41 (1955), pp. 45-63.

Vogel, Cyrille. *The Medieval Liturgy: An Introduction to the Sources*. William G. Storey and

Niols Krogh Rasmussen, OP, tr./rev. Washington, D.C.: The Pastoral Press, 1986.

————, and Reinhard Elze, eds. *Le Pontifical Romano-Germanique du Dixieme Siecle: Le Texte II.* Studi e Testi, Vol. 227. Vatican City: Biblioteca Apostolica Vaticana, 1963.

Von Fischer, Kurt. "Passion." *The New Grove Dictionary of Music and Musicians.* 1980 ed. Vol. 14, pp. 276-282.

Wagner, Geoffrey. "The Catenacciu: Holy Week in Corsica." *The Tablet,* April 21, 1962, pp. 375-376.

Walker, Joan Hazelden. "Further Notes on Reservation Practice and Eucharistic Devotion: The Contribution of the Early Church at Rome." *Ephemerides Liturgicae,* 98 (May-Aug 1984), pp. 392-404.

Walsh, Thomas. "Sevilla of the Images." *The Month,* 123 (April 1914), pp. 354-362.

————, ed. *The Catholic Anthology: The World's Great Catholic Poetry.* New York: Macmillan Company, 1943.

Warren, Frederick E., tr. *The Sarum Missal in English* (1526 edition). Two Vols. The Library of Liturgiology & Ecclesiology for English Readers, Vols. VIII (Part I) and IX (Part II). London: Alexander Moring Ltd., 1911.

Weakland, W.G. "Alleluia." *New Catholic Encyclopedia.* 1967 ed. Vol. I, pp. 321-323.

Weiser, Father Francis X., SJ. *The Easter Book.* San Diego: Harcourt, Brace and Company, 1954.

————. *Handbook of Christian Feasts and Customs: The Year of the Lord in Liturgy and Folklore.* San Diego: Harcourt, Brace and Co., 1958.

Wiley, Ernest. "Easter Comes to Anguillara." *Sign,* 14 (April 1935), pp. 566-567.

Wilkinson, John, ed./tr. *Egeria's Travels.* London: S.P.C.K., 1971.

Williams, H. Fulford. "The Diocesan Rite of the Archdiocese of Braga." *Journal of Ecclesiastical History,* 4 (1953), pp. 123-138.

Willis, G. G. "The Solemn Prayers of Good Friday." In *Essays in Early Liturgy.* Alcuin Club Collections, No. 46. London: Alcuin Club, 1964, pp. 1-48.

Wilson, Ian. *The Shroud of Turin: The Burial Cloth of Jesus Christ?* Garden City, New York: Image Books/Doubleday, Co., Inc., 1979.

————. *The Mysterious Shroud.* Garden City, New York: Doubleday & Co., Inc., 1986.

————. *Holy Faces, Secret Places: An Amazing Quest for the Face of Jesus.* New York: Doubleday, 1991.

Wiseman, Cardinal Nicholas. *Four Lectures on the Offices and Ceremonies of Holy Week (As Performed in the Papal Chapels).* New York: P. O'Shea Publisher, ca. 1838.

Yarham, E. R. "Medieval Easter Sepulchre." *Ave Maria,* new series, 55 (April 4, 1942), pp. 432-434.

Yattendon Hymnal. New York: Oxford University Press.

Young, Karl. *The Drama of the Medieval Church.* 2 Vols. Oxford: Clarendon Press/Oxford University Press, 1933.

Zoffoli, P. Enrico. *S. Paolo della Croce: Storia Critica.* 3 Vols. Rome: Curia Generalizia PP. Passionisti, Commissione Storica, 1963-1968.

Glossary of Selected Terms

Aer [Greek; lit. "air"]. A cloth used in the liturgy of the Byzantine Rite; it is brought to the altar during the Byzantine offertory procession, the "Great Entrance." It is used to veil the chalice together with the *discos*, that is, the paten holding the unconsecrated altar bread.

Ampulla [Latin; lit. "bottle"]. Within the context of Holy Week, the *ampulla* is a vessel for holding any one of the three oils blessed during the Chrism Mass on Holy Thursday.

Caeremoniale Episcoporum [Latin; lit. "Ceremonial of Bishops"]. A supplementary liturgical book of the Roman Rite governing liturgical functions as celebrated by a bishop. The *Caeremoniale* provides additional directions to those contained in the *Missale Romanum*; much of what it contains is applicable even when no bishop is present (such as in a parish liturgy). For example, the universal practice of kneeling at the moment of our Lord's death during the reading of the passion on Palm Sunday and Good Friday is specified not in the *Missale Romanum*, but rather in the *Caeremoniale Episcoporum*.

Capsa [Latin; lit. "box"]. Although this term can be used to refer to certain other vessels for the reservation of the Eucharist, in the context of Holy Week the *capsa* is the special tabernacle of the Holy Thursday repository. It is frequently in the shape of an urn — hence in the past this vessel was sometimes called the *urnula* (Latin; lit. "small urn"). Prior to 1970, the term *capsula* (Latin; lit. "small box") was used in the *Missale Romanum*.

Christus factus est [Latin]. An antiphon derived from two verses of the Letter of Saint Paul to the Philippians (2: 8-9) that in its complete form is used as the "Verse before the Gospel" for the Mass on Palm Sunday and for the Liturgy of the Passion on Good Friday. It also appears in the Divine Office for Holy Thursday, Good Friday, and Holy

Saturday, where it is used "incrementally," that is, in three successively more complete "stages" over the three days of the triduum (with the shortest form on Holy Thursday and the complete antiphon on Holy Saturday).

Creeping to the Cross. An English expression for the medieval custom of approaching the cross or crucifix on one's knees for the Veneration of the Cross during the Good Friday Liturgy of the Passion.

Depositio [Latin; lit. "Deposition"]. An extraliturgical Good Friday ceremony in which the burial of Christ is symbolically reenacted by the placing of a cross, crucifix or image of Christ laid in death and/or the holy Eucharist into an enclosure representing the holy sepulchre.

Discos [Greek]. The paten upon which is placed the Host in the Eucharistic liturgy of the Byzantine Rite.

Easter Sepulchre - see **Sepulchre**.

Ecce lignum crucis [Latin; lit. "Behold the wood of the cross"]. An antiphon of the Good Friday Liturgy of the Passion chanted by the celebrant each of the three times he elevates the cross during the rite of the Veneration of the Cross.

Elevatio [Latin; lit. "Lifting up"]. An extraliturgical Easter ceremony in which the resurrection of Christ is symbolically reenacted by the taking out of a cross, crucifix, or figure of the Risen Christ and/or the holy Eucharist from an enclosure representing the holy sepulchre. It is usually performed as the appropriate sequel to the Good Friday *Depositio* ceremony.

Epitaphios [Greek]. Although this term can be considered equivalent to *aer*, it is commonly used to refer specifically to the large cloth that in the Byzantine Rite is carried in procession and venerated during Vespers on Good Friday and again carried during the Holy Saturday Office of *Myrophores*. The cloth is in the form of a shroud-shaped tapestry on which is depicted the body of Christ laid in death. Among the Ukrainians and other Slavs the veneration ceremony of the *Epitaphios* is known as the *Platsenitsia* (Winding Sheet).

Euchologion [Greek]. A liturgical book of the Byzantine Rite, the *Euchologion* is in content analogous in some ways to the **Pontificale Romanum** and **Rituale Romanum** of the West in that it provides rubrics and prayer texts for the celebration of the sacraments, as well as for a number of other ceremonies; however, unlike the *Pontificale* or *Rituale*, it also contains the texts and rubrics for the Ordinary (unchanging parts) of the Mass, as well as for the Ordinary of the Divine Office.

Exultet [Latin]. A song of praise and rejoicing that arose as a formula for blessing the paschal candle during the Easter Vigil. Originally the text of the *Exultet* varied from place to place, but only one version of it is now in use — one attributed to Saint Ambrose; the words, traditionally sung by a deacon, express the jubilation of the Church and of her children over the resurrection of Christ.

Great Entrance, the. The offertory procession in the Eucharistic liturgy of the Byzantine Rite.

Hearse, *Tenebrae*. A special triangularly-shaped candle stand formerly used during the Office of *Tenebrae* on Holy Thursday, Good Friday, and Holy Saturday. These stands usually held fifteen lit candles that were gradually extinguished as succeeding portions of the Office were completed. They are still in use in some places.

Heilige Grab [German; lit. "Holy Tomb"]. German name for **Easter Sepulchre** — see **Sepulchre**.

Improperia [Latin; lit. "Reproaches"]. A composition consisting of nine "reproaches," that is, verses in the form of accusations addressed by our Lord to His own people and to all mankind; always chanted with the reproaches themselves is the **Trisagion** which serves as an antiphon for them. The *Improperia* are sung during the Veneration of the Cross in the Good Friday Liturgy of the Passion.

Lectionary. A liturgical book that provides the complete texts of all Scripture passages to be read at Mass on any given day of the liturgical year.

Lucernarium [Latin; from the word *lucerna*, lit. "lamp"]. A vigil service of the early Church that consisted of Scripture readings alternating with Psalms and which concluded with the celebration of Mass. The name is derived from the practice of lighting lamps at the beginning of the service. The current Easter Vigil may be considered the only surviving example (albeit in somewhat modified form) of the *Lucernarium* to be found in the present liturgy.

Mandatum [Latin; lit. "Commandment"]. The ceremonial washing of the feet of clergy or laymen by a cleric or monarch in imitation of the action of our Lord at the Last Supper in washing the feet of the Apostles. The name *Mandatum* is a word taken from the Latin text of the gospel reading (John 13:1-15) that has traditionally accompanied this ceremony over the centuries.

Memoriale Rituum [Latin; lit. "Remembrance of Rites"]. First issued by Pope Benedict XIII in 1725, the *Memoriale Rituum* was a supplementary liturgical book of the Roman Rite governing the proper celebration in parish churches of the liturgies of Holy Week, the Feast of the Presentation, and Ash Wednesday. It was discontinued after it had been superseded by both the 1955 revised Ordo of Holy Week and the revised liturgical books of the Second Vatican Council.

Mensa [Latin; lit. "table"]. The flat top surface of an altar.

Missale Romanum. The Latin name for the *Roman Missal*, the primary liturgical book of the Roman Rite governing the celebration of the Mass and containing the texts of all Mass prayers and Scripture Readings for the entire liturgical year, together with rubrics. The current **Sacramentary** and **Lectionary**, when put together, constitute the complete text of the *Missale Romanum*; before the era of the Second Vatican Council these were not published separately, but rather as a single Volume.

Monumento [Spanish; lit. "monument" — in Latin, *Monumentum*]. The name that has been given in Spain and other Spanish-speaking countries to the Holy Thursday repository of the Blessed Sacrament.

Myrophores [Greek: "Myrrh-bearing women"]. The Office of Matins (the first "Hour" of the Divine Office) for Holy Saturday in the Byzantine Rite. As reflected in its title, this office commemorates the bringing of spices by the holy women for the anointing of Christ's Body, and thus focuses on the theme of the entombment of Christ. It is held late at night on Good Friday and includes a "funeral procession" with the *Epitaphios*.

Mystagogical Interpretation. The Eastern tradition of interpreting the different details of the liturgy either as representative of the various events of our Lord's life ("Antiochene" mystagogy — first elaborated in the writings of Theodore of Mopsuestia [A.D. 350-428]) or as allegories of the soul's progress toward perfection ("Alexandran" mystagogy). See Father Robert Taft, SJ, "Commentaries," *The Oxford Dictionary of Byzantium*, ed. A. Kazhdan et al. (New York: Oxford University Press, 1991), Vol. I, pp. 488-489.

Ordo, Roman [Plural: *Ordines* (Latin)]. Any one of a series of medieval liturgical documents that provide rubrics of the liturgy as performed in Rome (although many of the documents that bear this title aren't genuinely "Roman" in content). Unlike a missal or **Sacramentary** a Roman Ordo usually lacks prayer texts; it does, however, in many cases indicate what prayers or Scripture readings are to be used.

Orthros [Greek]. The first "Hour" of the Byzantine Rite's Divine Office, equivalent to the first "Hour" of the *Roman Breviary*, the Office of Readings (Matins).

Palmesel (Palmchristus). A figure depicting Christ riding on a donkey used in medieval Palm Sunday processions, especially in Germany.

Pannuchida [Greek: "All-night service"]. A nocturnal vigil of the Byzantine Rite formerly conducted during the night of Holy Thursday to Good Friday but currently observed on the morning of the latter day. It features a series of twelve readings from the four gospels, arranged to form a gospel harmony so that together they provide a complete account of the passion. This vigil has another name — "Royal Hours" — a title it acquired in Constantinople, where the Byzantine emperors attended the service many centuries ago.

Paso [Spanish]. A sculpted figure or group of figures depicting a scene from our Lord's passion that is mounted on a portable platform and is carried in procession by lay confraternities during extraliturgical Holy Week processions in Spain and other Spanish-speaking countries.

Planctus [Latin; lit. "mourning"]. A medieval Good Friday chant in the form of a lament delivered by one of those present on Calvary as an expression of their sentiments on this occasion. Usually the speaker is the Blessed Virgin, expressing her grief as she watches her Son suffer and die on the cross. The earliest extant examples date from the twelfth century.

Platsenitsia — see *Epitaphios.*

Pontificale Romanum. The Latin name for the *Roman Pontifical*, a liturgical book of the Roman Rite governing the proper celebration by a bishop of the Sacraments of Confirmation and Holy Orders, as well as a number of other special episcopal rites, such as the consecration of a new church and the blessing of the Holy Oils during the Chrism Mass on Holy Thursday.

Quarant 'Ore. The Italian name for the "Forty Hours' Devotion," the practice of exposing the Blessed Sacrament for adoration over a period of forty hours; this devotion in its current form was introduced in the sixteenth century, but may have been derived from earlier customs associated with the Easter Triduum.

Quartodecimans. This term refers to those Christians of the early Church who believed that the annual observance of Easter — of the "Pasch" — should always take place on the "fourteenth day of the moon"(the day of the full moon) following the springtime vernal equinox regardless of what day of the week this "lunar fourteenth" fell on. Such a view, especially found in the East, was in contrast to the practice of the Church of Rome, which in remembrance of our Lord's rising from the dead on the first day of the week always observed Easter on a Sunday — the first Sunday following the "fourteenth day of the moon." In the fourth century this Roman practice was declared binding upon the universal Church.

Quem Queritis [Latin]. A *trope* for the Introit (Entrance Rite) of the Easter Sunday Mass that was later transferred to a position in the Divine Office for this day where it served as the nucleus for the subsequent development of the medieval *Visitatio Sepulchri* rite.

Redditio Symboli [Latin: "Return of the Creed"]. The term for a practice of the early centuries, the ceremonial recitation of the Creed by catechumens on Holy Saturday (on Holy Thursday in the East) as a final preparation for their Baptism at the Easter Vigil.

Reproaches, the — see *Improperia*.

Rituale Romanum. The Latin name for the *Roman Ritual*, an official book of the Roman Rite governing the proper celebration of the Sacraments of Baptism, Penance, Matrimony, and the Anointing of the Sick, as well as certain matters regarding the holy Eucharist, such as reservation and adoration of the Blessed Sacrament outside of Mass; the *Rituale* also provides rubrics and prayer texts for a number of other rites, such as the blessing of various objects.

Royal Hours, the — see *Pannuchida*.

Sacramentary. A liturgical book that provides both the rubrics and the prayer texts for the celebration of Mass throughout the year; it does not provide the texts of the Scripture readings assigned to the Mass on a given day, but does specify which passages from the Scriptures are to be used.

Santo Entierro [Spanish; lit. "Holy Burial/Funeral"]. Name used in Spain and other Spanish-speaking countries for the Good Friday devotional practice of the *Depositio* in its current form, which originated in Italy (the "Italian *Depositio*").

Sepulchre. Within the context of Holy Week this term has been used in association with two different practices. In the past the Holy Thursday repository was often called the "sepulchre." The expression "Easter sepulchre" refers to the representation of the tomb of Christ erected for the extraliturgical *Depositio* rite of Good Friday.

Sepulto Domino [Latin]. A responsory taken from Matthew 27 (66, 60, 62) and assigned to the Divine Office for Holy Saturday; currently it is said following the First Reading in the Office of Readings. In the Middle Ages this responsory was often also used during the Good Friday ceremony of the *Depositio.*

Sequence. Having arisen in association with the singing of the final *a* of the *Alleluia* in the first part of the Mass, the sequence can be described as a form of **trope** that is sufficiently developed to stand on its own when removed from its original liturgical setting. One example of a sequence still utilized in the current liturgy is the *Victimae paschali*, which is sung or recited just before the *Alleluia* preceding the gospel on Easter Sunday (and on the subsequent days of the Easter Octave).

Synaxis [Greek]. A service of Scripture readings and prayers originating in the Sabbath services of the Jewish Synagogue and adopted by the early Church. It was held as a complete non-Eucharistic liturgy of its own on days when Mass was not celebrated. The Liturgy of the Passion on Good Friday includes the only surviving example in the Roman Rite of a genuine *synaxis* in its primitive form (although it could also be said that the Liturgy of the Word of every Sunday Mass is in and of itself structurally identical to the *synaxis*).

Tenebrae [Latin; lit. "Darkness"]. The communal recitation of the first two "Hours" of the Divine Office — Matins (now known as the "Office of Readings") and Lauds (now known as "Morning Prayer") — on Holy Thursday, Good Friday, and Holy Saturday.

Traditio Symboli [Latin: "Delivery of the Creed"]. The term for a practice of the early centuries, the ceremonial teaching of the Creed to the catechumens preparing for Baptism at the Easter Vigil; in some places this rite was conducted on the Sunday before Easter (Palm Sunday).

Tre Ore. The Italian name for the "Three Hours Devotion," the extraliturgical practice of commemorating our Lord's agony on the cross with a special service from noon until three o'clock on Good Friday during which the seven last "words" (utterances) of Christ are recited, accompanied by appropriate prayers, hymns, and meditations.

Trisagion [Greek]. An ancient Greek hymn, perhaps of apostolic origin, and found in all of the Eastern liturgies. It is used in the Roman Rite as an antiphon for the *Improperia*, which are sung during the Liturgy of the Passion on Good Friday.

Troparion [Greek]. A refrain of the Byzantine liturgy analogous to an antiphon.

Trope. A formula added to, and elaborating upon, the official text of the Mass. We see a licit contemporary example of this in the optional formulas used in conjunction with the *Kyrie eleison* ("Lord, have mercy") in the current *Roman Missal.*

Typicon [Greek]. A liturgical book of the Byzantine Rite that provides the rubrics peculiar to the different feast days of the Church year.

Ubi Caritas [Latin]. A hymn dating from the eighth century sung during the *Mandatum* (foot washing) rite of Holy Thursday.

Urnula — see *Capsa.*

Vexilla Regis [Latin]. A hymn of the cross composed in the sixth century by Venantius Fortunatus. It is used in the Divine Office for both the Fifth Week of Lent and Holy Week; formerly it was also sung during the Eucharistic procession in the Good Friday Liturgy of the Passion.

Victimae Paschali [Latin]. A **sequence** dating from the eleventh century that is sung or recited before the Alleluia preceding the gospel during the morning Mass of Easter Sunday and (optionally) on each of the succeeding days of the Easter Octave.

Visitatio Sepulchri [Latin; lit. "Visiting of the Sepulchre"]. A medieval extraliturgical Easter Sunday ceremony in which the discovery of the empty tomb of Christ following His resurrection is symbolically reenacted by clerics and/or religious who assume the roles of the holy women, the Angels at the tomb, and in some cases the Apostles Saint Peter and Saint John.

Xerophagia [Greek]. An especially strict fast of the early Church wherein only one meal was taken during the day — a meatless meal at which only dry food, bread, salt, and vegetables were permitted.

Index

[438]

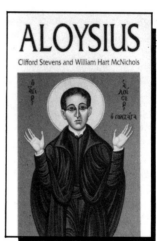